# THE WAR ON DIRTY MONEY

Nicholas Gilmour and Tristram Hicks

With a foreword by
Phil Mason

T0313948

First published in Great Britain in 2023 by

Policy Press, an imprint of
Bristol University Press
University of Bristol
1–9 Old Park Hill
Bristol
BS2 8BB
UK
t: +44 (0)117 374 6645
e: bup-info@bristol.ac.uk

Details of international sales and distribution partners are available at
policy.bristoluniversitypress.co.uk

© Bristol University Press 2023

British Library Cataloguing in Publication Data
A catalogue record for this book is available from the British Library

ISBN 978-1-4473-6512-9 paperback
ISBN 978-1-4473-6513-6 ePub
ISBN 978-1-4473-6514-3 ePdf

Cover design: Robin Hawes
Front cover image: iStock/chipstudio

# Contents

# List of figures, tables and boxes

**Figure**

**Tables**

**Boxes**

# Acknowledgements

We would like to thank our families for their encouragement and support as we undertook to author this book. We would also like to thank the many hundreds of prosecutors, colleagues, police and Financial Intelligence Unit staff from all over the world who helped us understand what money laundering really means.

# Foreword

*Phil Mason*
*Formerly UK Department for International Development (1988–2019)
and senior DFID anti-corruption adviser (2000–19)*

## One problem, two architects

Wherever you are in the world, *The War on Dirty Money* should make you angry. Few other sinews of modern globalism have woven such a powerful and effective network of cooperation as illicit financial flows, connecting every corner of the world. Dirty money leaves an impact everywhere – from poor, underdeveloped countries that are losing gargantuan amounts of public funds which should be contributing to the improvement of the lives of their people, to the streets of London, New York and many other cities in the developed world which witness the effects of the inrush of such funds in the form of block upon block of plush, newly built – and for the most part unoccupied – apartment buildings, all snapped up as convenient parking lots for foreign money, both inflating the area's housing prices and driving large numbers of local people out of the city in order to find affordable accommodation.

Those who want to move their dirty money need the willing assistance of others in the destination location to complete the movement safely. This has fashioned a huge conspiracy of silence and deliberate ignorance: between criminal perpetrators, on the one hand, generating the illicit funds, and, on the other, accommodating bankers, lawyers, accountants and estate agents who are disposed to not ask too difficult questions, to look the other way and not voice concerns. The unholy alliance is no better symbolised than by the classic triptych – the unseeing, the unhearing and the unspeaking.

## One problem, two fates

Two images are seared into my mind when, as an official working in the UK government department responsible for development aid, I started out on our efforts to combat the corruption that blights the developing world. The first snapshot shows two children knee-deep in a muddy drainage culvert surrounded by an assortment of battered but brightly coloured plastic buckets and containers. Hands on hips, looking like wizened old labourers, they stare with tired resignation into the camera. They can be no more than seven or eight years old.

They are collecting the family's daily water supply, from what appears to be a ditch. They had probably walked many miles that morning to reach this spot – instead of going to school – and faced the same trudge back to their home, bearing their now heavy loads. They did the very same journey yesterday. They will do it again tomorrow, and the day after, and the day after that, long into the future. They probably did it this morning, as you started to read this book.

The other image, by contrast, shows an evidently self-satisfied young man posing proudly for his picture, poolside and in front of a salmon pink mansion which fills the background. A faux classical life-sized statue stands behind him and the drinks seem to be ready on the umbrella-shaded table on the expansive patio in the distance.

This is Teodoro Obiang, son of the President of Equatorial Guinea, and he is here enjoying his US$35 million ocean retreat in Malibu Beach, California. The estate behind him occupies 19 acres (7.7 hectares) of prime real estate. The mansion itself is 15,000 square feet (1,400 square metres) in dimension and, along with the pool, boasts a tennis court and even its own four-hole golf course.

As he was enjoying his largesse, most of his country folk were surviving on less than US$1 a day. They still do. The two youngsters we encountered above could just as likely be scratching out their lives in Obiang's Equatorial Guinea as in any other place in Africa.

These two very different images epitomise the consequences of dirty money and money laundering. The abject poverty, ingrained injustice and lost life chances on the one hand; unparalleled illicit wealth, privilege and impunity on the other. All this is made possible by money laundering.

## One problem, so much damage

Understanding the exact scale of the haemorrhaging of resources from any country is difficult, not least because, by their nature, 'illicit' finances are secretive. Elected politicians occupying positions of public trust rarely advertise their hollowing out of their countries' wealth (although the impunity with which many go about their business suggests that few feel fear of facing any consequences).

What we can have absolute confidence about from a global development perspective, to give one example of the dire impact, is that the flows of dirty money, whether it be from corruption, organised crime or commercial tax evasion practices, dwarf the inflow of development funds going in the opposite direction. The UN Office on Drugs and Crime (UNODC) has estimated illicit financial flows to be in the region of 2–5% of the global economy annually – that is currently between US$1.7 and US$4.25 *trillion*.[1] Even allowing for a substantial margin of error on this estimate, compare it to the level of global development aid of around US$160 billion annually[2] and it is easy to see the size of the problem.

The holes in the bottom of the bucket are far larger in many, perhaps most, places around the world than the stream of foreign aid entering it. The development aid community is losing the game, and losing it big time. Developing countries and their people are losing big time.

Poverty and inequality are being perpetuated, public services are being drained of resources, the standards of public administration that most of the world's poor look to, and need to rely on, are being constantly corroded, all by dirty money. Not for nothing has it been observed that Africa is 'a rich continent full of poor people'.

This is just one illustration of the real effects of illicit financial flows. *The War on Dirty Money* will reveal many more. It is why we need to understand the problem of dirty money far more clearly than we have done up until now.

## One problem, so few obstacles

That corrupt elites and organised criminal gangs can accumulate riches on such a scale, hide the proceeds of their activities and transform their gains into 'clean' money to spend as they wish is down to the practice termed 'money laundering' – the transforming of dirty money into seemingly clean, legitimately acquired, wealth.

One of the most striking absurdities about money laundering is the apparent ease with which perpetrators are able to get away with it. The proportion of illicit finance actually intercepted and seized by anti-money laundering agencies is universally acknowledged to be woefully low. A commonly accepted figure, drawn from UNODC research, is that just 0.2% of laundered criminal funds is seized annually by law enforcement.[3] Put another way, anyone contemplating money laundering has a 99.8% chance of success. What other gamble in life offers such a promising rate of return?

If this was occurring in an environment that was a vacuum of attention, effort or control measures, it would still be an outrage but at least an understandable one. The shocking and dispiriting story of global anti-money laundering is that this occurs *despite* the enormous human effort and resource that has been devoted over the past three decades to building up the system that exists supposedly to combat this phenomenon. This system costs in excess of US$200 billion a year and absorbs the working lives of tens, if not hundreds, of thousands of operatives in the public and private sectors around the world.

As *The War on Dirty Money* reveals, there are oceans of data that are routinely (and laboriously) collected, mountains of analysis that are compiled (and diligently published) and legions (armed with their credentials-boosting certificates of proficiency in the discipline) deployed to run highly sophisticated networks of anti-money laundering specialists that now cover the globe. But all of these together, and working for decades, have had virtually zero effect on the problem. It is not getting anywhere near.

With any difficult law enforcement battle, for example with 'ordinary' forms of crime such as car theft or street muggings, drugs or firearms, it is expected to be an uphill struggle. No one thinks crimes like these will be eradicated completely, or that there will be rapid results, but one looks for, and expects to see, a measurable bearing down on incidents. Some return on the effort is usually visible. But with anti-money laundering, it seems that we are not even managing to scratch its surface. Despite all the forces and brain power applied, we are leaving almost no imprint at all on the problem. Not even a shadow.

How can we have set up a system at such expense and with such intense technical, intellectual and operational inputs to so little effect? That question is what this book seeks to explore. It is the unacknowledged scandal of our times. The failure of anti-money laundering is leaving large swathes of the world awash with criminality, decrepit governance, abject poverty and social dysfunction. But it does not have to be like this. It is time for a radical reset.

## One problem, so many absurdities

*The War on Dirty Money* argues that the battle against money laundering has been *made* more difficult than it needs to be. Mostly through accident, it has been the consequence of both a narrowness of vision and the incremental effects of carrying on down tramlines that were originally badly set and now trap us all in keeping going in the wrong direction (although it is unwise to discount the possibility that some interests have actually found it extraordinarily beneficial, and profitable, to see this overcomplication arise, such as the providers of training courses and expensive IT solutions).

Once embarked on a course dictated by bad initial premises, we see the evolution of the anti-money laundering community's response go increasingly awry as each attempted 'fix' to the system only makes things worse, more convoluted, less effective. The inability to escape from the rigidities of the initial framing has doomed the collective effort.

That the initial mistakes were made is unfortunate (but it could reasonably be argued that it was a new field and we knew so little back then). That we have not in the interim been willing to take a step back and reconsider the fundamentals is unforgivable. *The War on Dirty Money* is an attempt to look again at those fundamentals and propose what a reset would look like.

We will encounter many absurdities. Take, for example, Suspicious Activity Reports (SARs), the filings that banks and other financial service providers are required by law in every single country on the planet to make to a central Financial Intelligence Unit (FIU) in their country when they suspect that a transaction they are being asked to make may involve money of illicit origins. This is the backbone of the anti-money laundering defence. In the UK, for example, it has led to hundreds of thousands of reports piling up in our national repository. The reasons for this are not clear. Is it that our banks believe that there are an awful lot of suspicious transactions going on? Could it have something to do with the fact that by sending in the SAR the banks, by the simple virtue of having reported, immediately secure immunity from prosecution, however ill-founded the report turns out to be.

This creates a huge incentive to throw any questionable transaction over to the FIU. This conveniently passes the problem of digging deeper to discover the truth behind a SAR to an overstretched and poorly equipped law enforcement. The statistics show the remarkable upsurge of SARs over the past 20 years – from 14,500 in 1999[4] to more than 742,000 by 2020–21.[5] *The War on Dirty Money* explores the implications of this phenomenon. To some minds it represents a tsunami of undigested information that submerges law enforcement and incapacitates the system. But could it be a golden opportunity if the right resources were in the right place?

Or take the global scrutiny mechanism – the Financial Action Task Force (FATF) – that has been set up to ensure that every country and jurisdiction abides by the same set of rules that should, if applied, create the necessary barriers and prevent dirty money slipping through the financial systems of the world. A formidable industry of reviewing national systems of all 190-odd countries (plus non-sovereign jurisdictions such as the UK's overseas territories, many of which are substantial offshore financial centres) has grown up. The applied brain power devoted to detailed assessment of legal provisions, institutional operations and policy making is truly awe-inspiring. The resulting reports are incredibly rich in technical commentary and insight, frequently run to many hundreds of pages, and are all fully transparent, every one being published.

Yet none of this seems to change anything in the real world. Governments rarely seem to be concerned about the actual effects of dirty money on their economies or their societies. What they do worry about, immensely, is making sure that they get a good report from the FATF. Not to do so risks being placed on a watchlist of jurisdictions that are deemed not to be fully cooperating on applying the rules – the global naughty step. A consequence of being listed is that other countries might start to curtail their financial dealings with you. The vast majority of energy that is devoted to anti-money laundering has now turned to trying to pass the FATF 'exam', rather than to addressing the perilous effects of money laundering in the real world.

Once a review has finished – they happen every ten years or so, such is the burden of getting round to everyone who has to be reviewed – and assuming a country gets a reasonable mark, everything mostly returns to how it was, spared of further trouble from the global invigilator for another decade.

For some governments, this can be the lifeline for going back to doing just the things you were doing before. To external observers, it can prompt real questions about what world the FATF lives in. Perhaps the most egregious example in recent years is the UK's glowing review by the FATF in 2018.[6] So good was the assessment – it concluded that the UK had a stronger anti-money laundering regime than any of the 60 countries so far assessed in the current review phase – it enabled the UK Treasury to purr that 'UK takes top spot in fight against dirty money'.[7] This, the UK that in the real world had become a by-word to most anti-corruption and anti-money laundering campaigners as one of the most openly accommodating hubs for hosting dirty money from all over the globe.

*The War on Dirty Money* reveals many more absurdities like these that have now encrusted the anti-money laundering industry. It should make you angry. Very angry. Angry that so much effort is having so little impact; angry that few appear to be able to see this; angry, especially, because it is not hard to chart the changes that are needed to transform this mire, and they are not difficult changes to make.

Money laundering can be made to look complex, calling for sophisticated (and expensive) solutions. It has been made to appear difficult. What follows is intended to show that it does not need to be. It is a call for change, a call to action.

Not to make the attempt to change will consign many more youngsters across the world to continuing that daily journey to fetch water from a muddy ditch, and allow the Obiang Jnrs to continue to siphon off the wealth of their countries and relocate it for their personal enjoyment. I hope what follows shows that it is not impossible to stop all this.

# 1

# Global standards, governance and the risk-based approach

To succeed in life, you need two things: ignorance and confidence.

Mark Twain[1]

"Money is not the root of all evil", said the finance manager in the audience, "It's the love of money, which causes all the trouble". He was right, of course, and his contribution corrected all future presentations given by this author. There is nothing wrong with money itself, the evil comes from the bad behaviour of people. The behaviour is the 'evil' that makes good money dirty and has done since biblical times.[2]

Nowadays we use the word 'crime' to describe evil in our national legislation, across the world, and some lesser evils we describe as 'breaches of regulations'. But they too create dirty money. Every year, millions of crimes and breaches of regulations generate billions of dollars. Evil may be a strong word, but crime kills people or causes irreparable harm to our lives, our bodies, even our dreams and ambitions. Enabling all this evil is money laundering, the crime of handling dirty money. So, if you are not angry now, you should be. You, and everyone you know is worse off than they could be. Your water, the very air you breathe contains extra polluting particles that are there because someone, somewhere, broke an environmental rule to get some dirty money. There is no escape, everything you see about you is tainted by money laundering.

It does not have to be this way. The regime to control money laundering and its many evils, is not protecting us, but it could be so easily redesigned and at the same time, strengthened. This chapter, and those that follow are about how we tackle global crime by targeting the money. Even as you read this chapter, wherever you are, whoever you are, you too will likely have access to money. Money, by the way, in the context of this book, means money's worth. So, it also includes the home in which you are perhaps sat reading this book, or the device which you are reading it on, or the book itself. Laws will sometimes use the words 'property' or 'goods', so you will see these words too, but unless the example is very specific, we are referring to anything, because *any asset* with a monetary value is capable of being laundered.

We want to take you on a journey through your own world, just viewed from the perspective of dirty money, a world that is in turmoil, but could be a bit more orderly, more prosperous, more peaceful, more crime-free. The book has chapters with potential solutions at the end. These may sometimes seem minor even nit-picking points but in tackling evil we really think that the Devil is in the detail and the solutions add up to a comprehensive package, which is why we needed a whole book. After this introduction, we demystify the jargon of dirty money and then discuss some common myths (Chapters 2 to 5). You will have a view about money laundering because everyone does, we will just put some meat on the bones of the ideas that you already have. Then we will explain how governments look to monitor the financial sector and prevent it from being corrupted and distorted by secret and dirty money. We will show how this affects everyone, including you (Chapters 6 to 11). Once dirty money is identified we will show how it is arrested and prosecuted (Chapters 12 to 14). Dirty money permeates everything and can seriously damage your health and prosperity, we explore how it does this through terrorism, breaching national security, corruption and tax evasion and suggest simple, better ways to protect everyone (Chapters 15 to 18). Finally, we look at how the financial sector is directly exhorted to behave better and how that is going (Chapters 19 and 20). Through all of this we try to pick out and challenge the absurdities which are defended as normal.

We would like our book to become out of date, but we do not think it will. Beneath the apparent turmoil of a changing world are some stubborn realities that seem hard to budge. We will refer to research, indices and books that may seem old, but this is because the findings are still true. The many changes that were recommended have not yet happened, so we try to explain why and to expose fundamental issues with a critical and original eye. This comes from decades of our own practical experience and the knowledge of others who have written about and experienced the war on dirty money. If this interests you, or it is your job, or you simply wish the world to be a better place, a world with less crime and more justice, then we look to show how everyone has a part to play.

While many authors talk about crime and criminals, this book does the opposite by talking about the good guys and girls. The authors will praise the excellent work they do and encourage them to do better.

## God's work

If the pursuit of money is the root of all evil, then the pursuit of dirty money is the way to salvation. Tackling dirty money is a huge endeavour, a public–private partnership that costs over US$210 billion every year.[3] It employs tens of thousands of people, in every country. At the centre of this community-based army are the law enforcement officers who engage directly with the dirty money, supported by the rest of the criminal justice and regulatory system. At the flanks are the banks and the non-financial sectors, preventing dirty money from entering the system and providing intelligence and information – reporting back their suspicions as they are required to do by law. This community seeks to reach out to the wider public, encouraging civil society organisations to heed the call, recognising that many harms originate from the pursuit of money. Leading this fight are the national leaders, loosely coordinated, but globally by the dramatically named 'Financial Action Task Force' (FATF).

The multitude of good people trying to track the dirty money, constantly on the hunt for it and to recover it, come from many diverse backgrounds. The quotation at the start of this book came from an audience member at a presentation given 20 years ago by one of the authors – delivered high above the streets of London on the top floor of a police administrative building. The audience were mainly finance managers in suburban police stations. You may wonder how this audience could ever contribute directly to the fight against crime. Back in 2004, these people had a new role, to count the millions of pounds (in cash) that were suddenly being seized from criminals in the UK, since a new law, the Proceeds of Crime Act (POCA), had been passed. Amusing but real administrative problems had been created. The confidential document safes in police stations were simply not big enough to hold big evidence bags full of money, forcing it to be stored in cells and guarded by gaolers until it could be banked. It proved very difficult to persuade managers *not* to count the money as soon as possible, as was customary with loose change. Counting large volumes of money is very time-consuming, very hard to do accurately and can even be unsafe if it is covered in heroin or cocaine. These same finance managers had to solve myriad issues, from how and when to count it, through to how to disburse the government 'incentivisation' of funds back to local policing.

These and many other types of professionals are in the front line. They also include bank compliance staff, prosecutors and judges, people following the rules, reporting crimes and breaches of regulations. Everyone has a part to play, and every little helps. It may seem that none of this is seen, coordinated, or cared about, but it turns out that there is a global infrastructure to join everything up. It is not well known, but things are more coordinated than you may have thought.

## The FATF

Established in Paris in 1990 and hosted there by the Organisation for Economic Co-operation and Development (OECD), this quite small, independent secretariat, has had a remarkable global influence. Its meetings are regularly attended by government ministers, its public statements generate global news headlines, and its recommendations have changed national laws across the world. Awareness of money laundering and the FATF mantra of 'follow the money' has spawned many films, TV series and books across the globe. But all is not well with the global AML regime. David Lewis, former Executive Secretary of the FATF (2015–2021) observed, in 2020, that the global AML community was "doing badly, some not as badly as others". His condemnatory conclusion about 'his community' is in the context of a Strategic Review of the FATF focused on "how FATF evaluations of countries can better promote and enable more effective and efficient AML/CFT measures".[4]

This seems like a good idea in the context, but how did it get to be so bad?

The global governance of AML which has grown and evolved over many years was matched by national legislation to follow the money. This spawned new police units to conduct financial investigations and, over time, the utility of financial investigations to address all crimes motivated by money was recognised. It is now central to understanding *how* we tackle crime itself. It is particularly applicable to transnational organised crimes, such as drug and human trafficking but can be used against any crime committed in the pursuit of money. Solving crime efficiently relies on good intelligence and financial intelligence is some of the best available to modern-day police forces. Financial intelligence has been used to solve all kinds of crimes, including crimes of violence, public disorder, terrorism and contract killings. In this sense, every crime is covered by financial investigation. *How* financial intelligence makes its way over to law enforcement is what decides the outcome of the fight against crime. So, it perhaps goes without saying, we must improve the lines of communication to the front line.

In the beginning, the FATF's aims were modest. At the G7 Summit in Paris, in July 1989, a review of money laundering was requested that led to a report in April 1990 outlining 40 Recommendations. A small secretariat within the OECD then met to implement these Recommendations. It is worth noting that the decision to review money laundering was reached by the G7, which at the time was Canada, Japan, the USA, France, Germany, Italy and the UK. The rest of the European Union was represented by the European Commission. Since then, the 40 Recommendations have been accepted by over 200 countries. The FATF's regional work is conducted by associate members and observers, including various global and regional agencies such as the United Nations Office on Drugs and Crime (UNODC), Europol and Interpol. Its coverage truly is global.

The original concerns at the Summit were about the fortunes being made by drug traffickers, especially the trade from poorer countries producing narcotics for consumers in richer countries – particularly the G7 countries. The specific issue at the time was the risk of dirty money entering the legitimate financial system and tainting it. The risk-based approach adopted by the global financial sector still forms the basis of the FATF policy even today. Since the FATF describes itself as a 'policy-making body', this has proven central to its *raison d'être*. This self-acclaimed title implies a risk that some money will enter the system, and that the policy is there to manage the risk. All well and good, in theory.

The money laundering report created a list of the 'predicate' crimes, the sort that generate 'dirty money'. This list had its own self-fulfilling logic, for example, the illegality of the drug trade created high prices and an 'alternative' society where all sorts of crimes were committed by drug takers to obtain the money to buy drugs. Since the list of predicate offences made up by the FATF needed to be understood globally, it was framed in everyday English rather than jargon. Today, it provides a clue as to what was on the crime agenda back in 1989. The original list was very widely drawn, to include every conceivable way to make money through crime, the only notable exception was tax evasion, although this was later added in. Money laundering was a threat to the whole economy and to society in general and derived from every type of crime recognised by criminal law. The idea was to view all crime from a financial perspective; this would provide new ways to tackle age-old problems. It had (and has) the potential to revolutionise the way we tackle all crime with new efficiency and effectiveness. In particular it offered a way out of the problem of displacement.

Historically, law enforcement would focus on a particular crime type and succeed in suppressing it, only to find that criminals moved their efforts to another type of crime that was less well policed. This could lead to criminal justice agencies playing a version of the fair-ground game of 'Whack-a-mole' whereby scarce resources would follow crime types as they spiked. Specialist police squads would be formed and reformed to successively tackle shoplifting, armed robbery, then fraud, then car theft, then burglary, then street robbery and then back to shoplifting in a never-ending game of catch-up. Each crime type ended up with a residual small squad to manage ongoing crime until the crime type came back into 'fashion' and became a priority again. The discovery of a thread called 'money laundering' that connected all crime could have allowed the formation of police squads to tackle dirty money and follow it back to the predicate crime, deterring, disabling and dismantling the finances that underpin organised crime as they went. There would be no displacement because the dirty money would be the priority. It is the ultimate example of thinking like organised criminals in order to tackle them in the most effective way possible. Criminals are (obviously) aimed at making money. Law enforcement would be meeting them head on, no longer following, but tackling the current crime issue – whatever it was – head on. Over time, the financial crime squads would get better and better at their specialism, more and more effective, using the latest financial methods to tackle every type of crime. This could, over time, help develop crime policy, helping to identify systemic weaknesses that help all sorts of crime, such as: the ability to form companies to help transport drugs, trafficked people and counterfeit goods; the use of enablers to provide professional accountancy and legal services; allowing the police to seize dirty cash (the ultimate crime enabler). None of this happened. Governments and policy makers instead tried to fit the new miracle into the existing bureaucracy. A new all-encompassing concept was reduced and folded down until it could fit into an existing pigeonhole. This is what they did:

Convoluted efforts by governments and policy makers tried to narrow down the money laundering agenda to economic, financial crime, fraud and to similar 'white-collar' offences. Perhaps this was an attempt to make money laundering more logical to bankers and financial policy makers. Whatever the reason, the effect was disastrous. Responsibility was passed to the people in charge of criminal justice, but those people were unfamiliar with the world of finance and lacked guidance that money laundering was of general relevance to *all* crime. In their ignorance they passed it down the line until it ended up with one of the smaller residual police squads mentioned above. Money laundering was handed over to the 'Fraud Squad' or 'Economic Crime Unit'. It is an absurd and counterproductive effort because, by its very own definition, the *crime* of money laundering cannot exist without a predicate *crime*. If money laundering is an economic crime, then all its predicate offences are economic crimes too. This decision would have brought money laundering into the mainstream of policing and criminal justice where it belongs. The techniques to tackle money laundering would have come too. The incredible breadth of financial intelligence, the hugely impactive powers to freeze assets could have transformed policing. Instead of following the traditional approach of forming a little squad to tackle a new crime, the policy makers should have made it clear that AML was a new approach, a new way to tackle crime, a new technique of 'financial investigation' that required a new profession of 'financial investigators'. The 1990 report heralded a new concept which became known by the mantra 'follow the money', but the policy makers never followed through. They still have not. We know much more about financial investigation and have repeatedly tested its efficacy against crime in the real world but sadly our criminal justice system has not moved with the times.

There is merit in listing the FATF predicate crimes in full as it reminds us of the basic principles underpinning the regime. Doing so, helps us to understand that everything on the list is an economic or financial crime. This means that everything on the list in Box 1.1 is what the global AML regime is *for*.

---

**Box 1.1:  Crimes that are necessary for money laundering**

**Designated categories[5] of offences means:**

- participation in an organised criminal group and racketeering;
- terrorism, including terrorist financing;
- trafficking in human beings and migrant smuggling;
- sexual exploitation, including sexual exploitation of children;
- illicit trafficking in narcotic drugs and psychotropic substances;
- illicit arms trafficking;

- illicit trafficking in stolen and other goods;
- corruption and bribery;
- fraud;
- counterfeiting currency;
- counterfeiting and piracy of products;
- environmental crime;
- murder, grievous bodily injury;
- kidnapping, illegal restraint and hostage taking;
- robbery or theft;
- smuggling; (including in relation to Customs and Excise duties and taxes);
- tax crimes (related to direct taxes and indirect taxes);
- extortion;
- forgery;
- piracy; and
- insider trading and market manipulation.

This list of economic and financial crimes has had two additions since 1990. In its Annual Report of 1996, describing 'new developments', the FATF observed that two members had introduced innovative draft legislation, one to tackle terrorism and one to tackle tax. These new areas were formally added to the global list in 2001 (terrorism) and 2012 (tax). No need to rush, then.

Interestingly, tax evasion had been *specifically omitted* from the initial comprehensive global list of predicate crimes for over 20 years, contrary to the original view of the US Permanent Sub-Committee on Investigation in the 1980s (to be discussed later) until its inclusion in 2012.

Although the original list was aimed at serious crimes only, many countries have since adopted the 'all crimes' concept, for the practical reason that it would be absurd to allow criminals who have amassed a criminal fortune to escape confiscation of that fortune via a technical defence. Many crimes with low penal sanctions can be very lucrative when committed on an industrial scale not envisaged by law makers. The use of confiscation by the UK's Environment Agency shows a potential way forward to the global problem of waste disposal. In a typical case, the operator of a disposal site permitted toxic waste to be treated as normal waste.[6] This reduced the cost of dumping 3,500 tonnes of waste from £288,000 to just £9,000. Many countries have not adjusted their penalties to match the terrible damage caused by environmental crime and the UK is no exception. The *penalty* for the crime was therefore a suspended prison sentence and some hours of 'community service'. A confiscation order, however, required the offender to repay the proceeds of his crime. This was calculated at over £800,000 and was enforceable against his personal assets, which is likely to have had a greater impact than the criminal penalties. This is a crucial point in the weaponry against dirty money. Confiscation orders are sometimes viewed as a fine or akin to a prison sentence. They are neither, they are a mechanism to restore the status quo to the time before the damage of the crime was done. After that, a deterrent penalty can be considered.

This common-sense approach has not, however, been adopted everywhere. and absurdly there are still many countries permitting fortunes to be kept by convicted criminals based on purely technical defences based on local, narrowly drawn definitions of money laundering, defences which would not be available if the local drafters had understood that money laundering was intended as a routine aspect of existing predicate offences.

Still, the tangible results of the FATF approach are nevertheless impressive. Every country has established a governmental FIU to receive reports about suspicious financial transactions. They have also created a mechanism to coordinate stakeholders, and legislated money laundering as a specific crime. Moreover, every country is now subjected to peer-reviews on a regular basis conducted under the premise of a mutual evaluation. Non-compliant countries are placed on watchlists, although being placed on an FATF list is not taken seriously by a few rogue nations. The FATF has achieved a longevity and momentum which few other policy-making bodies can rival, and in the field of money laundering and terrorist financing the FATF is unrivalled. There is simply no other body which comes close. Despite its long history, the FATF has surprisingly managed to avoid the type of organisational scandals that have tainted other global bodies. Perhaps it is for this reason its reach across the globe makes it a serious policy leader. Yet are its policies still 'fit for purpose'? After all, money laundering and the harms of its predicate crimes continue to plague the world, meaning there are still many questions to be answered.

Despite its global reach and acceptance, there are critics who feel the FATF is unfair, tending to favour the wealthier founding member states. There are others who feel that the whole structure was secretly rigged from the start. Others, like the authors, still feel that the problem of *international* crime will simply be missed by a system that focuses largely on *national* performance. How can the FATF fairly evaluate a country which copes well with its own predicate crimes, but whose economy is based on laundering the proceeds of predicate crimes committed elsewhere? Even more fundamental, is how the FATF focuses on prevention, yet acknowledges that regulation, prosecution and confiscation are also necessary. The reality is, the FATF has chosen to focus on doing only really the first half of the job and it must know by now, that no one is doing the other half. As the appointed and self-styled global standard-setter, it clearly has a responsibility to make the entire system work. Of course, fostering global cooperation and establishing a level playing field is never going to be easy, particularly when some countries are better equipped than others. Still, doing nothing is an option that should no longer be offered to the table.

## Was the FATF approach rigged from the start?

G7 Summits do not make spur-of-the-moment policy moves. G7 Summits are the place where they are *announced*, drinks are sipped from awkward cups on ill-fitting saucers and people mingle. In the run-up to the formation of the FATF in 1989, unsurprisingly, there were extensive discussions between officials – mainly those working in the USA and UK in the administrations of President Reagan and Prime Minister Thatcher. Several years later, two researchers from the University of the West of England, Mary Alice Young and Michael Woodiwiss, researched previously unseen correspondence from 1987 and published their findings in April 2020.[7] An abstract from their paper has this extraordinary summary:

> [T]he core of the current, global AML regime, was not the destruction of drug money laundering and banking

secrecy, nor the ending of criminal financial enablers and with-it hot money; rather it was the protection and leverage of national trading interests on both sides of the Atlantic. And the drive to protect these interests would see crime control laws made, amended, and changed to cater for the interests of the US and UK banking and finance industries.

They are suggesting that American officials and their counterparts in the UK Treasury collaborated to design an almost ideal AML system to protect their financial industries, at the expense of crime control. To do this, it was necessary to take control of the instruments of international crime control and ensure that they concentrated on prevention rather than enforcement: 'The US government was then largely responsible for setting the organized crime control agendas of national governments and international organisations, notably the UN, the FATF, the Basel Committee on Banking Supervision, and international law enforcement agencies such as Interpol.'

The critical importance of these discussions was in the framing of a narrative that was both plausible and acceptable. The narrative was based on three main assumptions: that the US system worked; that the illegal drug trade was the main threat; and that tax havens could be adequately policed. This 'prevention' narrative would allow the Americans to get British help to control their own tax-dodging citizens who used British islands. In return, the Americans would allow the British to market their islands' financial services to the rest of the world. Both countries over-estimated their ability to control events by preventative means. The assumptions were imperfect, but this was to be the controlling narrative for the foreseeable future. We will explore later whether the narrative still holds true.

Other narratives existed about how to tackle organised drug crime through a change of focus or curbing bank secrecy, but these did not survive the debate. Essentially the needs of bankers, an American tax-starved Treasury and a beleaguered British government managing the remnants of empire came out on top. An American Government study in 1983 found that 'bankers, lawyers, offshore politicians and gangsters used offshore banking facilities as part of organized criminal enterprises'.[8] The 'gangsters' aspect was something of an afterthought in this list; the concern of the committee, as revealed in the published report was primarily the proliferation of 'white-collar' crime and the loss of taxes. The concern about drugs was largely an American phenomenon.

At the same time, a separate group, the UK Home Affairs Committee was discussing the 'misuse of hard drugs' and had recommended 'immediate steps to reform the laws of banking to remove the secrecy which protected the international drug traffickers and made the "laundering" of their money easy'. We recognise, the report noted, 'that this will call for a basic and dramatic reform of international banking law'.

It is worthy of note, that a call to end banking secrecy was thus already firmly linked to the trade in hard drugs and had already been made by a high-level Parliamentary committee. This was viewed as radical at the time, yet it has still not been addressed, more than 30 years later.

The researchers into the 1987 events, concluded that the discussion 'elevated the role of bankers to criminal policy makers, whilst minimising the role of international law enforcement bodies such as Interpol'.

This is still highly relevant to today's global money laundering policy. In 2019, the UK's financial sector officially assumed the 'elevated role' of criminal policy maker, being formally assigned significant membership of the UK's newly established Economic Crime Strategy Board.

Back in 1987 these discussions were informal and had been classified as secret – as was normal for diplomatic correspondence at the time. This is not to say that they were deliberately suppressed, simply released under the normal 30-year rule on public disclosure in the UK in 2017.

The result was that organised drug crime would be approached through the sole medium of preventing illicit financial flows via financial system compliance. Options such as lifting bank secrecy, promoting criminal justice enforcement, or ensuring the transparent ownership of companies were simply not taken forward. The idea that some government officials (in finance) were undermining the policies of other government officials (in operations) will likely come as no surprise to anyone who has worked in government. There are, however, some important caveats when considering the notion that the FATF's purpose was fundamentally weakened from the start. The officials concerned should not be seen as pro-crime advocates, they were merely working in the national interests as they saw it. Equally, they were not pro-money laundering, more pro-financial sector viability. Nor did they necessarily succeed, either at the time or over the next 30 years. Policies (and officials) change, lose importance, or get overtaken by events. Having said that, it is important to realise that anti-crime and AML policies do not always have universal approval in government, or anywhere else. Like any public policy, it must fight its own corner, have its own logic, its own supporters. Even once a policy has been accepted it has to be implemented. Again, anyone who has worked in government will know that many excellent, universally acclaimed policy initiatives have stalled and withered away during the implementation stage. The authors will discuss more about the gap between policy ambition and reality throughout this book, while making practical suggestions on how to bridge it, notably in relation to AML.

## Is prevention better than cure?

At the core of implementing its 40 Recommendations, the FATF runs a very sophisticated and expensive evaluation process. The idea is that compliance with the Recommendations will automatically prevent money laundering through the financial system. The results are publicly available in detailed 'Mutual Evaluation Reports' (MERs) which give a snapshot of a country's compliance with the AML Recommendations set by the FATF and a grading of their operational effectiveness. The FATF has broadly succeeded in walking that regulatory tightrope of being seen to be both independent but not distant, tough but not insensitive. The final versions of MERs are eagerly awaited by those who recognise their importance to national commerce and reputation. An adverse report can be damaging, and the consequences can last for many years. The existence of these reports is a significant global achievement, it is hard to think of another global standard in any human activity which has such a wide policy scope and that is so regularly and thoroughly reviewed and evaluated. The process is impressively thorough, and the results are informative for the country concerned, its neighbours and trading partners. The process itself raises awareness of crime and its consequent money laundering in the context of a specific time and place.

As an homage to the FATF, the chapters of our book broadly follow the same order of the listed criteria for operational effectiveness evaluated by the FATF. The authors believe that the FATF criteria follow a logical order. To help explain this, we have chosen to include the criteria, in full. But before you read the criteria, there is a noteworthy health warning: The FATF is very fond of words, so Box 1.2 is for technical wunderkinds. To help, we have condensed what it says in Table 1.1, which is much shorter and more appropriate, for the executive in a hurry, or normal people – like us.

---

**Box 1.2: The FATF criteria for evaluations**

**FATF Methodology for assessing the effectiveness of AML/ CFT systems**

The 11 criteria below are to be used to assess whether AML regimes are not only technically compliant (that is, possess AML legislation) but that their laws and regulations are effective in delivering outcomes that support the High-Level Objective.

**High-Level Objective:** Financial systems and the broader economy are protected from the threats of money laundering and the financing of terrorism and proliferation, thereby strengthening financial sector integrity, and contributing to safety and security.

Intermediate Outcomes: A to C. Immediate Outcomes: 1 to 11:

A. **Policy, coordination, and cooperation mitigate the money laundering and financing of terrorism risks.**
   1. Money laundering and terrorist financing risks are understood and, where appropriate, actions coordinated domestically to combat money laundering and the financing of terrorism and proliferation.
   2. International cooperation delivers appropriate information, financial intelligence and evidence, and facilitates action against criminals and their assets.

B. **Proceeds of crime and funds in support of terrorism are prevented from entering the financial and other sectors or are detected and reported by these sectors.**

  3. Supervisors appropriately supervise, monitor, and regulate financial institutions and DNFBP's [Designated Non-Financial Businesses and Professions] for compliance with AML/CFT requirements commensurate with their risks.

  4. Financial institutions and DNFBP's adequately apply AML/CFT preventative measures commensurate with their risks and report suspicious transactions.

  5. Legal persons and arrangements are prevented from misuse for money laundering or terrorist financing, and information on their beneficial ownership is available to competent authorities without impediments.

C. **Money laundering threats are detected and disrupted, and criminals are sanctioned and deprived of illicit proceeds. Terrorist financing threats are detected and disrupted, terrorists are deprived of resources, and those who finance terrorism are sanctioned, thereby contributing to the prevention of terrorist acts.**

  6. Financial intelligence and all other relevant information are appropriately used by competent authorities for money laundering and terrorist financing investigations.

  7. Money laundering offences and activities are investigated, and offenders are prosecuted and subject to effective, proportionate, and dissuasive sanctions.

  8. Proceeds and instrumentalities of crime are confiscated.

  9. Terrorist financing offences and activities are investigated and persons who finance terrorism are prosecuted and subject to effective, proportionate, and dissuasive sanctions.

  10. Terrorists, terrorist organisations and terrorist financiers are prevented from raising, moving, and using funds, and from abusing the NPO [Non-Profit Organisations] sector.

  11. Persons and entities involved in the proliferation of weapons of mass destruction are prevented from raising, moving, and using funds, consistent with the relevant UNSCRs [United Nations Security Council Resolutions].

You will see straight away that the FATF have put their criteria into three groups: A, B, and C addressing policy, prevention and prosecution, respectively. These groupings are useful because they 'belong' to different parts of the public sector: policy is the business of government; prevention belongs to financial and other regulators and prosecution belongs to the criminal justice system. All of these will engage with private sector bodies and the general public to be operationally effective. The scope of the criteria is incredibly wide, so these groupings are necessary to provide some clarity. You might have thought that AML is a rather niche activity, but money is everywhere, so money laundering is too. It follows that AML is a global effort that reaches every aspect of life. This means you, whether you like or not, so you may as well know what they are up to.

The FATF attempts to evaluate an entire country and that means everyone within its sovereign boundary. For example, in 'group A', dealing with '*policy, coordination and cooperation*' means evaluating the coordination of the public and private sectors of those who might manage, or have information about dirty money. That could be you, it could be someone you know. The FATF have what they call 'a risk-based approach', and the money laundering risk applies to everyone. There is always a risk that existing money might be the proceeds of crime and legitimate or clean money might become dirty if it is used for crime, evades tax laws, or is used for terrorism. So far, we have only looked at the first criterion (of 11) and already everyone in a country is within scope. As we go through you will see how the criteria is cross-cutting and involves many ordinary roles in business and society.

The second group, 'group B', looks at preventing money coming into the financial system and 'other sectors' (which is really every other sector that handles, as opposed to manages, money). These criteria again affect you as the reader, because if you have a bank account, or you use a shop that has a bank account, then you are automatically included. Although direct involvement in the AML regime carries some legal obligations to report certain financial transactions, most people are not the subject of such routine reports, but they are part of the system, nonetheless.

The final group, 'group C', concerns the criminal justice system. Straight away it is interesting to note that six of the 11 criteria are in this group, all relating to sanctioning criminals and depriving them of criminal assets. Interesting too, because we do not think that the level of resources applied to the global AML regime is in any way balanced towards improving the 'operational effectiveness' of criminal justice. Criminal justice relates to victims, witnesses and criminals, that is, anyone and everyone connected to a crime or attempted crime (consider the many attempted scams on your email or phone to see if this means you). Witnesses (whether they give evidence or not) also include any one of the hundreds of thousands of people connected to financial compliance and the world of Currency or Suspicious Activity Reporting.

The three groups set out the scope of the FATF evaluations to include the entire population of countries being evaluated, who are, in effect, thought to be at risk from the harms of money laundering. These populations are being, more or less, protected from these harms by the 'operational effectiveness' (or ineffectiveness) of the regime according to the specific criteria, below.

Table 1.1 shows the 11 FATF criteria, in brief, along with the chapter references in this book where we look a bit closer under the bonnet of each one.

## Does the FATF's snapshot national approach miss the point?

It was not always like this. From its inception in 1990 to a change of approach in 2012, the evaluation process examined compliance with the 40 Recommendations. The logic was that compliance with the Recommendations would prevent money laundering. Over time, the FATF refined its understanding of the impact of the Recommendations and recognised that some were more important than others and these became 'core Recommendations'. The grading system (Non-compliant, Partially Compliant, Largely Compliant and Compliant) being used sought to assess how the Recommendations were working in practice, but over time this proved really quite difficult, eventually becoming a tick-box

**Table 1.1:** Condensed FATF criteria for evaluations

| FATF Methodology for operational effectiveness, in brief. Mutual Evaluations will look at the things below to see if they work. | Chapters in this book |
|---|---|
| Group A: Risk reduction | 2, 3 |
| 1. Coordination of organisations and people | 1 |
| 2. Cooperation with other countries | 6 |
| Group B: Preventing dirty money in the system | 20 |
| 3. What regulators do | 5, 8, |
| 4. What service providers do: banks, lawyers, accountants, etc. | 9, 10 |
| 5. What companies do: beneficial ownership | 4 |
| Group C: Sanctioning criminality where prevention has failed | 21 |
| 6. Information sharing | 7, 11 |
| 7. Investigating crime | 12, 13 |
| 8. Confiscating criminal assets | 14 |
| 9. Prosecuting terrorist finances | 15 |
| 10. Preventing terrorist finances | 16 |
| 11. Preventing weapons of mass destruction | 17 |

exercise accomplished by having a policy in place, without actually implementing anything. The process could be cynically likened to a medical procedure where everything went according to the hospital policy and therefore no blame could be apportioned at the coroner's inquest into the death of the patient.

At a personal level, the authors used to read MERs in the pre-2012 era, and after finishing 300–400 pages of dense text would be none the wiser as to whether the country was any good at AML/CFT. It was simply hard to tell from a pre-2012 report. There were too many Recommendations, too many grades, too few tangible measures. Not only was it hard to tell if a country was any good, but it was also impossible to tell if it was getting better or worse. The evaluations, every eight to ten years or so, were too far apart to tell. The reports did not distil the findings into meaningful groups of conclusions. Instead, the reader was faced with a matrix of 40 scores, many of them interlinked with others. The effectiveness was implied rather than stated. The 'core' Recommendations were identified but their impact on 'lesser' Recommendations, which might be different from country to country, was not clear. The issue of international money laundering could be looked at from the evaluated country's perspective but without knowledge of its partner countries it was of limited use. The approach of taking a snapshot of an individual country's compliance with the Recommendations had three flaws: a lack of *comparative* measures over time or between countries, an absence of information about *international* AML and no *direct* assessment of operational effectiveness.

The FATF had started with a blank slate and achieved a great deal over its first 20 years. It took a long time, however, for the FATF to start to evaluate AML regimes. Before they could do this, they had to create the laws, institutions and understanding that underpin such regimes, normally from scratch. So, they can be forgiven for being distracted from their initial objectives. The FATF was created by countries which had established financial centres and strong institutions. It quickly discovered that many countries had neither. They also lacked laws and regulations, and these needed to be put in place across the entire globe. It was a Herculean task. Raising awareness of money laundering from next to nothing to being a criminal offence in every national criminal code was no mean feat. The creation and continued existence of an operational team – an FIU – in every country, along with a national multi-agency supervisory mechanism, was and is an incredible achievement. Without institutions and regulations, no systematic compliance could be evaluated. For this reason, the initial objective of evaluating compliance with the Recommendations was hobbled from the start. The essential groundwork of building institutions and legislation took over two decades, but by then the FATF had learned a great deal and could embark on a brave new world.

## The great leap forward, the FATF New Methodology

In 2012, the FATF launched its 'New Methodology', which added 'operational effectiveness' to the way it evaluated countries. It decided to keep the tick-box compliance aspect but, to be frank, the operational effectiveness element is much more interesting and useful to non-AML specialists such as policy and law makers, police and prosecutors. Put simply, if a country is not compliant, common sense (and the FATF's own logic) means that the country is also not likely to be operationally effective. So, it is just easier to look *only* at the evaluation of operational effectiveness. To a large extent, the technical compliance element is a legacy from the days of institution building and regulation writing that consumed the FATF's early efforts.

The current MERs can be likened to the results of a road safety test on a vehicle: the operational effectiveness grading tells you whether the vehicle has passed or failed and lists parts of the vehicle that are working correctly. The technical compliance part is only for the mechanic as a checklist. Before the New Methodology, only the checklist was available, and it did not really tell you if a country's system was working effectively. Now that the 'New' Methodology approach has been tested on well over a hundred countries (since 2012), it may be time to reconsider the value of the checklist.

## What are the FATF Recommendations really for?

The old logic was that compliance with the Recommendations would prevent money laundering, but now that we can directly evaluate operational effectiveness this logic is called into question. To put it another way, for which we will probably be burned as heretics, we question if the compliance industry is central to AML/CFT. The operational effectiveness that is desired seems to include the compliance industry of course, but in partnership with government policy makers and the criminal justice sector. The criminal justice sector in particular is central to the majority of the 11 operational criteria, yet until now it has seemed peripheral, which does not seem right in a crime prevention system.

Since 2012 there are only 11 'operational effectiveness' criteria instead of 40 Recommendations (about money laundering) and nine Special Recommendations (about terrorism). Why bother yourself with the 49 technical compliance details when just 11 criteria tell you what you need to know? In fact, of the 11 criteria only ten are commonplace. The eleventh criterion is the risk of funding the proliferation of weapons of mass destruction; we think that this is a very niche topic. Important, but niche.

The New Methodology has transformed the utility of the MERs. Most of us can grasp the top ten of something. So, it is far easier to understand the evaluation of the top ten criteria for a country. The 49 Recommendations remain, for the truly dedicated.

So, the FATF New Methodology has enabled us to see through the fog of war on crime and money laundering, meaning we can see some gaps that were not clear before. Some of them flag up things that are *incredible*. We should stress that the FATF does not use the terms 'pass' or 'fail', but in a four-level grade system, being in the bottom half of the grades is probably an operational failure. For criterion 8, which relates to the confiscation of criminal assets, only 20% of countries can do this effectively. To put this in lay terms, 80% of countries let crime pay.[9]

This should be a significant issue for the FATF's huge global community, who are constantly judged on how much is recovered compared to how much is available to be recovered. It turns out that the *cost* of compliance does not compare well with the *benefit* of depriving criminals of the proceeds of crime when measured in monetary terms. The estimates for the amount of dirty money out there is always far more than that which is recovered. Dr Ron Pol's research on national recovery rates across the world indicates that only about 1% or less is recovered.[10] We think that this is a simplistic approach, but there is no doubt that governments and commentators are drawn to it as a way to explain something that they see as complex. We think that more should be said about the *impact* of confiscation on criminal behaviour and the social benefit of recycling criminal assets back to victims and the wider community. We also think that far more confiscation could and should be done by the authorities. We think that the high level of scrutiny applied to the financial sector should also be applied to the criminal justice sector.

## MERs explained

We have briefly asserted that we see the MER process as robust and thorough, so here is a quick summary of the process. The

MERs are normally organised by FATF-style regional bodies (FSRBs). The 'rounds' of MERs are published in advance, allowing countries time to prepare for their evaluation. The process is time-consuming, and the impact of the COVID-19 pandemic has meant some changes have been made. It takes ten years for all the FATF member states to be reviewed. So, once you have been evaluated and get the 'green light', you are good for 8.5 years before you need to think about improving yourself once again. That is when the panic sets in, and countries are forced to catch up. As of 2022, the FATF is in its fourth round of evaluations with no real end in sight for this approach.

---

**Box 1.3: Who evaluates countries?**

There are small secretariats, modelled on the original, the FATF Secretariat in Paris, dotted around the world. They are: Moneyval for Europe, ESAAMLG for East and Southern Africa, GIABA for West Africa, the APG for the Asia-Pacific, CFATF for the Caribbean, EAG for Eurasia, GABAC for Central Africa, GIFILAT for South and Central America, and MENAFATF for the Middle East and North Africa. The FATF also does some of the evaluations, of the largest countries and to check the consistency of its FSRBs.

---

Each evaluation involves a group of nine evaluators who are selected for their representation of large and small countries, their diverse skills and some for their regional knowledge, as they are likely to be from adjacent countries. Think of it as a bit like the Fellowship in *Lord of the Rings*.

The evaluation starts with a questionnaire being sent to each country, which the evaluators assess before a week-long site visit to validate and clarify the answers; this is followed by a report. The report, once complete is then sent to the country for comment before being presented in plenary session of the FATF, prior to publication on their website. From start to finish, each evaluation takes around 18 months to complete. For the evaluated country, there is a very substantial amount of work required. Typically, some officials will be assigned *full-time* to respond to the requests of the evaluators.

The MER process has been criticised as:

- Too infrequent (at eight to ten years)
- Too stage-managed (cold calling might be more revealing of normal procedures)
- Too political (the inclusion of neighbouring countries exposes the 'Eurovision Song Contest risk', whereby neighbouring countries vote for each other, irrespective of the tune)
- Too forgiving (the evaluations tend to be generous)
- Too unforgiving (some countries whose populations have low access to banks feel aggrieved)
- Too inconsistent (how can anyone be sure that far flung countries are treated consistently, despite the FATF's efforts to guide its FSRBs?)
- Too detailed (consider 400 pages about 49 Recommendations)
- Too vague (despite the length of many FATF publications, at critical points the explanations can leave officials bemused about what to do)

Any global system will be open to criticism and we merely highlight that there are critics. The FATF seems very open to constructive criticism; it recognises that reform is needed. In October 2020 its president, Marcus Pleyer, accused the 'vast majority' of countries of not tackling money laundering. Our focus is on things which are mission critical or could be cheaply and easily fixed and that are worth doing.

There is a systemic missed opportunity in the MER system, when compared to some other similar evaluations. For example, the European Union carried out a multi-disciplinary review of 'financial crime and financial investigation'[11] between 2008 and 2012. The report for each member state contained recommendations for the state to consider but also good law and practice by the member state which had been identified by the review. These became recommendations by the member states to fellow members. Thus, over a four-year period, successive examples of good practice were promulgated across the Union. It is worth saying that, given the snail-like pace of change in most countries, the European Union (EU) recommendations of 2012 are still worth considering by any country looking for working examples of operational effectiveness.

The FATF MERs identify examples of good practice in the course of evaluating a country's progress. But the reasons why some countries are operationally effective is not proactively promoted by the FATF. Each national achievement is judged at the time compared to its last evaluation and then shelved. There is not a mechanism to promote the specific good practice by competent authorities and law makers that may have been identified. Indeed, the FATF publishes what the criminals are up to instead, by reporting on illicit financial flows around human trafficking, wildlife crime and trade-based money laundering, for example.

Citing good practice between countries is a missed opportunity; it does not have to be negative or embarrassing. Evidence-based learning seems to be a missing feature of the FATF evaluation process. The irony is that in many countries the competent authorities and policy makers are thirsty for information about how to do better and visit countries that they perceive as being competent, based on MERs. The visits are necessary because the MERs observe that a country is operationally effective but rarely identify why this is so. It is certainly more difficult to work out *why* a complex system works, rather than just observe that it does, but this seems a potentially important route for the FATF to pursue.

## Is the regime biased towards rich countries against the poor?

On this topic, we know of quite a lot of unhappiness and a quick surf of the internet will find much more. At the time of writing (July 2021), political economist Shakeel Ahmad Ramay of Pakistan's *Daily News* had this to say:

> It [the FATF] was created as a technical institution, but it is trying to behave as a political organ of the G-7. Pakistan is seeing the worst impacts of political manipulation. The G-7 is using it as an economic hitman. The media is using this opportunity to malign Pakistan and undermine its status. It also has

economic implications for us as the international business community avoids doing business with grey-listed countries. There is a broader consensus among independent scholars that the FATF is being used against Pakistan as a pressure tool. It is being used to compel Pakistan to bow down in front of the US and Western demands.[12]

Criticism in national media can be seen as a good thing, it shows that the FATF matters. It is hard to comment on the validity of a particular critique, but this type of criticism shows that the FATF and its work are perceived to be of political significance. The FATF tries hard, and broadly succeeds in producing fair MERs, but it cannot escape accusations of specific unfairness, the same is true for any umpire.

A more systemic problem is the potential for unintended consequences from the Standards themselves. In the same week, Wendy Delmar, speaking for the Caribbean Banking Association, said, "My sector has been significantly and adversely affected by FATF standards". She went on to describe how a brutal wave of de-risking activity between 2015 and 2018 had left Belize (for example) with no correspondent banking relationships and so it could not trade outside its borders; 'an entire county had been de-risked'.[13] Most Caribbean small countries were adversely affected by de-risking and having to spend 'burdensome amounts of money on the purchasing of compliance related technology and software'.[14] The FATF responded to criticism of this sort by establishing a project in February 2021 to address it[15] and delivering a high-level synopsis in October of that year.[16]

### Is evaluating one country at a time effective?

A significant problem for the FATF is that countries vary enormously in all kinds of categories. Trying to be fair is perhaps impossible. More seriously, it might not be the best approach for evaluating money laundering at all. It is well known by the FATF that criminals and their money cross borders easily, while the competent authorities just cannot.[17] Some countries have little crime of their own but are terribly busy laundering other people's money. Other countries have had all their money stolen and it has been laundered elsewhere. The FATF does evaluate 'international cooperation', but a country-by-country approach can never do this justice. The approach needs to recognise that countries are not isolated places but operate in a financial network.

We think that this is a fundamental flaw and offer these workable solutions. The FATF (and its partners) could look at a networked approach, whereby a country is evaluated, and its international partners are also visited. This could also be approached from a regional perspective, whereby close partner countries are evaluated in succession or even concurrently. This could either be based on finance and trade networks or crime networks or perhaps ideally a mix of the two. This need not be as complicated as it sounds. All countries already do a dynamic (that is, constantly changing) National Risk Assessment (NRA) based on FATF criteria, but these primarily look at the internal functions of a country and can only note external risks without exploring their origins. A networked approach would require countries to engage with partner countries in evaluating money laundering risks to mutual benefit. It should be quite easy for each country to map its main trade and finance partners and its main crime partners. Our experience as international AML consultants, means that we have specifically asked officials to list countries they have trade, finance and crime links with. We have found that most countries have an extremely limited network of 'crime partners', normally their immediate neighbours or a few more distant countries with strong historical links based on language, colonialism or diaspora. Similarly, finance and trade networks will be limited and grounded in historical logic.

Rather than evaluating how a country operates in isolation, the evaluation would look at specific cooperation and coordination with its networks. This would bring some logic and practical reality to evaluations, which we feel is currently missing.

## The AML community

The FATF is not the only global organisation concerned with tackling dirty money. The World Bank and UNODC have a

Stolen Assets Recovery Initiative (the StAR Initiative includes an interesting database explaining the details of the few cases where corrupt monies have been recovered). Interpol has a money laundering section, although on their website it is a mere subset of financial crime, which is itself listed as just one of 15 predicate money laundering crimes. This is an important criticism. If Interpol think that money laundering only applies to financial crime, who in their organisation is addressing the money being laundered from its other crime categories, shown in Figure 1.1?

There are other less well known (to the public) global organisations, devoted to dirty money. The Egmont Group is the secretariat of all the national FIUs. The Camden Asset Recovery Interagency Network (supported by its regional offshoots, with global coverage) has its secretariat in Europol. This informal group of law enforcement and prosecution specialists tries to cut through all the barriers to tackling dirty money erected by national governments.

Other global bodies have an interest in dirty money derived from crime. Transparency International has a keen interest in dirty money from corruption, so has the World Wildlife Fund.

Activists of many stripes from Avaaz, to Greenpeace, to DeSmog, have increasingly shown a keen interest in dirty money

**Figure 1.1:** In Interpol's crime categories, money laundering is a subset of 'financial crime'

| INTERPOL | Who we are | Crimes | How we work | Our partners | What you can do |
|---|---|---|---|---|---|

— CORRUPTION

— COUNTERFEIT CURRENCY AND DOCUMENTS

— CRIMES AGAINST CHILDREN

— CULTURAL HERITAGE CRIME

— CYBERCRIME

— DRUG TRAFFICKING

— ENVIRONMENTAL CRIME

— FINANCIAL CRIME

— FIREARMS TRAFFICKING

— HUMAN TRAFFICKING

— ILLICIT GOODS

— MARITIME CRIME

— ORGANIZED CRIME

— PEOPLE SMUGGLING

— TERRORISM

— VEHICLE CRIME

— WAR CRIMES

as they have joined the dots between the various evils and the pursuit of money. Some have always made the connection, such as the Tax Justice Network.

There are also national and regional organisations interested in tackling dirty money that have significant reach. There are too many to list here but to give you an idea of their diversity they would include: Germany's aid body, GIZ, which has a 'Global Programme against Illicit Financial Flows'; the International Centre for Asset Recovery in Switzerland; and France's strategy to assist the United Nations' 2030 Agenda and Sustainable Development Goals.[18]

## But first we need to talk the same language

All these organisations have an interest in dirty money and its counterpoint, asset recovery. But they are not all on the same page, they cannot even agree to use the same words. 'Asset recovery' at the World Bank is different from 'asset recovery' everywhere else. They are not even sure how to describe money laundering. Money laundering by placement, integration and layering is a common definition used by the bankers and the financial sector the world over, but the UN Conventions on which all the money laundering crimes are based do not even mention placement, layering and integration; they do not use the words 'money' or 'laundering' either.

The fact that there is neither 'money' nor 'laundering' in *any* money laundering definition matters; the term is misleading, and people put their own interpretation on the words. If you want to understand what journalists and expert commentators are really saying, read on. Our bluffer's guide to the jargon of dirty money comes next.

## 2

# The war on dirty money is mostly being lost in translation

In the world of asset recovery, the meaning of simple words causes serious, even grave, problems. As Kimon Friar, an American translator of Greek poetry observed, "Even the simplest word can never be rendered with its exact equivalent into another language". Kimon Friar was working with poetry where nuance, subjectivity and personal emotion are vital elements. You might think that legal translation is dry, objective and more susceptible to objective definition. But the stock in trade of lawyers the world over is to argue with each other over the meaning of individual words in their own languages. Not just lawyers but law enforcers and law makers. In an attempt to make international AML and asset recovery work, the globally agreed international language of cooperation is English. This chapter gives a series of examples where even simple words with narrow meanings have been misunderstood. The Kimon Friar problem was actually relatively simple compared to international legal cooperation. Mr Friar was working from Greek into English, whereas international lawyers make requests in one local language (such as Greek), have the words translated into English and then translated into another, different local language (such as Turkish). The answer to the request is then created in Turkish, translated into English and then into Greek.

These multiple translation steps have one important result, time after time: a failure of international asset recovery to work.

For example, over an 18-month period, German authorities refused to help with a series of Albanian police financial investigation requests for information about specific crimes committed in Germany by Albanians.[1] The request was made in English, the language of financial investigation. The German translator had used the word 'grave' to describe the legal threshold for providing assistance, the Albanian translator had chosen 'serious' to describe the crimes in the requests. The words did not match so the Germans, quite correctly, refused to help. As none of the investigators spoke English themselves, they did not know what the problem was. No blame is ascribed to anyone, but getting lost in translation hurt the victims in Germany and Albania, because solvable crimes went unsolved. This kind of thing is multiplied by the number of frontiers in the world and the number of crimes.

If you are thinking 'that couldn't happen here', think again. This kind of problem happens everywhere, all the time. The math works like this: the universally understood predicate crime of theft, for example, is described differently in every legal code in over 200 countries, so a request about theft might go from one country to any other country (200 squared).[2] Theft can be committed in separate ways – consider robbery, burglary and pickpocketing, for example – so there is a multiplier effect for each subclass of crime. Theft is just a small subsection of the 21 types of 'predicate' crime that create dirty money (see Chapter 1). The formal requests about dirty money from one country to another must define all the crime(s) committed and the evidence or information needed.[3] The potential for misunderstanding increases exponentially with each crime, each type of crime, each frontier, each language. All requests must get through this matrix of misunderstanding. Very few get through, which means very many are never tried. This has a serious impact on the international cooperation upon which international asset recovery depends.

Legal jargon is one part of the problem, so it is easy to blame lawyers, but it turns out that everyone is at it. We are going to try to define some misunderstood terms, starting with 'money laundering', 'asset recovery', 'confiscation' and 'offshore'. This will upset experts, keen to promote their definition, but we do not want to upset anyone, just explain why definitions really matter and what happens when they go wrong.

## Money laundering

According to Jeffrey Robinson, the term money laundering was first 'coined' (we saw what you did there, Jeffrey) by the *Oxford English Dictionary* in relation to political donations and the Watergate scandal in 1973.[4] As a specific type of crime, it began in 1986. The confusion began in the late 1980s as the two halves of the 'dirty money' army took the definition of money laundering and twisted it out of recognition.

One half, the financial and banking sector, aided and abetted by academics, went down the route of defining levels of difficulty in finding dirty money and produced a three-stage process of placement, layering and integration to describe greater and greater distance from the predicate crime. This has led to many, many people thinking that money laundering is complicated. We agree that the definition is complicated, but not the act of money laundering.

In the other half of the dirty money army, criminal lawyers produced a quite simple definition and showed how easy it was to identify and prosecute dirty money – which they defined as 'any property derived from or obtained, directly or indirectly, through the commission of an offence'.[5] It really was that simple. For example, when Eve picked the fruit of the Forbidden Tree in the book of Genesis, she became the first money launderer (directly). When she gave the 'property' to Adam, he became the second (indirectly).[6] Every criminal who acquires property through a predicate crime, is also a money launderer, by definition. We do not necessarily have to *prosecute* them for this crime, but it should inform our *investigation*.

London's police officers boiled this down to 'handling dirty money' and added a useful comparison to an existing crime: 'It's like handling stolen goods, except you don't have to prove that the goods are stolen.' This was a definition that was understood by operational officers. It was something that they could use because it was delivered in terminology that they understood (whether we can understand it does not matter). The result was that during 2003, hundreds of arrests for money laundering were made. Convictions for money laundering followed in subsequent years, showing that the courts agreed that the arrests were for the right crime. This shows that it can be done. Keep it simple and the rest will look after itself. Unfortunately, it was an isolated example of success against money laundering.

In most other countries, money laundering has not been explained to non-specialist officers, so they wrongly think it has nothing to do with them. There are few statistics for the number of police financial investigators as a proportion of the total number of police detectives, but the authors would hazard an educated guess at between 1% and 2%. A similar statistic, from the UK, is that there are 1,700 officers and non-police officer staff working on 'economic' crime out of a total of 135,000 officers and 75,000 staff,[7] less than 1% of the combined total. The category 'economic' crime in the UK includes both fraud as a crime type and financial investigators tracing assets from all sorts of crimes. Given that 40% of recorded crime is fraud, there must be considerable pressure on the fraud investigators, meaning that the number of financial investigators engaged against money laundering is a small fraction of 1%. Failing to engage the vast majority of investigators in the concept of money laundering massively reduces the resources available to the war on dirty money. It really is an absurd imbalance of resources.

Meanwhile the criminal lawyers, having started so well, managed to confuse the entire world. The way UN Conventions work is that the legal definitions that have been agreed are adopted into the local law in each country. A few countries simply pass a law that refers directly to the Convention, so that the *exact wording* is transferred into the local law, nothing is lost or gained. Unfortunately, many countries tinker with the wording, ensuring *decades* of chaos, criminal justice failure and a criminal jamboree. The EU has tried to fix the problem created by the UN among its member states. A series of Money Laundering Directives, agreed over many years, are still trying to 'harmonise' the definition of money laundering, showing just how difficult it is to unmix a cake.

The UN made one mistake; they did not make it clear that money laundering is an integral part of every predicate offence. This was an important thing that the UN could have said and one that is still worth saying by the FATF and, indeed, by anyone who seriously wants to fix the global crime problem. As a result of not understanding the integral nature of the crime, many legal drafters tried to define a new, separate crime and changed the original wording. Some decided that only 'serious' crimes would count, defining 'serious' according to local tradition: the length of a prison sentence; a crime on an existing list; the monetary value of the harm; the monetary value of the gain; the monetary value of the profit; the value of the gain as a multiplier of average income; and so on. This is without the boundless variety of choice and confusion to be gained from translating the UN Convention into the local language, amending it, and passing it into local law and then translating it back into English for the purpose of legally binding international agreements. It is impossible to exaggerate the chaos that ensues from this. It is the root cause of a global failure against transnational crime. Any national crime where the money is sent across the national border becomes effectively unsolvable. Every single change made to the law on either side of the national frontier must be understood, negotiated and then agreed in the circumstances of each part of each request.

Just to complete the mess, in addition to limiting the types of predicate crime, many countries limited the types of people who could commit it. Some excluded the original predicate perpetrator from money laundering, on the basis that they would be committing two crimes on the same evidence. Some decided it had to be organised, so they had to find two or even three suspects to complete the offence. In short, needless and significant barriers to international cooperation were created, not by criminals, but by law makers.

There is a global problem but potentially a global solution. There is an opportunity to transform crime fighting across the world. We accept that harmonising all 200 legal codes is impossible, but could the UN get everyone to agree to use the same definition of money laundering in their local law? It does not seem a big ask. Because money laundering is integral to all the 'predicate' offences, so international requests could be simpler for all predicate crimes. A request could simply ask for help with a money laundering crime (which everyone would understand and agree is serious) and then the predicate crime(s) could be described. At the same time, we could agree to ban the 'placement, layering and integration' definition, something we discuss in Chapter 3. The different jargon causes real-world problems. Someone in finance might discover some 'layering' and report it to someone in law enforcement. But yet, 'layering' means nothing at all to the recipient, it meets no definition of any crime and therefore is of no use.

It may help to describe what money launderers do rather than what money laundering is. Money launderers manage dirty money *and* they do not tell anyone that it is dirty. It really is that simple. Money launderers deal in *information*. They separate the *information* about the crime from the *information* about the money. The task of the anti-money launderer, therefore, is to put information about crime (and criminals) and dirty money together, ideally with evidence about who knew what, when. Again, it really is that simple. The world is full of massive databases about crimes and criminals and has massive databases about dirty money. We could just merge the two datasets together if we were serious about AML.

## Asset recovery

Asset recovery is a handy global term for a bunch of legal procedures which journalists (and therefore the public) often confuse. Impress your friends with your knowledge of legal jargon. Box 2.1 shows your bluffer's guide.

---

### Box 2.1: Bluffer's guide to asset recovery

- **Asset recovery:** This is the general term for taking assets away from criminals.[8] It is illustrated by the existence of an 'Asset Recovery Office', responsible for doing this, in every European Union member state (and many EU neighbour states too). Asset recovery is achieved through a series of actions by the authorities, starting with:
  - **Seize:** Physically take something away to preserve its value.
  - **Restrain:** Preserve something's value by court order preventing its disposal.
  - **Freeze:** As above.
  - **Sequestrate:** As above, Eastern European translators particularly like using this word. Which is a shame as it carries with it an inappropriate sense of authoritarianism, being originally used to describe seizure by a monarch from a traitorous subject. There is nothing authoritarian about depriving criminals of the money they stole.

After the court case, the ownership of the property is decided by a court order to confiscate or forfeit the property.[9]

- **Confiscate:** In most countries this means that the actual property ownership is transferred to the state. In many English-speaking countries, confiscate imposes a debt on the convicted person equal to the value of the assets.
- **Forfeiture:** Everywhere, forfeiture means that the actual property ownership is transferred to the state. At least we all agree on that one.

Simple, so far – so good. Now we come to the tricky bit.

- **'Non-conviction-based' confiscation:** It is also called 'civil recovery', or 'administrative' confiscation or, by Latin enthusiasts, 'in rem' confiscation. This is where no one is prosecuted, the actual property is the subject of the case. This leads to cases in the USA named 'The People versus US$123,456', or whatever the sum involved is. You may wonder what happened to the person, who should, surely, have been arrested. Well, this method of asset recovery is widely available, globally, where that person is no longer available for trial because they have died, run away, or become mentally incapacitated. It also applies where cash has been found that should have been declared at a national border. It is considered a waste of time to detain a traveller for trial, so Customs just litigate the money. Many countries have extended this latter, legal power inland and made it available to other competent authorities.

The 'competent authorities' is another bit of jargon, by the way, not flattery. The FATF use the term to describe all public bodies in a country that are engaged in law enforcement, financial regulation or prosecution. Each of these legal bodies has legal limits to its remit and its powers, collectively known as legal 'competence' to do what they do.

## Offshore

Where is offshore? You may well think that it would be an island, perhaps a sun-kissed one in the Caribbean or a little archipelago just off the coast of France. From a technical point of view, it just means a different country from yours, so Germany is offshore from France (if you live in France). As a parlour game, you can have some fun linking big countries to little ones. So, Germany and Liechtenstein; France and Monaco; Italy and the Vatican; the USA and the Bahamas; China and Hong Kong; Australia and Niue; the United Kingdom and Gibraltar, the British Virgin Islands, Jersey, Guernsey, the Isle of Man (et cetera, et cetera). In the advanced version of the parlour game, you can link Europe and Luxembourg, everywhere and Switzerland.

You will recall that, after 20-odd years, the FATF finally added 'tax evasion' to the list of dirty money crimes. This brought tax havens (or as the French say, 'les paradis fiscaux') into sharper focus. Companies and people exploit different tax rates by putting their property in different countries. The competent authorities all stop at their border and then ask for help from other countries, entering the Kafkaesque chaos described above.

Tax havens would argue, and we would agree, that different tax rates are not really the problem. We think that their secrecy is the problem, which is why activists such as the Tax Justice Network keep a Financial Secrecy Index which 'ranks jurisdictions according to their secrecy and the scale of their offshore financial activities'.[10]

To keep it simple we use the term 'country' in this book. But in the world of dirty money there are plenty of places that are not countries that often have a disproportionate, even inverse, importance compared to their size. The northern part of Cyprus is known and recognised as the Turkish Republic of Northern Cyprus (TRNC) by just one country, Turkey, which keeps an army there. It has just three major towns with populations of less than 70,000, and 27 casinos. For many years, its minister of finance could not leave the island for fear of arrest by the British police, by whom he was wanted for fraud.

It is, frankly, unfair, to pick on Northern Cyprus, there are so many other little corners of the globe which are not countries, US states for example. We selected the TRNC because, technically, it is part of the EU, whose oversight is, in fact, minimal. The world of 'countries', 'territories', 'jurisdictions', is extremely confusing; sometimes it feels that some of these places *only* exist because of secret (and therefore potentially dirty) money. Our point is that trying to control money laundering by focusing on geographical locations is doomed to failure. We quite liked, therefore, the title of Oliver Bullough's book about kleptocrats, *Moneyland* (Bullough, 2019),[11] which, in one word, describes the diverse places where their dirty money exists. The route to control the problem is not by studying geography but by studying the people in Moneyland and the people who enable their behaviour.

## The meaning of success

The confusion about dirty money is worsened by the way that it is described. Next time you read a news story about dirty money, see how often they describe how much was seized, against how much was eventually confiscated following the final court judgment. Indeed, see how rarely confiscation is mentioned at all. Confiscation is important because it is a real loss of profit for the criminal (noting of course that in English-speaking countries a confiscation order still must be enforced). Then compare this with news about the seizure of drugs at a frontier. The value of the drugs is typically quoted at the street value, that is, the value after distribution to wholesalers inland, mixing, division into single doses, distribution to street retailers and sold to end-users. In other words, the value is, quite literally, a 'gross' exaggeration of the actual loss to the drug importer. These distortions matter because we cannot really tell the difference between gross and net profit from crime. This means we cannot really get anywhere near the impact on criminal behaviour. We obviously congratulate the competent authorities anywhere who make an exceptionally large seizure of, for example, a ton of cocaine. It would be churlish to point out that global production exceeded 1,700 tons in 2018.[12]

We cannot do much about how drug seizures are reported. But we could, and really should, be able to know how much property is seized and confiscated from how many people each year. This has been the subject of an FATF Recommendation for over 30 years and we *still* do not know these simple statistics nationally and globally. There is, quite simply, no excuse for this.

The significance of 'seizure' is worth discussion. As the bluffer's guide explains, if something is seized the criminal does not have the use of it anymore (unlike something restrained by court order;

a criminal can continue to live in a restrained house or drive a restrained car, they just cannot dispose of it). 'Seizure' normally happens unexpectedly, often on arrest, when the criminal first discovers that they are in trouble. The impact is normally devastating. Imagine, if you will, being a courier for an organised crime gang. You are driving the boss's car with the boss's cash across the border, and both get seized by the authorities. Who are you going to call? Remember, the cash and the car represent real, not imagined, profit. Criminals really do know the difference, even if the competent authorities do not. Suddenly your life may be on the line. The impact of cash seizure on criminals is insufficiently researched. Governments and agencies are distracted towards the nature of crime bosses, corrupt politicians and their monetary worth. They should pay more attention to the impact of what they do on the behaviour of those people; the sudden loss of cash is a serious, possibly life changing occurrence, not merely an occupational hazard. Criminals change their behaviour when it happens, so should the authorities.

Confiscation orders come at the end of the litigation. They are normally for a much larger amount than the value of property that was originally seized. But typically, a criminal has had at least four years to adapt to their impending loss. It may be far longer. The Abacha fortune, looted from the people of Nigeria by the former Head of State was first frozen in the late 1990s and some litigation is still going on now. The impact of confiscation on criminals is important and it has even been studied by academics (inconclusively), but we feel that more research is needed on the impact of *seizure* on criminal behaviour.

Additionally, the number of people being litigated matters. Far too often, people are simply missed out of asset recovery statistics. The UK, unusually, began publishing detailed asset recovery statistics in 2017, starting with a five-year review.[13] Well done, the UK! Their report begins by stating that the purpose of asset recovery is to cut crime: 'by disrupting criminal networks [*of people*] … depriving *people* of their proceeds of crime, removing criminal roles [*people*] from society, deterring *people* from becoming involved in crime and … can also be applied to foreign politicians or officials … [*people*] who may pose a particularly high corruption risk'. We have highlighted their emphasis on people.

The report then gives extensive statistics about *money* recovered without mentioning any information *at all* about the number, or type, of people from whom it was recovered. Rarely has an official paper so thoroughly missed its own point.

Talking of people, the army tackling dirty money has two flanks: the finance people and the crime people. They are tackling an army of criminal people (including their money laundering people). Our experience is that good criminals are often extremely poor at money laundering. In fact, the skilled financial investigator versus the criminal is a very uneven, unfair struggle. In many ways, the money is the 'soft underbelly' of the hardened criminal.

---

**Solutions toolbox**

• Can we just all use the same words to describe money laundering? Let us use the wording from the United Nations Conventions:

The acquisition, possession or use of any property derived from or obtained, directly or indirectly, through the commission of an offence.

Can every country put the same words in the same order into their criminal code so that requests to trace and confiscate criminal property can cross borders as seamlessly as the property we are all chasing?

• Can we engage with the other 99% of detectives who already investigate predicate crimes to also consider the money from those crimes?
• Can we merge the data from SARs with the data held by police about criminals and crimes?
• Can we consider losing the term 'offshore' and instead gain the term 'Moneyland' to describe the secrecy that criminals use to keep, store and spend their money.

---

Financial investigation is an opportunity that is often missed by the competent authorities whose collective leadership does not know what money laundering is, let alone the many diverse ways that financial investigators can solve everyday policing problems if only they were tasked to do so. Nor do they understand that financial investigators are the forefront of their army, frequently not only working at the front line but behind enemy lines, striking at their supply lines and quartermasters.

This is a failure of education which this book is trying to address. So, what do we know about money laundering? The financial sector and its regulators are in a far better position than law enforcement to know about money laundering in their sector. Let us see what is known and how we can use our understanding of the problem to deploy our forces better.

# 3

# How much do we really know about money laundering?

If the United Nations definition of money laundering does not include 'money' or 'laundering', or 'placement', or 'layering' or 'integration' – what then is money laundering?

The authors

Many of the world's population – even those with little interest in crime – will, with any good fortune concede dirty money drives current affairs and global politics, and cultivates corruption. Avid viewers of films via Netflix, Amazon Prime and similar, will quickly appreciate money laundering is one of those activities naturally connected to illicit drugs, fraud, corruption, human trafficking and many other serious crimes. It is even considered a threat to national security; something we have decided to discuss in Chapter 16. However, what is missing is how it impacts on people's lives.

The movies, first-hand accounts and crime thrillers, demonstrate how understanding of money laundering sits only as a general topic. The knowledge gained has, in many cases, chosen to ignore the backdrop of global businesses and social activities which have sped up the way people now connect and interact with, and equally choose to disconnect from, the outside world. These are factors which we think now complicate understanding of most problems, let alone understanding as to how money laundering impacts on all of our lives.

Choose to review the current and earlier Europol Serious Organised Crime Threat Assessments side by side and you quickly begin to understand today's issues with establishing what is really taking place in the world of money laundering.[1] All we have are two Organised Crime Threat Assessments written years apart with no real material variation. The only difference is a more sombre and defeatist tone in the latest version. We think that this shows that the problems are intractable, thanks to the same mindset and techniques over the last 20 years.

Burkhard Mühl, Head of the European Financial & Economic Crime Centre at Europol was able to confirm the gloom and misery (albeit perhaps not his sole intention) when answering a question via an online seminar in June 2020 as to how criminals were managing their money laundering.[2] His response was to say: "We are still learning, still gathering the intelligence picture." Although most likely true, this must raise eyebrows among those involved in preventing serious crimes across Europe, and throughout the general population. Mühl's response clearly highlighted a losing battle. If Europol are still gathering the intelligence picture – against a problem that drives current affairs and global politics, and certainly fosters corruption – who could be trusted in Europe as knowing what is really happening today?

Is this why Interpol has now apparently stepped in, to do what Europol cannot manage at a local level? Interpol's *new* Financial Crime and Anti-Corruption Center will apparently fight the exponential growth in sophisticated transnational financial crime. Or will it? Is this move simply a rebranding, a fear of missing out or a drive for a stronger global existence? Or is it another "centralizing of [the] international response to transnational financial crime and corruption", as said by Interpol's Secretary-General, Jürgen Stock. A response that will create further toe treading and a more centralised *black hole* of unusable and unobtainable information no doubt.[3] Whatever the real reason(s), the hope is for better understanding and quickly – especially if we are to alter the sombre assessments and get to grips with a problem which is seemingly all too problematic.

Further troubling is how Europol will soon lose control over the secure communications network – FIU.net – with the introduction of the AML Authority (AMLA) – the EU's pending body with a direct supervisory role over large financial institutions. In doing so, the AMLA will control the AML/CFT database currently managed by the European Central Bank, meaning it will control a significant amount of data. Not only is this a massive blow for Europol, it causes a severe blow for establishing a real-time intelligence picture.

## Written in stone

If you take part in AML – and there are many weird and wonderfully titled roles to choose from – you will have already recognised just how many experts there now are. Of course, if a common literal meaning of expert is *someone having comprehensive or authoritative knowledge in a particular area* and we match it to money laundering, an activity having held an official place in society and business for nearly 40 years, then it is likely there are some true experts. But 'experts' in what exactly?

In 2020, the former FATF President Dr Marcus Pleyer criticised the gap between theory and reality when it came to AML, suggesting this was a reason so many criminals continued to succeed in the financial system. He was right. We think many experts in money laundering have been wandering round with their eyes closed and fingers in their ears. If theory and reality are so far apart – a strong assessment by the FATF at the time, have we, by the very pursuit to deal with money laundering, created experts not in preventing money laundering but in supporting AML compliance checklists or tick-lists (covered later in Chapter 8).

This distortion between prevention and compliance expertise is largely being driven by the profitable area of AML compliance – the meeting of expectations. We, therefore, recognise that globally the focus has matured towards developing solutions and support mechanisms that are compliance aligned, not necessarily aligned to preventing money laundering. While there can be an argument that AML compliance obligations are seeking to prevent money laundering based on the evidence in initially creating them, expertise largely comes from leading entities to strictly follow the compliance obligations.

What we now see worldwide are experts qualified at preventing money laundering driven by a belief that AML compliance equals prevention. Prevention is something different – it is the stopping of something, in this case money laundering, as opposed to meeting expectations outlined in AML compliance requirements. If AML compliance was working as a preventative activity, then money laundering would be on the decline. And it is not. We think this lack of clarity has created a distortion in global appreciation of the efforts being taken to tackle money laundering. A noticeable appreciation that fails to recognise how preventing money laundering requires understanding money laundering intricacies over and above a common money laundering typology definition. Equally it is not just about how a section of legislation can be applied, how time can be saved in managing monotonous checks, and where evidence of compliance can be best proven to an auditor.

Still, we could argue that the fewer people who know how to successfully undertake money laundering, the less likely they are to do it themselves or help others to do it. With 99.99999% of AML/CFT professionals having never been intentionally involved in money laundering – coinciding perhaps with the theory *opportunity makes a criminal* in criminology[4] – the worry remains because these experts are still too influential. Many are instrumental in shaping the course of measures to prevent money laundering – some having little experience. What assurances does anyone now have that these same experts are true AML and even CFT experts, and that their abilities, knowledge and appreciation of the many facets are relevant in today's criminal world? The answer for most will be zero – there are simply no assurances. It is far too easy to become an AML expert and get lost in the swath of pointless online chitter chatter at the same time matching compliance standards to business practices. Gone has the need, so it seems, to first understand the problem of money laundering, and this is why we are losing the war. We feel the real experts in money laundering face a tough ordeal at getting their voices heard. Has anyone ever considered asking the non-expert what they think? We suspect not. Even those true experts working in AML compliance struggle to be heard. The reason is that, for many, there is little benefit to what they have to say. Few like spoilsports, whistle-blowers, and those who ruffle feathers and lessen the ease with which things once happened. Instead, we now exist in a world where the same questions are being asked, with the same answers being given. If money laundering is to then be promoted as a terrible threat on the back of clearly non-expert opinion, then one would quickly think there would be an obligation to know the details of such threat(s)? But, in terms of money laundering, there are still few facts capable of anywhere near deciding the scale of money laundering as a problem – even its threat to everyday society. This may be hard to understand – what with so many experts and 30 years of effort – but the reality is, and it is a terrible reality, these experts, individuals, companies and international organisations benefit from making us all believe the threat is significant and even on the rise. Since we know the US has been a primary claims maker in the terms of defining money laundering, maybe these experts only need to rely on the US to determine the scale and promote their very existence.

What seems to be happening is that the figures we hear and read about are easily attracting the necessary attention. Equally, most are justifying what then follows as almost certainly necessary – however obscure it may seem to those with an ounce of common sense. The commonness of such information has a common tendency to skip over the finer details. Yet, these finer details you would expect an expert to be able to tell you. But they do not, because doing so can lessen a problem that is still accepted as being vast, huge, troubling, a global threat. So, despite the many experts in money laundering and the storytellers, it seems we now know a lot less than we should. But then without a problem, there would be no need for experts, nor would there be any need for AML compliance experts – so *why start to even think about cutting off the hand that feeds you?*

## Identifying money laundering

Fear not, if you have not been party to preventing it, money laundering can be a difficult activity to recognise. For many people it is considered a clandestine activity, committed by so-called 'threat organisations'; those criminal enterprises that are usually transnational and hierarchical – many of whom are suggestively portrayed as exciting in Hollywood movies. This is why you find many experts are also storytellers. Unfortunately, these same perspectives equally describe many worrying presumptions that can easily be decades old. Yet, such public assessments have become widely accepted without ever challenging what organisations such as the FATF, World Bank, International Monetary Fund (IMF), Egmont Group and similar continue to tell us.

Take a look at the Canadian Financial Transactions and Reports Analysis Centre (FINTRAC) website and fraud will be described as a predicate offence to money laundering. Look at the Australian government's financial intelligence agency (AUSTRAC) website and you will see how they proudly announce how organised criminals use *cuckoo smurfing* as a method of laundering money,[5] despite having already shown case studies of cuckoo smurfing way back in its 2012 typologies and case studies report.[6] Amazing as these statements can appear even to the avid reader, it is the details, such as these, that are now inhibitors to better understanding. Simply, the basic principles are being used repeatedly. But after 30 years of effort, you would be expecting agencies such as AUSTRAC, FINTRAC and similar to be leading the charge and sharing new characteristics about money laundering. But they are not, and if you take a moment to ponder this, the information we are being fed can quickly become a lot less relevant and believable if you are also intent on understanding today's money laundering endeavours.

What these statements and the associated glossy publications do tell us is that no one is really keeping up to date with understanding the problem of money laundering. Statements are continuing to be repeated as if there is simply no need to prove understanding. Yet, these statements also come from agencies that have the most up-to-date information at hand. So, does this really mean that when statements such as those mentioned are being published, accuracy is by and large being ignored?

Have, as our experience has shown, too many people fallen foul to the kudos of these publications, statements and similar because of the simple credentials of the authoring organisations? It seems so, because as authors we have seen the raw information, we know new knowledge exists and yet all we read in the public domain are historical perspectives that are no longer entirely relevant. It is simply illogical to think that the same snippets of information remain relevant year on year when confronting money laundering and the people involved. It is also challenging to understand how such meaningless publications, statements and those watered-down case studies can still be allowed to reflect demonstrable proof in leadership across AML/CFT compliance and/or financial intelligence.

## The knock-on effect

All this regurgitation of common sense means that money laundering, again as the guidance material will have us believe, fits a three-stage process of placement, layering and integration. Yet, critically, this is a model that has not been updated since it was first developed by the US Drug Enforcement Administration in the 1980s. Although, strangely, defence[7] as a fourth stage has since been added without any warning whatsoever – if you believe Kate Beioley at the *Financial Times*.[8] The result is that this original model has distorted the true understanding among practitioners and made it difficult, in fact almost impossible, for academics to operationalise it in their research. Nor have the processes' exceptionally weak conceptual foundations and vague definitions added anything helpful.[9] Yet, the model remains and continues to be used extensively while lessening the scope to ever begin questioning money laundering as a practice in the 21st century.

It might be thought we are about to head onto a better track with recent developments in the EU, as member countries create regional bodies intent on dealing with transnational crime, money laundering and terrorism financing. Yet, look a little closer and it appears nothing new is about to be brought to the table for discussion anytime soon. That is, if there is such a table in Europe where people are allowed, even encouraged, to bring something new. Is this why banks, professional entities and even countrywide regulators suffer from a lack of knowledge and any impetus to challenge the status quo which has continued for at least the last decade? When was the last time a table was set up, a round robin was initiated, a chance for everyone in the room to give an opinion? We think *group think* has taken over, steam rolled through the obstacles and made a path without any care for the destruction left behind or the true direction of travel.

It is possible that today's risks are not being found because lapses in compliance controls are allowing money laundering and terrorism financing to routinely take place. Lapses not just elsewhere, but in Europe too, despite its coordinated approach. This means new and existing problems are not being fully addressed, especially those within particular industry confines. The consequence of this alone is that national FIUs (talked about more in Chapter 7) do not then receive the details that allow them to return support to the regulators and regulated sectors with risk details capable of supporting AML/CFT compliance. Although this obvious circle of knowledge may exist in theory, when knowledge is missing and the trends in sectors are not reported, then the national threat cannot be shown to all relevant parties through the NRA. We agree, the practice of discussing what is already known may be reassuring for many, but we as the authors think that it leads to the war on money laundering being as practical as a one-sided game of tug-of-war. If there is no relevant resistance from those who look to stop it, then why bother turning up?

### 'One potato, two potato, three potato more'

Initial guesstimates, and that is what they are – simply guesses – openly illustrate to us that the amount involved in money laundering is a large figure. Initial and commonly referred estimates date back to 2009 when the UN first put the figure at US$2.1 trillion.[10] In real terms, such figures are now less relevant, almost invisible thanks to global monetary figures attributed to global trade and the many aspects associated with COVID-19. Yet, with money laundering, the US$2.1 trillion figure still offers a way to attract the interest of the reader, especially if it is feared their attention is fading.

Maybe you couldn't make this up if you tried, but since 2009 there have been countless attempts to put a figure on the problem of money laundering. Yet the obvious challenge, something that would probably have been clear right from the start, is that it is almost impossible to figure out the total illicit value laundered each year. The more thought given to this, the more absurd it is to even begin such a task – a task similar to counting waves when at sea. Still, economists and financial experts around the world from various universities, global bodies and state-specific law enforcement and governments have tried and failed. They fail because they contradict one another in their assessments of the legitimate economy. It is here, in the legitimate economy, where understanding is still underpinned by independent audits, external analysis, public statements and credit reference agencies. Add in the checks and balances of shareholders, regulators and the market itself and you are left with different perspectives and the inconsistent foundation for any assessment.

If it is obviously impossible to understand the legitimate economy, the basis or foundation for calculating money laundering, how then, without a magic wand, is it possible to put a value on crime – never mind money laundering? One would now hope for a 'light bulb moment' to finally happen. Why, because calculating the value of money laundering is impossible when changes to type, values and frequency change as often as the weather. Equally, the black market or illicit economy is enormously non-transparent. No real surprise there, but this means it can never, even with the biggest of magic wands, be quantified. Equally, it is here in the illicit economy where the most influential and the wealthiest criminal organisations unsurprisingly decide, with little persuasion, to undertake their business. Most of these criminal organisations are supported by no public presence, no formal offices, no staff, nor operations – in complete secrecy.

So, to then think is it possible to decide a figure would be like guessing a better guess to simply try to find 'a more exact guess of an earlier guess' as to the size of money laundering. Still, it is worth glancing over the more interesting estimates (and we really mean best guesses on older guesses) that reveal the true absurdness of any attempt to put a figure on money laundering.

Headlines by the UK *Financial Times* in 2017 claimed **£90 billion** of criminal money was laundered through the UK each year.[11] Yet, a year earlier, a Parliamentary Home Affairs Committee report had estimated that around £100 billion of illicit money was being laundered each year through the London property market. The 2015 US National Money Laundering Risk Assessment has us believe nearly **US$300 billion** is laundered through the US financial system on an annual basis. So, with the UK and US roughly totalling **US$400 billion**, this then leaves only **US$600 billion** for the rest of the world when matched against the hyped up and extensively referenced UNODC study claiming **US$1 trillion** is laundered each year.[12] The non-profit organisation Global Financial Integrity has also suggested that transnational crime is worth as much as **US$2.2 trillion** each year. So, can this mean only 40% of the illicit funds is laundered, if this figure is again aligned with the UNODC figure being used time and again as a policy pushing benchmark figure? No, because they are all guesses, not even best guesses just more guesses that have been taken forward by most because someone with authority said that is what the amounts would be.

These figures, even those from the most prominent organisations are then duplicated, referenced and drawn upon to support various crime policies. This means it is difficult to find a government document which does not rely on such a reference in its opening chapters as a way to justify the generic chatter that then follows. Advocates may argue that these figures are a step in the right direction – as a means to add some clarity or parameters to the problem. But while all these estimates may appear fine – how do they truly relate to today's world when estimates suggest the cybercriminal economy in 2018 (that is pre-COVID-19) was, on its own, already worth **US$1.5 trillion**.[13]

Looking a little deeper at these estimates, there are many questions that need to be answered – especially if you have some understanding of money laundering practices. First, is there a process of avoiding double counting? We bet there is not, and this question is made all the more difficult to answer when no effective high-value money laundering operation is ever truly centralised. By centralised, we mean it stays in only one country – meaning illicit funds only ever circulate the same counting method once. Could this issue alone mean that the figure of money laundering is possibly much smaller than the guesstimates? Second, is all that has been counted (to create these fictitious values) been laundered through the typical three-stage process of placement, layering and integration or has a value – and to what percentage – simply been self-laundered?[14] Is it possible the figure is therefore much higher?

The widespread lack of critical thinking or even basic analysis attributed to this scenario has allowed these figures to remain so widely accepted and relied upon. Knowing this as so many do, why is there so little effort to question these numbers when they are so terribly informed by the data used to create them? It is perhaps recognised behind closed doors, away from the tables where people are hopefully encouraged to come together to discuss solutions that it is impossible to count money laundering. Impossible, in the same way it is impossible to count corruption, or is it simply, as we have suggested already, not at all necessary because existing figures still manage to serve a purpose?[15]

## The reality of money laundering behaviours

Today, almost anyone can undertake money laundering. It can be the student, single parent or unemployed elder who chooses to allow their account to be used to deposit and transfer funds derived from criminality. Or it could be a professional criminal intent on laundering billions. Equally it can be the complicit bank teller, accountant or lawyer allowing their individual services to be accessed without raising suspicion and circumvent AML/CFT controls. This means, it can be difficult to pinpoint exactly who is responsible for money laundering, complicated too by the incessant flow of social media and spam emails offering desirable rewards for simple *deposit and transfer* schemes. Nevertheless, in the effort to combat the threat of money laundering, a knee jerk reaction has led to the passing of laws as the best technique for making the problem easier to deal with. A practice many will recognise as being derived on what was clearly an absence of knowledge right at the start and now a practice of legislating our way out of a social problem.

Still, as critical as money laundering is, no money launderer will knowingly describe in detail how they manage to launder illicit funds belonging to them or someone else. Today, we recognise a few may inadvertently discuss behaviours and activities during interviews with law enforcement, but money launderers do not as a matter of course *kiss and tell*. This obvious reluctance to say too much is probably because money laundering is an activity with strong links to organised crime. Equally, money laundering is the most important part of the criminal journey, with typical practices staying applicable year on year.[16] This makes it difficult to find out what is going on.

We have seen money launderers becoming experts at using every practical opportunity, while, at the same time, assessing activities for risk in the same way that legitimate businesses decide their risk of taking a new product or service to market. Since many money laundering methods are long-term, understanding risk is essential to them. Money launderers can and will use a variety of options. Many, despite the efforts to stop it, still use banks – highlighted quite nicely by the suspicious trades worth over Aus$600 million at Danske Bank between 2012 and 2015.[17] Similarly, the Commonwealth Bank of Australia (CBA) in Australia – a reputable bank with what would be considered strong AML/CFT policies and processes, permitted criminals to exploit vulnerabilities by depositing illicit funds into accounts via *hole in the wall* cash machines. This is an interesting scenario to grasp going into the 21st century when we match it to the widespread and strict AML/CFT legislative and regulatory environment that has surrounded banking institutions for quite a while now.

Take a moment too to look at drug seizures at the borders of most countries and ask yourself, 'How were the organised crime group(s) behind the import going to launder the proceeds of the drug sales?' We acknowledge cash may be on the decline in society,[18] equally 'cash may still be king',[19] but drug sales still produce a huge amount of physical cash. If 320 kilograms of cocaine is going to be shipped to a country like Australia,[20] someone somewhere has a tried and tested money laundering plan already in place.

Of course, despite the prosecutions, regulatory action and large fines, the reality or biggest issue is that none of the finer details are routinely uncovered, especially during law enforcement investigations. Nor, from our experience, are they routinely searched out or documented for future reference and analysis. As problematic as this may sound, worrying too, interviews with law enforcement officers over the last 15 years highlight just how the intricacies of money laundering operations are less of primary concern. Of course, charts depicting links between criminals, their activities and possessions are often seen as worthwhile, but this material only seems to make interesting office wallpaper, a reason to turn on a large infrequently used printer or form part of future case study presentations. It does appear that the underlying *red mist* aura surrounding investigations is doing little to support policy and preventative measures beyond the circumstances being investigated. The raw data exist, but the lack of effort to tie this to the problem suggests something somewhere is very wrong.

Money laundering, it seems, is almost certainly permitted to take place because we do not understand it. We know this is a brave and perhaps quite simple statement to make, but a lack of imagination by those claiming to want to prevent it is giving the money launderer a whole raft of opportunities to then exploit. While it is difficult to predict tomorrow's money laundering escapades based on yesterday's events, something academics are all too profoundly keen to do, there are still too many missed opportunities passing us by. What is taking place every single day are many thousands of mini failures that combine to make a global money laundering frenzy. Money laundering is not necessarily an actual *mistake* but learning from your *mistakes* can reduce the chance of future *mistakes*. The key here is *learning*.

With a little imagination, focused interest and a change in attitude, the outcomes could be enormously different and thus extremely beneficial. Perhaps this obvious light at the end of the tunnel is why the UK Financial Intelligence Unit (UKFIU) senior manager, Martin Cox, made a simple suggestion at the 20th anniversary conference of the Institute of Money Laundering Prevention Officers in October 2021. Cox highlighted (and we are glad he did) the importance of professionals from all parts of the regulated sector keeping up to date with evolving trends and themes aimed at tackling financial crime. Still, despite Cox's enthusiasm, the captive audience, and the obvious relevance to his statement, when the trends and activities are not being captured, knowledge only ever arrives in snippets. Such snippets then do little to figure out true trends and themes – something we see all too often in money laundering typology reports. If there was a greater focus on the entire landscape, we feel it could finally be a less tortuous process than that of cutting out the letters from tabloid newspapers to make a copy of *War and Peace* having never read the book.

## Training for an event that never happens

Our consistent lack of knowledge on today's money laundering behaviours is, to all intents and purposes, depicted by the lack of clarity in public-facing documents. Of course, documents need to be redacted while keeping readers interested in the excitement attributed to organised crime, but historically what happens is a failure to inform those struggling under the pressure of AML/CFT obligations. Typology reports only add to a simplification by repeating yet again the basic principles, and purposefully singling out those already-known definable money laundering types. Add to this the overly intense micro-credential subjects focusing on specific methods of money laundering – created by academics relying on FATF documents that equally create little real-world value or understanding. Yet, by lessening the grasp on historical knowledge, ignoring weak centric analysis, and turning to look at today's money laundering behaviours, it is possible to devise an entire range of more applicable training solutions.

Many of today's training solutions and the ill-informed repetition comes at the same time that the FATF and regional bodies are emphasising the importance of training as a key part of the ongoing fight against financial crime. Yet, in any training session, you are likely to see far too much evidence being credited to historical case studies. Of course, this misguided judgement then usually influences how money laundering is prevented and detected. So, with training solutions also being broken down into micro detailed certificates, diplomas and seminars, choosing to ignore the entire topic creates many problems. None more so than the threat to those organisations relying solely on these same training solutions as a measurement of knowledge and comprehension.

As will be discussed in Chapter 4, money laundering is not complicated, simply hard to spot. But you would be forgiven for thinking otherwise from a quick review of the courses and training material now available. Money laundering is a straightforward process, it really is, but this is not always clear to see, hear or read about. Perhaps it is the mere fact that money laundering is linked to organised crime, which has attracted widespread complication. Nevertheless, the landscape of training opportunities now available suggests there are not enough years in the average lifetime to cover all the topics.

## Revisiting some basic principles

Amid all the hype surrounding the problem of money laundering, the general viewpoint has somehow failed to remember that money laundering is 'not a place, not a person' (although there are so-called professional money launderers), it is a series of actions. It is not the behaviours that make the illicit funds appear clean; it is the transfers and purchases that take place right underneath our meaningful gaze.

These particular transfers and purchases involving illicit finance are intended to mimic those which law-abiding people have the opportunity to undertake – with the main intention of appearing normal. By identifying money laundering as simply transfers and purchases it is possible to see how money laundering is both simple and difficult to identify. Yet, importantly, this perspective provides evidence that money laundering cannot be defined by type – something, again, we discuss in Chapter 4.

One transfer and a single purchase or many transfers and many purchases are what constitute money laundering. A transfer we see simply as the movement of illicit value, hand to hand or via a formal and regulated financial transaction. A purchase we see as being goods bought with the illicit value.

Sadly, the focus on behaviours as a means of detecting money laundering through technology (something discussed in Chapter 9) is managing to conceal what is taking place – even distract us from the obvious. Instead of understanding money laundering as two quite different yet inextricably linked areas of *prevention* and *enforcement*, the focus has been on keeping them apart at all costs. We have become obsessed to the point of addiction with the behaviours of customers using vulnerable money laundering avenues and have ignored too many other basic details.

The mere fact that money laundering prevention has become so distinct from enforcement suggests a void of misunderstanding; a void that allows money laundering to thrive beyond its wildest dreams. AML/CFT prevention is now all about how money is moved and who owns it. Although the cost of compliance may be declared as a significant burden for many businesses, it is their approach to discouraging regulatory punishment for failures in the AML/CFT practices which delivers the best long-term results. Yet, in the financial world, AML/CFT is still poorly resourced, perhaps only attracting enough attention when the penalties have consequences far exceeding the original cost of doing business. The details surrounding money laundering and terrorism financing are unfortunately of little interest to most people. Although a business may be looking at customer behaviours, the tendency is to simply follow (ideally to the letter) the guidance supplied by regulators. The result of this is an AML/CFT compliance culture that is ill-informed, ill-aligned and way too costly, with prevention taking a back seat behind compliance.

Put to one side the glossy manuals, guidance and sales material incorporating those all too painful historical money laundering cases, and you begin to see how knowledge of money laundering is still bound by rules and compliance needs for most affected professionals. Little is known about the real intricacies of money laundering despite valuable data being captured by financial institutions and regulated sectors each day. Money laundering typologies scattered across the desks of AML/CFT professionals are, without doubt, too heavily relied upon. This means the complexities beyond these commonly distinguished behaviours are not always considered – seen in many cases as being out of scope, not relevant or simply not prescribed by regulatory obligations. "When it is a problem, we will be told it's a problem", is how one professional in AML compliance responded when asked what they were looking for.

With most knowledge among AML/CFT professionals coinciding with neatly formed and specific typologies, some dating back longer than the role of AML compliance officer, the ability to notice new avenues for money laundering seems to be dwindling. Perhaps, to those working in AML compliance, prevention is literally someone else's task. Perhaps this is a true assessment if considered literally. Yet, largely thanks to the heavy reliance on placement, layering, integration, typologies and duplicated training sessions, any understanding through the eyes of a bad actor is also of little interest to many professionals. So too are the workable opportunities to disprove existing beliefs or even understand those threats which are characteristics of new products. Prevention has become obsolete, a burden, an afterthought. Compliance instead has become the principal feature in the war on dirty money.

## You can keep the money

Meanwhile, in the law enforcement world, money laundering has become somewhat of a bolt-on addition that distracts resources from *real* policing and criminal justice. Here there is a lack of interest in money laundering. All too often, money laundering is only dealt with if it can pay for itself. While we accept confiscation continues to deprive criminals of their ill-gotten gains, when not recycled back to those that collected it, these same agencies naturally lose their desire to continue in their efforts. Still, this practice of taking the money has become a key performance measure that brings pats on the back for senior officers instead of anything concrete.

Still, it seems law enforcement has chosen not to do any more about money laundering than what is sufficient for securing a prosecution – and then, not necessarily a prosecution for money laundering. Hence why money laundering details are all too commonly missing from prosecution case notes. We have seen first-hand, because we have gone looking, the absence of critical details that could pull pieces of the investigative jigsaw together. Needless to say, it is common for cases of money laundering to be exchanged for a guilty plea on a predicate offence. But doing so can mean an offender keeping the money. A notion as absurd as it sounds yet all too often seen in practice. Crime really does pay.

Take, then, the disparity that also exists between prevention efforts and the direct and sometimes short-sighted enforcement-specific approach to securing a prosecution for a predicate crime. Knowledge gained and details uncovered can, in many cases, miss being recorded, shared or even acted upon. So, with the added hesitation in handling large-scale and cross-border investigations, the opportunity for making a dent in current money laundering activities has naturally become a whole lot more difficult. Is law enforcement really covering its eyes and blocking its ears to then focus only on the immediate challenges? We hope not, because if there is to be any chance of making a dent in criminality, then there needs to be more focus on money laundering through post-case analysis.

## Media portrayal or media betrayal?

While bad journalism can make people believe money laundering is less important than it really is, hype created on various aspects of money laundering does nothing more than create excessive noise. Much of this noise comes through over-quoting of relevant bodies, and the unnecessary excitement around the link between money laundering and organised crime. Then there are the ad-hoc issues, such as money laundering through the use of pre-paid cards or money laundering using cryptocurrencies – both of which are nothing more than a reaction to modern-day financial and business offerings by the criminal.

Still, once these reports are published, a path of *truth distortion* then begins. This leads to the true relevance quickly becoming obsolete, as details are then copied and applied to various arguments for greater legislation, more regulatory oversight, innovative technology solutions and even more red flags. If only it could be recognised by those in any way linked to money laundering that there has never been a set way of money laundering, then such reports would cease or at least dramatically decline.

Of course, it takes time to verify a source, analyse the data and question the meaning of statements; and who has the time to do this? Needless to say, it is not always the truth that matters, more a case of getting the message out there first, quicker and even profiting from what was apparently said. There is no doubt that the overwhelming amount of reference material now appearing on social media and professional networks such as LinkedIn is partly to blame. Much of what is being created is driven by businesses looking to deliver compliance solutions and provide IT services. Much of the hype is about raising profiles, meaning too few are willing to verify a source, analyse the data, and question the meaning. Therefore, it appears that the information being provided to customers is never scrutinised, especially if it can be attributed to a globally recognised entity, organisation or *expert*. We feel this is a major oversight which is fostering a downward spiral of neglect to actually understand money laundering.

It is possible to argue that our lack of knowledge and progress towards preventing money laundering (and terrorism financing) coincides with what Atul Gawande (2011)[21] – author of the book *The Checklist Manifesto* – describes as errors of ignorance. Errors of ignorance are what Gawande claims are the mistakes we make because we do not know enough, driven by how we make mistakes because we do not use the knowledge we have. The book goes on to talk about checklists, something the authors – you will note – hardly feel comfortable with in the context of AML/CFT compliance, yet the premise of these statements by Gawande are correct. We know mistakes are still being made because our understanding is limited – no more so thanks to a lack of detail surrounding today's money laundering activities and behaviours. The ignorance to understand or even consider the unknowns of a problem is further leaving us in a spin, explaining why money laundering is so successful.

Take, for example, trade-based money laundering (TBML), considered by many to have been conducted in the same way for 14 years. Why 14 years you may ask? Well, because the guidance from the FATF took that long to update.[22] Does this mean it was still relevant all that time? What we think happened is the FATF made the initial assessment, and everyone continued to think it was relevant. We also think no one dared to question the need to update it; it served a purpose for training by *typology guided experts* and the selling solutions while the focus was elsewhere. The problem is that this single form of money laundering distorted what happened in those 14 years in terms of prevention and compliance. We suggest it is still leading us down the garden path, despite the update.

## One man's money launderer is another man's investor

The belief that knowing the true scale (not the value) of money laundering can then support calculations of the harm being caused, we think, inadvertently ignores money laundering as integral to the predicate offence.[23] Scale is simply associated with the spread and frequency of money laundering, whereas to understand the harm requires understanding the characteristics of the many individual predicate offences which lead on to money laundering. These harms are created by actions such as human trafficking, illicit drug sales, online child abuse – or, as we would say, 'the actual crime' – not the laundering part. Since money laundering activities generally occur a long way from the first predicate offence, the laundering process can only ever be socially harmful in the country where it is taking place. And then, only if it undermines democratic controls and legitimacy or perhaps leads to greylisting or blacklisting.

It is also worth remembering, because we feel it is largely ignored, money laundering is a process that can and does cross borders. What we mean by this, is that where one country is laundering the money from crimes in another country, then both countries are equally responsible for creating the harm. While there may be harms to businesses caught up in money laundering scandals, no one is anywhere close to quantifying how big a social harm this really is. Nor must they try. As in the case of trying to calculate the size of money laundering, there are too many variables and opinions that need to be continually addressed, even if the end result could drive change and create legislation and stronger controls.

## Analyse this!

At the heart of any solution is, of course, the need for quality research and analysis – especially if your intention is to understand money laundering. Yet, research and analysis require focusing thoroughly on current cases and deciphering the changes in habits which have occurred. And, where possible, the reasoning behind them. Predicting future trends is critical if understanding is to match strategic desires.

We feel there is an opportunity right here. We suggest that to be strategic requires bringing together practitioners, new and experienced, to critically review existing money laundering beliefs. This would involve pulling apart the assumptions, mapping out processes as well as challenging original principles. With experience in analysis, the authors recognise this is no two-minute task, but a long-term exercise requiring commitment to ensure the full value is realised. Equally it is an essential programme of work that, if done right, can dovetail the real meaning of prevention and investigation together. Increasing knowledge on the problem of money laundering will only help to improve clarity. Improving clarity will better focus intervention efforts. We acknowledge the efforts by many, as well as the research and analysis that has already happened. However, the efforts to date have been largely wasted because if we really knew what we claimed as a collective to know, there would be clearer evidence of success in tackling the problem of money laundering.

## Acknowledging reality

Let us not forget, however, that we know more about money laundering than when it first came to the table as a topic for discussion among G7 leaders in 1989. The 1,000 plus reports written by the FATF alone, suggest knowledge levels will have improved.[24] Yet even now our level of knowledge seems all too connected to the perspectives of old. It is this obsession with money laundering traits of old that impedes the willingness to explore beyond the methods often released by the FATF. We feel many, including the experts, are unwilling to admit our knowledge is no longer entirely relevant because that would mean the experts are experts no more!

Perhaps the world will simply wait for all countries to fully adopt the 40 Recommendations set by the FATF before something new and more relevant is conjured up. It would be nice for all countries to catch up, but despite the effort, by 2022 only 76% of countries supervised by the FATF have only satisfactorily implemented the 40 Recommendations.[25] Many, like us, will feel this is a somewhat poor achievement, as *satisfactory* is a less than perfect grade against the global problem of money laundering. *Satisfactory* is a basic benchmark – nowhere near a demonstration of full commitment to meeting expectations and dealing directly with a problem causing harm to so many people.

If the global approach is to keep believing that the old, now outdated characterisations of money laundering are still relevant, then the only possible fate, we think, is a continuation of small successes and large-scale policy and operational failures. If 76% of countries supervised have now *satisfactorily implemented* the FATF's 40 Recommendations, why do we not see a reduction in crime, not just money laundering? The simple reason is 76% are also not entirely satisfactory across the entire 40 Recommendations. There are always going to be gaps in what has been implemented and it is these gaps where money laundering is going to continue. If a country is satisfactory overall, but non-compliant in dealing with DNFBPs, the opportunities for money laundering remain.

Of course, no solution is ever simple, and we acknowledge this. To find a solution we first suggest ignoring what the 'Global heads of ...', 'Regional heads of ...' and 'Chief heads of ...' and 'Directors of ...' associated with AML have to say. These people are usually far from knowing the details still being ignored when it comes to money laundering. These people may look and sound great on stage, but we are confident they are more people managers than authorities in money laundering. These people are managers of those who have the knowledge and we think the best ideas can only then come from listening to the people at the coal face – those who see and hear what is happening in the real world.

Solutions will take time to be formed, especially against problems as vast as money laundering. But can time complicate matters even more and effectively work against what we are trying to achieve? It has been over 30 years since the G7 meeting in 1989 when the process of money laundering started to become more complicated than it needed to be. Has the fear of needing to be *super chickens* (as author Margaret Heffernan describes the situation of giving the most powerful in the room all the resources and all the power) inadvertently forced some potential leaders in fighting money laundering to hide away?[26] To understand money laundering we must collaborate and bring together people without fear of competition. Indifferences among individuals, not just within public–private partnerships (PPP) is needed. If we want to learn how this has been successful, we only need to look back to Bletchley Park in the UK which became the Allied centre for code breaking during the Second World War. What happened there, and could easily happen again in the war against dirty money, is brilliant minds were brought together and people were accepted for their abilities, not who they were. If we chose once again not to suppress the skills and knowledge of others, it is possible to understand money laundering as it is happening today, not regurgitate how it once happened decades ago.

## Solutions toolbox

- We feel there is a need to first clear desks, clear the bookshelves, clear the mind, and begin again to understand crime and its association to money laundering. Imagine, if you can, you are a money launderer. Focus on how it is possible to circumvent today's preventative AML compliance obligations to launder a single one-off amount or a continuous flow from ongoing criminality. We feel money laundering must be understood in the context in which it is happening and the social relationships in which it is embedded. By ignoring the evidence to date, it is possible, if the willingness exists, to unveil new evidence of money laundering practices.
- Clear the schedule and the diary, switch off the mobile phones, close down the emails and review those money laundering cases that perhaps never received the analysis they deserved. And by review, we mean 'review'. So, map out what you think happened, find the knowledge gaps, and immerse yourself in the process that was taking place. Ask questions of those involved while seeing what those involved saw, did not see, did not go looking for. Try to walk in their shoes and open your eyes to the world of money laundering so many people still ignore. It will surprise you just how many other activities, people and locations are usually involved but are never investigated.
- Take action that moves away from the baby steps which might not always garner 100% public approval. Money laundering and terrorism financing are significant forces that require immediate controls and measures to stop the harms being caused. Not all will be accepted by professionals, but stronger controls and measures need to be taken.
- We think there is a need to create cross-dimensional think tanks. The need to combine the perspectives of people who are willing to leave their egos outside the room, not be those damaging 'super chickens' seeking to peck all others to death. This means bringing together people who have experience but may not always be the loudest in the room. Tacit knowledge from analysts, researchers and investigators can almost certainly provide far more insight than any senior manager who once led a team involved in investigating money laundering.
- If you have any interest in money laundering, if you are intrigued how it is happening and wish to find ways for it to be stopped – then do not just think 'outside of the box'. Think as if there was never a box in the first place. Imagine the ridiculous, the far-fetched, the opposite to all the

preconceived notions that have ever come to bear and that is where you will most likely find the answers to all your money laundering questions. Consider the actors involved in money laundering and the spaces in which money laundering is still allowed to take place.

• FIUs, we encourage, must start to focus on understanding the transfers and purchases which are money laundering. This requires ignoring the set typologies for money laundering and using the intelligence and investigation material to create a more elaborate picture of how money laundering is still managing to exist. Suspicious Transaction Reports (STRs) may provide some of this information, but existing understanding of money laundering by typology is narrowing down the scope of thinking.

Now is the time to find answers to the problem of money laundering. As a collective we simply know far too little. We need to start questioning the many sources of published material and contesting the supposed facts which have clearly led to the widespread duplication of misleading truths and general myths. This we think means focusing on solving problems – rather than figuring out repeatedly if the problem still exists.

In the next chapter, the scope for money laundering is shown as truly immense, not simply because of the number of studies, typology reports and assessments in circulation, but more appropriately the ability, confidence, and brazenness of the criminal, or the more aptly described money launderer, to manage their business in a professional manner.

4

# The obsession with defining
# money laundering

> Those involved in the fight against money laundering,
> or the financing of terrorism rely on the most current
> information on typologies.
>
> IMF[1]

Imagine just for a minute you have the pleasure of being a
money launderer.[2] You appreciate AML/CFT compliance
professionals are supposedly watching your activities, you know
law enforcement officers have an interest in asset recovery, yet you
need to launder money for a cartel whose leaders are not going
to take too kindly if you fail.

What do you do? Do you go with a well-publicised method
of money laundering that you know has red flags, is considered
risky and is likely to be detected, or do you choose the best bits
from lots of methods to limit your risk of raising suspicion? If you
chose choosing the best bits, you are probably like many other
professional money launderers – so well done, because life just
became a whole lot easier. But if you chose going with a well-
publicised method, you are equally as good, perhaps just a little
more discreet. In this chapter we shall explain why.

## The principal premise

The principal premise behind money laundering is to *make the
illicit value usable*. Dirty money, which is money gained through
crime *can never be made clean* – despite the word laundering

implying that when it comes out of the three-stage process of placement, layering and integration it is then somehow clean. Equally there is no need to hide the illicit value, because if it is hidden, how can it then be spent?

It is the change of appearance where money laundering is most effective. Although there may be many definitions of money laundering, the principles are always the same: illicit money should appear clean so that it can be enjoyed without fear of raising suspicion. The less suspicion, the less chance of having to hand it over to law enforcement and thus having wasted time committing the predicate offence which provided it.

Various definitions of money laundering exist, a handful of which were captured in Chapter 1. Many definitions also derive from the EU Directives that show money laundering as: '[T]he conversion or transfer; concealment or disguise of the true nature, source, location, disposition, movement, rights with respect to, or ownership; acquisition, possession, or use; of property, knowing that such property is derived from criminal activity.'

The concern here for the authors, especially with the EU Directives and United Nations definitions, is that they never mention placement, layering or integration. Nor do they mention *money* or *laundering*. Yet, from the start some 30 years ago, these terms and defining principles of money laundering have fostered all that has followed, especially training material across various nations' law enforcement and private industries.

To simplify things, it is possible to think of money laundering as like the game of snakes and ladders.[3] As the money launderer you may find an easy passage to the top after climbing up the placement, layering and integration ladders one after another. Yet as you reach the top, you then land on the snake – inadvertently showing the money to be dirty (by, for example, not spending it wisely, spending it in the wrong place or simply attracting the wrong type of attention). Thus, you find yourself slipping all the way back down to the start, almost certainly into the welcoming arms of law enforcement who gladly try to confiscate it.

As the game of snakes and ladders suggestively depicts, three specific ladders are widely considered critical to a successful money laundering process. Ladders which, when combined, have become synonymous with defining how money laundering happens.

In doing so, these ladders have meant (albeit erroneously) that method has then been confused with 'purpose', these methods have become the definition of money laundering with the 'purpose' attributed only to high-level definitions.

Such lack of clarity and distinction between 'purpose' and 'methods' is perhaps why the AML/CFT world has divided itself so evidently into prevention and enforcement and, in doing so, ensured that the two shall never meet. This overused placement, layering and integration mantra has also caused deep confusion by extrapolating money laundering into something far more complicated than a series of transfers and purchases. It is especially confusing to those people who need to connect with law enforcement officers and prosecutors, since many are working to entirely different definitions or not in the slightest attributing the three stages to their investigation. We see this as a terrible case of confusing the already confused – for no real benefit. Such an old characterisation of money laundering through this three-stage rhetoric may be why we finally see it becoming less of a focus in later published documents.

Still, the need to define money laundering has likely taken the greatest toll on generations of bankers and compliance officers. As a disservice to them, the definition has forced them to divert their attention away from efforts to understand their clients and their money. The push, and it is a strong one, has been to focus on the money, but not where the money came from or even where it is going – instead on how it behaves in between the stages of placement, layering and integration. This distraction has played into the hands of money launderers worldwide who know that even those in the financial institutions are still fumbling, many years on, with something so important yet irrelevant to their organisation.

This is something we think is set to continue. Looking at the April 2022 AUSTRAC and Fintel Alliance[4] report 'Preventing the Criminal Abuse of Digital Currencies'[5] helps to prove this. The glaring push for money laundering to be understood as a three-stage process hits the reader on page 6 with a stunning infographic on page 7. Yet, despite the disservice of this idea of money laundering on bankers and compliance officers, it is the Fintel Alliance that is represented by these same people. Are the confused confusing the confused or is it something else? Are they in fact annoying everyone who they supervise by somehow expecting them to determine the difference between 'serious crime' and, if it really does exist, 'non-serious crime'?[6] Is this an intentional message or simply evidence of an unwillingness to think critically about money laundering in the 21st century? The authors think it is something much worse – simple ignorance to really understanding money laundering and apply common sense to solutions.

## Money laundering typologies

Integral to the placement, layering and integration mantra is the tortuously wordy 'typology report', a document coincidently supported by the IMF's belief that 'those involved in the fight against money laundering, or the financing of terrorism rely on the most current information on typologies'.[7] These reports – which the FATF devotes significant resources to creating – cover a wide range of money laundering types that define the step-by-step process to prove, and in the strongest conceivable way, just *how* and *where* money laundering is happening.

Such reports can do this by listing an abundance of red flags at each of the three stages, suggesting for all intents and simplistic purposes that anyone can spot money laundering if they attribute one or more red flags to what is presented before them. By doubling down on the idea money laundering is complicated, money laundering apparently follows a pattern each time and can be spotted by anyone with only basic understanding of red flags as indicators. So, no wonder money laundering is still hard to stop. Yet, as the authors are keen to stress, red flags do not match the methods of money laundering defined by typology reports. If they did, then money laundering would be struggling to exist – easily spotted by those with access to the many lists of relevant red flags and IT solutions which look for them.

Still, even with the strongest of cautionary notes sitting alongside such red flags, it is difficult to imagine how a series of red flag indicators can abstain from limiting the mindset of the reader. An alert by FinCEN in the US in early 2022, advising on increased vigilance for potential Russian sanctions evasion attempts, provided seven quite specific red flag indicators.[8] In doing so, it automatically meant any reaction would purposefully align to the same specific set of seven key points. Whether good or bad, the seven points would be instrumental in limiting the overall response and lessening the scope and propensity for finding more vulnerabilities.

Nevertheless, the authors argue there are no *types* of money laundering, despite the increasing number of typology reports. Money laundering is simply money laundering; the premise of **making the illicit value usable**. What then constitutes money laundering is nothing more complicated than a series of transfers and purchases. One *transfer* and a single *purchase* or many transfers and many purchases. A transfer we see as simply being the movement of illicit value, hand to hand or via a formal and regulated financial transaction. A purchase we see as being the goods bought with the illicit value. Such transfers and purchases happen each day in the billions, both as intentional money laundering activities and similarly as practices that are, or at least appear, legitimate.

By evaluating TBML to once again evidence this argument, the FATF guidance document demonstrates there is no clear assessment of TBML against the three stages of money laundering: placement, layering and integration. Does this mean that without these stages it is impossible for money laundering to take place? Remember TBML, defined in the 2006 FATF report, is 'the process of disguising the proceeds of crime and moving value through the use of trade transactions in an attempt to legitimise their illegal origin or finance their activities'. So where is each stage of the money laundering process when considering this definition?

Right back since it was first developed by the US Drug Enforcement Administration in the 1980s, placement, layering and integration have needed to be present. It is these three stages which apparently constitute the act of money laundering. Without them, is there perhaps something taking place which is not really money laundering? In the FATF TBML typology report, placement and layering stages are indicated by the statement: '[I]n the case of TBML specifically, money can be laundered through the international movement of commercial assets, which are normally traded or shipped for purposes of commercial profit.' Nevertheless, one critical stage is still missing. The defining stage of integration. Still, what the typology tries to define as integration is: 'Summarises key TBML/TF risks, reflecting on newer methods of cash integration such as the exploitation of surrogate shopper networks, and the infiltration of legitimate supply chains that do not rely on misrepresentation of any aspect of the trade process.'[9]

Fastidious, perhaps, even awkward in our need to pull this apart, but why does TBML not follow the placement, layering and integration mantra? If it was possible, and the same form of thinking was needed in every instance, then the clarity would of course only serve to provide the end-users with further certainty in figuring out those all-important red flags. Does this mean TBML is not a true method of money laundering or are the authors of the report confident there is now no need to perhaps show relevance between this type of money laundering and the three-stage process? Surely, as the literature, training and micro credentials suggest, you cannot have money laundering if the three stages are not present: together and complete. Or can you?

In the absence of the three stages, it therefore would appear TBML does not amount to money laundering. This is actually true, although the FATF would probably disagree with the authors on this point. It is not because the three stages are not clearly defined but because money laundering, the real series of transactions and purchases – as the authors see it – use trade as part of its process. This means there is no such method of money laundering as TBML. Why is this? Well, because by rights going with the state of play and the growing library of typologies – surrogate shopper networks would also be a method of money laundering in its own right. This would mean, like TBML, there would then need to be a specific typology report. This would be impossible as readers would quickly recognise the impossible task of then defining the three-stage mantra against this specifically labelled method formed round surrogate shopper networks. As with TBML, surrogate shopper networks do not equal, or represent the entire three stages of money laundering which we are told must exist. Instead, they only support a purchase and even a transfer depending on how they are categorised.

Look further afield and its clear to see the FATF reports are not alone in what seems to be a necessity to omit some of the critical analysis that disproves certain activities are methods of money laundering. If you look at AUSTRAC's cuckoo smurfing report and then look to apply the placement, layering and integration mantra, you find placement and integration are nowhere to be seen. Is this a mistake, intentional oversight, or a clue that placement, layering and integration are no longer relevant after so many years of creating confusion among so many professionals? The only weak association to placement and integration, or stages 1 and 3 of the money laundering process, is shown in: '[O]rganised criminals use cuckoo smurfing as a method of laundering money to disguise and integrate their funds across borders to profit from and further enable their illegal activities.'[10]

Yet, the description given aligns more to placement and layering than it does to integration. Perhaps if intentionally omitted, then it is hoped readers will see cuckoo smurfing as an actual method of money laundering – not as a single action, like trade, which *supports* TBML. Or, more appropriately, just money laundering and money laundering that is, in practical terms, just made up of a series of transfers and purchases.

Similarly, Free Trade Zones have attracted a typology of their own too. But are Free Trade Zones really a method of money laundering or simply an aspect of money laundering? Free Trade Zones, which the FATF call money laundering and terrorism financing threats and the EU parliament calls for them to be phased out, are becoming more popular.[11] China and the UK are setting up new Free Trade Zones with Dubai having had bonded warehouses which are known to allow criminals to store and break up shipments. But is this again a method of money laundering requiring a typology report or are Free Trade Zones acting as a tool to help money laundering and the series of transfers and purchases behind it?

Why does all this critique of the commonly believed typology material matter? Surely the guidance written in the many typologies highlights the scale of the problem and the vulnerabilities which support money laundering activities. A step in the right direction, so to speak. The actual issue is that such defined typology reports are complicating money laundering.

This, in turn, creates a sea of consultants needing to be employed for vast sums of money to deliver solutions only they, it seems, could possibly deliver. Or for experts, and there are lots of them from all professional backgrounds, to come to the rescue equipped with highly decorated commercialised qualifications and a tech solution to solve the extremely complicated issues apparently before them. Yet, issues surrounding money laundering are now being created in much larger quantities by the very same typologies. The reality is that all the answers already exist, as well as the knowledge as to *how* criminals can be prevented from laundering their illicit assets. It is the reliance on typologies and a lack of willingness to really know *how* money laundering is taking place today that is preventing the meaningful knowledge from rising to the surface.

The idea that money launderers follow a specific scripted typology report contradicts the idea that money laundering is a buffet with many choices, not a *table d'hote* with a prescribed menu. The scripted approach to money laundering contradicts how the money launderer instead chooses their opportunities as they see fit, thus considering the options presented before them. But since money laundering is simply a series of transfers and purchases – some real, some imaginary and interlinked but never prescribed by a typology or three-stage process – thinking continues to differ. Trying to match observed circumstances to written typologies has become a woeful distraction that has overwhelmed already scarce resources for no useful purpose.

## The growing library of publications

Despite recent publications like those of AUSTRAC, the FATF and the European Commission defining various types of money laundering, a glimmer of hope may be on the horizon. Documents such as that published by the FATF on TBML have begun to now outline risk indicators. These indicators are valuable because they inform risk assessments. Since the entire FATF approach is risk-based – despite the obvious problems in AML with defining risk[12] – there is hope that the two will begin to support one another. But whether this is an intentional move away from identifying specific red flags, a revamp in the overall approach to delivering guidance, or another feature to further complicate understanding, only time will tell.

We certainly do not need additional red flags. What we do need are peer reviewed and documented evidence on money laundering. Material that is far more relevant than, for example, the banking sector money laundering and terrorism financing risk assessments which have been released again by AUSTRAC in September 2021.[13] All close to 100 pages long, these reports expanded on problems and issues to such an extent it was difficult to see the specific relevance of each report other than to give a concrete platform upon which an entity's AML/CFT business risk assessments could be formed. Long documents such as these, with significant duplication, only serve to function as excuses for not looking further, wider, or more specifically at the problem in the context in which risk is being assessed. Such documents become doorstops because of their size and overall relevance, equally forming assumptions that are not regularly updated or clarified as still a risk or threat.

Much of the risk-based guidance being supplied is so generic that it has become largely irrelevant at preventing money laundering. If, as AUSTRAC says, 'the risk assessments ... are to identify, understand and disrupt serious criminal activity', then why is there an ongoing need to pigeonhole the problem and suppress any *outside of the box thinking*? Money laundering is not a singular, tight or limited process confined to a box. There simply is no box for the money launderer to contend with and pigeonholing money laundering against specific sectors and entities only further lessens the scope for then recognising the various transfers and purchases facilitating money laundering.

According to French anti-corruption judge-turned-Member of the European Parliament, Eva Joly, money laundering now represents an effective business model in which people are receiving significant returns.[14] Yet, it is hard not to notice that human trafficking and environmental crimes have been the main topics of discussion for many years. So, of little surprise, reports by the FATF and others have looked to quickly promote money laundering as an associated activity, yet no more relevant than discovering more specific typologies. An illegal wildlife trade report by the FATF may have raised awareness about the scale and money laundering techniques of environmental crimes, yet it could only really highlight how criminals often use trade-based fraud and shell or front companies to launder proceeds from environmental crime. While recognising a comingling of legal and illegal goods early in the supply chain made it harder to detect suspicious financial flows, the report well and truly skipped over the real problem, which is that it is unlikely a money launderer is following a script, nor do they always care where the illicit money came from. Even when this method is so elegantly publicised and referred to by AML/CFT compliance professionals, regulators, and technology solution pundits in every corner of the world, the problem is that money laundering has simply been added for publicity reasons. It has been added for the sake of making the initial crime more critical, serious and important, and so that those who push a policy for AML/CFT, even if outdated, remain equally as important on the global stage. A case of "remember me, I'm here again and look what I've found relevant".

## Putting it into practice

As Chapter 8 will highlight, transaction monitoring is fine as a practice, but perhaps not when the parameters are also based on typologies which create the multitude of red flag indicators AML/CFT compliance personnel are now drowning in. Since there is little knowledge as to the way money laundering is being undertaken today (something we raised in Chapter 3), it is possible our knowledge also requires us to place customers into nicely labelled pigeonholes. If this is the case, the struggle may also be just as difficult when trying to find customers to suit the expectations of the money laundering scenario.

The increasing recognition of criminal diversity is perhaps accidentally and critically a result of increasing typology reports. Not such a terrible thing to an outsider, because as we have already suggested quite strongly in the previous chapter, little is known about money laundering or the people behind it. But any benefit quickly disappears when typologies do not focus on a single method of money laundering and instead elect to also link activities with a specific crime type. Recent examples are the cases of wildlife trade and counterfeiting of currency. What then usually follows are imprudent judgements which are aligned to the behaviours of the money launderer against a specific crime type, as opposed to understanding money laundering as a series of purchases and transactions attributed to illegal wildlife trading and counterfeit currency. Another case of confusing the already confused?

For consultants and FIUs, the detailed typology report is good news, but for AML/CFT regulators it must be a headache. For those that benefit, it supplies a fall-back excuse as to why money laundering was missed. If activities do not correspond to a known typology, how could a reporting entity have possibly known that what was taking place was in fact money laundering when it chose to only follow a typology to the letter? Has the situation which has been created, now brought with it a get out of jail card for a reporting entity? While it seems that the answer lies in common sense in understanding money laundering, the prescriptive nature of defining money laundering in typologies is also being used dogmatically to manage compliance obligations and risks. Typology reports have, in theory, forced the money launderer and act of money laundering into a set format, complicating it way beyond the three stages, which were already an overcomplication. This quandary has removed any possible desire to think outside of the box – no matter how small the box may have been in the first place. Only by considering money laundering as a limitless series of opportunities unrestrained by boundaries can AML techniques start to work against current money laundering behaviours and become a source of further clarification for the regulators.

## Oh, so many red flags

Since day one, confusion has existed as to how money laundering can be identified. Then along came the red flag – a specific indicator (apparently) allowing money laundering to be easily identified. Like a knight in shining armour here to save the princess from the evil master, red flags were a solution that unfortunately too many professionals have since chosen to rely on all too heavily. With increased popularity, red flags have become more irrelevant than many will now care to admit. The regurgitation of red flags has forced compliance professionals into a corner in which they no longer need to look for the real red flags relating to a scenario before them. The money launderers know this as they too have seen the many lists and with this same knowledge have been able to reduce the likelihood of detection. So, it seems the generic appeasement of creating guidance material (typologies) that relies on red flags has simplified the problem of money laundering to a series of red flag indicators as opposed to showing the transfers and purchases that make up money laundering in today's global environment. It seems, overall, the guidance material has made things worse, instead of better. And by worse, we mean less functional at helping to prevent money laundering.

If we are to make any progress, red flags must no longer have a place in supporting AML/CFT behaviours and practices. There are simply too many of them for them to aid our efforts. Most focus on the trivial aspects, rather than assist in identifying the imagination of the money launderer and the transfers and purchases that constitute money laundering *to make the illicit value usable*. Then there is the expectation that a small sample of case studies can identify sufficient red flags to become entirely applicable to a specific method of money laundering nationally, globally and for a decade or more. As the number of red flags then increases, even with duplication, the process of money laundering becomes ever more complicated, rising from 'The Financial Action Task Force (FATF), an independent inter-governmental body, issued a report in 2013 highlighting the vulnerabilities of legal professionals to money laundering and terrorist financing, in which it identified 42 "Red Flag Indicators"'[15] to 'We have collated a unique database of over 10,000 Red Flags that have been defined by regulators, law enforcement agencies and banking associations around the globe'.[16]

So how could a money launderer possibly react to all these red flags intended to identify their behaviours and stop them from successfully laundering illicit funds? The answer is they take note, dismiss most, and continue as normal knowing that in AML compliance, chaos, disarray and misfortune are all very much still present.

There are simply too many red flags for anyone to worry about, especially if 10,000 is anywhere near true and not just marketing waffle. With 10,000 red flags there are obviously too many for every AML/CFT reporting entity to focus on. Hence red flags get dropped for fear of needing to investigate every customer or client – a waste of time and effort for an employee of a business reluctantly following AML/CFT compliance regulations. Or they get adopted by yet another IT solution promising AML/CFT compliance success beyond the current landscape of hidden chaos and disarray. If a red flag suggested a deposit out of normal activity could raise concern, then almost all of us at some stage would have been a suspected money launderer.

To the money launderer, the scenario of a red flag minefield is perhaps the equivalent of walking past a guard tower when escaping from prison but knowing exactly which way the guards will be facing at a particular time and what they will be looking for. So, if they are looking for a human, then moving past disguised as a sheep is extremely beneficial, especially if the guards are looking the other way.

By allowing commentators of crime to have their say and treat money laundering as an adjunct to many diverse crimes, money laundering is largely assessed by typology type and therefore, in many instances, way too complicated to investigate. This is something the authors feel is perpetuated by the unfortunate add-on approach taken by law enforcement and by the absurdity the *follow the money* approach creates. And yet the authors also note the contradiction which is occurring over the entire problem of money laundering. The systemic approach is both overcomplicated and, equally, too simple – it is simply made to fit. Although the latter is perhaps the response to the former, the leading down into the rabbit hole of confusion taking place worldwide is creating a mass activity of ineffectiveness that is now driving a global phenomenon of unprecedented cost.

### In practice and then in reality

Wildlife crime is of huge concern in a world where wildlife is literally being driven to extinction by the pursuit of money. Worthy research by specialised institutes such as the International Centre for Asset Recovery in Basel[17] and the Royal United Services Institute in London[18] has revealed the use of cash, anonymous companies and corrupted officials alongside wildlife crimes.

The result of this is a typology that presents a few operational opportunities to intervene in the trade and some expensive time-consuming ways to follow the illicit proceeds after the event. For the wildlife criminal specialists, it is a revelation, and they seize upon the few operational opportunities as genuinely valuable. For the seasoned financial investigator, the typology resembles a hundred other typologies for all sorts of predicate crimes. Sure, the specific companies will differ, the types of company that provide a cover for smuggling wildlife will also differ from those smuggling drugs and weapons, *but* in the end the generality will always be comparable. In fact, it is hard to grasp how such a typology can inform those calling out for more help when, by the very nature of its creation, it focuses understanding way too deep into a single issue. In this case – wildlife crime.

Take then the idea of creating *workstreams*. One such example, again by AUSTRAC, has seen the release of unprecedented amounts of information for the industries it regulates. But yet, the result is almost certainly a diversion of attention away from the prevention of money laundering. After all, the publicity and excitement of sharing specific material to specific groups is contradicted by the strict expectations that lie before them to manage their compliance obligations. The workstream guidance by AUSTRAC provides no critical evidence as to how to prevent money laundering. Instead, what we see is evidence of a pressure to align to regulatory expectations, and global recommendations, with the hope that they have been created on the basis of preventing money laundering. If only that was true and equally aligned to today's money laundering practices!

## Magic wand, anyone?

It was not our intention in this chapter to be pedantic, meticulous, or to go looking for faults with the process so far. We apologise too for using AUSTRAC as references to our arguments. Instead, we set out to highlight just how convoluted and distorted our understanding of money laundering has become and the terrible process we have set before us. Furthermore, we sought to show just how reliant we are on old knowledge dating back some 30 years, capturing details from investigations from as far back as the mid-1990s. We have heard the stories many times, the old school attitudes to the problems and the desire to prove expertise in something that yet no longer exists. Times have obviously changed, the world has moved forward in so many ways and it would be helpful if these old-time storytellers took a bow and stepped aside to let the truth finally come forward. And by coming forward, we do not mean in the form of typologies, workstream guidance, red flags all coinciding with what is an outdated three-phase process of money laundering.

It is clear that the FATF, the World Bank, the UN and similar needed from the start to provide some guidance material. We acknowledge and respect this because it is hard to create something from scratch. Had they provided nothing, those in AML/CFT compliance, investigation, policy and prosecution would have been left wondering what it all meant. Perhaps many of them still do, because from our experience, the lack of knowledge is widespread and worryingly low. The issue is not that there is a lack of guidance, it is that the guidance does not also consider how money launderers ignore the rules (in so many ways) to select what is right to them at a particular time. They eat from the buffet, not dine to a set menu. They take the best bits from typologies, and they understand what is being looked for in specific reports to stop them from laundering illicit funds through their transfers and purchases. Red flags give the clues as to how not to manage a money laundering business.

While typology reports are still the primary resource for governments, law enforcement agencies, businesses and researchers, typology reports should always be factually correct and timely if they are to continue being produced. They should also be geographically, socially and practically compliant – not a single global assessment on a problem. Unfortunately, typologies also serve to evidence the message given in NRAs, as it is these national assessments which describe *how* and *why* money laundering is taking place in a specific country. So not only can a typology report obscure risk calculation, but NRAs can also lead readers up the garden path altogether and create an accumulative error as the years pass by. If it is wrong at the start, what follows usually becomes more wrong. No sufficiently detailed typology report can ever be entirely globally applicable, because the facets of money laundering are not entirely universal.

With the term typology comes another problem – the distinction of a particular method of money laundering. Yet there is growing evidence that new ways of working, new ways of spending, new systems, and many new threats – not all of which can or must be given a label or considered distinct – are now being seen. So, any belief that a typology is entirely and factually correct, must be accepted with caution. The best system for the future would not be based on looking for specific TBML red flags – but rather, on identifying money laundering by identifying suspicious (rather than unusual) activities using trade. The absurdity that a money launderer considers undertaking TBML before moving to another method is worrying, if not ludicrous. There must be money launderers worldwide sniggering at the idea this is the belief the world has of their illicit behaviours.

One possibility would be to take the idea of a typology and throw it away. This would immediately dismiss the idea that money laundering can be split into *types* once and for all. Cancelling typology reports quickly provides an incentive to create comprehensive analysis of money laundering – now and into the future. The time has come to shed light on the facts of money laundering as they are happening today and ignore the contentious need to create ever more specific guidance material. Imagine throwing all typologies together and instead recognising money laundering to be a series of transfers and purchases; no red flags, no individual typologies, just pure money laundering. Of course, to do this correctly would mean less reliance on people who are TBML experts – because money laundering would be just that: money laundering with *trade* as a tool used to hide illicit transfers and purchases. If typologies were to have a bright future, then we would have already taken to labelling those involved as TBML money launderers, high-value commodity money launderers, cash-based business money launderers, and so on. If we over distinguish compliance roles, why not also over distinguish money laundering as official roles? The reason we do not is simple; there is no such professional (criminal) role. So why then do we continue to label money laundering types as if there is?

If the use of typologies is too globally ingrained, relied upon by too many, just too difficult to throw away – then change must be immediately considered. A good place to begin would be to start addressing money laundering for what it is – a series of transfers and purchases. Money laundering urgently needs to be defined in a more coherent way that reflects modern practices. It is no longer the three-stage process and, as we have shown, this process alone has confused all too many people for far too long.

## Solutions toolbox

- Money laundering needs to be recognised only as a series of transfers and purchases. It is not, and never has been a neatly defined process that can be followed step by step. So, moving forward this means dropping all reference to the three stages of money laundering. Money launderers do not follow the scripted methods we are bombarded with in typology reports and risk assessments. Nor do investigators and prosecutors of money laundering need to prove the three stages.
- Remove any reference to the term red flag. This would prevent the continuing narrow thinking and a silo approach to determining money laundering. Red flags are prescriptive, limited and linked in many cases to the three stages of money laundering and specific money laundering methods. Red flags are overwhelming AML/CFT compliance and IT solutions and not providing sufficient evidence in the prevention and detection of money laundering.
- The AML risk-based approach (RBA) relies heavily on Know Your Customer (KYC) procedures and money launderers know this. We suggest that by following the money back to the source and asking 'is this legitimate money' we can overcome instances which KYC has accepted as satisfactory because money launderers have exploited opportunities through which to appear normal, friendly and honest people.

Still, all this discussion and the suggestions for removing money laundering typologies and red flags becomes irrelevant if the predicate crimes generating illicit wealth are prevented in the first place. There really would be less confusion about finding, stopping and following illicit money – never mind the need to name it by the type of process used to make the illicit value usable. Step back for a moment and you will notice just how the AML/CFT process today is one which is heading in all sorts of directions. With a focus on red flags, typologies, case studies, workstream and tick-box compliance rules, it is difficult to see where the winners will come from. Some of the effort is consistent, having been the focus for a long time. Some of it is managed – but most is largely ineffective if we draw back onto the predicate offences of crime which are on the increase globally.

As Chapter 5 will discuss, it is not always whether the rules work, nor whether they produce intended outcomes, it is whether the problem we are chasing is fully understood. Have we made the role of money launderer something far too exciting? Have we given them superpowers and, in doing so, complicated further the idea of money laundering? Chapter 5 gives you some answers.

# 5

# Money launderers and their superpowers

Let me see if I've got this Santa business straight. You say he wears a beard, has no discernible source of income and flies to cities all over the world under cover of darkness? You are sure this guy isn't laundering illegal drug money?

Tom Armstrong[1]

## Celebrity status

In media entertainment, in films and TV, organised crime is associated with glamour. From Bond villains to McMafia, from the Godfather to the Jackie Chan film series, the baddies are seen in luxurious mansions and yachts, eating in the best restaurants, and hardly ever doing anything that looks like work.

These modern portrayals of organised crime get some added visual magic from the banking system. Consider the instant transfer of funds in the TV series *The Night Manager*, where the illicit arms deal is confirmed by a huge transfer of funds in a luxurious Egyptian salon, authorised from a laptop by a handsome young man after a single retina scan. In the film, *The Bourne Identity*, the government assassin gains instant access to multiple identities, cash and weaponry in a safety deposit box held in the tight but obsequious security of a sumptuous Swiss Bank. This miracle is achieved just by knowing a number and a scan of his palm print.

The sophistication of the criminals' lifestyle is matched only by the sophistication of how they deal with money. Yet we have conflated the two, instilling the criminal and their money launderer with superpowers. After all, ordinary people do not see themselves routinely jetting from mansion to yacht to private Caribbean beach; they may aspire to, but it is largely beyond their financial power. The worship of celebrity tends not to question the origin of wealth until an arrest is made. The wealthy may have their suspicions about each other, the same as any person in the street, but they still sit together in the best restaurants, mingle at charity dinners and walk through the same VIP doors. They also use the same professional help to manage their wealth.

This perception of money launderers has sadly been perpetuated by the authorities for far too long. As Janet Reno stated, while serving as Attorney General of the United States from 1993 to 2001: "Money laundering is a very sophisticated crime, and we must be equally sophisticated."

This sentiment was echoed from across the pond, by the then UK Prime Minister, Tony Blair, in a Performance & Innovation Report on asset recovery in 2000: 'As the criminals become more sophisticated in covering their financial tracks, they become harder to investigate and bring to court.'

This conflation of wealth and sophistication is corroborated and copied in media reporting. Reports of the arrests of wealthy criminals are accompanied by aerial shots of mansions, library footage of celebrity appearances and glimpses of cars and yachts. The later confiscation of these assets is much less prominent. The trial and prison sentence may get reported on, but the asset recovery stage does not. The predicate criminal and their crimes are unpicked in detail, but the money launderer does not get even the slightest mention. The air of mystery attached to the money and the money men[2] is confirmed by this lack of reporting.

Official press releases by governments and their agencies perpetuate the mystery. Predicate offending gets explained in depth, but the money laundering and confiscation of assets hardly receive the time of day. The reason is that our news is partially driven by human interest, and the assets and the money are, apparently, inert – meaning they are of little interest. There is also a lack of explanation by the authorities. When the EU compiled its first Organised Crime Threat Assessment in 2006 it listed, at some length, all the types of financial institutions that could be exploited, and then summarised their findings into one simple sentence: 'No specific and structured intelligence is available concerning the nature of the link between criminals and the operators in the financial sector.'[3]

Fifteen years later, in 2021, the same Threat Assessment noted: 'The precise scale of illicit finance generated through money laundering is difficult to assess due to serious intelligence gaps on criminal turnover and profits.'

This is not to say that they do not know how money laundering is done; the problem is that they cannot access the information, for the same systemic reasons that existed in 2006.

In the meantime, we have all become distracted by cybercrime, cryptocurrencies and the Dark Web. These modern phenomena are mysterious to the average person, mainly through their impenetrable jargon and rumours of improbably large amounts of money and increases in use.[4] They therefore excite speculation that they not only involve dirty money but have become the primary tool for the money launderer. At least we suspect that might be what is occurring. But perhaps much of the innovative technology is a distraction in the battle against dirty money. Viewed dispassionately, cybercrime provides new ways to commit old crimes such as extortion, fraud and theft. Cryptocurrencies may just be a modern-day South Sea Bubble (an investment scam from 1720 involving attractive but non-existent opportunities). Finally, the Dark Web provides ways to purchase illegal things anonymously. New technology does provide criminals with new ways to commit crime, but moving dirty money is, frankly, so easy that there is no particular *need* to innovate. For many criminals, the new technologies are needlessly risky when compared to tried and trusted transfers by banks.

## The barbarians would be at the gates if we had any

The battle for dirty money has not changed for 30 years, meaning the same fundamental issues remain. We knew what the problem was in the 1980s, and since 1990, it has been described repeatedly in the FATF reports, national and international threat assessments, and academic studies. We have chosen not to address the simple issues, but to talk about sophisticated new ones. We behave like children at a firework display, initially interested in the bonfire, but then distracted by the illuminated night sky while the bonfire burns slowly to the ground.

A typically pithy observation was made by Kofi Annan, United Nations Secretary-General in his Foreword to the Palermo Convention against Transnational Organised Crime in 2004: 'Criminal groups have wasted no time in embracing today's globalized economy and the sophisticated technology that goes with it. But our efforts to combat them have remained up to now very fragmented and our weapons almost obsolete.'

The international transfer of drug money across borders is what drove the creation of the FATF in the first place, yet the EU, a quarter of century later, in the Europol Organised Crime Threat Assessment 2006, was only able to observe: 'The pivotal role of money laundering in organised crime is widely recognised. Borders still provide shelter to money laundering activities, hindering investigations. Investing dirty money in countries other than that in which the predicate offence was committed is common practice.'

The issues that were clearly identified in the 1980s are the same issues being discussed now; they arise repeatedly, unsolved, unaddressed. Criminals and money launderers do not need superpowers, any old fool could do what they do. Merely a series of transfers and purchases. The defences are fragmented and the weapons obsolete, just as they were when Kofi Annan was reflecting on the past, back in 2004.

There are four separate issues which drive a coach and horses through our common everyday defences for money laundering. A coach full of dirty money being pulled by Four Horsemen of the Apocalypse, if you will. Let us focus on these, and for ease of understanding, the four horsemen are: cash, borders, companies, and law enforcement.

## Cash. Borders. Companies. Law enforcement.

### Let us start with cash (in our supposedly 'cashless society')

It has already been said that the money launderers' only task is to separate the information about the money from the information about the crime. The key tool for achieving this is the anonymity of either the criminal or the money. The anonymity of money is best achieved by cash because everyone agrees what it is worth, which is particularly important for criminals, who tend to be distrustful. Modern commentators tend to ignore cash because, well, who in modern Europe uses cash? We live in a 'cashless' society, and not just in Europe, but the populations of China and many developing countries now use their phones for ordinary retail purchases. Cash is becoming unfashionable, but it still provides vital cash-flow for banks, governments and criminals. Indeed, it is almost as if *only* banks, governments and criminals need cash, while banks and governments are persuading the rest of us to stop using it.

Cash was the sole medium used to commit: 'The largest money laundering case in history – that has come to light [up to 2015] – occurred in China in 2007. The case involved the equivalent of 633 million USD, being laundered over a period of two and half years and involved 68 different banks.'[5]

The EU finally stopped producing the €500 note in 2019, although it is *still* legal tender. This is despite British research from 2010 that revealed that 90% of the notes were used by organised crime:

> SOCA [the UK Serious Organised Crime Agency] says that an eight-month analysis of movements of the note in the UK revealed that it was almost exclusively used by money launderers shifting cash for major crime gangs. The British trade in the notes is thought to be worth some 500 million euros – but less than 10% of them are bought by legitimate tourists and business travellers.[6]

The UK stopped the trade in €500 within its frontiers, following research by the National Crime Agency's predecessor – the Serious Organised Crime Agency. Absurdly, the same argument exists for scrapping the €200 note – which is still being produced and traded – even in the UK. The absurd Swiss 1,000 franc note which is worth over €900 also remains in circulation. Meanwhile India scrapped all notes above the equivalent of just €6 under the pretext of AML and anti-fraud by locking out money that was unaccounted for – known as 'black money'. Then there are the

European Central Bank's calls for the elimination of the US$100 bill in America. The global approach is clearly inconsistent and almost entirely ineffective. Cash is still present, and eliminating cash will likely do little to reduce crime. Needless to say, the absence of effective cash controls drives a coach and horses through the battlefield of dirty money.

Our controls over cash, the most basic medium of money laundering, are not working. Moreover, when they have worked, the good practice has been largely ignored. Just to give you an idea of relevance and scale, let us note that in the CBA case, two men used 101 CBA accounts to launder nearly AUS$1.8 million in 255 different transactions. Cash which was physically deposited into CBA's Intelligent Deposit Machines or 'holes in the wall'. So, perhaps you really do not need to be an expert in banking, compliance or regulations to know that if £264 million in cash had been paid in by a single customer into a single branch of a bank in an average sized city in the north-east of England someone would have almost certainly noticed within the bank.[7] To suppose anything else is absurd. Surely, once noticed, something would have then been done. In fact, something extremely specific *was done*. Absolutely nothing.

This NatWest incident is far from an isolated example. With banks receiving fine after fine for AML/CFT compliance failures, it seems quite clear that there is a systemic problem which is not being fixed by the current approach. Does this then raise the question as to whether the focus is correctly aligned? Did, as what was possibly happening in many other cases, the operational side of the bank know what was going on and took the risk to carry on regardless? A strong suggestion, true. But someone, somewhere must have thought something was not quite right. Or did they simply think someone else was doing something about it?

The transit of cash over borders has long been recognised as a problem, although not necessarily a criminal one, since currency control and capital flight have historically been bigger worries for governments. Still, it is now relevant to the control of dirty money flows, meaning most countries now require travellers to declare amounts over a threshold of around US$10–15,000. Importantly it is still allowed, it just has to be declared. If not declared, then it can be, and normally is, forfeited to the state. This fact is noted by Customs, but few countries investigate the origins of the cash or the person carrying it.

In the UK, something interesting happened to frontier cash declarations in 2003. The law allowing law enforcement to seize undeclared or suspicious cash was extended inland. The implementation of the law allowing law enforcement to seize cash at the frontier had some significant differences when it was applied inland. At the frontier, the person carrying the cash is prepared. The cash is usually hidden, sometimes elaborately.[8] The person has documents and a prepared story. The circumstances inland are significantly different; the person with the cash is normally not ready for it to be discovered *and* normally they are under suspicion of the police. Cash is normally discovered during a search for evidence of *other* criminal offences. The added criminality and their response to the cash being found normally provides sufficient evidence to forfeit the cash. Before the law changed, cash found by police was left where it was, because there was no clear power to seize it. Once the law changed, police routinely seized and forfeited cash. The UK has an increasingly cashless society and criminals have had years of experience in using non-cash methods to launder money. Despite this, over the five years between 2015 and 2019 the UK competent authorities forfeited an *average* of £41 million in cash every year.[9]

The authors take the view that the amount of cash found (as opposed to seized) by the police was probably the same before and after the law changed in 2003. After the law changed the police did not venture out to specifically look for cash. We know this is true, because the police were given a new power to search for cash, which they did not use. The cash, which is today seized and forfeited to the state, is incidentally found while searching for evidence of crime. The fact that it is seized is a product of several factors. First, there is a power to permanently forfeit the cash if it is probably the proceeds of crime; second, there are financial investigators at local police stations to take over the work from the searching officers; and third, there are police lawyers readily available to do the necessary litigation. All three factors are necessary ingredients to success.

It is possible that the availability of cash to be found may have changed during the period. It may be that the amount available to seize became *less* as criminals sought cashless options for laundering, or it may be that there was *more* cash available because banks became more wary of cash deposits. Either way, before the power became available, substantial amounts of cash were being regularly found but not seized in the UK. This is an important finding and one which has been ignored by governments looking for ways to improve their asset recovery rates. We think that police all over the world find hundreds of millions of dollars in local currencies in the course of searches of premises owned or used by criminals and the cash is left where it is found for want of a simple legal power to seize it. It really is absurd.

Until fairly recently, outside the USA no country routinely seized cash within its borders. The law was changed to allow this in Ireland (1997) and the UK (2003). This suggests that in most countries exceptionally substantial amounts of suspect cash are being found by the police but not seized. It seems likely that, in countries which are more cash based than the UK, the amount *not being seized* may be proportionately larger.

It seems surprising to the authors that more police forces do not have this tried and tested legal power. The chances are many of them will first read about this power in this book. The idea of seizing cash seems to be a blindingly obvious way to hinder the coach and horsemen driving through our war against dirty money. The good practice of Ireland and the UK could then be used to drive forward a global opportunity in the fight against dirty money. In fairness, a few *practitioners* have successfully introduced this new power to a few Caribbean islands, but the effort lacks strategic support and recognition, for reasons that are unclear.

Cash seizure has other important benefits for the competent authorities. The seizure of large amounts of cash requires management to be involved. There are obvious issues of securing and banking the cash; the real problem of counting cash (humans are not particularly good at it without machines) and the potential need to test cash for fingerprints or excessive content of controlled drugs. Incidentally, all cash in circulation is tainted with some cocaine and heroin, normally just microscopic amounts.[10] Management intervention often leads to policy discussions about incentivisation (to seize more) and recycling (to compensate communities for the harms arising from crime) and, at the very least, a more professional approach to the proceeds (and financing) of crime. All of these are social goods that make the world a bit better.

The sudden emergence of cash forfeiture cases in the UK courts was instrumental in initiating hundreds of new cases of money laundering, prosecuted after 2003. Big bags of cash were, as we say in the trade, a clue, that even the most clueless could not ignore. The disincentive of returning seized cash became a major incentive to the authorities to make sure they kept hold of it. The authorities were motivated to explore how to prosecute the new money laundering offences. Outside of the UK, the default position among prosecutors is to not prosecute money laundering, something we explore in Chapter 13. The crucial role of cash seizure in the decision to pursue money laundering prosecutions in the UK is poorly understood.

There is even more cash seizure good practice to be had from the UK. A specific (but not unique) crime issue for the UK is the stealing of metal for its scrap value. This includes copper electric cable and the lead from church roofs and brass memorial plaques (these latter crimes can be very hurtful for victims). It is a well-recognised crime and scrap metal dealers have been traditionally heavily (if not well) policed since the 1950s. The UK's *Sunday Times* newspaper, on 13 September 2014, reported that 'metal theft on the railways had fallen by 95% in the year since cash payments for scrap metal were banned'. That is close to eradication, a rare event in the world of crime reduction. The number of incidents had fallen from 1,000 incidents to just 43. This near total eradication was part of a package of increased enforcement, but the article specified that the fall was due to the cash ban (and who are we to disagree with legendary journalist John Simpson)? The interesting bit of good practice mentioned was the ban (as opposed to a threshold) on the use of cash to buy metal. A PhD thesis on the topic observed: '[D]iscussions with practitioners and government officials in the UK and other European countries suggest that there is a perception in Britain that metal theft is a problem that has largely been solved, while in (for example) France, Belgium, and Germany it is seen as a current threat.'[11] It then went on to say: '[T]he ability to buy scrap metal for cash in Germany may have limited the effectiveness of cashless transaction laws in France, since thieves can transport stolen metal across the border to sell.'

The significant difference between the law in the UK and other countries was the 'total ban' on cash buying by traders, as opposed to a threshold. This meant that the casual metal thief could no longer hawk metal from place to place in small lots, if necessary; they had to open an account to make the sale and provide personal details and a proof of identity. This practice destroyed the vital anonymity that made the crime so worthwhile, because scrap metal dealers' books are routinely at risk of being examined by police.

## Borders: where crime crosses over, but law enforcement stops

The globalised economy has resulted in huge volumes of trade and money quickly crossing borders. Similarly, using the same mechanisms, dirty trade and dirty money cross borders with minimal interference. Some frontiers are extremely porous with cash simply carried across in bags. In 2013, although around a million euros *a day* were seized by EU border officials, this amounted to only 5% of cash volume thought to be on the move.[12] No superpowers were involved, the most sophisticated techniques included strapping cash to a leg and stuffing cash in children's pockets. Once again, in the war on dirty money we are faced with trying to show a negative, an absence of activity. These cash seizures normally do not lead to investigations, instead the cash is just forfeited by an administrative procedure. There is no follow-up. Statistics on international cooperation are hard to come by. For the authors, who have visited dozens of countries in search of asset recovery statistics, the reason is simple: an absence of activity against dirty money by the competent authorities is to blame.

The significance of international borders cannot be underestimated. Dirty money flows towards the most secretive states, ones with laws and procedures designed to prevent the sharing of information about wealth ownership. Once across the border the money is safe. It is the modern equivalent of the Wild West bank robber riding as fast as possible towards the state line. And frankly, no one can outrun the modern-day equivalent of a wire transfer. The war on dirty money is conducted in each country because legislation and law enforcement are done on a national basis. Effectively, the war consists of about 200 separate battles being fought with varying degrees of failure, monitored and reported on by the global referee, the FATF. Occasionally there are victories, but these are often not understood, seldom reported and any good practice is almost never shared.

There has been some effort to at least try to harmonise laws and criminal justice practices, particularly in the EU and especially in relation to dirty money. The harmonisation of European law is achieved by European Directives which direct national laws to conform with fellow member states. This is much, much harder than it sounds and the fact that the EU is currently about to launch its Sixth AML Directive is indicative of failure, not harmony. The latest Directive encourages EU members to extend criminal liability to legal persons, it is a huge understatement for us to observe, 'it's about time'.

There is truly little comprehensive information about international prosecutions. One of the few reliable sources is the World Bank. The topic of corrupt politicians in developing countries bringing their money to richer countries attracts much entertainment media coverage as briefly shown at the start of this chapter, and this merits a response from the competent authorities. The World Bank has helpfully set up the StAR Initiative, which provides written guidance and tangible training support to authorities, which includes a comprehensive public database of international corruption cases. This database provides the details of cases to help authorities approach future casework. The scope of the database is the entire world and the period covered starts as far back as 1977. This means there is every reason to think that the database is comprehensive in relation to international corruption cases. The World Bank is to be commended on such an achievement. On the one hand the database shows the range of possible approaches to asset recovery from criminal and non-conviction-based confiscation to voluntary settlement and private civil action. It also covers a diversity of countries and sectors. On the other hand, it is a depressing read. Most of the cases have taken **decades** to resolve and if 'justice delayed means justice denied', the cases suggest the entire world is losing out.

The diverse range of methods listed in the database to tackle corrupt money shows what can be done by some countries, but unfortunately many competent authorities do not have modern laws like 'non-conviction-based confiscation' available to them.

For a global database covering 40 years, less than 250 entries seems extraordinarily low. It hardly needs a database; they could have used a ledger. In the detail, it looks far worse, with many entries repeated. This means there are, in fact, less than 90 subjects who have been investigated since 1977. There are, however, a few reasons for optimism. One is that the database still exists nearly 40 years later, although it is a constant reminder and measure of where we are in the war on dirty money. There are also more cases starting now than in previous years. But overall, this is a sorry tale of global failure. Several of the cases involve companies, which introduces our next horseman.

## Companies: we need to talk about Kevin

The anonymity of criminals used to involve techniques such as highwaymen wearing masks. The modern equivalent is achieved by real people masking their identities with those of other, real people. Almost 50 years ago the film *The Day of the Jackal* was first shown. It was a hit, gaining 11 Oscar nominations and instructed a global audience on how to steal an identity in the UK. The gruesome method was to tour British graveyards and note the details of deceased children and young people. Armed with this information, it was possible to apply for a Birth Certificate and thereby assume the deceased's identity, including of course getting a bank account. This method was commonly used by illegal immigrants to the UK for the next three decades. Incredible, isn't it? For three decades, the UK authorities did nothing at all about this. When they finally did create a database that matched the names of the deceased with other people who were still very much alive, the British civil servants, with a mischievous sense of the absurdity of the situation, decided to call it Elvis, in homage to the persistent rumour that the rock star was (is?) still alive.

Meanwhile, for the purpose of committing crime, nothing really beats the formation of an entirely new person. This used to involve getting your children involved in the family firm, but these days it is so much easier to create a new, legal person. A company is a legal person. Forming a company is easy and cheap, using false details that are typically not verified before inclusion in national Registries of Companies. Once the legal person commits the crime and transfers the money, you just form another one. The USA has two million new companies formed every year, the UK about half a million.[13] The tiny British Virgin Islands (population of real people c.30,000) is home to over 500,000 corporate entities, 15 for every man, woman and child. We are not suggesting, of course, that all these companies are created for criminal purposes. But some are. This matters, because, if you consider *any* of the major multi-billion-dollar money laundering scandals in Europe and elsewhere, it is always legal people who are committing the crimes.

Imagine for a moment that you are a criminal intent on making money from the perfect crime. The *perfect* crime, of course, is one that is committed by someone else, but on your behalf. In this perfect world, someone else runs all the risks and you get all the money. Traditionally, organised criminals in search of the perfect crime used expendable associates or minor family members to commit predicate crimes, act as getaway drivers, cash couriers or straw men. The criminals had power over these acolytes through proximity, familiarity (often in the literal sense) and sometimes physical menace. The traditional counterpoint to organised crime was to recruit these same acolytes as informants or introduce them to undercover officers. But globalisation has changed the nature of organised crime, supplying both opportunity and challenge to those in search of the perfect crime. The opportunity of ever bigger markets for illegal products and to exploit hapless populations through corruption has multiplied the fortunes to be made by criminals.

The basic model of organised crime has adapted to globalisation by exploiting the differences between real and legal people. This has gradually become a fundamental problem. Legal (sometimes called juridical) people come in different varieties: limited companies, limited partnerships, trusts and so on but they are all 'people' for the purposes of the law. From a law enforcement perspective, this crime wave appears to be out of control, and this will continue until criminal justice is duly applied.

The heart of the problem is that the *real criminals* behind these crimes have successfully created *legal criminals* who are constantly getting away with it. The inequality before the law comes to light because *legal criminals* (such as a limited company, partnership, or trust) cannot be imprisoned or extradited. More significant, is the fact the courts are unable to decide the criminal intent, the *mens rea*, of *legal criminals*. Current interpretation of the law is that investigators of *legal criminals* must also find the *real criminals* controlling them. This is allowing both to escape justice. In practical terms, it is the opposite of double jeopardy – the risk that a person can be tried twice on the same evidence.

Corporate criminals appear to enjoy double indemnity for their crimes. Investigators have not only to find the guilty legal person(s) but also unpick the body corporate to find the real person(s) who had the criminal intent, before commencing a second investigation into them. It is wrong; *legal criminals* should be treated as what they are. Courts should treat a legal person as a sober, capable adult, and if they are found guilty, the court should confiscate their assets just like they do with real people.

*The Puppet Masters* is the title of a World Bank report from 2011. The World Bank recommendations, based on extensive detailed research, focused on trying to find the **beneficial owners** or *real criminals* through the medium of their *legal criminals*. These recommendations have been widely pursued globally but, over ten years later, we should accept that this approach is never going to work. Our simple enforcement answer to when things do not work is to change them and, when dealing with criminals, it is best to play them at their own game. The problem is that *real criminals* can create *legal criminals* far too easily. Bizarrely these *legal criminals* are registered with the authorities, meaning they have created their own Fifth Column.

Campaigners have been suggesting that company registries should include details of ownership; to distinguish from the 'straw men' routinely used by criminals to front companies. Campaigners commonly use the term 'beneficial ownership' or 'ultimate beneficial owner'. It is a *Day of the Jackal* situation, in which the true criminal is disguised by a false identity. The solution is to prevent that situation from being possible.

We need to talk about Kevin to find the answer. Kevin Brewer, an exasperated whistle-blower, who to this date remains the only person ever to be convicted by the British authorities of falsifying details to register a company.[14] His crime was to successfully register a company in the name of Vince Cable, the UK Secretary of State for Business, not for criminal purposes, but to show just how easy it was to abuse the system. That was in 2013, and over nine years later, the British competent authorities are still *considering* whether the Companies Registrar may, in the future, be given powers to verify the details that are published on its own Registry. In their defence, the UK authorities would argue that: 'The UK has among the highest rates of compliance with company filing requirements in the world – over 98% of annual returns and 99% of annual accounts are delivered valid, complete, and correctly formatted to the central register.'[15] We do not dispute these compliance statistics, we just think that they are irrelevant.

This is because Companies House does not verify the content of its own register. It does not know if any of the details filed, with 99% compliance, are true. The specialist world of AML is regularly amused by the work of Graham Barrow and other activists who publish on their websites and podcasts (for example, The Dark Money Files), ludicrous and obviously suspicious details found in the Companies House register which they, apparently, cannot find for themselves.

There is a public interest problem here that is not being addressed. Arguably the current approach wastes all the money spent on banking and private sector compliance associated with the battle against dirty money. All of it, every penny, cent, euro, and dirham is wasted, raising it as the crime of the century, and a crime of neglect. The scandal of company registries is one part of a problem with the 'competent authorities'. Another, even more serious problem is the neglect of and by our Fourth Horseman, law enforcement.

### *Law enforcement: all quiet on the Western front*

Cash, cross-border crime and the verification of company ownership are all problems that could be solved with a little investigation. Indeed, the reason we know about the prevalence of these problems is because law enforcement has repeatedly revealed them during financial investigations and consequent asset recovery. So, the answer is already known, just routinely ignored. Yet, these three problems have been significant problems since the first asset recovery investigations in the 1980s. Although, since then, the legislative tools available to law enforcement have improved enormously and global agencies such as Interpol have opened specialist departments. Cross-border agencies, such as Europol and Eurojust, have grown hugely in size and matured and now regularly report on burgeoning money laundering and transnational crime issues. The Council of the European Union has conducted a major four-year review of financial crime and Financial Investigations which delved into good practice across the continent (2009–2012).

## So, what is the problem?

It is certainly not a lack of money; the financial sector is spending billions on the prevention of financial crime through compliance every year. This buys an army of people worldwide, of which the Association of Certified AML Specialists (ACAMS) alone has 85,000 members. The Egmont Group has 164 FIUs around the world with the remaining FIUs endeavouring to meet the high standards needed for membership.[16] Staff numbers in FIUs vary from country to country, but even small FIUs – in the authors' experience – field 20 or 30 staff, and larger countries maintain 70 to 100 staff, so perhaps 5,000 people are employed in the global FIU sector. There is no shortage of equipment or information. The global SAR system is mostly computerised and generates around 35 million reports a year, with an additional 205 million reports about cross-border cash transfers.

This is a massive resource of people, material and information all devoted to identifying dirty money, preventing it from entering the financial system and generally understanding how dirty money moves around the world. Unfortunately, none of this activity *permanently recovers* any assets from criminals. None of it. It probably helps, but not in a quantifiable way. This huge effort to pass information about dirty money to the front line is mostly wasted, because of the way it is passed (or not passed) to the law enforcement front line. Meanwhile at the front line itself are a tiny handful of end-users, the number of financial investigators employed by law enforcement is so low it is hardly countable. The managers of the competent authorities, operating in criminal justice, the ones with the 'legal competence' to do asset recovery (hence the term competent authorities) do not even know there is a war on dirty money taking place.

What the competent authorities do know about is the 'war on drugs' and the 'war on terror'. The 'war on dirty money' – not so much. The 'war on terror' has gone rather well in comparison. This is not to understate the horror of the many terrorism attacks since 9/11, but the competent authorities can show many effective and swift responses to attacks, many more have been prevented, and many would-be terrorists are serving lengthy prison sentences. Organised attacks have been limited to unpredictable 'lone wolves'. Few would argue that the 'war on drugs' has gone equally well, but the competent authorities have at least tried.

Conversely, in the 'war on dirty money' the competent authorities are still not engaged, not organised and not structured. The well-resourced, global equivalents of the Egmont Group or ACAMS do not exist. There are a few national examples of good practice and some embryonic regional structures, but the competent authorities are fully engaged elsewhere, in yet another war, the 'war on crime'. More specifically, we suggest, they are engaged in an intractable 'war on *predicate* crime'; they just do not use (or understand) the meaning of the word 'predicate'. There is a deep irony here; the senior managers in competent authorities are trying to win the war on crime through expensive traditional, and demonstrably ineffective methods. Many have given up and have ascribed to Martinson's '*Nothing Works Doctrine*'. Today's senior manager and competent authorities do not fight crime, they just manage it.[17] Meanwhile, close by, there is a war on dirty money, led and conducted by a handful of front-line financial investigators.

The irony is that modern financial investigation is akin to a superpower. It is supported by a mass of high-quality intelligence from the financial sector. Its practitioners are supported by high-quality training and surprisingly strong (but informal) international practitioner networks. Financial investigators themselves tend to be well educated and very aware of their impressive legal powers and of the comparative vulnerability of organised criminals to financial investigation.[18] Indeed, financial investigation has multiple applications to all kinds of policing problems that senior managers are struggling to comprehend. Managers could easily access these super-skilled investigators, but there are too few and managers are simply unaware of who they are. In large part, this is due to the legal framework within which senior officers work – a framework which separates money laundering offences from ordinary predicate crimes. It is an odd separation of ideas, as any criminal knows *the crime* is just the precursor to *the money*. Trying to separate the two is absurd, yet that is what our criminal justice systems have done. Some will argue that the political will *is* present and can point to rhetorical exhortations for action. But in the hard world of the competent authorities, what gets done is what gets measured. And what gets measured is the 'war on crime', not the 'war on dirty money'. Because of this simple truth, we can be sure that the 'war on dirty money' has not yet begun.

The FATF emphasised the importance of asset recovery from its inception in 1990, but there are still, over 30 years later, no *global* statistics on *how* much is recovered from *how* many people or from *how* many cases. In 2003, the FATF, perhaps in exasperation of its own failings, created a specific Recommendation (number 33) just on statistics:

> Countries should ensure that their competent authorities can review the effectiveness of their systems to combat money laundering and terrorist financing systems by maintaining **comprehensive statistics** on matters relevant to the effectiveness and efficiency of such systems. This should include statistics on the STR [Suspicious Transaction Reports] received and disseminated; on money laundering and terrorist financing investigations, prosecutions, and convictions; **on property** frozen, seized and **confiscated**; and on mutual legal assistance or other international requests for co-operation.

## How did that go?

Ten years later, one of the best regional studies on asset recovery statistics was carried out by Eurostat, published in 2011 and renewed in 2013.[19] The report had data from three phases of the process: intelligence, investigation and asset recovery. For 'intelligence' categories, all 27 member states provided data. For 'investigation' only 15 of 27 countries provided data. 'Asset recovery' data were available from only six member states in 2013, a number that had declined from the original ten States in 2011. Basically, as the data get towards the interesting bit – the actual confiscation of real money from real criminals to help make a real impact on crime – the information starts to peter out like a pen running out of ink. Eurostat did not publish which member states provided data – unsurprisingly. Nor did Eurostat bother to do a more recent study, and nor has anyone else. Asset recovery lends itself to easy statistics, but there are none. Perhaps it is time for things to change?

There is a simple reason why there are no confiscation statistics for everyone to pick over. Embarrassment. Hardly any European country confiscates any assets from criminals. There is a simple reason for this too. There is no one doing the work. This is the reality. The authors, having had the privilege to work with dozens of law enforcement agencies across the world, salute the diligent and resolute experts in these units, we really do. It is partly in honour of these unsung heroes that we chose to author this book. At the heart of all asset recovery cases is the financial investigator. If there is no financial investigator there is no asset recovery.

So, if you can find out how many full-time, dedicated financial investigators exist in a country, you can then understand if there is a 'war on dirty money', or just a token resistance to it.

In our experience, the number of financial investigators is generally less than the staff in the national FIU. This is shocking and technically inefficient. The FIU is meant to distribute information to national agencies to tackle substantive predicate crime problems, but all too often it passes information to just a few units, sometimes to a single person tasked with 'economic crime' or even just 'fraud'. This could and should be a major focus point of the FATF evaluations.

## The war on dirty money has not yet begun, but it could

In the movies, we fear organised criminals because of their propensity for extreme violence. We also connect the technical wizardry of transferring dirty money to their luxurious surroundings. We are frequently left in awe of their abilities, but it is a trick, it is all just an illusion. It is the banking that is sophisticated, not the criminals, although moving money is rather ordinary: Nicely summarised in:

> 'I have never met a money launderer who was not a nice person. And yet, they launder money, which we both hate, because we connect the money to the crimes which cause immense suffering, harm, devastation, and the death of so many people. Money launderers need to be nice, because they are fraudsters, confidence tricksters who look to hide or misrepresent the ownership/origin of criminal property. They need people to believe in them and like them. I have encountered relationship managers who have protested, their clients cannot be money launderers, because they are nice people.'[20]

In a straightforward contest between financial investigators and money launderers, the legal superpowers of the investigators would surely win, hands-down, and every time. But the battle is not straightforward, the financial investigators are completely outnumbered and unsupported by their organisations.

### Solutions toolbox

- There is too much focus on cybercrime, cryptocurrencies and the Dark Web and not enough on anonymous companies, cash and routine transfers and purchases.
- Cash seizure and forfeiture is underestimated as a law enforcement tool, while consumer thresholds on cash usage have been over promoted as a solution. Meanwhile flows of cash within banks have been overlooked.

- Borders are a weak link in the battle against dirty money, specifically we need more investigation of illicit financial flows and less administrative nodding through.
- International cooperation is almost non-existent as it is not specifically resourced.
- Company registration is more of a facilitator of crime than a hindrance to it. Wholesale reform of Company Registrars is required.
- At the front line, the number of financial investigators is disgraceful when compared to the massive resources in banking compliance and the FIUs. There needs to be a transfer of human resources to law enforcement to do greater justice to the work of compliance staff.
- The FATF has failed to gain compliance with a key recommendation to collect statistics about confiscating assets from criminals. It should address this simple requirement as a top priority.
- We do have effective laws and trained people, but we have chosen not to deploy them in sufficient numbers.

The system provides unfair advantages by allowing anonymous cash, porous borders and anonymous companies to thrive: 'The common denominator of the most complex and effective money laundering scheme is the international dimension. As in other criminal fields, also in money laundering, organised crime groups display peerless skill in managing the international dimension while national and international authorities are constantly struggling with it.'[21]

To address the international dimension at a global level, it should be recognised that dirty money mostly flows to those countries with the least resistance to stop it. International organisations look to control illicit financial flows by exposing countries perceived to have low resistance and then publicly listing them to raise awareness. The universal problems of cash, porous borders and poor enforcement are overlooked in the making of these lists, instead regulatory weaknesses and other criteria are applied. The results of this, very public, process can look rather bizarre, as we now explore.

6

# Global watchlists: money laundering risk indicators or something else?

> Whether they are 'things to do', 'things to remember' or 'things to forget', lists can help, that is until your name appears on a list, a list which is titled 'watchlist'.
>
> The authors

The appeal of an AML/CFT watchlist has well and truly elevated political egotism. The exposure of a country's failings or neglect to do anything worthwhile towards preventing money laundering and, to a lesser extent, addressing the threat of terrorism financing, has driven a global media frenzy against a side line of smugness. The most prominent of all AML/CFT watchlists is that of the FATF; it would have to be, would it not?

In 2000, the FATF implemented a Non-Cooperative Countries and Territories (NCCT) list. The process exposed the approach towards enforcement following the 9/11 attacks in the United States while adding counterterrorism financing to the FATF's remit. In 2007, the NCCT process was replaced by the International Cooperation Review Group (ICRG) that ran until 2009. The ICRG's use of MERs was instrumental in later creating two lists: the greylist, making up countries with significant deficiencies in AML/CFT practices, and the blacklist. Of the 23 countries that were initially listed as NCCTs (15 in 2000 and 8 in 2001), today only Iran, North Korea and Myanmar are present.

In 2010, the FATF members altered the process to its current-day setting – thus seizing ultimate control. During all this time, only Iran and North Korea have faced major calls by the FATF for countermeasures, with Myanmar joining them in late 2022 following unaddressed failures dating back to 2018. Still, it has not been plain sailing for the FATF watchlist process. As far back as 1991 in the FATF Annual Report the idea of *whitelists* was raised – those countries with strong AML/CFT systems but not fully compliant. Yet this option failed to generate sufficient consensus, suggesting the solution was never truly set to gain full global appeal, instead a level of appeal attributed only to a select group of countries. Perhaps countries which wanted a level of fairness in what was about to come tumbling down upon them?

The FATF watchlist has since spawned other lists, many helping the FATF's defensible position of making companies think twice about trading with those on any watchlist. Transparency International's Corruption Perceptions Index (CPI) is one such list. This list has many opponents thanks to an ironic lack of transparency surrounding its funding, yet somehow seems to take second place when watchlists are mentioned. The US International Narcotics Control Strategy Reports list of major money laundering countries ranked according to their *presumed* money laundering vulnerabilities and regulatory weaknesses also comes close to the FATF's. Although here we raise the idea that *presumed* is perhaps not an ideal measure for money laundering threats.

The EU of course has its own lists, two to be specific. The AML–CFT list is the most reputationally damaging of the two – it acts as the sharp knife that certainly knows how to wound. The second list is designed for non-cooperative tax jurisdictions that consistently refuse to play fair on tax matters. The European Commission also publishes a list of countries – countries it considers a high-risk financial crime threat. Yet *considers* could be used nicely for political reasons if the intent were there. The remarkable thing with this list, is that it just happens to overlook all European Economic Area members.[1]

Inconsistency and opaqueness we feel do not stop there. When Saudi Arabia was due to find itself on the failing list, the European Commission decided (out of the blue) to veto the crucial decision – alongside American Samoa, Guam, Puerto Rico and the US Virgin Islands. The reason for this – Saudi Arabia and the US were the West's geopolitical allies. Not only did this prove how political interference was able to distort such watchlists, but it also undermined the credibility by not naming and shaming those close to the author.

What makes the FATF's list stand out from the crowds is that it proves the FATF's global impact on how it administers AML/CFT expectations on countries. With no power to enforce compliance, messages with an imperial or commanding tone from regional bodies and organisations are still not enough to ensure the tasks laid on countries are adopted. Recognising this, it seems the FATF has chosen to fall back on the principle of *naming and shaming*.

The end result may be a series of watchlists, but what exactly are we watching for?

## Creating lists

The basis for AML/CFT-related lists has, however, not always been obvious. The UK's Financial Conduct Authority (FCA) list of countries it considers *high risk* for money laundering purposes is, wait for it ... not publicly available. This is despite the necessity for regulated entities in the UK to apply measures to countries for which they do not have the relevant names. Having a list is fine, a step in the right direction, but not sharing the list for fear of damaging relationships with other countries or international organisations shows just what a pointless activity this is. You would think someone would then question this predicament as it is like needing to supply answers to a quiz, without knowing the questions. Any wrong answers, well that would then result in regulatory action, national naming and shaming, perhaps even a large fine, but less likely prison time. Maybe this is the reason no one then questions the absurd dilemma of a hidden list, because if there is little consequence of meaningful punishment, not knowing details of a hidden list serves as an ideal defence.

While the UK example may be dubious, the benefit of a watchlist is clear. The premise is that it raises a country's profile – clearly not positively – thus allowing investors to make judgements, or so we are led to believe. Or does it? There is a strong belief that countries cannot afford to ignore the FATF because banks use its ratings as a proxy for risk in their dealings with countries. While this may appear correct, banks also base judgements on perspectives that matter to them – not everyone else – even if a failure to recognise glaring risks aligned to a particular country could result in troublesome consequences. Watchlists are instead considered to play only a part, not be the authoritative resource. After all, banks manage risk every day, it is just what they do, and they are good at it. Watchlists also reflect the approach taken by entities in dealing with due diligence of customers. Although Enhanced Due Diligence (EDD) of persons from watchlist countries is ideal, EDD is not always mandated, nor are the FATF watchlists always the primary list.

How much of a role the FATF's watchlist played in 2020, when Commerzbank was fined £38 million by the UK FCA, is not really known. But we can speculate that it was minimal. Whether it was minimal because 40 high-risk countries were found to be missing from the bank's AML/CFT transaction monitoring tool,[2] or entirely instrumental, no one really knows or is letting slip. Perhaps no one gave the FATF watchlist a great deal of thought. Perhaps like many others they still do not.

Reaction to these watchlists, particularly the FATF's, is almost certainly indicative of the fear imposed through the FATF membership. Certain countries are always more vocal in highlighting countries not meeting the FATF's expectations and falling onto the FATF watchlist. Whether grey or black, the destination is not positive nor is it incredibly helpful. Nor can it be purposeful, as financial transactions have been performed with countries on watchlists for years. This is all despite knowing the obligations to close correspondent banking relationships and local branches in troubled countries.

So, we are led to believe, conforming to the FATF's expectations and standards is considered a way to improve regulatory regimes and set up a global set of AML/CFT standards and norms. Watchlists are seen as a suitable control measure for a process which simply measures *buy in* to the standards. By creating discomfort, countries are pushed towards strengthening their rules towards a material impact on countering money laundering and terrorism financing. Hence, the principal basis for the introduction of watchlists has always been the need for a collective approach, not in any way, shape or form an avenue for political bullying. Anything less than a global regime would weaken the results, no matter on what basis the results are decided. Yet imagine if half of the world's sovereign states decided to ignore the FATF watchlists. Would this create a divide, force a more proper means of strengthening rules towards a material impact or simply lengthen the watchlists? Maybe it would just come down to which countries decided in the end to say goodbye.

Even so, not making it onto a watchlist apparently shows all is well. The reality of this is almost certainly very different. Whether this is because of inconsistencies in the assessment, political interference or simply being left off a list altogether, the truth is typically obvious, yet never really addressed because the truth may not be what people want to hear. While an approval tick from the FATF (or similar who claim a presence for fear of missing out) can show all is well, below the surface evidence can suggest that *coming top of your class* leaves opportunities for crime.

Still, many countries do take the threat of being named on a watchlist seriously. Ensuring compliance with AML/CFT standards and being suitably prepared for the FATF mutual evaluation process is, by and large, part of a necessary process or a game which we see as having some questionable fairness issues around its rules. The need to receive the all-important seal of approval is still somewhat essential as it helps to add authenticity to the actions being taken by the state and the many people playing a role.

New Zealand's 2020 approach (despite being identified as an avenue for money laundering in the 2016 Mossack Fonseca Panama Papers exposé)[3] highlighted the country's desperation to conform. As a member and advocate of the FATF since 1991, New Zealand took measures to ensure it was prepared for the international peer review by appointing and seconding staff into full-time preparatory roles before conducting a mock-evaluation. It was like they were valeting their vehicle before taking it for its annual safety inspection, hoping because it looked clean inside and out all would seem to be mechanically fine. Yet, this was despite knowing full well servicing requirements had not taken place since the last inspection or had simply been rushed through with inadequate care.

New Zealand is not alone in taking such a desperate approach; the UK did something similar, suggesting a common approach now exists as part of the rigmarole that precedes many a MER.

A rigmarole that has highlighted the disconnect between FATF judgements and what is actually taking place. A disconnect so absurd that it has allowed the UK in 2018 to achieve top marks for its MER despite being considered by critics the world over to be a major money laundering hub.

Equally, Vanuatu's leaders, realising their country could soon plunge into an economic abyss, set about an ambitious drive to overhaul Vanuatu's financial system to ensure compliance just before the country's pending MER assessment. In a rare act of unanimity, the government and the opposition in Vanuatu quickly passed dozens of legislative amendments and laws as part of the FATF's prescribed action plan, suggesting how the scared and overconfident can both be manipulated to perform when the time comes.[4]

## The greylist

The FATF greylist is for those countries who are not *toeing the party line* or doing as is expected and even causing some embarrassment to the 39 more influential FATF members. The greylist is essentially the FATF's tool for persuading countries to conform to globally recognisable AML/CFT obligations. By increasing monitoring, labelling these countries as committed to swiftly resolving the identified strategic deficiencies within agreed timeframes, the FATF simply provides reassurance to other more influential countries while further establishing its own presence.

Like those on the blacklist, countries on the FATF greylist are considered to present a much higher risk of money laundering and terrorism financing.[5] Nevertheless, despite the method for deciding list additions and deletions, most countries do commit to working with the FATF to develop action plans that address their AML/CFT deficiencies – something which occurs even if this is out of desperation or annoyance for what is judged by some as a failed assessment tool. The increased monitoring is administered by the FATF, but the leg work is typically conducted by FSRBs who report back to the FATF on progress of rectifying deficiencies. But since they are regional, it would be unsurprising if some decided to add their own agendas to the mix, thus making sure they get their own ounce of flesh out of neighbouring states' assessment processes. Childish perhaps, impossible maybe, but off the cuff comments by FATF assessors have indicated some truth in this practice.

It is only by taking a closer look at those countries on the greylist that you begin to see potential reasons why countries can fall foul of the FATF authoritative system in place. Take as a recent example Malta. Having adhered to a Moneyval assessment in which it achieved a high compliance rate on various recommendations, it later joined the FATF greylist in 2021. Yet Malta was at the time also in the spotlight for various reasons, some creating embarrassment and the shaking of heads. You may be aware of some of these reasons through the media reporting, but would you believe Malta is one of only five countries having been assessed by the FATF to be largely or fully compliant with all 40 FATF Recommendations? Still, the Panama Papers, the assassination of anti-corruption journalist Daphne Galizia, Malta's alleged money laundering through its gaming sector, links to foreign high net worth individuals nevertheless was enough to encourage or cause Malta's final entry to the hall of infamy – the FATF greylist. Yet, in Malta's case, through a determined effort to make change, the visit to the Grey List was only for 12 months. Justifiably perhaps was the initial greylisting or was it the golden passports saga that brought out the most disgust of the FATF members?[6] In response, Malta's Prime Minister, Robert Abela, accepted the *unjust* placing on the greylist and insisted that the government would respect the decision and work together with the FATF to resolve any shortcomings. But to what extent the failings exist, to what level they call for greylisting and to what extent the scandals influenced the shift, is unclear.

Was this an example of substantive AML/CFT failures being punished, or a means to punish for other political failures, and would a *whitelist* listing possibly have been more appropriate to deliver the necessary AML/CFT changes instead of discrediting Malta's entire situation? Whatever the real reason, within six months reports were suggesting some 24 companies had renounced their licences to operate in Malta following the greylisting, heightening uncertainty in Malta's financial services industry.[7] But the listing had also closed the door for accessing the EU via a golden passport. Marlene Zammit, Principal Auditor at National Audit Office Malta summed up the situation when she wrote:

> [O]ne of the 3 countries voting for our [Malta] greylisting is actually worse than us [Malta]. I am in no way justifying the mistakes made, but this proves that what is good for the goose does not apply for the gander and the sanctions only apply for the little powerless fish.[8]

There is also the issue with Morocco's inclusion on the FATF's greylist as Morocco has a relatively lower money laundering and terrorist financing risk profile than most countries not greylisted. Whatever the viewpoint, the listing on the FATF greylist is unfortunate because it tarnishes Morocco's image internationally despite reports of it being safer than most European countries.[9] A remarkable feat for Morocco, yet something most FATF member states are unlikely to achieve despite widespread and globally recognised AML/CFT failings.

That then brings us to the UK and Australia. No sign of a greylist for miles around despite the UK being considered to be the global hub for money laundering and Australia choosing not to implement Tranche 2 despite strong criticism by the FATF in its MER way back in 2015. Whether Australia's circumstances are linked to the FATF pausing their assessment of Australia in 2019 following expectations that they would be added to the greylist is difficult to ascertain. Yet even a follow-up assessment never took place, despite an assessment taking place in the meantime across other countries. Was this a case of intentionally forgetting Australia had failings or simply passing over Australia because it is one of the 39 FATF members? We are confident many other countries would have also liked such a consideration to have played out for them in this way, but it seems there was only one winner in this instance – Australia – who by early 2022 had still not taken real action to implement Tranche 2 to bring them in line with the FATF's expectations.

Of course, there is also G20 member South Africa, with its failure to pursue serious cases, especially those linked to so-called *State Capture* as raised by the MER adopted in the June 2021

FATF Plenary meeting. A predicament that gives peace that the UK example was not alone. A particular problem in South Africa was apparently with: 'corruption where businesses and politicians conspired to influence South Africa's decision-making process to advance their own interests. It helped generate substantial corruption proceeds and undermined key agencies with roles to combat such activity.'

Equally, South Africa must make better use of financial intelligence and proactively collaborate with international partners to detect and seize illicit cash flows. So, it must be helpful being a G20 member when these points are highlighted. Yet equally, it was a brave move by the FATF to then raise such dismal and critical aspects. Still, you would think someone was 'pulling your leg' if this were told to you in 2021 and placement on an FATF watchlist was not forthcoming. Australia and South Africa, we think you are two incredibly lucky countries.

Then there is Canada. Canada has failed to include the accountancy profession into its AML/CFT regulated sector, going against the FATF Immediate Outcome 3 – supervisors appropriately supervise, monitor, and regulate banks and DNFBPs)[10] – therefore leaving a major loophole in Canada's AML/CFT regime. But still, no greylisting for Canada. Oh wait, Canada is also a founding member of the FATF and a G7 member.

Let us not ignore Switzerland and Luxembourg. Both are major financial centres offering offshore services and yet largely non-compliant with the FATF regulations.[11] Neither of these countries have been near an FATF watchlist, never mind on the FATF blacklist. Do these examples therefore suggest or prove double standards and the need to deflect attention? Or is the entire FATF naming and shaming process so flawed that it is chosen to be ignored by some? It is clearly 'business as usual' for some countries?

## The blacklist

The blacklist on the other hand, this is something unique. Countries assessed as non-cooperative end up here, as this is 'the' list reserved for those countries who have no regard for the FATF nor implementing the FATF's AML/CFT standards. For these 'blacklisted' countries, there may be little or no willingness to ever conform, having little fear as to what the list purportedly signifies.

Countries added to the blacklist are those needing to be punished for not adhering to rules of the rules-based order, run by the FATF, and some would argue steered by the G20. After all, the Western perspective of a rules-based order is reassuringly familiar and uncontroversial, like the rule of law. Yet, the 'non-cooperative' significance of the blacklist is perhaps a contradictory perspective, assessment or judgement. What would be more fitting is a label that recognises less a defiance to conform to Western ideology and to international best practice, and instead identifies that a limited scope of regulatory infrastructure because of a lack of resources can quickly prevent these countries from fully enacting the FATF's standards. The irony is that these same countries are those which have a unique perspective, typically as dictatorships or nonconformists to international agreements. While these countries equally benefit from not conforming to AML/CFT standards set by the FATF, the entire approach to making positive change seemingly does little to stop them from remaining on the blacklist.

The FATF approach to blacklisting overlooks one major issue: the widespread failure of intermediaries to accurately enforce customer due diligence laws. With countries on the blacklist nicely segregated – as a warning to others to stay away – the fairness of the FATF blacklisting process raises questions about the severe economic harms it causes. Considered deficient in their AML and counterfinancing of terrorism regulatory regimes, is the accuracy of this perspective drawn from the overall failure to tick the FATF generic tick-lists? Or, more worryingly, is it an under-the-table political tool for punishing others? After all, only Iran, North Korea and now more recently Myanmar are the subject to heavy ongoing sanctions pushed largely by Western rules-based countries.

## Utilising watchlists

If the process of placing countries on watchlists raises concerns, so too will the consequences of countries willing to *right the wrong* of not meeting global expectations. It is these same expectations which are neither sympathetic nor entirely flexible. For many countries, the consequences are soon clear, for others they take years to come to fruition. Increased levels of corruption, a reduction in effort towards the standards and long-term economic issues can come as a result. All of this happens despite the official intentions of the watchlists: to raise deficiencies in internationally agreed AML/CFT standards. To us, the uniformity of these intentions and the later reaction is far from universal.

If the intention of the FATF listing is to bring all countries into line, then there needs to be improved appreciation of the consequences. That is unless it is the FATF's intention to keep most countries fearful as to what might happen. If, on the other hand, the FATF greylisting is focused towards reducing payment flows, it appears to only be the long-term case, despite insinuations of capital flight following a greylisting announcement.[12] Equally, a country may try too hard to move off a watchlist by only focusing on the immediate problems and choosing to ignore those issues below the surface. A quick win can of course equate to a long-term loss, but does that always really matter?

The Prime Minister of Saint Kitts and Nevis described blacklisting as an "existential threat" to small economies.[13] Neighbouring Saint Lucia's Prime Minister added that small countries are grappling with restrictions imposed with no "credible evidence of wrongdoing" wreaking "irreversible damage".[14] Whether it is placement on a blacklist or the less serious greylist that creates the impetus for change, the willingness to 'get off' can be instrumental in deciding a country's long-term success.

Depending on the severity of the failings, many countries still look to counter their failings with urgency. Those on the greylist may understand the notion that the lists are still a relevant signal to investors about country risk. Yet those countries on the blacklist are more likely to be dismissive of the placement ritual – meaning the consequences matter little. Hence, the entire premise of placing countries on the blacklist is somewhat contradicted by the very process created.

Worryingly, it seems that the FATF have carte blanche to name and shame – leaving those countries moved to a watchlist to pick up the pieces and deal with the various levels of punishment apparently handed out by banks and investors. Simply by agreeing to be supervised by the FATF, countries, of course not all of them, run the risk of failure and subsequent placement on a list. Still, putting your hand in the fire, means you are likely to get burnt. Yet, what happens within a country after it is placed on a list appears to be of little concern to the FATF. Had there been interest and concern from the start, we think the process would now be very different from that initially created. Still, perhaps it is the flexibility which is to the detriment of the entire process so far; that flexibility to pick on some countries and not others.

Whatever the desire and reasoning behind naming and shaming, the process contradicts a push for financial inclusion. The services, the economic impact and the long-term challenges which result from ending up on a watchlist are usually not the fault of the general population. Yet it is these people who typically suffer the most. So, whether they are 'intended consequences' handed down by the FATF or 'unintended consequences' felt by the receiving country's population, the consequences are in fact the same.

## Watchlist absenteeism

The mechanism behind moving countries to watchlists, particularly the FATF watchlist, is the mutual evaluation process – a process which has two basic assessments: effectiveness and technical compliance.[15] Evidence from a country needs to show its measures are working and delivering the right results. As shown, some countries are simply far too important to ever go anywhere near a watchlist, while others are added in order to make an example of them. We think it would now be remiss of us as the authors to not highlight that, as far back as the 1980s, the UK and US were making compromises that would inevitably see the creation of an AML system capable of protecting the richest countries. Is this why we now have the FATF watchlists?

For those countries which seem to enjoy protection from their political allies, literally all can be fine. Examples include those countries hidden under the UK umbrella enjoying the reputation of their 'guardian' without necessarily deserving of good grades. Referred to as 'overseas territories', the British Virgin Islands, Bermuda, Jersey, Guernsey and the Isle of Man are, according to IMF research, 'the eight major pass-through economies'. The countries of the Netherlands, Luxembourg, Hong Kong, the British Virgin Islands, Bermuda, the Cayman Islands, Ireland and Singapore, according to the IMF, host more than 85% of the world's investment in special purpose entities, which are often set up for tax reasons. Three of these are British territories and three are European member countries. Yet quite ironically, none of these countries has been FATF blacklisted.

Then there are the discernibly poor levels of effort by those countries teetering on the edge of a watchlist. While some frantically do what they can to remove themselves – many times with no extra effect – countries like Switzerland still commit to the absolute minimum in terms of AML efforts. When they do, it is then only because of foreign pressure.[16] Perhaps this is the reason money laundering is more prevalent in countries with a stronger economy, a prominent financial sector, a stronger rule of law and a means to control corruption.

This begs the question, 'So which country must the focus really be on?' Should it be the country not on a watchlist or the country doing all it can to get off a watchlist, even if the effects of doing so may have a detrimental effect on its long-term stability, levels of corruption or ability to meet the FATF standards. Equally, who is to blame: the country for passing the peer review or the FATF as the authoritative organisation for allowing countries to pass?

By removing the rose-tinted glasses, we can easily see it is the FATF who are at fault. The notion that the entire process looks to serve them and key FATF members quite nicely is perhaps more correct than many wish to admit. Although the MER process may address domestic money laundering, it does not evaluate international illicit financial flows to and from individual countries. What it does do is evaluate international cooperation in a bilateral way, without placing a country in the context of its network. The FATF process is about measuring effort, activity and processes – not the true effectiveness of AML/CFT interventions against today's real, usually unseen, money laundering activities. Nor is it affecting money laundering flows. It is an approach which does not so much distract from dealing with the intrinsic effects of money laundering and illicit financial flows, but rather changes the entire tactical and strategic approach by the country. The process measures outputs rather than outcomes so the assessment views what the country is doing, as opposed to what, if anything, it is achieving. A process of ticking boxes then becomes a blunt instrument with which the FATF can control countries from afar. In the end the process never really ends up affecting money laundering flows, suggesting why, for some, asset confiscation is seen as a tick-box winner – a result determined solely by the monetary figures recovered. But what the situation achieves is then only to focus law enforcement on the individual criminal as opposed to preventing criminality and the money laundering that enables it.

## The watchlist effect

Let us raise some simple points once again about this 'technically neutral process'. The criteria underpinning the inclusion in AML/CFT blacklists is methodologically flawed and less transparent than might be expected. This is all alongside a tendency for a geopolitical bias, with countries penalised because they do not formally align with those Western countries who assist in determining those heading onto a watchlist. It is true, there may be strong influence on how countries deal with AML/CFT, many following them to the letter of the law, or introducing laws to meet the FATF's requirements. But where the water gets a little murky, it can be seen that political influence is perhaps managing how the FATF approach is mastered and followed.

Take, for example, Pakistan and its placement on the FATF greylist. As of 2021 it was found to be 88% compliant with FATF expectations. This was in contrast to countries like the USA having non-compliance of 78.5%, Israel 87.5% and Japan 72.5% who never ended up near the greylist.

We feel that the FATF examination mindset can actually be detrimental to any long-term AML/CFT regime. While countries may focus all their efforts on the 'exam', the premise of infrequent and condensed assessments does nothing to deliver consistency. Rather than driving concern about the intrinsic damage money laundering is having on an economy, the entire process pushes for superficial fixes. These include laws, bodies and processes (that clearly cannot take place in each country at the same pace) as opposed to actual action or a focus on outcomes instead of policies or procedures. Nor does the current approach account for differences in risk types and risk levels. Common risks may be clear, but the level of risk may not consider or show where the risks really are in each country.

High risks in relation to placement and the opportunities to open bank accounts to deposit dirty money can have a different impact on a country's vulnerabilities. If a country is susceptible or even obliging at creating shell companies, corporate opacity is likely to be a far more important vulnerability than the level of cash used within the local economy. Nor does the 'one-size-fits-all' approach assessment suit countries who launder other countries' money. The money laundering risk in these countries is always different from a country with high domestic crime or one that exports criminals to commit crime elsewhere before sending the money back. The country-by-country approach does not work because of these practical circumstances. Hence, the long-lasting consequences of the entire watchlist process needs to be urgently reviewed if it is to achieve what it is actually promoted as seeking to do.

Then comes the problem of de-risking, often attributed to blacklisting and the AML/CFT regime. De-risking always calls into question a fundamental assumption about the drivers of the FATF's impact. Given the much-needed attention as of late on enhancing the effectiveness of the AML/CFT regime, there is a need, many will agree, to address the reasoned criticism from those countries suffering the most from economic sanctions. This means, and this can be uncomfortable for some, a complete U-turn on the global practice of naming and shaming, because the desired effect has not always been improvements in money laundering standards.

## Revisiting the overall approach

If there is a need to segregate, raise awareness and support countries to deliver more effective AML/CFT regimes, then clarity from the FATF is urgently needed as to how watchlists really work. How this will come about is difficult, since it is obvious there are few scholars unable to go beyond simply critising the existing FATF approach. Any viable solution must of course be able to limit, even counteract, the downward spiral of worthless effort that governments, businesses and individuals are clearly focusing too heavily on. Whether the FATF is capable of the clarity now needed we are not sure, but it is necessary if current efforts are to be assessed against the abundance of existing money laundering opportunities.

A strong place for the FATF to start would be the need for countries to overcome the obsession of passing recurring 'peer review assessments' that provide little benefit in preventing money laundering. Passing the assessment currently indicates a need to do nothing more until just before the next assessment, with failure instead forcing a reaction to rush and do all you can to correct apparent wrongs. We think the assessments can cause more harm than good. The process that exists can mean neglecting what is happening below the surface and the long-term effects. The result of the FATF assessment process is a crude list of countries that serves to refute any idea of an interconnected international fight against money laundering.

Then there are the notable inconsistencies that need to be ironed out to prevent punishing countries not considered to be abiding by the rules. The FATF blacklist is a formidable instrument – a political construct and equivalent to a global sentence of bureaucratic isolation, yet it is not the blacklist that is the most important to most countries. With only Iran, North Korea and Myanmar enjoying a place on the blacklist, it is the greylisting regime that has attracted the troubling day-to-day ramifications by complicating international fund transfers, foreign direct investment (FDI), and correspondent banking. It is therefore crucial that countries which genuinely fail are added. With Vanuatu's greylisting in 2016 amounting to full-on economic sanctions for a country struggling to achieve developing nation status, the ramifications can be severe. Yet the punishment was in fact for weak legislation and oversight that was simply considered 'not tough enough'. So, did the punishment really fit the crime?

This then leads us to the idea that the FATF needs to be stronger on those countries which do not technically make the lists, yet still have failings. There are countries yet to supervise DNFBPs[17] – and some with little or no apparent intention to do so – despite being a 'major' country and an FATF member state.

Straight away this should raise concerns for many as the process is clearly ironic but also openly arrogant. If you expect a police officer to be prosecuted for unlawfully exceeding the speed limit, would you not expect an FATF member state to be reprimanded for not adhering to the rules it was instrumental in creating? Are we living in a system of 'do as I say, not as I do' when it comes to global compliance with FATF expectations? The answer is almost certainly 'yes' if you take a critical view of what is taking place.

If the existing and poorly derived assessment method for some unfathomable reason must stay, then there would need to be a focus on issuing warnings – an action more aligned to those countries which could be on the greylist, but whose failures do not run the full breadth of their systems and processes. This is particularly important when they have only one or two key, but critical, issues needing to be addressed – not a true systemic failure.

We recognise bringing change will be difficult, largely because a cultural change is needed, and changing organisational culture is always fraught with opposition. However, the stigma and egotism that coincides with placing countries onto watchlists must also be eliminated. The current process adds no value to the unintended consequences deriving from both the de-risking phenomenon and the international isolation of (alleged) risky jurisdictions. There is unlikely to ever be an exact model for assessment which categorically proves that only particular countries truly present a heightened risk of money laundering and terrorist financing. Nevertheless, countries can be labelled all too easily with poor effectiveness despite substantial improvements. This suggests there is a need to consider whether another category that reveals 'work in progress' or something similar is then introduced. It could be argued this already exists in the results of the FATF assessment – but that would only align with a work in progress list if the country assessed was intent on correcting the failures found. Hence, a 'whitelist' is now needed to capture the warnings issued.

If Australia is to be an example, following its assessment failure in relation to DNFBPs[18] – it is clear the FATF assessment sometimes does little to motivate corrective action.[19] Although, until recently, the US also had no requirement for DNFBPs to identify the beneficial owners of their clients[20] – a somewhat commanding problem in the face of money laundering prevention – Australia is certainly dragging out the process. It seems in this instance that the political might behind greylisting and blacklisting is not strong enough for Australia to adopt the obligations – and quickly. Why has the FATF not yet found the courage to hold Australia to account? Perhaps the recent submissions to the Legal and Constitutional Affairs References Committee by various interested, commercially driven professionals somewhat ideally placed to comment will instigate the necessary change. So too, perhaps, will the idea that Australia still is one of only three states (Haiti and Madagascar being the others) yet to commit to bringing lawyers, accountants and real estate agents under the umbrella of AML/CFT laws.

Through the naming and shaming process that takes place, the FATF clearly makes no apologies for destroying economies and reputations. Nor does the FATF seem to have interest in the negative press that accompanies the publication of a country assessment. The FATF, it seems, simply sits back and watches the turmoil unfold. The awkward truth is that the assessment may not even be factually justifiable, as the underpinning assessment is methodologically flawed. Assessments can be undertaken by FATF representatives with inadequate experience, fail to address global inconsistencies, and report on factors that must never be seen as a means for failure. All on a one-size-fits-all checklist. Where can you then head to when you feel aggrieved by the findings of an FATF assessment – nowhere. There is simply no arbitrator for countries to raise issues with, hence why the media storm following any FATF announcement is typically strong from both sides.

If the global approach to AML/CFT is to be truly global, adopted to a satisfactory level and moved forward collaboratively, then foundations need to have integrity as opposed to the showmanship currently taking place.

### Solutions toolbox

• The FATF MER approach needs to be thoroughly reviewed to primarily ensure fairness of the methodology across all member states. Too many countries are too easily falling foul of the consequences of a poor MER assessment while, at the same time, equally failing countries somehow manage to avoid any consequences. We accept changes will be made in the near future as the FATF develops, but like adding more vanilla flavouring to a cake made of rotten eggs, the outcome is never going to be pleasant, no matter who says they made it.

• Empirical evidence is needed to determine the consequences on a nation state when they are greylisted. These consequences can then be managed for long-term compliance with the FATF recommendations, rather than short-term political mischievousness.

• Greylisting and MERs are both blunt instruments. MERs could focus on various 'things' that MUST be fixed, rather than a lengthy list of tedious tasks. MERs and greylisting should both be in the context of a country's international partners. So, if the problem is an illicit financial flow between two countries, then both countries are named by the FATF as responsible for fixing it.

• Consideration should be given to issuing warnings for countries which could be on the greylist, but whose failures do not run the full breadth of their systems and processes. This is particularly prudent for when a country has only one or two key, but critical, issues needing to be addressed. Not only does it improve integrity in a system which is receiving increased criticism, it also reduces the adverse effects of 'greylisting'.

• Perhaps identifying illicit financial flows should be included in MERs. This would help to identify, for example, the flow of kidnap ransom money into the Nairobi real estate market.

• There now needs to be a concerted effort to end what is seen by many as a politicisation of AML/CFT. If there is to be unanimous 'buy in' to the FATF recommendations and a truly global approach that finally delivers the absolutely necessary results, then there needs to be less political influence. To date, political influence has potentially led to the greylisting of poorer countries when there were insufficient reasons to do so, or the ignoring of particular countries failing to adhere to the rules, the same rules they were instrumental in approving. Too many times we have observed MER findings that signify possible political interference thus leading to adverse effects that contradict the FATF's underpinning goal of preventing money laundering and terrorism financing. Integrity in the current process would automatically see the FATF's founding member countries marched off to the 'greylist'.

• Any one-size-fits-all approach to assessing whether a country should be placed on a watchlist needs to consider how money laundering risks

in countries are always different based on circumstances such as high domestic crime.
- A truly interconnected international fight against money laundering and terrorism financing is needed. Some 30 years later, interagency cooperation and international cooperation are still absent, and even now agreements are finally being signed between states[21] – and emirates[22] – to foster 'better cooperation'. All this groundwork should have been in place decades ago. Crime is international, so should be the response.

## Caution required

As impressive as the intentions may appear, the results of the process of adding and subtracting countries from the FATF-controlled watchlists, are still extensively debated, contested, and not entirely appreciated by all. Whether change will come soon, could be down to the commitment of the current and future FATF presidents or simply to the various underlying factors within the FATF's origins. With more than a decade of grounding already in place, the likelihood of change is nonetheless doubtful, and made less likely if the FATF presidency continues to come from a strong Western-based ideology and rules-based system that are not always transposable onto every country. This is something assured until at least 2024, with the appointment of Raja Kumar from Singapore as the successor to Dr Marcus Pleyer from Germany.

Whatever the future holds, the current path, even with a small step to the left or right along the way, is not necessarily unwelcome news for the FATF whose focus has now swayed towards financial inclusion as opposed to de-risking. It seems the delivery is on the premise of seeking greater control, not pushing the problem underground. By doing so, the problem then becomes an issue for those sectors strongly encouraged to manage the risks. The result – greater compliance, and regulatory scope for the FATF to manage. Of course, financial inclusion expands scope for profitability – a new venture that along with regular publication of typologies and a push for the use of technology solutions strengthens the FATF's global presence and dominance even further. It also acts as a powerful defence against the accusation that watchlists are politically, not technically engineered.

It seems that no matter whether AML laws work, the threat of the FATF's watchlists is enough to encourage action by close to 205 countries and jurisdictions that have embedded to varying degrees the FATF's standardised template in their laws. Whether the lists once mattered or matter a little less now, most responses are just posturing alongside obligatory responses – many of which are soon forgotten unless there are remarkable results to shout about.

Shouting about results takes us to the next chapter, in which we look at FIUs. It is clear they shout, but is their message worthwhile, necessary, and correct? Hence, we discuss the role of the FIU and how it has almost certainly become a depository black hole for the abundance of material it continues to receive.

# 7

# Financial Intelligence Units or data black holes?

[T]he Council takes the view that the section on
Financial Intelligence Units must be strengthened.

The Parliamentary Assembly
of the Council of Europe[1]

The national FIU is one of the main components of the global
AML system. Established by individual countries, the national FIU
is an expectation of the internationally agreed FATF standards.
The collective group of FIUs are supported by the Egmont
Group – a global semi-official organisation whose secretariat is
in Canada. The number of FIUs has grown from 12 members
in 1995 when it began, to 164 in 2020, as a way to generate
mutual knowledge.

As a depository for AML/CFT data, FIUs have gained
importance thanks to increasing need for suspicious transactions or
suspicious activities to be reported. Sending such reports directly
to law enforcement is impractical, due to the vast size and varying
levels of quality and scope. Sometimes it can also be a lack of
trust in law enforcement's ability to deal with SARs sensitively
or even sensibly, that has triggered a country's FIU to become
the first 'port of call'.

Yet, it is here, in the FIU, where the details received can then be
analysed and decisions made as to whether to take further action.
The FIU acts as a buffer between law enforcement and the provider
of the SAR. Still, the anticipation involved in sending a SAR to
an FIU is like that of throwing a stone into a well and waiting

for it to reach the bottom.[2] Only in this instance, seldom do you ever hear the sound of any contact no matter how big the stone. As the Egmont Group highlights, for effective collection and disclosure of financial intelligence related to money laundering derived from corruption, the most important requirement is the need for FIU operational independence and autonomy.[3] Yet for those FIUs run by law enforcement personnel, independence and autonomy can be far from realistic. Still, according to the Egmont Group there are four models of FIUs: (1) the Judicial Model which permits seizing funds, freezing accounts, conducting interrogations, detaining people and conducting searches; (2) the Law Enforcement Model that exists within law enforcement systems; (3) the Administrative Model, which is a centralised, independent, administrative authority, which receives and processes information and disseminated accordingly; and (4) the Hybrid Model that provides a disclosure intermediary and a link to both judicial and law enforcement authorities.[4]

So, no matter the model, the FIU's vital role in AML/CFT and its position as recipient of all SARs within its remit, has raised the notion that FIUs should have most of the answers. Equally, the FIU should also see what threats are on the horizon and offer some insights.

The real issue is perhaps the process within the FIUs, not the idea of a national FIU. Internal processes are quite often preventing knowledge from coming to the surface or being received by the end-user. While this is made all the more difficult when SARs are poorly written and there is lack of sufficient detail, these issues cannot be entirely to blame. Still, whether intentional or because of poor understanding, this circumstance of poor details being received by FIUs plays right into the hands of the money launderer whose only obligation is to separate the information about the crime and/or criminal from the information about the proceeds. It is this 'gap' which is successfully exploited time and time again while lessening the influence of the FIU.

## SARs – but only briefly

It is a common belief that the AML/CFT regime benefits from the submission of SARs. These 'items of information' are critical for figuring out trends and finding money launderers. However, the flipside to this is that the amount of information that exists and the scope of understanding as to 'what is suspicious', means there is – through the very nature of the process – a significant amount of 'noise' or just utter rubbish being created. So, with few law enforcement agencies having the funding to successfully analyse the torrent of SARs filed by banks alone, the issues then become a lot more troubling.

Then there is the addition of low-quality or unnecessary reports. Such reports that are filed as a 'back-covering incentive' to justify compliance with AML/CFT regulations and possibly give legal immunity to prosecution. A genuine incentive if ever there was one. What this means, is that the information, no matter how great it is, rarely receives sufficient attention because it is not always appropriately aligned to the SAR reporting ethics. As a result, the information becomes lost, or simply adds to an internal system generating false positives.

Think of it this way. If unreliable information goes in, with little analysis once inside, what comes out is typically of limited value to the end-user. This is an absurd situation, more so when considering FIUs and money laundering. Even now, what comes out of most FIUs are those details that were asked for, not those following careful analysis of the collective mass of data. The largely significant material is lost in the hype, so we do not see 'intelligence-led targeting' but instead 'targeted intelligence', supplied by the FIU based on the answers already known by law enforcement. So, as the FIU provides further details to support an already commenced law enforcement operation or confirm already 'known knowns', the model being created delivers only short-term results.

## Incoming data – by the bucket load

Globally, banks on their own send over five million SARs a year. In America, over 1.2 million were sent by deposit-takers in 2020.[5] Most of these fall effortlessly into the ether and create more noise for the US FIU: the Financial Crimes Enforcement Network or FinCEN for short. The then 'knee jerk' reaction to submit, submit and submit more SARs on a global scale, is somewhat due to the fines attributed to non-compliance within AML/CFT regulations. This current practice of sending SARs resembles when a doctor taps on the tendon below the knee, no matter the type of shoe on the foot, the size of the leg or who the leg belongs to; the knee will react in the same way every time – to send more SARs! Yet sending greater numbers of SARs as a clear demonstration of meeting AML/CFT obligations is not necessarily the right indicator of measuring compliance or a benefit for FIUs.

Still, even with the underpinning problem of 'rubbish flowing in', FIUs have us believe that a single SAR can be critical in detecting wrongdoing. A case study example usually given at a conference or seminar is usually enough evidence to provide this notion and make attendees 'feel worthwhile'. This may be true in a few instances, but it is also an infrequent observation, despite the sheer number of SARs being sent to almost all FIUs. It is the sheer number of SARs and the poor use made of them which makes this notion hard to really believe. When SARs are neither shared nor used proactively, instead being kept in a 'black hole' depository, it is typical for SARs to be found relevant long after a key event or investigation.

As discussed in Chapter 3, our understanding of money laundering is extremely limited, so SARs are not always linked to actual money laundering, but instead a historical money laundering typology. Still, while there is no such thing as poor information contained within a SAR (see Chapter 10), when a SAR is forcibly matched against expected standards or a money laundering typology the value can become a lot less usable. Still, we are confident that most entities with AML/CFT obligations do not spend time simply fabricating SARs just to show their commitment to AML compliance. Nevertheless, when a red flag notification, or an artificial intelligence (AI) determination of possible wrongdoing is raised, there does appear, from what the authors have seen, a need to overjustify the final sent SAR. The problem is that the justification is commonly shown against a typology report within an NRA to appease the FIU's gatekeeper.

Beyond the SARs issue, the FIU has no doubt become a much bigger 'depository for information'. Many of the issues preventing the FIU from achieving its potential success are perhaps beyond its control, so it could be argued they are not entirely to blame for the part they are not now playing in preventing money laundering. A hesitation to report a SAR, or the overreporting of less meaningful activity, almost certainly works against the FIU and its purpose. Despite these issues, which are of course critical, the FIU still has an obligation never to withhold relevant information from law enforcement – that really does mean 'never'. Withholding information which the FIU knows or should know eases the acquisition, retention, use or control of criminal property (by virtue of it not being investigated) is wrong and not helpful. Such a practice creates only a depository within the FIU and a useless one at that because the information is only ever in one direction – inwards. The idea of sharing is there not to weaken the FIU's status, but to use what is known to have influence and support other investigative agencies.

In the UK, under s. 328 of the POCA, 2002 it is a criminal act within the UK to withhold such information from law enforcement. However, globally it is still unclear as to why many FIUs still insist on not sharing this critical information. It may be a cultural default common within intelligence units worldwide, but the policy of not sharing information that has not yet been assessed as useful within the FIU is partly why the activities associated with the prevention and detection of money laundering and terrorism financing are, we think, so terrible. It is this dire predicament that creates the absurd situation of FIUs acting in the same way as money launderers. A process in which they keep, and there is no rhyme nor reason for doing so, the separation of the information about the money from the information about the crime. This is an unfathomable situation which most who sit outside of an FIU can struggle to even begin to understand.

## The FIU: a black hole for data

The idea that the FIUs are a black hole for data is no fairy-tale. No matter how valuable the information going in, the belief that it could then be effectively analysed for relevance under current circumstances and quickly shared is foolish. FIUs hold a tremendous amount of data, even too much thanks to excessive and unnecessary SAR reporting. So, whether it be raw information or analysed information presented as intelligence, there is no shortage of it, and it appears the FIU is the one place still happy to hold it all. Yet, like pieces in a jigsaw puzzle, sometimes only part of the picture is created, because the other pieces are then never found.

As is in the case of FIUs, more pieces are always being thrown into the mix, meaning the pile of pieces is getting bigger but the picture is becoming less clear. This might be why when ministers for justice and home affairs met in Brussels in late 2015, they expressed that in the Fourth Directive on money laundering and terrorist financing, "the section on Financial Intelligence Units must be strengthened".[6] Is this because as the FIU may manage to 'get to grips' on one issue, information will be received that simply changes everything? Hopefully, yes. Yet the most amusing point here is that new pieces of the jigsaw are typically sent to an FIU only when an entity feels a need to share, confess some existing knowledge or wrongdoing or add to an existing and perhaps distorted picture that was beginning to form. It may even be shared to help meet a monthly target. Still, the timing of a submitted SAR can equally throw a 'spanner into the works' for any FIU. However, that is still no reason for an FIU to decide not to share what it receives. The idea that 'sharing is caring' is surpassed here by the mandatory 'obligation to share' principle no matter how mixed up the pieces may be.

Still, there is the 'all singing, all dancing goAML solution',[7] provided by the United Nations to help FIUs sort the pieces. Perhaps goAML is the original AI tool to solve the FIUs' dilemma of incompetence, yet the application is used by only a quarter of FIUs globally to 'gather intelligence based on the suspicions of reporting entities to help FIUs in combating money laundering and the financing of terrorism'.[8] Just with this statement alone, you could be led to quickly think all is well before realising that with the increase in crime and values associated with global money laundering, the solution may not be quite all it seems.

All this black hole information and still no real intelligence is then likely to raise questions as to 'what is really going on?'. Is it really intelligence that goAML is creating or is it simply categorised data that analysts then search through to support the answers to the already determined problem? A lot like searching for keywords to show something you knew was and always has been a problem as opposed to looking for potential problems existing under the surface.

The goAML specific solution does not stop there. A search of the UNODC's website on goAML explains just how successful goAML is at meeting 'the data collection, management, analytical, document management, workflow and statistical needs of any Financial Intelligence Unit'.[9] The reality is that goAML is a database – it has nothing to do with intelligence. Intelligence comes from analysis, drawing conclusions, testing hypotheses, matching sources, hence why FIUs are full of intelligence analysts. Still, without goAML, just imagine how disorganised an FIU data storage centre would be. But would such disorganisation make them any less efficient than those that claim all sorts of goAML user benefits? A rethink of goAML and its role in aiding how FIUs receive, analyse and share information and intelligence is seemingly long overdue if there is a desire for the remaining 75% of FIUs to adopt goAML. Not only is the current system adding to the problem, without it the black hole of each national FIU becomes more 'inaccessible'.

## National Risk Assessments or just risk expectations?

The reason the NRA has in some cases become just another publication is, we think, threefold. First, they rarely say anything new, despite years of new knowledge having been captured as to how money laundering and terrorism financing are changing. Most rely heavily on expert opinion without following any uniform approach of eliciting expert opinion. Second, they are written in such a generic format for fear of releasing sensitive intelligence. Third, they ignore risk, instead focusing on methods of money laundering while aligning to other more influential and authoritative publications by the FATF, the UN and regional bodies. None of this is the fault of the FIU ideology, more a failure from leadership. But if the FIU is the pivotal point for all relevant information, it would be expected that NRAs actually delivered a lot more. After all, we cannot see how it is possible for a risk-based AML strategy to succeed if a country fails to research and explain their risks.

It seems the obligation to produce an NRA is more an obligation (a tick-box exercise) rather than a means to inform regulators, reporting entities and the public sector as to the threats and risks a country faces. In Europe, Article 8(4) of the proposed 6th AML Directive will soon require EU member states to keep their NRA up to date and review it at least every four years. What will then apparently distinguish EU member states from other countries is the European Commission's risk assessment of the risks of money laundering and terrorist financing affecting the internal market and relating to cross-border activities. Of course, like the story which has been told to us before, no doubt one NRA will be a copy of the earlier version leading to just a series of pan-European threats and risks. But we must remember, the FIU is really an entity of its own. Its authority, its power and its response are all decided by how it performs and uses the information it has available. This means NRAs are essential in deciding how to design and execute countermeasures against financial crime that make sense, preferably using a risk-based approach going forward. If EU member states decide to copy and paste NRAs, then the insights needed as to how criminals behave in a particular country will be missed and therefore fail to qualify the prioritisation of future resources.

## Ordinary SAR submissions

Typically, all the data received by FIUs are based on the processes which create suspicion. Yet suspicion on money laundering does not always come in the form of demonstrable and visible evidence. Transaction monitoring processes administered by banks assess values, volumes and the frequency of the transactions against sets of rules. These rules are typically built on peer group and historic and/or perceived normal account activity, thus creating almost predetermined results. However, in some instances, data linked to jurisdictions (such as those countries named on watchlists – the FATF grey and blacklists) are also considered. Business type and product may then be incorporated in the assessment to provide further clarity. Yet, and this is where the problem becomes more noticeable, cash may also be considered a higher risk. When these factors are combined, it is possible to see how the volume of potentially reportable suspicions to the FIU becomes infinite in practical terms.

This highlights the almost inconceivable problem of matching SARs with keywords: those *words, names, addresses, businesses* already attributed to money laundering and terrorism financing activities and typologies. A real problem of 'facts becoming facts by repetition'. This is particularly a worry when keywords are being used as a means of deciding themes within the datasets contained in a national FIU's black hole of ever-increasing information. But what happens when keywords are wrong, old, or even included by money launderers to deceive?

Although particular keywords will almost certainly appear many times in a mass of data, most relating to money laundering are, we now feel, too prominent to allow genuine analysis. Hence why goAML may be best suited but still poorly adopted by the majority of FIUs. High-level keywords such as *cash, cannabis, unknown, reason, car, house* coinciding with 'hits' can then all too easily be used to create an extremely naive picture of what is happening across a sector, or worse across a national money laundering landscape.[10] The trouble is, they are just words with little relevance, even if they are needed to evidence the creation of a SAR.

So, if you were going to analyse data held by an FIU, you would not start with searching for common keywords. Most of the time these keywords are unable to figure out anything more than what is known far outside of the FIU confines. With so much data now available and more arriving daily, just how closely aligned are they to what is considered or thought to be money laundering as opposed to the realities or unknowns of money laundering as it is happening today? The difference between red flags indicating money laundering and the reality of today's money laundering activities is most certainly wider than most professionals are led to believe. Why would a money launderer raise red flags by suggesting, identifying or even mentioning keywords such as *cash, cannabis, unknown, reason, car, house* if these and other keywords are what the bank teller, compliance officer, AML analyst are looking for?

## Data overload

It is widely recognised that the amount of data is already becoming problematic; hence, FIUs and law enforcement agencies are now reassessing what they need to have in place going forward. Interestingly, the Hong Kong police have upgraded the computer system for their new AML squad. The intention is to speed up the screening of a vast number of suspicious financial activities, which surged by 10% in 2020 to more than 57,000 reports. Yet, to what extent is computing power going to help deal with the problem and for what is it really needed? Is the upgrade instead for a process which has been too complicated from the start and simply snowballed into a situation which needs an overhaul not tweaking?

This move by Hong Kong also coincides with the UK's history of managing computer systems not able to cope with the amount of SARs data being sent. Problems faced by Australia similarly suggest widespread issues. In 2021, AUSTRAC engaged in a System Transformation Program designed to update and upgrade how the Australian financial sector filed suspicious matter reports in a first step to counter a negative narrative within the region about AUSTRAC's capabilities.[11] A perspective helped by New Zealand in 2017 when they introduced goAML in preparation for an influx of SARs resulting from lawyers, accountants and real estate agents finally being added to AML/CFT compliance obligations and a pending MER assessment.

Do these reactions to add and update technology solutions signify another knee jerk reaction? Almost certainly, yes. As when the doctor taps on the tendon below the knee and there is a reaction, for FIUs it comes in the form of failure, criticism or downright neglect. However, is it possible in this instance, that not only the hammer needs to be reassessed but also the doctors' abilities to do it right first time when it comes to more technology? If the reaction is necessary, then it ought to be proportional and transparent. Accepting increasing numbers of SARs into a data black hole will more than likely create missed opportunities to use what may only ever be a small percentage of worthwhile reports. Adding fuel to the fire will not necessarily extinguish it, so why seek more SARs when the quality and the quantity are already overwhelming FIUs worldwide?

To date, the collection of data in each national FIU black hole has little proven evidence of purpose. We acknowledge there have been successes and options for sharing details with overseas law enforcement agencies, but the time spent, even wasted, by reporting entities writing, sending and even resending SARs to their national FIU, has been on the rise for some time. After all, does a business in a high-risk sector go with the notion they must submit reports to meet expectations, or do they attempt to stay below the radar of regulators and look the other way when suspicious behaviours are identified? We agree, both options can work for a while, but both, if investigated correctly, can unearth many problems. Is the best approach to occupy the middle ground, 'sit on the fence' so to speak? A wobbly fence to sit on, some would argue, but equally, a case of 'damned if you do, damned if you don't'.

If what was received by FIUs worldwide was prompt, accurate and relevant then the situation FIUs now find themselves in could be improved. If Europol are not able to recognise any more than about 400 top-level professional money launderers in Europe, there is another sign, a warning light even, that relevant details are clearly missing. According to Europol, these 400 'professionals' are 'apparently running billions of illegal drug and other criminal profits through the banking system with a 99 percent success rate'.[12] Does this level of severity show that there are more details to be found, or is there evidence that the current focus is not where it must be?

If FIUs know there is a problem such as this, then why are the data being held by national FIUs not being used to tackle and abolish the problem? The answer is simply that the process of data collection by FIUs is ad-hoc, disjointed, inadequate in quality and not strategically delivered. It is also very one-sided, even when partnership arrangements are in place. All national FIUs hold a treasure trove of information capable of impacting on investigations. So, if you have ever listened to a Head of a national FIU speak at a conference, this 'control of power' oozes through in their tone, language and case studies – clearer than night follows day. But what the FIU manages to deliver is only a fraction of that which is possible.

## FIU independence

This brings us back to the issue of operational independence and autonomy of an FIU, which is something considered a fundamental condition to an effective AML/CFT framework. FIUs simply need to be able to manage their priorities without external influence. If not, the credibility of an FIU with members of the private sector and domestic law enforcement is weakened. The FIU's ability to gather information it needs domestically and to exchange information with international partners can also be negatively influenced. This suggests the quality and scope of investigations relating to money laundering, terrorism financing and predicate offences such as corruption can be further weakened.[13]

It is not uncommon for reporting entities to see their role as one which is supporting law enforcement, as opposed to simply keeping their AML/CFT obligations. Many can react by sending more SARs and overloading the system, at the same time becoming frustrated that they are continually being brought into the role of law enforcement, a responsibility which they are not in business to fulfil. The only way to overcome this is to leave the FIUs to be what they are – Financial Intelligence Units and not simply an extension of law enforcement. It may be that FIUs contribute to the *war on dirty money*, but apart from receiving and later sending SARs to competent authorities and even using urgent temporary powers that are then taken forward by the competent authorities, the FIU is only ever best placed to be a Financial Intelligence Unit.

## FIU potential

Ideally, an FIU must not be seen as a 'sorting house' or as a 'library' only open for law enforcement to borrow material, but only as the FIU then allows. To be effective, FIUs must instead be used for the purpose of connecting the proceeds back to the predicate crime or, better still, the criminal mastermind. So, either what is going into the FIUs is rubbish, or the analysis and dissemination is poor and wrongly aligned, because connecting the proceeds backwards is not happening. Since FIUs do not pass intelligence over to law enforcement does this, in practice, suggest FIUs replicate the behaviours of money launderers? A practice of keeping their tacit knowledge to themselves to prove the importance of the role they hold. Equally, the less they tell, the fewer questions can be asked, and any wrongdoing then identified.

In the fight against money laundering, not only are we asking the wrong questions of the wrong people, in respect to FIUs we still do not understand what they really have to offer. It is the mystique surrounding FIUs that is perhaps hampering the submission of information from certain aspects of society. Much of the information being sent to FIUs is believed by those in AML/CFT reporting entities to be solely for law enforcement purposes and a compliance obligation when the time arises. It stands for information that will be used to prosecute, recover illicit assets and, therefore, hopefully in preventing the illicit activities which generate trillions of USD annually. Yet, this belief misses out the FIU as an entity, dismissing it as simply a collection point or email recipient for SARs.

Now is the time – before the tremendous amount of data becomes more of a complicating factor – to define key principles so everyone knows what to expect from a national FIU. Doing so would work towards negating hesitation that reporting entities may have in sending SARs. Knowing SARs will be managed by an FIU, can create a more sympathetic appearing recipient as opposed to an aggressive gang busting team. This is important in times when trust in law enforcement is low and when many people only interact with law enforcement in an emergency.

## Revising basic beliefs

With experience working in and alongside various national FIUs, the authors understand the challenges, the issues and the opportunities. But hearing the Parliamentary Assembly of the Council of Europe (CoE) criticise, in 2021, the efforts to combat money laundering and terrorism financing, brought many of the opportunities to the forefront of thinking. The CoE nicely pointed out the need to strengthen FIUs across Europe.[14] The authors recognise first-hand the potential FIUs can offer in the overall AML/CFT regime, it is simply a matter of realigning FIUs towards achieving their full potential. As the CoE suggests, strengthening national FIUs to match the FATF and Moneyval standards is key, but these standards also need to be assessed. It is quite possible that these standards are no longer relevant because, as noted in

Chapter 4, the obsession by the FATF to create typologies is more detrimental to the AML/CFT regime than it is helpful.

Not wanting to use the perspective too many times, take again for a minute the 'rubbish in – rubbish out' scenario and match it to intelligence sharing. How possible is it to stop being so secretive with the knowledge and instead share it more widely, on time and for a purpose? The problem is if the level of knowledge about money laundering is not lifted, then what an FIU shares will only be based on that old, regurgitated information read many times before by the reporting entities. The same information that is told again and again at annual conferences run by the same organisations. Yet, it is possible to break this vicious circle of wasteful energy by using the FIUs as a hub of knowledge on trends and activities in a preventative way – not as an echo for the FATF, UN and World Bank. This would enable FIUs to bring an exact localised perspective to the problems while, at the same time, using the critical details and forming intelligence for use by law enforcement for the purpose of connecting the proceeds back to the predicate crime. Since law enforcement is not there to always prevent crime but, instead, to uphold the law and bring to justice those who break it, then it is down to the next in line to add something relevant. It is here the FIU has noteworthy potential. A 'share to prevent', rather than a 'provide only on request to support an investigation' approach.

If the FATF is not going to introduce a novel approach to educating AML/CFT practitioners across the globe, then it is down to FIUs to educate within their national boundaries. Whether this will become a widespread practice, will only be decided if a single FIU takes the reins and leads from the front. But in doing so, the idea that others will follow will show more forcefully the need for a global FIU, not simply a supporting agency such as the Egmont Group. Perhaps a global FIU already exists in terms of the FATF; after all they do collate material from countries to support the creation of typology reports. This is seemingly a widespread presumption which of course ignores whether what is shared with the FATF is relevant and of good quality. Or could the Egmont Group take the reins and replace the FATF altogether, since at least they have been working with FIUs as opposed to just verbalising various principles to them?

**Solutions toolbox**

- There is a need to define the key principles of an FIU, so everyone knows what to expect from a national FIU. With over 200 national FIUs there is little clarity globally. Equally, there is little clarity nationally. This needs to be corrected – and soon – as statements from heads of FIUs can leave professional reporting entity audiences baffled and equally worried what and just how much they should share via SARs reports.
- NRAs are no longer fit for purpose and need to be corrected to suit the audience's needs. NRAs largely reflect FATF typologies and red flags, rather than the actual risks that a country recognises and needs to address. The value of an FIU comes from informing those who need specific knowledge. This allows the user to apply it to their own entity or entire sectors' AML/CFT risk assessment.

Despite these opportunities, the creation of a global FIU is unlikely. Why? Because those with 'intelligence' always seem too scared to share it. But is there an opportunity for an 'all EU 27-member state FIU', an 'Asia-Pacific FIU' or a 'MENA FIU'? Or would this again be too difficult to agree upon, manage and thus keep control of the information and intelligence? Something must change if there is to be a global approach to a globally diverse and stateless threat.

If not, then the world – and particularly Europe – is set for many more years of individual countries trying to transpose new directives into local law and then trying awkwardly to prosecute money laundering years after the event. Still, with Europol unable to access all the data that already exists, the absence of an EU-wide tax structure, and little political will for change, then perhaps there is still hope for a more effective solution to appear.

This brings us to the idea of prevention and the notion that we can prevent money laundering, when it is on the predicate offence where the focus should really be directed. Preventing money laundering has created jobs, fancy titles and amazing technology solutions but, as we see in the next chapter, preventing money laundering is based on 'wishful thinking' instead of something solid.

# 8

# The 'fingers crossed' approach to money laundering prevention

Stopping money laundering is about saving peoples' lives.

FATF[1]

Failures to prevent the more conventional forms of money laundering usually bring about particular types of response. The 'we need to ...' or 'We have now looked at our failings and are addressing them' and, of course, the 'We strongly regret ...'. Yet such statements are almost irrelevant, and they rarely transform the effort towards preventing money laundering. You could argue it is all just 'lip service'.

Yet it is true, change can take place, updates can happen to existing practices, more regulations may be added, but change is usually minimal outside of improvements in AML/CFT. The real problem here, is that the entire approach to preventing money laundering is wrongly and inconsistently attributed to compliance. Modern-day behaviours and those of today's criminals, and the consequences of the harm caused by their activities, are being ignored, with many remaining misunderstood. Is this perhaps why David Lewis' (a former FATF Executive Secretary) statement, "Stopping money laundering is about saving peoples' lives",[2] could be one of the most important statements of recent times?

If you want to know how wrong we have the idea of prevention, look at German digital bank N26 who found out the hard way after been fined US$5 million over the delayed submission of SARs. In May 2021, N26 was ordered by a regulator to implement safeguards to prevent terror financing and money laundering. N26 was also ordered to close loopholes in their IT monitoring/CDD processes. However, since N26 ran out of time they were hit with penalties. A statement in response to the fine (because there always needs to be a statement), noted how N26 "takes its responsibility in the fight against the growing threat of global financial crime, and in the prevention of money laundering, very seriously". If statements such as these are to mean anything, then we think what goes before it needs to be looked at in a little more detail.

What we find is preventative measures are being reinvented time and again, but few are hitting the nail on the head, so to speak. It is true, 'things' are happening and much of it is aligned to a business-like strategy and surrounded by a deep belief of needing to be effective at prevention. Yet, any strategy can easily be regulator driven and nowhere near focused on preventing the actual problem. Instead, the focus can be aligned to identifying and reporting under the banner of compliance. The problem is, we already know AML and CFT compliance can never be 100% effective. Where the true effectiveness can be measured is not our focus as the authors, but since criminality circumvents the measures being enforced, efficiency is always going to be less than perfect for the perfectionists.

With the value of money laundering continuing to grow, as a direct consequence of increases in crime, it is clear the preventative measures that have existed for so long are not working. Again, this level of detail is not ideal in what it suggests, but evidence of something which can quickly appear wrong to many. It seems for too long policy makers have been able to introduce flawed policies thanks to the media's depiction of organised crime and the apprehension this causes to the public. What we now face is a situation in which strategies are absent, ill-informed, or guided towards the ambitions of individual organisations. Governments and international bodies simply choose not to admit just how bad the problem is, attributing it to a threat to national security, we think, as a means of disguise. When the need does arise, many fall back on a 'finger in the air' guesstimate that is now too old to even mention. Yet, if money laundering figures were calculated today, nobody would like the answer – particularly if the figure captured all predicate crime types, something we see commonly missed out of earlier 'guesstimates'.

In their defence, national governments have created legislation, much of it accompanied by strong statements. It seems when it comes to AML/CFT everybody loves a good strong statement! But that is usually where preventative efforts come to an end. We think you could match today's approach to preventing money laundering with that of reducing climate change. Lots of talk and promises but only ever minor changes (sometimes actual changes) by the main polluters. Where preventative action for climate change has taken place, failures have also arisen since the problem has been improperly assessed from the very start. Producing electric plastic cars with little interest in the environmental impact of mining materials for manufacturing batteries is one notable example.

Review what is happening, and it quickly becomes apparent that in money laundering, preventative efforts have focused on the point where the money launderer is most vulnerable to detection – the inevitable depositing of cash. Yet, reporting of suspicious transactions and behaviours is not always limited to cash. Nor are successful money launderers unaware of the basic principles being deployed by front-line staff to detect them and such activities. Is this really where our effort should be directed? If it is, then prevention has failed, either because we have failed or because the money launderer has outsmarted us. We think this should cause concern. If this is where the problem of money laundering starts, with *placement*, and we have convinced the biggest sector – the financial sector – to actively participate, why has money laundering grown as a threat?

As a rule of thumb, the regulated sector, as in those businesses with AML/CFT obligations, is not paying staff to prevent money laundering. We are sorry if this statement offends any readers, but the focus of most is on keeping the AML/CFT regulator at bay, at arm's length. If you do not believe the statement and think we are wrong, consider why a bank, for example, would accept a law enforcement role when it is a commercial enterprise. Catching money launderers is for law enforcement, as most in a bank will tell you. Most will also tell you commercial entities do enough through the reporting of suspicious activities and transactions to the national FIU. What more can we expect from them?

Is this then why the 2021 Basel Index found jurisdictions to be consistently scoring even worse for the prevention of money laundering than they do for enforcement. This finding alone must raise grave questions about whether jurisdictions are serious about dealing with money laundering and terrorist financing risks.[3] If Basel Institute are saying this, the evidence for many must also be plain to see. We think this assessment raises many questions as to what is actually happening to stop money laundering.

While technology has been able to reduce so-called false positives – perhaps, but we hope not, by ignoring areas where alerts could be detected – the same technology solutions are still only as effective as the information used to develop them. Then there are the issues arising from where it is used. Within retail banks, the products and services being offered have different data requirements. In private banking, clients are diverse in their activities and AML/CFT risk profiles. Any off-the-shelf solution is, of course, unlikely to provide anywhere near 100% protection for these users. Yet the reliance on compliance software solutions is growing fast against a backdrop of what is clearly decades old knowledge on the problem.

Let us not forget, AML compliance may be established on preventative principles but, as time has gone by, the compliance obligations are obviously no longer suitable for preventing money laundering. We see *true prevention* is only possible when the activities behind money laundering are understood. When this happens, we can substantially increase risk for the money launderer and introduce specific measures to directly stop money laundering. For a technology solution to achieve this, an understanding of money laundering is needed right from the very start.

## Wishful thinking – ticked

The notion that businesses and international organisations are actively preventing money laundering is wishful thinking if today's criminal environment is anything to go by. Yes, international and national organisations have given us many recommendations and regulations, most adopted into national laws, but after 30 years, the international AML/CFT regime has never been assessed as to the extent activities have managed to even reduce money laundering, never mind prevent it.[4] Instead, with no absolute authority, the FATF has had a major impact on the lives of so many. Most AML/CFT policies rely on FATF evidence, yet is what is being told to us serving the agenda of a few? Are we suffering from confirmation bias that makes us still believe what we are doing is working?

We think it really is 'wishful thinking' to believe global efforts to prevent money laundering have been worthy of the time and cost so far. Even in 2022 a plethora of vulnerabilities across the globe exist, which, although frowned upon when the spotlight is shone towards them, still offer options to launder illicit wealth. Take for example the numbered accounts held in Swiss banks thanks to Article 47 – which makes it a criminal offence to disclose information about a bank's clients, even if it is in the public interest to do so. Then consider countries such as Dubai and Singapore apparently being exploited as safe havens for money laundering. Coincide this with the approach to preventing money laundering still based on decades old understanding that formed compliance obligations which are still not globally implemented. These are not hidden, small or unsolvable issues, but while they remain, they equally allow money laundering to exist.

If we could start to see 'on the ground', 'at the sharp end', and at the 'coal face' the opportunities that are exploited by money launderers, then we could start to feel positive once again. Unfortunately, it is in these same areas where AML/CFT compliance hopes are typically destroyed.

We do not see how it is possible to stop money laundering if we do not know how it is happening. Is this why AML/CFT risk assessments can be more focused towards technical compliance with requirements rather than the effectiveness of the businesses' combined efforts to prevent and even detect money laundering? As the Wolfsburg Group suggest, 'this exercise typically concludes in an enterprise-wide risk assessment which tends to be too long and complex and focused on data, documentation, and process rather than outcomes'.[5] For many businesses, the idea of staff going beyond compliance obligations is as beneficial as paying more tax than is required. It is not necessary, nor is it helpful and it certainly leaves no one feeling more satisfied. If a failure happens, it is unfortunate, but it is merely a temporary headache, a small cost of doing business.

## Top-down persuasion: compliance culture vs actual prevention

AML compliance is about just that, complying with rules, expectations and obligations considered to be effective at preventing money laundering. The trouble is, as we see it, money laundering is on the rise, still largely unhindered and somewhat elusive in nature. We are not suggesting for a minute that compliance efforts are, in their entirety, a waste of time but we do feel the blindfold needed to be removed a lot sooner. What we are suggesting is that today's efforts provide only a partial control – an obstacle not a barrier. True prevention is about introducing and altering the barrier to match the pressures being exerted on it. We believe that as money launderers alter their activities, so too should the preventative measures.

One glaring issue we want to raise at this point, using an example, has to be the problem that AML compliance obligations are always historical. If AML compliance is to be adopted, it needs to be timely. Yet, in terms of Tranche 2, the inclusion of lawyers, real estate agents and accountants as professional entities into AML compliance – based on the idea they are gatekeepers or enablers[6] to money laundering – widespread implementation has been anything but. It has, to date, been over a decade since these professional sectors were identified as capable facilitators of money laundering and still there are huge gaps in the global effort to prevent money laundering, with countries such as Australia so far dismissing the need to add these sectors to its AML/CFT compliance regime. Ignoring this obligation is clearly a critical failure in the global efforts already adopted to prevent and detect money laundering and terrorism financing. Equally, we think this approach can be a wilful neglect to recognise the proficiency of money launderers.

## No motivation, meaning few benefits

We think the peak in motivation for AML/CFT compliance has been reached. The effort applied to AML compliance and to creating typologies has been overwhelming. Time-consuming and costly activities have had little influence on money laundering. Fines continue, costs are rising and the need to be managed by technology solutions is perhaps leading far too many to turn away when there is an easy opportunity to do so.

Let us look back to 2012 when the FATF introduced the requirement for countries to conduct an NRA. Since then, less than a third of countries now have one, and where they exist, they range from two to over 200 pages. Some are four to six years old, despite the intention to shift from a rule-based AML/CFT system, where regulated entities followed procedures specified by law and regulation, to a risk-based approach. This is the risk-based approach which requires the identification of 'threats'. With NRAs lacking a methodology allowing them to be replicated, issues with defining 'threats' and little evidencing of change to policy decisions, if motivation were going to start dwindling, it would be here. Why would a business focus on managing risk when few fall from grace even when things go horribly wrong?

## Warning: the disconnect is extremely scary

We see how it can be difficult to motivate compliance professionals when criminals are buying up properties, living luxurious lifestyles and circumventing laws through corruption and an exploitation of the gaps that remain. For the outsider looking in at all this, it does not take long to see how some 'questionable people' are enjoying a better lifestyle than the majority.

Criminal money is truly making the world go round, thanks primarily to being embedded in a global financial system not entirely motivated to identify, never mind remove it. All this while working in the shadows of a wealth that is underpinning economies and countries which few ever seek to question. Is this perhaps why things never change – all despite strong statements of discomfort and condemnations by those in power or those caught napping?

The MER is perhaps the only obvious motivation for countries to do anything near preventing money laundering and terrorism financing. It is thought the consequences of a poor MER form deep cracks in an economy and damage the wealth and status of the elite. Yet the same MER process only requires giving the right answers to already-known questions. It is not surprising countries go out of their way to achieve a good MER but, after seven rounds, has the MER process done anything to stem money laundering? No, we suggest, not if the volumes of money laundering today are anything to go by. Still, a seal of approval by the FATF equates to a licence to continue to do more of the same or, in some cases, forget to do anything meaningful.

So, despite huge fines – something we cover in Chapter 20 – the motivation is again perhaps dwindling within the FATF member countries to prevent money laundering. We think perhaps the problem has become too great, with fines no longer having the desired effect. The process now being adopted on a bigger scale than before is one of keeping active, about seeking an immediate diagnosis of AML/CFT issues quickly followed by assurances that a technology driven cure can quickly be implemented. Yet, these very systems and processes remain underfunded, cohesion between the application of AML/CFT rules and regulations is still absent. To us, it seems too many people are busy ticking boxes that do nothing to really improve processes and procedures that are designed to prevent money laundering. When the regulator does come knocking, as in the case of Swedbank, one of Sweden's largest banks identified in a large-scale money laundering scandal in the Baltics, de-emphasising negative information and taking a literal or narrow reading to certain requests can still be seen as an acceptable practice.[7]

Where scepticism about a lack of motivation for AML/CFT compliance can be quashed is in a review of SAR reporting. As a method of preventing money laundering, the results are not great. Numbers may be increasing, details may be aligned to common expectations, but raising specifics as to who may be using an entity for illicit purposes is not an ideal situation to be in. The problem is SARs can demonstrate the best intentions of a team player, but equally some feel they can expose an 'assortment of problems' that lead to a visit by the AML regulator. It is then possible that the 'dammed if you do, but not always dammed if you do not' principle may be an important consideration among AML/CFT regulated entities.

## The authenticity of something fake

Just how authentic the current approach to preventing money laundering and terrorism financing really is, depends on where you stand. If you believe it is authentic, then headlines such as 'Swiss bank UBS agrees to pay a €10m penalty to end an Italian money laundering case' and 'A New Zealand company, Jin Yuan Finance, is fined US$2.7m for not complying with AML laws', may change your mind. These are not simply 'bad apples'. Calls in Australia for a royal commission after leaked CCTV footage from Melbourne's Crown Casino showed a man in a tracksuit exchanging 'bricks of cash'[8] worth hundreds of thousands of dollars for gaming chips in one of the casino's high-roller rooms adds to the quandary now before us. Should you still be clinging on to optimism, then look again at how NatWest Bank in the UK allowed the payment of over £264 million in cash to one account between November 2013 and June 2016.

In AML/CFT compliance, the focus on stopping money laundering is only ever taken seriously when the fines exceed profit, shareholders get jittery, or someone is teetering on the edge of going to jail (see Chapter 20). Banks have managed the monitoring of financial flows and the finding of money laundering occurrences for decades, yet increasingly higher fines are continuing for failures in this one area alone. These common scenarios suggest AML/CFT compliance has become a bragging right, a monopoly within organisations and the creator of significant bureaucracy – not an effective prevention tool. At the same time, firms such as HSBC and JPMorgan Chase have added nearly 5,000 specialists focused on fighting financial crime and more than 20,000 in risk and compliance. Either someone is looking the other way, people are ineffectually too busy to notice, or the system is flawed beyond our initial assessment. The idea that we are working towards preventing money laundering seems to be misguided.

Given that the prevention of money laundering has been advocated by various actors in the field for some 30 years – the FATF, the EU, the UN and the World Bank to name the key vocalists – evidence of what works must now be apparent. Yet, even as the EU's plan to ban cash payments above €10,000 is being seen as a strong indication of intent, the reality is most people do not have a genuine need to carry that amount of cash. Is the banishing of cash in society an almost pitiful attempt more akin to a practice of window dressing than actually implementing a preventative measure? After all, countries that have implemented bans on using or holding cash have not seen any significant reduction in money laundering, bribery or corruption.

We have found it difficult to find evidence of real money laundering prevention successes. By this we mean those successes which focused on stopping money laundering at the time and have managed to continue to do so. Instead, we see successes in detecting money laundering come mostly from 'lucky wins' faintly attributed to prevention activities. Some arise from the results of compliance lucky dips, some resulting from the submission of an accurate SAR rather than the introduction of a measure which prevents money laundering from taking place. We admit prevention is hard to measure and therefore is a worrying performance indicator for many managers, but the entire approach to money laundering is one of prevention.

Worrying, too, is that most successes come to fruition long after the initial predicate crime. Many are law enforcement exploited successes, those quick and easy wins resulting from criminal stupidity and mistakes which in essence have little bearing on all others involved in crime and money laundering. The impact of these efforts is negligible, the scope is usually limited and the obligation to prevent something can be hard to swallow for those whose performance is measured by managing the consequences.

Prevention successes may sound impressive within the media, supported by suggestions of intelligence-led, targeted and multi-agency and multi-jurisdictional efforts – yet most results only ever come from stumbling across cash or recognising obvious strange behaviour. If prevention is to happen, there need to be efforts to identify the activities surrounding transfers and purchases. We do not believe money laundering is a three-stage process of *placement*, *layering* and *integration*, nor is it a practice that can be separated into typologies. We see money laundering as *transfers* and *purchases* that are equivalent to those happening each day across the globe. They are managed in such a way as to appear no different to those that are for non-illicit purposes.

If the world is waiting for the FATF's standards to prevent money laundering, then we think it is going to be disappointed. After 30 years, there has been only minor change, with the problem exceeding any initial expectations. As the saying goes, 'the best time to plant a tree was 20 years ago'. For money laundering, then, perhaps it was 30 years ago that real effort should have started to understand exactly what the problem was.

The weaknesses revealed by the Basel AML Index are, we think, the result of the continuous evolution of financial crime typologies. Cryptocurrencies ten years ago were scarcely discussed; now, as the Basel Institute finds, regulators and reporting entities are scrambling to get on top of the associated risks. The failure to profile customers, a general failure to effectively monitor transactions, and the failures arising from a reliance on red flags to detect money laundering, all show – just like 'fool's gold' at the end of a rainbow – how prevention of money laundering has been unsuccessful. Nor is it likely to ever be successful while policy writers remain separated by the huge gap between generic beliefs and the real world.

If adding law enforcement to the money laundering prevention regime somehow suggests improved opportunity – sadly, the reality is, it does not. We know it is still a challenge to create a hostile environment at a global level because of a lack of capability and capacity in law enforcement. Yet, the response has been to bolt money laundering on to the existing criminal justice system, not have it incorporated within. Nor has prevention ever become the role of law enforcement, mainly because of the clear monetary rewards to be had for successful investigations into money laundering. It is clear, law enforcement and preventing money laundering will never truthfully exist together in the same sentence. The reality of 'policing for profit' is all too obvious alongside a preventative approach that is 180 degrees off target and which expects compliance to find the necessary successes. If law enforcement is to support the prevention of money laundering, we think there needs to be a clear obligation for ensuring this can and will happen.

## Giving AML/CFT a second chance

Imagine, that an international body, which most countries had signed up to follow, provided a set of rules – rules that were no longer based on the accurate behaviours and activities in today's world. Imagine too that these same rules were so strong that every country, and all the people who could be linked to the problem that the rules were related to, had to do lots of time-consuming and costly *things*. Imagine then, that the time-consuming and costly *things* needing to be done made life difficult, could not be universally adopted nor could they be directly attributed to tackling the initial problem that caused the formation of the international body in the first place. And then to cap it all off, imagine that huge fines could be issued to individuals and companies who did not exactly follow these rules.

This may sound ridiculous, but that is exactly what is happening when we look at the global issue of preventing money laundering and terrorism financing as it sits today, in 2022. Fines are being handed out (like sweets at a children's birthday party) to AML/CFT reporting entities for not following rules which are pointless or, worse still, woefully wrong for preventing money laundering. Is this a mistake or something more mischievous? Or is it simply a problem now too hard to put right despite initial good intentions?

We feel it could be argued that if time is spent focusing in detail on what is actually happening, nothing will get done. This is perhaps true, but there is a need to start somewhere new by occasionally lifting our head up and checking our destination. We see the current head-down, even eyes-closed approach, forcing many to rely too heavily on what they hear and read. The AML/CFT auto pilot needs to be switched to the off position or, better still, disconnected altogether. This would help to overcome the lack of transparency; insufficient collaboration; and the lack of resources we feel are urgently needed to prevent money laundering. Anything less is simply helping to just poorly manage it.

It is clear, when speaking with those people in AML/CFT compliance, that motivation is dwindling. Can this be changed by bringing forward firmer motivations to be 'preventative in practice'. If you remember, we suggested David Lewis' statement, "stopping money laundering is about saving peoples' lives",[9] could be one of the most important statements of recent times. There is a need to express once more the realities of not preventing money laundering.

It could appear to some, as it did to us, that there may be no real desire to find a solution to the problem of money laundering. The global efforts, huge expense, and the ongoing desire to prevent money laundering has had negligible impact on the problem. Even as money laundering continues to rise, if what exists in terms of preventing money laundering now is deemed success, have we really given any thought about what the state of play will be in 2030? With so many countries all needing to 'play ball with the FATF' it is likely there will be many more fouls, offsides, the odd draw but lots of losses for many competitors, with the game inevitably ending in 'naming and shaming'. We agree, things have improved as time has gone by. We agree, the measures being put in place are sometimes worthwhile, but the lack of appreciation for the skills of the money launderer has left the attempts to find a solution in turmoil.

If the existing status quo is to be effectively addressed, then only two options feasibly exist. The first is to reduce the effort placed on AML/CFT compliance and use it to instead support the prevention and detection of the predicate crimes. What currently exists, only serves to highlight why AML/CFT regulations and systems are so ineffective at reducing the impact of the underlying crimes. A move away from the 'trying to shut the stable door after the horse has clearly bolted' principle is urgently needed. Most AML/CFT practitioners can clearly see that the stable is empty and that all subsequent efforts are unnecessary. The second option is to focus on the money launderer in the same way that cybersecurity professionals enhance the resilience of an organisation to potential attack and mitigate the threat by gaining insight into those likely to be responsible. This means focusing on understanding tactics, techniques and procedures, and creating value in real-time threat intelligence to move away from a generic blanket approach to presuming everyone is a money launderer.

We admit red flags and typology reports may have provided insight into money laundering, but such generic assessments are what the money launderers are exploiting. Using the premise that money laundering is a series of transfers and purchases, to prevent it we need to be able to identify those that are money laundering. As professionals we have been pushing for the need to think like a money launderer for a while now, proving in earlier research how it can open us up to appreciating the lengths money launderers will go to to be successful.

The blanket approach or behavioural obsession in AML/ CFT is a costly, time-consuming and non-motivational series of ongoing activities that clearly, at present, are of little interest to compliance professionals who are, nevertheless, obligated through a widespread perspective. Whether these two options have been considered before, we feel they play no real part in today's efforts at preventing money laundering. Financial institutions, lawyers, accountants, casinos and all other sectors captured by AML/ CFT compliance simply follow the guidance provided. When the regulator takes guidance from the FIU and NRA, one can be confident that the FIU copied their guidance from the FATF. Unfortunately, it can also involve adding in outdated and redacted case studies. Instead, to be effective, these activities which form the practices of preventing money laundering need new sources of data, an innovative approach to analysis and an intention to see money laundering for what it is today, not simply match it to former generic perceptions.

Still, both options require going beyond the minimum standards and understanding what the typologies are really saying: what is believed, what is known, how factually correct they are and what is simply added as a big fat guess. Introducing opportunities for creativity and allowing AML/CFT teams the time to be more strategic, creative and innovative will serve reporting entities well as a means to save money. Such blue-sky thinking will serve entities if they are to be expected to prevent money laundering, not simply report on meeting assumed preventative objectives. Thinking like a money launderer, to ensure all preventative controls are in place, is critical and, again, cost saving in the long term. Money launderers operate with few confines, they may not have entirely free rein, but they have too few restrictions within which to operate.

To support either possibility, a culture change is needed. No matter how many i's are dotted and t's crossed, prevention is currently a matter of chance – a matter of luck. Until regulatory punishments stop allowing those who allow money laundering to also go home, have dinner with their family and sleep well in their own bed, then the behaviours within their organisation will not change. Yet, whether there will also ever be a discussion as to whether the enormous number of resources currently being invested in prevention and detection are being used in the most effective manner, is unclear. Throwing money, people and IT solutions at the problem of AML/CFT compliance is not a guaranteed solution but has become an acceptable reaction. In most cases, such reactions only fix one small issue, not the entire problem. Likewise, if it is still about how much money an organisation spends, not how it is spent, the prospects for tackling the problem of money laundering become a whole lot less probable.

Mixing up AML/CFT policies and procedures only adds to the misery. Policies tell readers what needs to be done, when, and by whom, while the procedures tell the reader how it is done. So, whatever is the next step in preventing money laundering, vague policies and restrictive procedures must be dismissed. To be effective, all optional terms must be removed. This will limit confusion as to whether something 'should be done' or 'could look to be done' in the future. Processes must also be 'end to end' rather than the focus of an end goal, thus ensuring there is clear understanding as to the overall purpose of what the controls are really for. If it is not possible to set clear obligations, then recommendations only imply compliance is optional. Where there is a choice to not do something, it is certain in AML/CFT compliance it will not happen. If there is little enthusiasm, a belief that the effort is someone else's focus, and it is outside of normal practices, then it is naive to think for one second that a professional will go above and beyond compliance when their focus is rightfully on their initial business interests. To be successful, AML/CFT compliance must work alongside, ideally intermingled seamlessly into, profit driven businesses, instead of remaining the apparent burden it has become.

No one really takes ownership of the AML/CFT failures that keep arising, because the reality is, no single person needs to. Even though top-level banks and financial institutions have been caught up in money laundering prosecutions or shown to have poor AML controls, vacuous responses to the large fines imposed are generally accepted. Prosecutions do play a large part in driving forward AML/CFT prevention but, as Chapter 20 will show, *meaningful prosecutions* for AML/CFT failures are as common as seeing a shooting star during daylight hours. With a glaring lack of criminal money laundering prosecutions by all financial regulators, and without a trail of high-profile criminal cases, it is increasingly difficult to send a tough enforcement message. When a prosecution does go ahead, few end up going to jail for money laundering. So, unless an individual is in the dock then the payment of a fine is an easy solution and an extremely rewarding outcome for the regulator.

Despite there being ample criticisms of the overall AML/CFT approach, one which the authors could not ignore was that of the clear inability to apparently intercept anything more than a miserable 1% of the dirty money apparently in circulation. Since no one can accurately tell us what 100% is as a monetary figure, or what could accurately be determined to be the entire value of dirty money being laundered daily, monthly or on a yearly basis, why has 1% become the benchmark figure? Why would changes not have happened sooner if 1% was the current figure for success? Apart from the misinformation this type of headline creates, it also distorts the situation surrounding AML/CFT compliance more than many care to appreciate. Therefore, we cannot assume, or be confident that the 1% is ever accurate any more than a seizure rate of 99%. With no global value of money laundering available, suggesting 1% is only ever seized, is misleading. So, it seems the criticism of 1% actually tells us seizures are perhaps the worst metric ever from which to start trying to measure AML/CFT effectiveness.

As we have touched on many times so far in this book, the genuine answer to preventing money laundering is taking away the activities that underpin it – the predicate offences. This means introducing real preventative measures aligned to the crimes and increasing risk and effort for the subsequent money laundering process. It is not about locking the stable door; it is about ensuring the horse was never born and the trees were never felled to build anything which could resemble a stable. We need more of this if we are to prevent money laundering. We need never to realise there was going to be a horse, nor a stable. As we see it, understanding money laundering requires also understanding the people behind it.

The global approach to preventing money laundering as it stands today is not simply 'fingers crossed' – it is also blindfolded, in a dark room and perhaps intentionally blind to what is before it. Yet it is also very loud. Wherever you look there are comments about preventing money laundering, but most are statements, even a series of questions with those who offer to provide answers never indicating the details, just a lot of claptrap.

So many people have spent their entire professional careers on the problem of preventing money laundering and many more are continuing to do so. But are we at a point in the journey where it is possible to say that all that has gone before has been worthwhile? We believe not, because if we were on the correct journey, then we would have realised we first need to thoroughly understand the problem – not address it with more legislation. Nor does it look as if things are about to shift in the right direction anytime soon, if you take a look at the out of touch speakers standing up at conferences.

Whether it be ignorance or ineptitude that has led us here, money laundering is simply not being prevented. With no clear definition of what the AML regime is seeking to achieve, is it now time for the FATF to overhaul the global approach, rather than observe the continuous failures occurring at a nation state level year on year while ignoring those of other key members?

## Solutions toolbox

- The activities attributed to preventing money laundering need to be a primary focus of AML strategies. Money laundering is vast, but also specific. There are pinch points in the transfers and purchases that make up money laundering – people just need to be willing to find them and introduce preventative measures. Focusing on the entire problem of money laundering will not always serve as an effective blanket approach to stopping it, so the focus needs to be more appropriate to today's money laundering behaviours.
- There is a need to truly be 'risk-based' in the approach to prevention. It is impossible for AML compliance reporting entities to do everything, so there is a need to prioritise and focus on the most impactful outcomes to fight financial crime. A correct and more relevant NRA for each country would help achieve this.
- It is clear financial crime risk and compliance officers are too busy trying to meet tick-box compliance expectations. They are not, nor can they be expected to prevent money laundering when they abide by rules that are neither fit for the intended purpose nor consistently applied. For many compliance professionals, there is no requirement to focus on any sort of preventative opportunities, identify prevention or discuss it with others. Due to the need to meet compliance obligations, there is simply too little time to develop effective risk strategies and policies for the entity. Rather than micro-managing by standards setters, there is a need for greater simplification and flexibility of what is currently in place. Ever-tighter prescriptive measures with the idea that they are preventing money laundering and terrorism financing are strangling the sectors who have the most to deliver in the prevention of money laundering and terrorism financing.
- There is a need to ask the question, 'What can be done to stop money laundering?'. The answer to which *must not* solely involve 'AML/CFT compliance', 'increased legislation' or 'bigger fines'. There are better, more critical areas on which to now focus. Investigation, enforcement and prosecution of the money launderer and/or criminal is perhaps, (nudge, wink wink) a really good place to focus the effort.
- We must stop the ongoing effort to legislate our way out of the failures to tackle money laundering by tackling specific areas, professions and

countries. It is a global approach which is needed, not ad-hoc legislation which can be circumvented by the criminals and the users.

- We have done things, talked a great deal and created several professions in the last 30 years. We have also criminalised money laundering around the world and made it a focus of governments in almost all 200 countries. But do we want to be saying the same thing when we hit the 40-year mark? And then the 50-year mark? If not, then alternative and specific approaches need to be found. Meeting the requirements of the current AML/CFT legislation must no longer be an end in itself.

With the failures identified in this chapter, prevention has become something of a misnomer in the world of money laundering and terrorism financing, meaning AML/CFT compliance has misled prevention promises for too long – a situation which is unlikely to change thanks to the introduction of technology solutions all seeking to outdo one another.

There is now a need to let go of counting closed barn doors and the decisions not to give a second thought to the damage being caused by the escaped horse. In Chapter 9 we pull apart the idea that 'technology is a solution'. It is not. But should you feel it is, then we tell you where we feel you are perhaps being misled, in the hope that technology does finally become an aid to preventing and detecting money laundering and terrorism financing as opposed to a costly by-product aligned to AML/CFT compliance.

# Technology: the solution to all our AML/CFT problems

> Unveiled in 1949 to help France's large rural population the low-price 'umbrella on four wheels' the Citroen 2CV was designed to carry four people, transport 50 kg (110 lb) of farm goods to market at 50 km/h (30 mph) and across muddy, unpaved roads. One design feature was its ability to transport eggs across a freshly ploughed field without breakage. Yet interestingly, in all the marketing material, Citroen never decided to claim the 2CV could win Le Mans, the Dakar Rally or break the land speed record.
>
> The authors

There is money laundering: an exciting criminal offence attracting attention through prevention, investigation and prosecution activities, and depicted in numerous ways in blockbuster movies. Then there is AML/CFT compliance: the boring, monotonous daily routines and actions of so many involved in AML/CFT regulated entities. Today, many technology solutions or black boxes are pretending to be compliance, prevention, investigation and much more. However, with closer inspection and critical analysis, the reality is somewhat different and misleading. Here is why.

## Great claims

The exaggerated claims by solution providers suggesting technology can prevent money laundering are, we think, overstated. Still, this has not stopped high-level advocates for the adoption of technology solutions in AML/CFT compliance formulating equally exciting assertions. The most prominent of these has to be the FATF. The FATF propose innovative technologies have the potential to make AML and counter terrorist financing measures faster, cheaper and more efficient'.[1] This type of claim does not just stay with the FATF; claims go deeper into the now hugely commercialised world of AML/CFT compliance to excite potential adopters with costly, off-the-shelf solutions.

These products want to 'revolutionise' what is seen as a broken AML/CFT compliance regime, and the troubles associated with false positives – those annoying time-consuming beliefs that clients or customers are involved in money laundering or terrorism financing. Algorithms can apparently be trained, using data on financial transactions, to learn and therefore identify suspicious transactions 'even in cases that might lack the usual red flags that a human designer would program into an automated system'.[2] All of this is reinforced by industry experts who are understandably enthusiastic about how AI can seemingly create a more efficient and transparent AML/CFT compliance regime.

Financial institutions, we are told, must *now* embrace such solutions. Solutions incorporating *black boxes* to protect themselves from possible regulatory failures in the future. Not that the authors want to go there just now, but does that mean banks have not been doing what they should have been doing? Does it mean they are going to fail in the future – almost inevitably? And are only these technology systems able to save them? The fear of a need to embrace technology is clearly upon us and being pushed far and wide to generate massive profit for suppliers.

Take a moment to review the marketing material behind these technology solutions on preventing money laundering, remembering that, as we discussed in Chapter 8, it is not the role of financial institutions to take the lead in tackling this particular criminal activity – more to take a role. Algorithms and machine learning against big datasets apparently allow users to spot real financial crimes. Alongside these solutions are various products that claim to also improve ongoing monitoring of customers. KPMG suggests this is possible by 'mimicking existing research and investigative processes of analysts to organise information by relevance for an optimised review of information, or by providing insights that are withheld from conventional approaches due to system limitations'.[3]

Yet, all of this is managed by innovative technology to then bring optimised results and apparently drive meaningful change. But does spotting these details imply anything meaningful will come from it, such as reporting it to the national FIU promptly and with sufficient detail? The answer is not clear, and there may be a reason for this.

Driving all the sophistication, technology and algorithms is the premise that criminals are becoming increasingly more sophisticated in their approach to money laundering – a classification we believe has been introduced simply to cover up the fact that many money launderers remain relatively free to go about their business. Whether this is true (although the authors believe criminals are not becoming increasingly more sophisticated) or solely expressed for the purpose of promoting equally sophisticated and expensive technology solutions, what is evident is that, as we discussed in Chapter 3, money launderers are always finding new ways to circumvent AML/CFT controls.

What is meant by 'sophisticated' is also anyone's guess, but calling their methods sophisticated distracts us from our wider failure to do more. What is not a guess, is that there is no need for money launderers to create new 'sophisticated' methods, as they continue to launder money quite successfully without overcomplicating any part of it. As we have discussed – money laundering equates to *transfers and purchases*, so money laundering is perhaps only sophisticated when trying to sell an expensive solution or cover up an absence of knowledge as to how money launderers are still managing to remain so successful.

Is this practice, then, an intentional play on words or simply semantics, or is it a way to cover up failures and deceive? Perhaps it is only when the cases that come into the public domain are then reviewed, that we find most money laundering is far from sophisticated, and yet it has managed miraculously to dodge technology solutions in place. Or is it that, as one person once said in their headline capturing statement, 'money launderers were becoming more sophisticated' and everyone then copied it? Sadly, it is perhaps both.

Should you doubt that technology is not for AML/CFT as it is currently promoted, then there is always the 'marketeers case study' to push you to acceptance: 'Before turning to "Provider X", "Financial Institution A" had a screening system flagging 1,000 false positive transactions each day. Within months after turning to "Provider X", the number was down to 100 – an amazing 90% reduction in false positives.'

So, does this make critics, such as the authors of this book, wrong in their judgements? We acknowledge there is evidence that some technology solutions are helping to prevent sophisticated money laundering, but it would be wise to also contemplate whether these solutions are based on our very own basic understanding of money laundering or today's actual money laundering activities.

Still, solution developers typically confide with what the authors prefer not to call 'money laundering experts'. Many, and the authors have spoken to them, use former senior managers. Yet we recognise that these people were managers, meaning the intricacies of money laundering at the time would have been the concern of the people they managed – not necessarily them. Such a reliance on job title has, we feel, distorted the truth, but yet solution providers use this credibility and former titles as evidence for their newly created and inevitably sophisticated solutions, as if it somehow justifies their very creation. Yet there is an equal obsession among these so-called AML/CFT solution providers to follow the smoke – at the same time adding fuel to a fire and remaining excited as to how it manages to keep burning. Why try to manage a problem so that it then disappears, when you can complicate it further to gain long-term financial benefit? It is simply bewildering how this is allowed to happen, but it does, right across the global AML compliance platform. Perhaps everyone involved in AML/CFT compliance should now think long and hard about heading home, leaving technology to fight money laundering on its own. After all, that is what it can do, right?

## Trustworthy solutions

The issue we see with technology is not just *trust* – more the source of this *hypothetical truth behind it*. Not that we are calling anyone a liar, merely we look to raise issues which we see as distorting the true facts. A black box solution may seem a solution, but do users really understand the workings on the inside? We suspect not, because the push has been to adopt, rather than use a solution 100% fit for purpose. We agree, not everyone may wish to know what the black box does, because a wheel may be wheel. But it needs to be remembered that a tractor wheel is no use on a Ferrari as a replacement for a flat tyre.

Typically, the efficacy of most products is untested against knowable criteria. We know this because the end-user is almost never involved in evaluating what the technology produces. So, it is not the computer that is untrustworthy, it is towards these so-called sophisticated solutions and the people making and selling them that caution needs to be exercised.

Review any AML/CFT technology solution and you will quickly note there can be few credentials behind them. Coincide this with APIs, automation, AI and problems at the implementation and operational/project level and all the buzz words and claims quickly become anything but a cure for all money laundering and terrorism financing's evil deeds. Can these same providers really deliver the holy grail while they hold a business's single data sources as hostage? We suspect not, as it seems we are still to see or hear of an institution that is using technology to achieve 100% success in any aspect of AML compliance. Meaning, does an actual solution really exist?

Is the vast introduction of technology potentially helping to create a compliance catastrophe for the future? With solutions introduced in various forms across most large financial solutions, it is still unknown whether such solutions have ever been fully amalgamated, tested and verified. Does anyone know for sure whether these solutions are effective at preventing and detecting money laundering? It seems very few are willing to even think about peeling away the outer layer to see just exactly what is lying beneath. If this continues, will the catastrophe that happens finally expose regulatory failures that have occurred even in the entities using such sophisticated AML solutions?

## Line in the sand

Despite the solutions available, could there in fact be a line in the sand that many choose never to see or, when they do, simply then ignore. On one side, we suggest, sits preventing money laundering and terrorism financing, and on the other side sits managing AML/CFT compliance requirements. The line is solid and distinctly clear, illustrating the reality of what is a sharp separation in the real fight against money laundering and terrorism financing.

Technology solutions as such do not currently straddle both sides of this line, despite the marketing material. If they did, they would no doubt lose credibility, since the audiences for these apparent solutions are not, if we are being entirely honest, fully engaged in preventing money laundering and terrorism financing. The audiences for these solutions have a business focus and a model on making money and increasing profits. The role of preventing, detecting and then prosecuting money laundering sits, quite rightly (according to them), with law enforcement. Even regulatory fines come nowhere close to the line; they stay put as simply fines for AML/CFT compliance failings. Start to straddle the line, and the technology solution being put forward becomes a form of spyware, a means of finding problems that some would prefer to stay buried. Hence why former law enforcement officers, those with the detailed understanding of how money launderers really work, are never great for compliance roles. They quickly find wrongdoings, as opposed to doing nothing more than ensuring the business complies with AML/CFT obligations.

In defining the line in the sand, we can then begin to call technology solutions aimed at preventing money laundering: *Technology Solutions to Prevent Money Laundering (TSPML)*. Those on the other side of the line can then continue to be known as *AML Regulatory Technology solutions (AML RegTech)*. The latter is, as many will appreciate, a common term to associate sophistication to a new era of solutions that can sometimes serve only to confuse compliance professionals and detract attention away from the underlying problem of money laundering. Splitting the two may prove the line in the sand does exist, but it does not make it simpler to understand. In fact, it complicates the idea that technology is the new unsung saviour to all AML/CFT problems. So 'what is it technology can really do', 'how well can it do it' and 'how long will it be applicable' for a criminal practice which is apparently more sophisticated and continually changing? The answer to these questions is *no one really knows*.

## Technology concerns

Meeting all AML/CFT regulations can, of course, be difficult. But relying solely on technology solutions can present many added challenges for the user. As an example, the Danish Financial Supervisory Authority suggests the need to improve technology for monitoring and reporting suspicious bank activity, to reduce money laundering.[4] Although this may appear a straightforward suggestion – a positive suggestion too – the challenge obviously comes with using a technology solution that is unable to set up any parameters for detecting suspicion. What is suspicious to one person, may be normal to another. The level of suspicion may be based on prior knowledge or the lifestyle of the user. It is true, technology may be able to automate mundane activities to save time and money for the user, but addressing suspicion is but left to humans who have had the right training.[5]

Think of it in the context of the former United States Secretary of Defence, Donald Rumsfeld, and his statement in 2002, when he said, "There are 'known knowns', there are 'known unknowns' and there are 'unknown unknowns'". With the increase of technology as AML/CFT compliance solutions all claiming to be better than each other, are we not missing the point that there are also lots of 'unknown knowns'? We see these as those dirty little secrets that no one wants to talk about, although everyone knows they are there. We know technology will not solve the problem of money laundering and terrorism financing, yet we choose not to want to accept this is the case. Nor do we want to start to discuss it. We think these solutions are helping to prevent and detect money laundering, when we also know they are being used in such a way as to not raise any unnecessary suspicion of wrongdoing. This is a major red flag for society.

To date, the AML technology solution providers have done nothing to reverse the tide of money laundering, with many not even caring to mention 'terrorism financing' in their sales material. Monitoring for unusual transactions is fine and perhaps even possible to a limited extent, but the quandary arises when most people at some time have an unusual transaction. Are they then because of these solutions automatically considered money launderers or financers of terrorism?[6] They could, just imagine it, simply be guilty of an unusual transaction. So, what prevents the risk that these unusual transactions may be flagged for further investigation? After all, the FATF clearly states that AML/CFT activities are to be risk-based even if this does not always require looking beyond the risks presented by customers, countries, products and the avenues used.

Let us then go back to the principles on which many solutions are based – those annoying red flag indicators – accepting we have just raised one. As we said in Chapter 4, red flag indicators are the worst place to start trying to understand money laundering. Red flags continue to mislead – meaning later judgements are always faulty. Yet red flags are also the basis for many technology solutions claiming to detect money laundering and terrorism financing – though not always identified as red flags. Technology solutions to identify suspicious transactions are known to employ automated systems that find transactions associated with red flags. Many can then align to a transaction amount, a location, or simply some form of deviation from a customer's typical activity. Given the collective belief that money laundering is becoming more sophisticated and clandestine in nature, how can these solutions see success tomorrow, when today's money laundering practices will remain hidden for some time to come. Even the smartest software designer is unable to predict tomorrow's money laundering behaviours and create a solution that immediately works. Perhaps even the smartest software designer also struggles to really understand money laundering. After all it is sophisticated.

Drop into the scenario the challenges caused by COVID-19 and the problem becomes a whole lot more difficult to deal with. COVID-19 has created a scenario of trying to incorporate unknowns into systems developed using largely unconfirmed knowledge. A reset of the system has taken place because of COVID-19, meaning time must pass before the data are available to again establish any new normal. With AML/CFT frameworks being based on the examination of patterns of behaviour, will there be a need to recalibrate existing data to manage a response to the new and unfamiliar environment in which we are now? How will these systems cope, how quickly will they adjust and what credibility will decisions relating to suspicious behaviour have in the meantime? More data will not equal better understanding. We think better understanding will only come from a willingness to remove the confusion that exists around money laundering.

On top of this, you have the problems attributed to the creators' ideas, beliefs, their outside input and their reliance on the success of the outputs of the final AML/CFT solution. What if the smartest AML software designer struggles to understand money laundering? These are all variables which mean that the solutions available are always going to be fighting among one another to claim superiority. How solutions are then developed plays a critical role in the product, something that controls the way in which it is eventually applied by the customer. Algorithmic bias hidden by a corporate black box developed using common data – as opposed to the data held within the AML/CFT context presents its own challenges. With restrictions on data sharing and training, the capability for AML/CFT solutions to form the basic results is always going to create significant bias due to a lack of generalisation of data from across society.

## AI or a best guess scenario?

Whether it be 'artificial claims in preventing money laundering' or 'artificial claims in detecting suspicious activities' – the term 'artificial intelligence' plays a significant role in the push for adopting technology solutions. If AI is to be considered the walls and roof, machine learning will be the foundations upon which AI is built.

As a subset of AI, machine learning teaches computers to learn from data. By finding patterns, it is apparently possible to make decisions with minimal human input – a process of data analysis that essentially automates analytical model building. According to the FATF, machine learning offers the ability to learn from existing systems, therefore reducing the need for manual input into transaction monitoring, identifying and reducing false positives, and illustrating complex cases, as well as facilitating risk management.[7]

Perhaps the best way to distinguish the difference between machine learning and AI, is that AI knows nothing despite the near-mythical status it may conjure up and apply, it is machine learning that provides AI the ability to learn. Like 'organic', 'unprecedented' and 'pandemic', AI is used frequently to market solutions as a redeeming feature for entities large and small hoping to manage AML/CFT. Yet, how intelligent is AI? Labelled artificial – perhaps the entire purpose of it is to make its behaviour or outputs appear more authentic – more intelligent. We see this as a genuine façade, behind which is almost always a fake.

So why a fake? Well, because the idea of being able to mimic human thinking is absurd. More so as a practice when it comes to detecting money laundering and terrorism financing. The idea that AI can be so successful in detecting the activities undertaken by professional money launderers suggests some people have lost their sense of reality. The data or intelligence held within AML/CFT solutions can only ever be best guesses. Not only are there still issues across the board at finding money laundering and other associated activities, but the data provided to the underpinning machine learning process are nothing more than a ridiculously small snapshot of the past. Think of money laundering as *transfers and purchases* and you quickly begin to realise that the AML/CFT IT solutions successes are, to date, not entirely effective at preventing money laundering and terrorism financing.

Proponents of AI (including the FATF) nevertheless claim that AI performs tasks that typically require human intelligence, such as recognising patterns, making predictions, recommendations or decisions. Perhaps this is true. But is what is happening relevant? Such techniques apparently obtain insights from diverse types, sources and quality of data[8] – sometimes marketed as 'improved software'. Opportunities to fix the inefficiency plaguing transaction monitoring and due diligence have not yet created a clearer understanding of AI, just more marketing jargon such as 'Robotic Process Automation'. Are these systems really trying to build solutions from public-facing typologies or is it something much worse? Are they simply mimicking the thinking of the creators? These solutions do not learn as we are led to believe, nor can they apply reasoning in the same way as AML/CFT professionals can, despite the attributed terminology.

So, where are the innovative ideas, the real solutions to the problems of preventing and detecting money laundering and terrorism financing? AI seems to be capable of replicating current failing processes – in a more costly way – rather than offering something different. One must not be fooled by the aspirational and sometimes delusional terminology being bandied around. Adopting innovative technologies can help entities identify and encourage reporting of money laundering and terrorist financing suspicious behaviours, that is certain. But if money launderers do what they always have done, technology solutions will almost never detect their transfers and purchases because there are too few opportunities to identify what *appears* normal from that which *is* normal.

The widespread and almost obscene adoption of technologies now before us is solely driven by the growing obsession to comply more efficiently with AML/CFT regulations. How do we know this is true? Well, because these solutions offered are focused towards saving money, reducing time, diminishing false positives and supporting internal compliance investigations – not preventing money laundering. If they were about reducing money laundering and terrorism financing, then they would be a different solution altogether.

For a start, they would be a solution that would look to detecting 'false negatives' – those missed opportunities which are money laundering and terrorism financing but are deemed as, well, simply just OK transactions, purchases and other everyday financial activities, that is, the so-called normal types of 'transfers or purchases' that raise none of the many red flags. Reality suggests these false negatives will only be dealt with by the next generation of IT solution creators, and solutions truly based on bigger data sources than those which are contained within a single entity.

We also think the problem with the machine learning model is that in AML it is left to the data scientists. These are the cavalry captains who have never even seen a horse. With little or no involvement from money laundering and/or compliance specialists, it is almost impossible to create AI technology capable of detecting the vast majority of criminal activities. The consequence of this is ineffective compliance teams.

## So yes, it is artificial

It is about here the authors thought it poignant to drop in the idea that actually AI is as distracting in the fight against money laundering as the use of inflatable tanks were in northern France during the Second World War. Back then, German forces were distracted, in the same way we think users of technology solutions are today when AI is marketed as an AML solution. Whether intelligence, information or carefully aligned data, AI is of little relevance to preventing money laundering and terrorism financing.

Still, there is scope for something a little less artificial if you take the Netherlands project of sharing transaction data (TBNL)[9] between organisations. This particular project, driven by the Netherlands' data protection authority will allow more than 160 financial institutions to share information about fraudsters to help fight financial crime. We think this is an interesting widening of scope within the fraud arena that can only serve to make positive change. Yet, within AML/CFT, this is almost impossible because of the lack of protocols, institutions not being allowed to exchange data large-scale, and the lack of any appropriate central database or blacklist of offenders like those in the fraud area. Needless to say, when you add in the problem of managing reluctance and any obligation to share, the idea of real-time intelligence appears only ever successful on paper or when chatted about at conferences.

While the Netherlands project is worthy of a mention, we think small, siloed approaches will only lead to criminals having to put just that little bit more effort in to make sure they continue to succeed. We do not think for one minute they will revolutionise the AML/CFT sectors in the same way as the fraud sector. This may be because of the differences in the crimes and how they are facilitated, or it could simply be that fraud costs these entities a great deal more than what a slush fund for an AML/CFT compliance breach needs to produce. Furthermore, until these partnerships become cross-border and data are tracked, accurately gathered and carefully analysed at every stage of the value chain, any effectiveness is best only promoted by those taking part or facilitating the venture with a technology solution.

The instability of many AML/CFT compliance IT solutions seemingly comes from a wish to create a one-size-fits-all universal product for everyone, justifying the cost by linking it back to the FATF red flag fixation. The trouble is, financial institutions and other entities captured by AML/CFT regulations believe technology really does play a critical part in satisfying the regulator. Still, not embracing technology solutions can raise unwanted questions. Questions such as 'does the entity have something to hide?' This suggests the options are made simple – run with the masses or risk questions being asked by regulators who themselves are pushing for technology solutions to be adopted. This is something increasingly encouraged by the FATF, the European Banking Authority (EBA), the UNODC and others – as well as their own business needs in the creation of supervisory technology (SupTech). SupTech is yet another term intended to create sophistication around technology solutions that we think again helps to hide those *unknown knowns.*

AI is therefore not extraordinary. It is a system programmed by humans to extract patterns from training datasets, and then it learns (by induction) what data patterns are associated with identifiable categorisations. Link those categorisations to money laundering typologies and red flags and you quickly triple the artificial aspect. In the same way tha spam filters, for example, still allow emails promising fortunes to arrive in your 'inbox', AI is unable to prevent money laundering or terrorism financing. The likelihood of anything improving has just been put to rest for quite a while, thanks to the COVID-19 data reset. AI is not going to suddenly start finding the new ways in which money launderers have reacted to cashless societies, changes in public spending habits and the ongoing lack of social interaction between huge swaths of the world's population. The data are simply not there and nor will they be for many years. Starting from now, AI is creating another new false positive, grasping at straws, guessing a new benchmark, all based on a format of what was once considered normal behaviour.

Then there are the annoying infrequent events. Those events which are money laundering but are also generic transfers and purchases sitting among all other generic transfers and purchases considered legitimate. How can AI possibly link two or more payments together in what we seek to believe is a sea of legitimate transfers and purchases? The sharing of information from multiple sources, as opposed to a single entity's customer base, could help set up other comprehensible datasets, but as the dataset then expands, the approach by the money launderer or terrorism financer will inevitably change. Thus, we then have an altering of the initial benchmark on which understanding is based, while leaving AI systems chasing ghosts – searching for something that is no longer present.

## Is this the end of the money laundering reporting officer?

With the introduction of AI is there now a need to say goodbye to the money laundering reporting officer (MLRO) or AML/CFT compliance officer role? Surely their role is now obsolete. Well, not quite, not if there is an argument for wanting to reduce the likelihood of money laundering scandals and costly compliance failures in the future. We believe that the role has essentially become far more important. No matter the label given to the position, their role is critical. There are always going to be benefits to using technology to make the mundane tasks easier to manage – but in doing so the human element must never be removed. It is here with the MLRO where the magic happens. The problem, then, is that it is not always the magic we need for preventing money laundering.

Magic in AML/CFT is not an illusion, nor is it the same as pulling a rabbit from a hat. It is more – a lot more. It is the intrinsic value in an MLRO's decision making; the insightfulness, tenacity, deliberation, teamwork and the skill to bounce ideas off others. AI can certainly learn from the data available, but when the data are more often than not missing, an AI solution cannot be expected to then become an investigator.

Common wisdom would stress humans make mistakes, miss patterns, are slow, too methodical and are a huge financial cost to a business – all of which suggests humans should be taken out of the equation to improve efficiency. Perhaps this may be the case in some instances, but clunky systems can equally generate more headaches than they can solutions. AML compliance is no different. A single dashboard allowing compliance officers to see and understand apparent key trends in their financial crime and compliance risks is only as good as the knowledge used to collect the data. To all intents and purposes, dashboards and many technology solutions are only ever adopted to allow compliance boxes to be ticked a little quicker. Many solutions may claim to showcase multiple metrics capturing rich and relevant management information. But since this 'output' is almost certainly built upon illogical understanding of money laundering trends, any further synthesising of essential information can quickly indicate the little value it has at preventing money laundering.

AI and machine learning may be more attuned to transaction monitoring than the KYC process. It is the KYC process that requires a critical and analytical assessment of a client or customer and the information they provide, either at onboarding or during reviews. It is here where people are better equipped to do this than machines. KYC is not a tick-box exercise and NatWest Bank Plc. in the UK learned this in their 2021 AML failings when they were fined £265 million. The fine was partly for not recognising when a client (a gold dealer) had forecast revenue of just £15 million a year and was instead depositing around £70 million. Could an AI solution have recognised this? We think it is very unlikely.

A good MLRO, compliance officer or analyst, also has empathy, compassion and instinct. Many have years of experience, allowing them to make sound judgements on what to investigate and how to investigate what is before them. Their parameters of moving forward are not always constrained by specific data points. They may even decide to pick up a phone and have a conversation with someone in a different entity or send a request to gain ad-hoc access to a different dataset. A good MLRO, compliance officer or analyst adds value that a machine has not yet been able to do. Despite the marketing literature, AI is simply unable to learn from human decisions and refine the alerts in the same way. Nor will it for some time. This is unless the humans involved start to prioritise, documenting their every decision made in such a format that the technology can use it. In the end, AI will only ever be able to learn from what it receives.

Remember, although the MLRO may be vital, their role is aligned to AML/CFT compliance, not prevention. Saying that, we really see the MLRO being best placed to change the mindset in many organisations to one which is more preventative in nature. If entities can see they have a corporate social responsibility not only to meet AML/CFT compliance regulations but, equally, to prevent money laundering and terrorism financing, then we feel the role of MLRO will continue to grow in importance.

## Successes to date – are there any?

Apparently, there are many AI, Machine Learning (ML) and AML/CFT compliance successes. Suggestions of wonderful things having taken place are frequently marketed, but these successes often equate to extinguishing a fire with a flammable liquid. Despite hundreds of RegTech, AI, ML and advanced technology solutions promising great benefits at reducing money laundering and terrorism financing, their combined influence on preventing money laundering is nowhere near obvious.

Still, financial crime is now the fastest growing category of RegTech; seeing an increase from 120 products in 2019 to over 400 two years later.[10] Does this indicate everyone is blind to the truth about what AI can deliver, or is it a case of you need to be in to win or just be among them in order to hide? Or is the reality somewhat different? Perhaps, as we suspect, it is a case where no one really understands and with so much pride at stake, no one is willing to raise their hand, ask the questions and begin developing sensible solutions that do more.

## Moving forward, one step at a time

The hype surrounding technology in the AML/CFT arena is largely driven by systemic absurdities. Technology solutions are simply one small tool in a large toolbox full of opportunities to prevent and detect money laundering.

Machine learning still has a lot to do as it builds a new dataset following COVID-19. Going beyond current expectations will never be possible while machine learning has access to only a fraction of the data. Until access is granted to the rest – the information about crime and criminals – then machine learning will continue to distort the truth. Still, technology companies continue to vigorously push their costly solutions to address AML/CFT because it seems not having a solution can raise uneasy questions for some entities. This now means more and more entities are 'jumping onto the same train, bus or plane' without ever considering the destination, the costs or what they will be provided with along the way.

Clearly, the problem with AI is that its potential is exaggerated. We accept there is a level of automation available to AML compliance, but AI is not a simple solution, nor a true solution because it still requires human expertise. Missing data need to be identified, as well as the relevance of the data identified and whether anomalies are statistically significant or simply 'red herrings'. Disregard for data science and combining of facts in the solutions offered must stop immediately and solutions must reframe from being labelled just that: *solutions*. There is no single solution to the problem, as money laundering has chosen to prove by its increasing resilience as a single act. Money laundering simply changes to meet the resistance it sees itself obliged to address. Adding in 'linguistic analysis', 'smart process automation', 'robotic process automation' and 'process orchestration' does little to advance true understanding of a solution's capabilities – it simply baffles those whose real focus is elsewhere.

The safest 'solution' of the future will be that which derives from partnering with vendors willing to collaborate and build capabilities responsive to risk profiles that grow over time – a solution that rethinks transaction monitoring to reduce high rates of false positives and focuses on the actors and the action-centric point of view. Many actions can be the same but understanding who is behind just one of these actions can be a significant win in the fight against money laundering and, equally, terrorism financing.

One day, when this happens, and a solution can ingest many data sources and understand behavioural anomalies, there may be an appetite to apply it to all existing data to see just how much money laundering and terrorism financing has been missed. After all, it is impossible to believe how a single entity could possibly have a comprehensive picture of a customer's financial position when customers – good and bad – are known to use multiple banks and access various sources of finance.

Still, there is a risk that the enthusiasm for AI is already fostering what the authors recognise as a false sense of security within many institutions, leading to a dangerous overreliance globally on highly imperfect solutions. This is especially an issue where regulatory oversight is more stringent. So, with poorly labelled datasets providing the backbone for AI, it is extremely unlikely AI will deliver quality results anytime soon. Introducing synthetic data, or specialised models that predict rare incidences, may deliver incremental improvements over existing automated review systems, but it appears a robust model in the AML/CFT context is still some way off. All this is, of course, occurring at the same time money launderers and terrorism financers continue to revise their transfers and purchases to flout legislation and other preventative measures being put in place. Just as they always have done.

Of course, experience will be critical in formulating any real solution. Knowing and understanding money laundering is very different from knowing how to meet regulatory compliance requirements. Helping a business tick the correct boxes at the same time as being friends with the regulator is not preventing money laundering or terrorism financing, even if the people believe they are money laundering experts. All too often these issues are becoming more obvious as money launderers are proving they know this by what they are managing to achieve.

Preventing money laundering or terrorism financing requires in-depth knowledge and yet we have inadvertently become reliant on the idea that technology is the solution. It is just a tool not a solution, because in the real world, AML compliance and the prevention of money laundering sit at opposite ends of the technology spectrum. RegTech is just that: regulatory technology – about meeting regulatory measures and making life simple. RegTech is not about detecting money laundering or terrorism financing – that is the role of law enforcement. Reporting entities simply play a supporting role by offering up suggestions of suspicious activities or transactions when it suits them to do so. Little thinking is taking place inside regulators, technology companies and many compliance offices – because with the push of a button answers can be displayed. The problem is, no one appears to be questioning whether the answers provided are the right answers. Everyone just seems content that there are answers to look at.

**Solutions toolbox**

- We think there is a need to stop developing technology to raise even more SARs based on outdated understanding. Quality not quantity is what is needed.
- We should pull the plug on technology solutions that are not fully explainable, transparent and understandable to the user and instead develop solutions that focus on delivering results – results more than those based solely on just saving time.
- Rather than seeking one solution for all our AML/CFT problems there is a need to identify specific solutions/datasets for specific requirements.
- There is a need to urgently develop technology solutions for the other side of the line in the sand. Law enforcement would benefit significantly from the computing power that is now clearly available. Thus, we should look to stop reinventing the wheel, creating unnecessary applications, and give resource law enforcement the necessary funding to work with technology providers.
- We also have the opportunity, with the computing power that now exists, to move away from using technology as a reactive tool and instead develop systems that are proactive. Systems that are looking forward as a means to identify ways to strengthen prevention as opposed to detecting facets of the AML/CFT compliance regime that can have negative influence on a business.

If technology is going to provide a real AML/CFT solution, it needs to be based on understanding and preventing the transfers and purchases which depict money laundering as it is happening today. Perhaps there is now a call for Preventative Technology Solutions for Money Laundering (PTSML) – solutions termed as 'PrevTechAML'.[11] Or perhaps, just maybe RegTech and PrevTechAML could work alongside one another to align with the expectation of the FATF's standards towards preventing money laundering and terrorism financing while meeting compliance obligations. After all, the marketing material suggests this is already happening, even if the impact on money laundering and terrorism financing to date is less than perfect.

Somewhere there must be a vendor who has the courage and the wisdom to confront the current failings and offer something profoundly different – the desperately needed PrevTechAML solution. If so, they are more than welcome to contact the authors for our support.

This brings us to an output of many technology solutions, the pleasing 'Suspicious Activity Report', created in their millions worldwide for the adding into the treasure trove of information held by FIUs. In Chapter 10, we look at how SARs are used and how they do not always need to clog up a system that seeks to achieve success, not prevent it.

# SARs: millions and millions of them

For want of a nail the shoe was lost.
For want of a shoe the horse was lost.
For want of a horse the rider was lost.
For want of a rider the battle was lost.
For want of a battle the kingdom was lost.
And all for the want of a horseshoe nail.

Anon

Each year tens of millions of reports about dirty money are made to the police.[1] They are regarded as either crucial information worth killing for or debris clogging up the fight against crime. We will explain the legal reason this divergence of opinion exists and take a peek into the world of intelligence. Part of this is secret, so sorry we will need to give you a blindfold. But first, Box 10.1 gives some views from the front line.

---

**Box 10.1: Evidence about SARs**

In many countries, filing a SAR can be a death sentence. Whether it is the fentanyl trade, human trafficking, terrorism, child exploitation or wildlife crime, the world's most ruthless criminals will kill to get their hands on illicit money. Once they have obtained it, they will kill to keep it. The author of this article met with an AML officer in Karachi, Pakistan last year who has two armed guards at home on rolling shifts to protect his family. Wherever he goes, he is shadowed by an armed escort, paid for by his employer. In Pakistan, this is just a cost of doing business as a major bank and keeping staff safe.[2]

The resulting high number of low intelligence value and poor-quality submissions puts unnecessary strain on the UKFIU while making it more difficult to detect actual crimes.[3]

---

A SAR is a formal report to the designated national FIU under AML legislation.[4] Most reports are submitted by banks but the law in some countries requires lawyers, accountants and others to submit reports. A typical report happens when a bank official observes a transaction or series of transactions that seem suspicious. There is no definition of suspicion, but the bank official will have been trained in the meaning of suspicion. So, at the beginning there is a bit of suspicion, an inkling, if you will.[5] They will raise the suspicious circumstances of the activity with a line manager. If the line manager also thinks it is suspicious then it goes to the organisation's MLRO, who is formally responsible to the Board for making such reports. If the MLRO thinks it is suspicious too, then a report is made to the country's FIU for a fourth opinion about whether the circumstances are actually suspicious.

## The Duck Theory

You can teach people to be suspicious, you really can. Most people are not naturally suspicious, but if you expose them to suspicious scenarios they will learn how to suspect. An effective way to learn is to join the police and meet the public in a series of situations where police have been called. An added frisson is that your life may depend on calling it right. This is why the police are particularly adept at handling Suspicious Reports, which is useful because this is where they end up. For the rest of us, learning suspicion in a classroom can be rather good fun. Students are given a scenario and invited to mark their personal rating of its suspiciousness on a 'Suspicionometer'. The variety in marks given by the students is discussed and the objective and subjective rationale for different choices is debated. Students may be given the Duck Theory. If it looks like a duck, waddles, and quacks like a duck, it is a duck. Applying this to banking; the first official thinks a scenario looks like a duck, the line manager thinks it waddles and gives it to the MLRO. If it quacks at this stage, it goes to the FIU.

One might suppose that by the time the suspicion has escalated to become a formal SAR to the FIU it **really, really is suspicious**. This is a reasonable conclusion too, but it does not make the report more *usable*. Its *usability* is determined after it has left the FIU, which is a clearing house for distributing SARs, to the end-users in the police and other investigative agencies. It is these end-users who actually decide if the SAR is any use and, if they can, they will use it.

Here, one of the authors has to declare an interest, as he was the end-user of SARs being reported in London, back in the day. More precisely, he was the manager of the relevant police departments that used SARs. In this capacity, we can state, categorically, that no FIU anywhere in the world has ever received a SAR of 'low intelligence value'. It is also impossible to 'clog up' a computerised system with too many SARs; that is why we invented computers, to stop all that clogging. Although you might be thinking this is not what we said in the chapter on FIUs, there is a reason for this. Read on.

### The 'needle in the haystack' theory

It is perfectly true that many SARs do not contribute directly to the fight against crime. This is because they only contain half the information needed to be useful. Their usability is created when they are combined with the information about the crime or the criminal. The point of being a money launderer, remember, is to separate the information about the money from the information about the crime, normally by the simple mechanism of keeping quiet about the origin of the money. Imagine, if you will, two haystacks, each containing straws and half-needles. As soon as they are put together, the half-needles get combined with other half-needles through the magic of a 'computer-dating service' and the needles fall out for further investigation. This is also the gift that keeps on giving. As thousands (perhaps tens of thousands, depending on your country) more half-needles arrive each day, more complete needles are created. Some are the other half of a crime from years ago, some will be the vital clue in an ongoing enquiry, a few will become the beginning of an entirely new enquiry. This is an important point; far more SARs contribute to existing enquiries than initiate new ones. This is because they are immediately and obviously useful to the police; unfortunately, it is also a fact that the police are generally starved of resources, they cannot spare them to start work on a new 'needle', unless it is *so* shiny and sharp that it demands their attention. Good quality needles are all over the place, but there's no one free to pick them up. The US$210 billion being spent each year on AML just does not go to the people doing financial investigation or asset recovery, sadly.

The analogy of the needle in a haystack, often used when discussing SARs, is a useful one. The reason that there are too few needles being used to sew up criminals arises from several factors. Most are absurd.

Many FIUs fail to pass on SARs to the police for reasons that they themselves, all too often, cannot explain. The psychology of intelligence folk means that the default position for FIUs is to carry on analysing instead of passing the intelligence on for use by the end-user. This is something that the FATF could address. An FATF Recommendation that SARs should be passed on **unless there is a compelling reason not to do so** would tilt the balance of usefulness in the right way.

Additionally, despite the massive investment that has been made globally to computerise SARs being delivered to FIUs, this still only generates half a needle. Meanwhile, the police generating the other half of the needle, the information about crime and criminals, may lack computers altogether. This is a serious issue. The imbalance of resources means that the banks have automated the production of their half-needles while law enforcement are still making theirs by hand. It really is absurd, and this applies to all SARs, both routine (the vast majority) and urgent.

The extreme absurdity of the situation is best illustrated by what happens with urgent SARs. The key problem is that there are not enough end-users − financial investigators in the police and other law enforcement agencies − to make good use of SARs, even urgent SARs related to the imminent transfer of suspicious money. The SAR could relate to a crime in action and urgent investigation is needed to prevent the loss of money or the receipt of the proceeds of crime. Once the money has been transferred it may be irretrievable or the evidence surrounding the suspicion may be lost. Urgent SARs go through the escalating suspicion process described above, at a fast pace, culminating in the MLRO seeking consent from the FIU to make the transfer. This consent will provide a valid defence if a crime is subsequently found to have occurred. The FIU will not normally have the information it needs to make an informed decision; it should consult with the end-user first. But it is the FIU that is the legally responsible authority to make the decision to allow the transaction to proceed. Delaying a transaction is serious. It may relate to a house or company purchase or the import/export of goods or services, and a delay might lead to the loss of the deal and cause for genuine complaint, even damages. Because there are not enough end-users to make an informed decision for the FIU, it allows the transfer to go ahead. All that effort to train staff to detect suspicion, to raise the casework to managers, the management time spent assessing whether to alert the MLRO, the transfer to the FIU and further analysis there. All that preparation and, for want of a financial investigator in the right place, the transfer just goes ahead.

This means at the crucial point where an urgent report might prevent a crime, we have a faulty system baked-in, in every FIU, across the world. Once again, we are grateful to the excellent UK National Crime Agency (the UK's FIU) for its detailed statistics. In its annual SARs report for 2019, the UK National Crime Agency disclosed that out of 34,151 requests for consent (now termed 'defence against money laundering' requests), just 1,332 were refused. In other words, over 96% of requests were granted – on activity that the requestor itself had thought suspicious – and the transactions proceeded.[6]

The system is at the heart of the RBA promoted by the FATF. In effect, it transfers the risk for allowing money laundering to go ahead from the reporter to the FIU. The FIU, meanwhile, is objectively unable to make an informed decision because the information about crime and criminals is held by the end-user. In lieu of an informed decision, the FIU just allows 96% of urgent potential crimes in action to go ahead.

Something could be done to improve this dire situation. That something is to get the urgent SAR to the end-user so that an informed decision can be made. An *informed* decision would be one based on existing data on crime and criminals held by the end-user or by a professional judgement about whether the suspiciousness of the transaction can be corroborated in some way and action to freeze assets can be achieved. Can this be done? The author used to do this for a living, so the answer is yes it can, if the end-user has enough skilled people to do the work.

The vast majority of SARs are not urgent, but they may still be just as valuable in addressing predicate crime, they just need to be transferred to the end-user. Now, law enforcement in the UK is relatively well-supplied with computers, so the question for the UK is why the SARs are not transferred directly to the computers of police financial investigators at the front line. Surely, it must be possible to write a programme that just pops the data into the police intelligence system. There would seem to be global requirement for such automation – to get the SAR data to the front line – yet the emphasis so far (meaning the last 20 years or so) has been to automate the reporting process to the FIU only. There has been substantial investment to automate and generally improve the reporting process. The United Nation's 'goAML' computer system is a genuine example of improved efficiency.[7] But we think that there is an important gap in the system; the connection between the SARs and the operational users who do the work. In an intelligence-led system it is the equivalent of the nail that connects the horseshoe to the horse. What we improved is to speed up the decision to allow suspected money laundering to go ahead. We have, very specifically, failed to improve the chance of identifying and stopping crimes in action, using urgent SARs, by not having enough staff in the right place. We have also computerised one half of the system, as far as the FIU, but then failed to computerise the rest of it. The SARs race towards the front line and then stop, just before they get there. It is ridiculous.

The UK has been very transparent, the FIU at the National Crime Agency produces regular reports lamenting that the SAR preventative safety net is more hole than net. We should not criticise the UK for reporting this, by the way; we should be applauding them. They are publicly saying what everyone else is doing in private, across the world.

The needle in a haystack analogy suggests that there are too few useful SARs hidden among a lot of non-useful SARs. But, as we said earlier, there is no such thing as a SAR of 'low intelligence value' at the FIU. This is because the FIU does not have the information about crime or criminals; they simply *cannot assess* whether the SAR is useful or not. The thing they can and should do, is pass it on to the police as soon as possible (unless there is a compelling reason not to), so that the police can match the data and see if it is useful. It may be, of course, that it has no immediate use, but can be kept for later, hopefully for years. Here comes another important point about money launderers. Their task is to separate the information about the money from the information about the crime. While the use of legal people (companies, partnerships and trusts) provides excellent cover, it is also handy to use real people, ideally with no criminal or police record, 'clean skins' in the trade. For this reason, SARs about 'clean skins' need to be kept. Sooner or later, they may sully their skin (after all they are already mixing in bad company) and then their previous money laundering role could be really, really useful information. Money laundering intelligence about 'clean skins' has a very, very long shelf-life. Far too many dim-witted people responsible for police intelligence think it should be deleted after some randomly short period of time. Let us be absolutely clear that these people are enabling serious crime.

## Criminals do not attend the briefing

Many police officers, over the years, have lamented that criminals do not attend police briefings about forthcoming police operations and so do not know what is expected of them. The result is that they do unexpected things when the police turn up (like not turning up themselves as they are supposed to or just not being in when the police call to arrest them). This can, however, work in the police's favour when it comes to SARs. In a perfect world, SARs will not contain information about predicate criminals. They should contain information about the relatives, friends, criminal associates and professional advisers of predicate criminals. These 'clean skins' have been selected for their apparent innocence and for their distance from both the predicate crime and predicate criminals. Occasionally predicate criminals and predicate crimes might appear in a SAR, but that is when criminals are being incompetent. Fortunately, criminals persist in not doing money laundering very well and frequently do appear in SARs all over the world. The problem is that SARs are not reaching the front line.

## An army of millions to fight crime

In the late 1990s, modern police forces started using computers for intelligence data. This had previously been done on paper, typically card-index systems. As the computers improved, it was realised that information about previous crimes and existing criminals could be matched to predict what might happen in the future. The crime sciences of 'hot-spot mapping' and 'intelligence-led policing' were born. It is impossible to overexaggerate the importance of this to modern policing. Scarce resources were deployed in advance of crimes happening, and efficiency and effectiveness were hugely multiplied. Unsolvable crimes became solvable, through the magic of data-matching. Policing turned out to lend itself to computerisation. The use of big data was extremely effective, and SARs are an excellent example of big data. The only problem is getting permission to combine the SAR data with law enforcement data, even though both datasets are being specifically produced for the purpose of fighting crime. You might think that such permission would be easy to obtain; it should be, if we were serious about wanting to fight crime and understood the utility of SARs.

Perhaps the FATF could explore making a 'recommendation' or 'a core issue to be considered', that SAR data should be merged with police intelligence data. This has been done, with interesting results. Sorry, but at this point the blindfold means we cannot reveal where the merge of data took place, nor the results.

## Low intelligence

So why do these myths about 'low intelligence value' SARs and 'needles in haystacks' persist? There are two explanations: confidentiality and mixed objectives. Together these factors mean that the public debate is confused, and obvious mistakes go uncorrected. We will do what we can here, to explain.

The 'FinCEN files', the leaking of over 2,100 SARs in the USA in 2020, led to a very public discussion.[8]

A key message emerging from the FinCEN files is that the raising of a SAR does not, in itself, end the movement of suspicious money, and the reports raise questions about the motivation of global banks and the effectiveness of law enforcement response. The reports also note that the submission of a SAR is not necessarily indicative of criminal conduct or wrongdoing. When journalists have approached banks for comment, it appears they have not responded with detail on individual cases; however, this lack of response is to be expected in line with their legal responsibilities. There are clear requirements contained within the POCA 2002, and equivalent US legislation regarding disclosure of information linked to SARs, which prohibits the release of this information.

The confidentiality of SARs also applies within law enforcement and hinders feedback to the reporting sectors. The banks, quite rightly, demand to be protected from exposure to criminals, so the police do not reveal that banks help with most confiscations and, probably, all money laundering prosecutions and organised crime cases. The banks then complain that they get no credit for SARs. It is a vicious circle and finding a solution is difficult. Feedback about a particular SARs contribution to the reporting bank exposes the risk of information leakage and there is no time limit on criminal revenge against a whistle-blower. As a result, the police do not tell the FIU and the FIU, in turn, cannot tell the bank, because they do not know. This keeps the source of the information safe. The whole system depends upon it.

There is something else going on too. The police receiving the SAR cannot use it as evidence directly. What they can do is corroborate the information contained in the SAR in some other way and present the corroboration as the evidence. We are delving into what the Europeans call 'special investigative techniques', so I am afraid the blindfold has to go on now, sorry. But, in short, one police unit is busy using the content of a SAR to investigate their case and another police unit is busy trying to bury the fact that a SAR is involved. This is not an occasional happening, this happens *all the time* with *every SAR* that is used. In fact, there is every chance that some or most officers working on an important case do not know where some specific information came from. This is the meaning of a 'need to know basis'. There is every chance that the senior officer in front of the camera or the press officer at the courtroom has no idea that the crux of the case hinged upon a SAR. The lack of feedback from police to the banks in individual cases is a necessary part of protecting the identity of compliance staff from being revealed to criminals. It is a success story, of a sort, but one we cannot really talk about. Frustrating but true.

Meanwhile, some in law enforcement and the legal profession are, unhelpfully, peddling the 'needle in a haystack' myth. The myth arises from some specialists who are only concerned with their own specialist area. They cannot see the wonderful breadth and utility of financial intelligence of which SARs are a part. *All* types of crime can, and are being, solved with financial intelligence. If you want to test this yourself, just watch a detective series, any one will do, from any country. Watch for the point in the story where intelligence from a financial source reveals the motive or the suspect. This is genuinely what happens in real life. SARs are incredibly valuable when used as big data, the bigger the better.

## Mixed messages

Not everyone sees the same part of the battlefield against dirty money. Author of *Moneyland*, Oliver Bullough, expressed it thus:

> Britain is currently bundling three different kinds of financial flows into the one laundering concept: domestic criminal money earned in the UK, foreign criminal money passing through the UK, and foreign criminal money being spent in the UK. All three of these are massive problems, which could overwhelm a law enforcement agency on their own.[9]

This neat summary of three different uses for SARs is a useful framework to look at how the resources of law enforcement are applied to money laundering. The UK model is not substantially different from that of other countries, so we can think of this as being globally relevant. SARs are incredibly useful for domestic criminal money *earned* in any country, all the police need to do is match information they already have about crime and criminals with incoming SARs. It is like shooting fish in a barrel. The UK's National Crime Agency has estimated that this is about £12 billion annually, which is very nearly the amount spent on the entire criminal justice system, prisons, courts and all. The primary agency for this objective is the police, as it is in every country, so immediate access to SARs by the police is something which should be high, if not top, of the FATF agenda. This part of the battlefield against dirty money should be a walkover, a rout. The UK police have a good record for ILP and SARs can very easily be simply added to the data that underpin the UK model. The UK police have been using ILP for 25 years and there is a wealth of expertise to draw on. Countries that lack ILP can import it into their own policing strategy, perhaps with FATF guidance and international donor support.

Bullough's next financial flow is foreign criminal money passing **through** a country. This suggests that the information about the crime is in another jurisdiction and the information about the criminal spending the money is in yet another. It may, indeed, be a rare SAR that gives you all the information that is needed if that is the particular haystack of interest. More importantly, what does law enforcement do about this financial flow? In the UK, the FCA might take an interest, perhaps the Serious Fraud Office or the National Crime Agency itself, but frankly, the more you look at this financial flow the harder it is to imagine that any national agency in any one country is going to divert scarce resources to investigate someone else's crime and someone else's criminal. Then, who are you gonna call? If this financial flow is to be addressed by financial investigation and confiscation, then a multinational capability will be needed. Over 30 years, we have created the multinational network of FIUs and created a global reporting process to identify money laundering through MLROs and an evaluation process through the FATF and its FSRBs. What we lack is the same enthusiasm for actually investing in money laundering investigation and asset recovery. The global infrastructure that the FATF and national governments have created could be used to develop an enforcement model. In many ways, the hard groundwork has been done. Now we need to shift excess resources in the prevention model over to the enforcement model. This would require serious investment in resources which are absent in many countries and stretched to breaking point in others, but we already have an extremely expensive prevention model, so we just need to find a way to transfer resources to another part of the same system.

The final financial flow is foreign criminal money being *spent* in the UK. This is a bit easier, because of the sheer scale of the spend. The 'Gold Rush' scandal, exposed by Transparency International in 2008, continues unaddressed (at the time of writing) and is merely one of many exposés of the problem.[10] The UK Strategic Assessment for 2019–20 observed: 'It is highly likely that over £12 billion of criminal cash is generated annually in the UK, and a realistic possibility that the scale of money laundering impacting on the UK (including through UK corporate structures or financial institutions) is in the hundreds of billions of pounds annually.'

There is a significant political problem here. Foreign criminal money is a subset of FDI. Many, perhaps all, countries are trying to attract FDI. To what extent does the minister of finance, who is typically in charge of attracting FDI, want to vet FDI, in case some of it is found to be criminal?

### Solutions toolbox

- One definition of intelligence is 'information for action'. This embraces the concept that unshared intelligence is not really intelligence at all. Any Intelligence Unit retaining its product without good reason is failing in its fundamental duty. This is an accusation that can be widely applied to FIUs; far too many do not send SARs when they should. It would be useful if the FATF recommended that 'SARs should be passed on to the competent authorities as soon as possible unless there is a compelling reason not to do so'.
- The imbalance of computing resources managing SARs should be globally addressed. The reporting sector and FIUs are generally well computerised, but the end-user, typically, is not. The result is that the whole system is failing across the world, a waste of billions of dollars that could be easily corrected.

## For want of a nail

At the heart of the global AML system is the humble SAR. The Egmont Group reported that in a single year its members received 34.6 million of them.[11] Every one might be useful, but only if they are shared with the right people, in the right way. Only the law enforcement part of the global system can advise of their utility. Unfortunately, the advice is shrouded in secrecy and mixed messaging, but fundamentally the SAR is a good thing, which contributes enormously to the fight against dirty money.

Which brings us to the issue of sharing information. The perennial debate: "I'll show you mine, but only if you show me yours first."

# Information and intelligence sharing

They have all the money and none of the awkward
rules, whereas we have all of the rules and none of the
money to do anything worthwhile.

Anon

The Cambridge Analytica story, which broke in 2018, gave
an indication as to the way in which enormous amounts of
confidential information could easily be extracted from a vast
number of people via a single system. Even before then, society
was becoming quickly accustomed to the gathering and sharing
of personal data. In terms of AML/CFT, the FATF perhaps do
just this as they capture details via MERs. Later, they share these
details of money laundering and terrorism financing activities via
typology reports – most interwoven to foster partnership working.
A point often iterated in the closing comments of conferences
organised by law enforcement and commercially interested AML/
CFT organisations.

Yet are partnerships simply a practice of 'smoke and mirrors',
within an already inefficient 'global AML/CFT regime'? Are
partnerships simply a cover for mediocre performance? Or are
partnerships and the demand for information and intelligence
sharing agreements the foundation of a much bigger excuse ready
when questions are asked as to why things have not improved?

We think it is worth adding some context to partnerships before
we move on. There are, of course, various partners involved
in such partnerships, sometimes making the term partnership
unclear. Simply, we should not conflate all those who take part
in preventing, detecting and prosecuting money laundering

under the term partnerships. We recognise Public Private Partnerships (PPPs) try to separate public organisations from private entities, but that is only part of the description which we see is not always appreciated against the backdrop of conflicting motivations and drivers and the protective mindsets (for obvious commercial reasons) of financial institutions. Alongside this are the different drivers and institutional jealousies within the public-sector FIUs and across law enforcement. At the same time, most partnerships are operationally focused, leaving little scope for strategic opportunities.

These differences are, perhaps, why partnerships have become a priority opportunity for some. An opportunity, perhaps driven by one's own ineffective and fruitless efforts to date, concluded by the idea that "it's not just our fault!" when things go wrong. Still, the split between the financial sector and law enforcement has always been driven by a need to preserve each side's own intentions. The idea of partnership working is not necessarily a means to support one another; the cynics may suggest it ensures one's own house is in order and protected.

## Ignored contact details

The reality, unfortunately, is that law enforcement investigators and prosecution agencies tasked with addressing money laundering offences barely speak to one another. Law enforcement is not always trusted with financial information because it might use it to arrest people, and arresting people can highlight there is a problem needing to be addressed.[1] And nobody wants to highlight unnecessary problems, unless they can be resolved openly by parading high-value cars, homes and motorcycles seized following an exceptionally complex investigation. After all, targets for prevention of money laundering are hard to measure; hence why asset recovery and fines have come to the rescue. Taking money from the criminals and administering fines to businesses which, even if they failed to meet their obligations, could not have allowed money laundering or terrorism financing to take place, have become a discreet fail-safe measure of performance.

It seems the attention now being given to the sharing of information and intelligence is perhaps a distraction from the absence of money laundering investigations, successful prosecutions and meaningful confiscation. Although FIUs are rarely at the centre of partnership working, some may question whether an FIU must share intelligence in the first place; after all it is intelligence, not the less valuable gossip and mere speculation at stake. Still, we feel what has been created is a case of "it is mine and I am not telling you", in order to protect the intelligence.

Financial intelligence is extremely useful at tackling all manner of predicate crimes, not just the follow-on problem of money laundering. Having already been used to solve domestic violence, football disorder, wildlife crimes and breaches of building planning regulations, it seems remarkable that for money laundering the problems still exist. Is it a lack of imagination or the limited intelligence available that somehow forces the intelligence to remain in an FIU instead of adding benefit? We understand how intelligence associated with predicate crimes can never be split from intelligence associated with money laundering, but we are baffled as to why it is so preciously controlled.

If it is a lack of imagination that stops the sharing of information and intelligence held by an FIU, then we are in for a long war. Not just in the war against money laundering but in changing the thinking of FIU leadership. FIUs are financial intelligence hubs, meaning intelligence and the raw information has widespread use. Thus keeping FIUs outside of law enforcement is one way of improving sharing practices with partners. FIUs must not be allowed to maintain a level of seniority and prestige that in any way thwarts the use of what they hold for tackling crime.

On the other hand, if it is the lack of intelligence held by the FIUs that is causing the problem, then FIU leadership has lost all sight of their responsibilities. Admittedly, the war on money laundering has raised the profile and responsibilities of the FIU – not always positively. So, thinking an FIU exists primarily for the fight against money laundering and terrorism financing only ignores the wider benefits financial intelligence can have towards preventing crime within society. Even where information can be received via a SAR, the belief that it is only linked to money laundering (or terrorism financing) is an indication of poor intelligence practices. A good SAR is one that reaches its destination. Widening the physical gap between FIUs and law enforcement, as well as widening understanding of the value of FIU-held information to fighting crime, we feel would immediately strengthen the FIU core business practices.

In our experience there are still too few discussions taking place to raise awareness about how financial intelligence is inhibiting a system capable of delivering a lot more benefit. The concept of getting financial intelligence to the front line is rarely discussed in the habitual reviews of SARs, as well as those unfortunate episodes in which dirty laundry is aired. In fact, the end-user is hardly ever discussed. It is as if they do not really exist, or worse still, do not matter.

If you think that everything seems to be moving in the right direction with the sharing of intelligence and information, then perhaps consider some of the results to date. Of course, partnerships are often praised, but scratch away the gloss and there are too few case studies that **convincingly illustrate** just how financial intelligence has helped law enforcement catch serious criminals. Whether at conferences, online webinars or in editorial content, the reality is that case studies lack unquestionable evidence of partnership working between agencies and a demonstration of a true sharing of intelligence. Equally, these partnerships are rarely evaluated to see if they are working. Many yield obvious working limitations, suggesting some partnerships are merely a disguise covering a broken underbody of prevention, detection and investigation of serious crime and money laundering.

## Control versus partnerships

'A problem shared may be a problem halved', so the expression implies, but the sharing of information, never mind the sharing of sensitive intelligence means a total loss of control. It is human nature to protect something you have worked so hard to collect, collate and analyse. So, if the sharing of commercially sensitive business data is uncommon, how could an outsider expect an FIU to share its information and intelligence with anyone else – whether government bodies, AML/CFT regulators or overseas law enforcement agencies. Data breaches of late, such as that by Cambridge Analytica, indicate the risks are ever present. Therefore, retaining control of intelligence, whether intentional or as a matter of course, has led to FIUs becoming natural hubs of centralised knowledge. Yet, FIUs have also become instrumental in creating partnerships, in which meetings take place to discuss trends, issues and concerns. Perhaps an obvious contradiction, but behind the friendly discussions, the shared meetings and the one-to-one chats over coffee, the fear of sharing too many details looms in plain sight for FIUs worldwide. Add in the problem of how shared intelligence then fits into the hidden activities of their partners, and the risks become unsurmountable.

Of course, information and intelligence should not be shared when it can inform those to whom it relates. Equally, there is an obligation to prevent 'outsiders' from knowing insider details about money laundering behaviours. Yet, there is still no line in the sand delineating what is 'necessary' and what is not. Does it then come down to the character of those attending partnership meetings, the agenda behind them, the level of trust, or simply naivety?

To be effective these issues need to be overcome if partnerships are going to have any real benefit. Although impractical and yet still a critical component of an effective AML/CFT regime, partnerships evidently help distribute the massive amount of data held across relevant agencies. All the transfers and purchases that make money laundering possible exist within multiple businesses and organisations. What this means is that communication is critical because it improves awareness of the underlying issues, risks and potential conflicts of interest. A perspective equally disclosed by the FATF:

> [P]ublic private partnerships have such enormous potential. I say potential, because even good examples such as the Joint Money Laundering Intelligence Task Force in the UK, have great scope for growth and improvement. The authorities need to give banks more specific information and the intelligence required to find real suspicious activity and to focus their huge investment and resources on activity that makes a difference. We need to break down the barriers to more effective information sharing, including the myths and realities that remain around tipping off and data protection. None of this is new, but I've never

seen such a strong appetite and consensus to get it done combined with the ready availability of the tools and technology to do it.[2]

Still, the sharing of information will only ever be determined by underpinning privacy laws that exist to prevent mishaps. And yet many of these laws can already exist, many setting out potential legal risks for organisations, suggesting the arduous work may have already been done. We now need to establish the intentions of those involved in promoting and facilitating partnership working, and not rely on the mere fact they are in place.

## Anyone can keep a secret

To date, there has been widespread hesitation to share information and intelligence even with the push for PPPs. The keeping of secrets about the behaviours, activities and persons involved in money laundering has been easy. What has been difficult is the next step, the losing of control in a controlled manner. Like the FIU placing its faith in the hands of the professional who straps them to the bungee cord – the sharing of valuable and sensitive information needs to be protected by skilled information managers through carefully managed processes. So far, few seem to have been brave enough to take the leap forward. Many have gone forward, only to be found hiding below the platform declaring success despite never jumping and experiencing the excitement of momentary freefall.

This whole idea behind sharing needs to be put into practical terms – something still poorly understood and yet the basis of a shaky foundation upon which the whole AML effort now seems to need to be built. We agree, sharing has taken place, but look at it in detail and it is usually ad-hoc, purposeful and covered by a mutual legal obligation or for the sole intent and purpose of one party. Yet, to be useful, information needs to be shared correctly, frequently and not for the wrong reasons. Something acknowledged when the Egmont Group suspended Nigeria from its platform between July 2017 and September 2018 following concerns surrounding the protection of confidential information and perceived lack of independence.

Is it a hesitation to share, a need to retain control, or is it simply poor management that is preventing partnerships from doing more to tackle money laundering? The sharing of information clearly remains a problem inside many organisations. It is still possible for AML/CFT teams to be located away from fraud teams, meaning they are isolated from the data allowing for greater understanding of the full lifecycle of a particular account. What is then shared is only ever limited, wrong or of little relevance. A case of sharing, because a policy says it must happen, instead of an approach to sharing to prevent criminal activity – either for commercial purposes or to protect national interests. This is something to which the cybersecurity and fraud sectors have become accustomed – basic sharing principles, as opposed to AML/CFT teams where the focus is largely on reporting suspicion.

Again, sharing by a national FIU brings about caution, and rightfully so as a central depository for SARs. Yet, it quickly becomes clear that information is primarily shared by FIUs in their attempt to gain access to further relevant details. Something which a receiver may note comes as a request for information that also lacks noteworthy context. A case of, "Please help us, but since we cannot trust you, you need to guess all the details we are seeking".

Should we be looking to the fraud sector for guidance? After all, it is here where profit losses can be so significant that action is driven towards the problem, rather than playing a role in a problem that never seems to go away. The Netherlands' example of partnership working as referenced earlier in Chapter 9 is perhaps a good example.[3] Still, sharing too many details can also mean losing control, or worse, losing a competitive edge. Perhaps this is why banks and other businesses never truly share what they know, raise concerns or identify problems, even if they are part of a formal partnership working agreement.

## Intent on success

At this point, you could ask where has the FATF been for the last 30 years? Time and again we are reminded that criminals are getting away with lucrative profits because the AML/CFT industry does not use its collective power. All well and good, but who in their right mind would 'tell all' to complete strangers? Surely the FATF has realised this. Or are the FATF's messages simply directed towards its membership, to force them to do something at the national level? Still, at least by doing so, the FATF can assertively demonstrate its governance role and global AML/CFT policy lead.

Coincidently, PPPs and information sharing now set the undertone for the FATF, country regulators, FIUs, law enforcement agencies and others with interests in selling AML and sometimes CFT solutions and training. Perhaps the main reason for this is FATF's immediate outcome number one – 'Risk, policy and coordination', one of eleven outcomes now used to assess the apparent effectiveness of a country to prevent money laundering and terrorism financing.[4] Clearly, all interested parties and vocal advocates are just following suit. We actually think they are all in it together a bit too tight, all equally aware that progress so far at preventing money laundering and terrorism financing has been pitiful but still with the obligation to demonstrate partnership working.

The former FATF President, Dr Pleyer, naturally had a vision of a more cooperative and collaborative future. Why would he not? It is, after all, an easy motion to suggest. Yet, like the idea that we must do more to stop climate change, we think he failed to consider that 'no one in their right mind' is ever going to share information, and especially intelligence, beyond an immediate need for supporting their own objectives. That is, unless they are obligated to – which they are not and nor does it seem the FATF or anyone else will be able to do so anytime soon.

It is also not a discussion anyone, including the FATF, really wants to raise. We agree, PPPs sound great, but since the FATF has no ability to reprimand countries failing to adhere to the 40 Recommendations, then perhaps the FATF is hoping someone else will take control. There may be the ideas, the intentions, the possibilities, but we see that without the obligations to share there is little hope of partnerships working out as intended.

Still, Dr Pleyer's predecessor, Raja Kumar is almost certain to continue pursuing partnerships as a focus for improving AML/CFT. Not only are partnerships easy activities to push for, they offer no means through which to assess success. While we agree with the idea of partnership working in AML/CFT, the prevention of money laundering and terrorism financing cannot rely on officials from various sectors agreeing to share a pot of tea and a plate of biscuits once a month.

## A lack of trust

With significant pressure being placed on a commitment to sharing, one important feature is consistently overlooked – *trust*. Already the Egmont Group facilitates robust cross-border exchanges of actionable financial intelligence and, in doing so, trusting that a member FIU will not misuse the information it receives from others is paramount. But how are we to manage open partnerships if trust is being brought into question when Uganda, Serbia, India, Tanzania and Nigeria are not playing by the same rules as other countries? Those rules that forbid abusing the country's AML/CFT legislation for the alleged purpose of silencing critics and running smear campaigns.[5]

Of course, it is not just the trust held with the organisation, but equally the representatives fronting such meetings and those who are then made privy to information and intelligence that has been shared. While PPPs may seem to be the ideal avenue through which to build trust, we think the ad-hoc structure only serves to work against them. Trust is not the same as being seen as a team player or appearing to work alongside law enforcement and turning up at meetings.

## Odds are stacked in favour of criminals

The AML/CFT regime, it seems, is being enhanced by PPPs working through the belief that sharing of information and intelligence can improve understanding and aid preventative measures. Yet, the reality may be more a case of networks of so-called dependable parties coming together to share in what could easily be argued as a means to keep sensitive material hidden. Whether these agreements work, depends on the details, the culture, the relationship and the ambition to prevent and detect money laundering and terrorism financing. How shared information is then implemented into AML/CFT seemingly raises many more questions. There is clearly a difference between sharing for 'sharing's sake' and sharing to make systems, processes and of course investigations stronger. Is this why law enforcement agencies are typically the drivers of such a partnership agreement? Do partnerships give law enforcement an avenue through which to elicit details from 'its partners' in a more discreet manner?

The Fintel Alliance – a PPP launched in 2017 – has sought to change things. Introduced by Australia's combined FIU and supervisor – AUSTRAC – the idea was simple, to publish financial crime guides within the Fintel Alliance and bring government and private sector members together to work in the fight against financial crime. Yet, despite creating what is still promoted as a successful approach to improving industry partnerships, the Fintel Alliance is a minuscule step in the right direction towards the sharing of threats in a real-time, or near real-time, manner. While it may please those involved, it is the details which are either too sensitive to share, irrelevant or so redacted that they still only provide a Wikipedia-style explanation.[6]

Still, the real threat may come as smaller entities address pressures from dispersed workforces and departmental separation following COVID-19. This situation, and the practices that will now evolve, will support criminality to gain access to information known about their behaviours. Sensitive documents now in home offices, on insecure computers, will likely provide greater opportunities for individuals to be compromised, meaning the container into which shared information was going to be hesitantly added has just sprung yet another thousand leaks. Whether it be the MI5 computer left on a tube in the London Underground,[7] or a lost USB stick, these same issues which are so often observed in large and sensitive government organisations, will inhibit external communications and information sharing for AML/CFT efforts. If full and frank communication between AML/CFT and HR, fraud, IT and risk teams inside the same four walls of a single organisation is still a problem, how can we expect PPP to do any better? It seems many advocates of PPP are willing to push the idea far and wide, but few are keen to take a leap of faith because of what could go wrong.

As reality indicates quite strongly, public and private sector organisations do not share secrets relating to their business, customers, services or activities – in the same way criminals choose not to expose their activities. Sharing leads to greater competition and a loss of profit. Yet, the difference between the AML/CFT regime and criminals, is that criminals have evidence of continuing to work together to solve problems and achieve a desired result.[8] Despite several EU member states having formed Financial Information-Sharing Partnerships since 2017, at the same time Europol was developing the world's leading cross-border financial information-sharing partnership – yet the evidence of success half a decade on is still absent. What the evidence equates to is a series of weak case studies that could have equally been written in the 1990s when the idea of working together was there, but no one wanted to push the idea too soon. Perhaps this hesitation came from the fear that the results would not be anywhere near reasonable or meet public expectations. Perhaps it was just too hard, or perhaps it would never work – and still will not.

## Time to look again at the jigsaw

It is not in the simple sharing of intelligence where all the answers are to be had, it is the lack of a comprehensive intelligence picture where effort is really needed. Although a national FIU may have half of it already, a single piece of the jigsaw is certainly worthless on its own, even if it is shared with partners with the hope they can place it. So why is the focus always on providing snippets as opposed to the full picture? The reason, and it is something to consider above and beyond the excitement of PPPs, is that public-sector intelligence is power, and in the private sector it is profit. It is these simple reasons why PPPs will never really work.

These priorities make intelligence sharing difficult right from the start. National FIUs still do not share with law enforcement. Cases such as the Bank of Credit and Commerce International only serve to limit sharing – not increase it. In this instance the BCCI was a bank owned by organised criminals. It operated for years using a British banking licence only to collapse following an initiative-taking investigation by the then New York District Attorney. The revelations genuinely shocked the British, driven by the idea 'everyone knew but no one knew enough'. Following the incident came the public–private Financial Fraud Intelligence

Network. To this date, how much of what is now shared is genuine is anyone's guess.

In Europe, a mechanism for sharing police intelligence with other agencies does exist. The 4 by 4 system which provides a rigorous method to judge risks and consequences of sharing has been adopted by Europol after originating in England in the mid-1990s. Formalised in 1999 in the National Intelligence Model, it was used to solve one of the most difficult and persistent problems in policing – the need to share valuable intelligence with other police officers and other law enforcement agencies. Still, its adoption in Europe (let alone worldwide) has been patchy, most likely due to the simple practical aspects associated with securely sharing intelligence. We feel if the 4 by 4 system could be introduced, it would move the risk of sharing intelligence away from the individual and onto the agency or entity. To do this, the agency or entity would centrally evaluate and grade intelligence in a standard way, including an assessment of which other types of agencies or entities it could then be shared with. The 4 by 4 system would simply overcome information being retained by individuals, causing inefficiency, institutional ignorance and risk.

## Until death do us part?

Even though the authors are not optimistic about the sharing of information and intelligence outside of an immediate group taking place, we feel there is still significant benefit to 'all singing from the same hymn sheet'. Although there are still obvious failures and a fixation on trying to catch the horse that has bolted from the stable, opportunities do exist. Yet, it is in the middle ground where these opportunities sit; the void between intelligence and the AML/CFT compliance information.

Needless to say, there is a degree of objective reasoning required behind collating intelligence to better understand money laundering. Intelligence needs to be timely to demonstrate its true value. We see having intelligence which indicates the horse will bolt from the stable after the horse has bolted as not the ideal situation. Even to the layperson, this signifies an intelligence failure.

It is perhaps the current reliance on the term intelligence where the problem lies. Intelligence has a level of mystique, commonly associated with spies, spooks and law enforcement. Yet, it seems intelligence can act as a smoke screen for deficient performance and even a lack of knowledge. Intelligence is clearly an inhibitor to sharing, despite the fact it conjures up excitement for those involved.

Imagine if a digital platform could be used to help Customs officials share information on trade transactions in real time to understand money laundering. No 'intelligence' would ever be involved. Instead, there would be real data, allowing entities across the globe to begin putting together pieces of the puzzle – in real time – to identify the transactions that facilitate money laundering using trade. Imagine too if this solution was solely fact-based, not analysed data formed on an incomplete picture. We believe such solutions are clearly possible when it comes to money laundering. The problem is the fact they fail to generate the excitement needed to implement them.

## Surpass expectations – dream big

It is far from normal practice for law enforcement and FIUs to share knowledge, never mind intelligence, with the wider law enforcement community without first considering the details being shared. The authors recognise that not all details can or will ever be shared. Nor should they be. Still, the authors, like so many others, have felt the frustration from having to redact documents for public consumption that are no more detailed than an FATF assessment or, worse still, an open source 2,000-word undergrad essay.

Getting **knowledge** to the front-line end-user must be an explicit objective for the FATF if the premise of preventing and detecting money laundering and terrorism financing is to be fulfilled. Specific analysis and assessment can flow from FIUs via NRAs and partnerships, but the FATF too should be focusing on less generic material. This means little or no repetition for the sake of enlarging documents to demonstrate superiority. The FATF can have their say, but the national aspect must come from the individual FIUs. Money laundering and terrorism financing are a series of transfers and purchases; we do not see the need for them to be illustrated as confusing typologies. NRAs are a source to many AML/CFT professionals, so if they lack credibility, so too can all practices which follow on.

Sharing knowledge with the front line is possible. Belgium is achieving this by increasing the level of collaboration between financial services and state agencies through the exchange of information and expertise on developments, trends and new risks related to money laundering.[9] Such a move can be effective if, and only if, solutions also look beyond AML/CFT compliance tick-boxes. So, imagine placing competent law enforcement and FIU staff in private sector entities to improve understanding and cross-entity working. This practice is not too dissimilar to 'liaison officers' found across various areas of government and industry, many scattered across the globe. With greater determination to meaningful sharing and partnership working opportunities are available, provided the designed solution is targeted, relevant, timely and impactful on the AML/CFT regime.

Still, it is clear there is more road to be travelled if Europol is still pushing for a strong, integrated operational response driven by international cooperation – a call they make in their report titled 'The law enforcement perspective in the wake of the Pandora Papers leak'.[10] An excuse perhaps to cover up for a lack of progress by what could easily be classified as entities woefully incapable of tackling the problem of money laundering?

Does this then lead us right back to the start – a need to question if there really are any good examples of effective information and intelligence sharing partnerships? Examples of partnerships that cross the 'public-sector intelligence-driven closed door workings' and the 'driven by profit private sector'? Or has the answer been staring at us all this time, for the last 30 years – it is just not possible? After all, we still have an undertone of seniority and an obsession with competition in law enforcement and the private sector. At the same time, we have hierarchical systems constrained by rigid structures as opposed to those valuing collective responsibility. Is it possible there are just too many super chickens to make partnerships the weapon that helps win the war on dirty money?

## Solutions toolbox

- There is an opportunity to industrialise partnerships to match the scale of the money laundering problem – similar to the way insurance industries have done so to prevent claims from being made numerous times by the same individual. But to do so, first we also need to understand the motivations/drivers that operate in the private–public sector relationship.
- Authenticity is required to foster effective partnerships. The need to be collaborative to succeed better together is not just formed on a partnership, but an agreement to collaborate at the operational and strategic levels. It is clear that PPPs and information sharing are at the heart of preventing and detecting money laundering and terrorism financing, yet, so far, they have had little positive influence on these two problematic crime types.
- Still, there is a need to be realistic about any key principles for effective PPPs. Leadership will typically come from those who have the most to gain, trust will need to be earned, and technology will always hamper the sharing, thanks to the 'types' involved. Legislative clarity and governance may be raised as principles, but they need to be established long before a partnership is even considered.
- One solution is, of course, to educate people so they can flatten structures, remove obstacles to cooperation and communicate without fear of being repraoched. Effective collaboration takes effort and requires attention to be paid to the 'people' aspect of the equation, creating a shared narrative of shared endeavours. It is not about managers and leaders seeking glory for establishing a partnership that in the end delivers little. True cooperation is only possible with the blending of organisational cultures and working practices.
- The 'us and them' approach that exists in PPPs needs to end, and end quickly. Greater collaboration is required to allow for the identification of genuine money launderers, not those who have an additional charge added because they bought a house with the funds resulting from a drug deal.

Yet, lessening the obvious restraint of convention and protocols of information flow can only serve to benefit prevention and detection of money laundering and terrorism financing. Too many hurdles and hesitations around the sharing of intelligence, and the lack of relevance of the information being shared, are limiting the effectiveness of the global push to prevent or even detect these two crimes. So too is the poor alignment of preventative efforts across the public and private sectors – which if viewed from afar seem entirely focused on generating profits rather than on prevention. Similarly, the anxieties of change need to be put to rest. Change is essential, as the current 'standoff' with regards to intelligence sharing is clearly no longer viable if the results are to get anywhere near matching the intended AML/CFT efforts.

To date, few are still choosing to question or explore the partnerships and sharing frameworks in place, even if the outcomes are obviously poor. Only time will tell if we have simply hit a small bump, or whether we are still acquiring the ability to make them work. As the next chapter will discuss, investigating money laundering and terrorism financing is dramatically different from what is being claimed. So, without partnerships, and information and intelligence sharing, is what we are already claiming as a success, meaningless or misleading?

# Investigating money laundering

Our effort was mocked by some police supervisors: has
the computer caught Ted yet?

Robert D. Keppel[1]

## Eve was the first money launderer

When Eve took the forbidden fruit from the tree, having been
told not to, she acquired the proceeds of her crime and thus
became a money launderer. You may remember this from our
discussion about 'jargon' in Chapter 2, where we introduced the
United Nations definition, which has since been transcribed,
more or less unchanged, into every country's law.[2] When she
gave the fruit to Adam, they both committed another element of
money laundering, transferring the property knowing it to be the
proceeds of the earlier theft. At the time, police and prosecutors
had not yet been created, but if they had been, they probably
would not have bothered charging Adam and Eve with money
laundering. This is because the fruit was gone and confiscation was
not an option, given the couple did not have a fig leaf between
them. Instead, they would have indicted Eve for theft and Adam
for handling stolen goods (or some variation). Money laundering
was *always* there, integral to the predicate crime, but its utility as
an offence was not yet relevant. It has taken a few thousand years
for the legislators to catch up — and there are two good reasons
for that — social change and modern technology.

## Legal origins

In 1989, the OECD commissioned a report on drug 'money laundering', created the FATF, and the rest, as they say, is history. The reason they decided to create the crime of money laundering was because the laws at the time could not address all the money being made from drugs. This is the 'social change' part that makes the crime of money laundering relevant and necessary to modern society. Interestingly, modern society has such a need for money laundering to be a crime, that it has backdated its existence to include the American gangster, Al Capone, who made a fortune from trading in illegal alcohol. Al Capone is commonly regarded as the first modern money launderer, famously using coin operated launderettes to launder the proceeds of his crime. Except this is a myth. Al Capone was convicted of tax crimes; the crime of money laundering was not created until *decades* later. He did not use laundromats either, not for washing money anyway. But society has accepted the myth because it meets a societal need to have some historical depth to types of crime and the crime of money laundering is no exception. Money laundering *should* have been a crime back in the 1920s, but the lawyers and politicians had failed to do their job. To make up for the shortfall, the myth makers *pretended* that they had, and the chattering classes of society repeated the myth until it became 'true'. It is still not true. Al Capone pleaded guilty on 6 June 1931 to tax evasion and alcohol prohibition offences.

No sooner had the FATF looked into drug money, than they discovered a string of other predicate offences which generate money. Now police and criminals have always understood that it is all about the money, but the law has not. It was only when the *fortunes* being made from ordinary crime by ordinary criminals became too large to ignore that the legislators finally took action to investigate it and take it back via confiscation of the proceeds of crime. The law is always a bit behind social change and, in this case, the social change was driven by globalisation and the mass consumption of recreational drugs by Americans and Europeans.

Now, between the investigation and the confiscation of drug money, there needs to be a successful prosecution in court, for a crime. Predicate offences had normally been drafted without a financial provision, because the amount of money being made was typically small and already spent, by the time the defendant appeared in court. In the absence of such a financial provision, or a perceived need for one, across the breadth of criminal offences, the legislators created a brand new crime. They called it 'money laundering' and the rest, as they say, is chaos.

The fact that money laundering was *integral* to a huge number of existing crimes was not explained by the UN and, as a result, its member countries then created chaos by bolting on to their criminal code something which should have been integral to it. This is the legal equivalent of adding an egg to an already baked cake. The results are messy and unpleasant.

Thirty years on, we are still trying to sort it out. The EU, for example, is on its *fifth* Money Laundering Directive, *still* aimed at harmonising the mess, and that is just in Europe. There is a powerful argument to go back to the United Nations and agree on one definition of money laundering and then *command* everyone to rewrite their laws using the same words, in the same order.

As is usual with messes created by other people, the police have been called in. And, as usual, the police have sorted it out. It may not be perfect, and you certainly would not have wanted to start from here, but their solution does work. The solution is called 'parallel investigation'. One criminal investigator investigates the crime, and a financial investigator investigates the money.

Looked at by the uninitiated, parallel investigation appears to be time-consuming, starting with the fact that *two* investigators are needed instead of just one (criminal) investigator. The reality is that financial investigation is typically quicker, and therefore cheaper than traditional detective techniques. This is because almost all financial intelligence-gathering is done online (by email, intranets and the internet). It is also better, because the evidence is being provided by witnesses who are professionals (accountants and bankers) presenting explanations and documents. This contrasts with ordinary members of the public who are giving evidence, as best they can, in criminal cases. Financial investigators are also capable of multiple enquiries at the same time because many of their techniques can be done from their desks, whereas criminal detectives are literally pounding the streets looking for clues. So, financial investigators are better, quicker and cheaper than ordinary detectives.[3] So why are they not used more widely, or just instead? An important part of the answer lies in the frustration expressed by Robert Keppel at the start of this chapter. Mr Keppel was using computer analysis to try to sort a mass of data into something that we would now call 'intelligence' or 'information for action'. In his case it was to identify a serial killer, the now infamous, Ted Bundy. Financial investigation uses computer analysis and a host of other innovative techniques to link people to places, people to other people and people to events. The sheer modernity of financial investigation is a cause for distrust and fear by traditional investigators, prosecutors and courts.

The crime of money laundering itself is also regarded as new and the managers of law enforcement agencies have not yet caught up with modern techniques. This is where 'modern technology' enables the new crime of money laundering. Modern technology allows us to *solve* this new crime by leaving money trails and even explanatory emails. Paper files can no longer be shredded or lost in the fire/flood/dog. Instead, the trail, or even its absence, can be presented as circumstantial evidence. This aspect is not popular with what Mr Keppel describes as 'some police supervisors'.

Maybe a younger, more tech-savvy generation will recognise that the crime of money laundering is only possible because computers made it possible to investigate it. Note that money laundering was always possible before computers, but now there is a trail to follow which can be given in evidence.

## Circumstantial evidence

There is an important point about modernisation here. The far-sighted drafters of the United Nations Conventions in the late 1980s, starting with the UN Convention against Narcotic Drugs and Psychotic Substances, recognised the importance of circumstantial evidence in money laundering casework. The original law makers who wrote the UN Conventions came from countries familiar with circumstantial evidence, so they added that handling dirty money was only a crime if you knew what you were doing, and explained how this could be proved: 'Knowledge, intent, or purpose ... may be inferred from objective factual circumstances.'[4]

This simple guidance just does not work in many countries. You may think that Anglo-Saxon jurisprudence is rather reluctant to use circumstantial evidence (and it is), but many other countries, in practical terms, just will not convict anyone without a confession. The UN did not, and does not, really get involved in implementing its conventions. So, if we are serious about the crime of money laundering, we really need to address this fundamental problem that lets money launderers walk free in countries whose delivery of justice falls short in this crucial area. The fact is that the evidence against money launderers rarely includes a confession or an eyewitness, it almost always relies on circumstantial evidence. The world's most famous detective, Sherlock Holmes, answered Watson's conventional plea to 'stick to the facts', with a very modern riposte:

> Watson: Let's just stick to the facts.
> Sherlock: Once you rule out the impossible, whatever remains—however improbable—must be true.[5]

Money laundering transactions are **supposed** to look normal, so the fact that it is hiding dodgy money has to be proved by ruling out all the normal explanations that might explain it. Once this is done, whatever remains is money laundering.

## You would not want to start from here

Money laundering investigation has a bad reputation for being very complicated, time-consuming and ineffective, much like the early computers that preceded Mr Keppel's success. But money laundering investigation's reputation has developed because it is being done badly at the direction of 'some police supervisors'. No disrespect to the practitioners being directed by donkeys to do the impossible, but what is going on is absurd. More importantly it is a waste of scarce skills and other resources that really could be winning the war on dirty money. As ever, the absurdity arises from good intentions and misunderstandings rather than deliberate folly. What happens is this: every now and then a politician or senior civil servant is caught with their hand in the public purse.

With a few notable exceptions for any particular country, this is a rare event (being caught we mean) and it is often accompanied by regime change, which may make the politics of the investigation complicated. It is also a major problem for the local police and prosecutors. There is no international rescue for this situation. The local agencies are *alone* responsible for investigating and prosecuting. It is, very probably, their first investigation of this type and scale. It is very likely that they are already under-resourced for money laundering investigation, because such investigations have an international reputation for being complicated, time-consuming and ineffective, so no one bothered to create such a national resource. It is also very likely that none of the practitioners have ever frozen or confiscated anything more complicated than a bag of drugs cash, because 80% of countries do not do this activity (according to the FATF evaluations). It may also be the first time that they have made international requests to recover stolen money; the global database of these cases, maintained by the World Bank, has less than 90 entries for the entire period 1977 to date. Finally, they are also trying to follow the money long after the crime, when it has already left the country, and when the perpetrators have already left too. Furthermore, the absconded baddies are fully alerted to the investigation, and have armed themselves with expensive lawyers from Europe and America. Any one of these factors makes the case 'mission impossible', but together it is like a plucky hillwalker trying to climb Everest without a tent or oxygen. It can be done but you would not want to start from there.

## Mission possible

Financial investigation by law enforcement agencies, even across borders, is, like riding a bicycle, easy when you know how. The first difficulty for financial investigators is usually 'some police supervisors' and their institutional structures. There are some organisational factors that need to be adjusted.

Preparation is key. Trained and experienced *criminal* investigators can be easily enhanced into *financial* investigators, likewise with prosecutors. Financial investigations are always urgent and covert, so the resources need to be placed in the right part of the criminal justice organisations. There is no point at all in trying to trace assets after an arrest, all but the very dimmest criminals have an escape plan for their money, if not themselves. Therefore, financial investigations need to be *proactive* rather than *reactive*. This is not new stuff; all law enforcement agencies have some proactive capacity. The mental leap is for them to realise that a financial investigator is just like any other proactive criminal investigator. The only difference is that financial investigators are better, quicker and cheaper to deploy. They also *generate* money for the state rather than being an expense.

## Fraud and financial investigation

Fraud and financial investigation are sometimes confused, so here is a bluffer's guide (see Table 12.1).

It is an unfortunate truth that many senior police officers lack an investigative background or investigative skills. A wide-ranging and important UK report lamented the absence of such skills in its senior managers, but the gap in skills is common across the globe.[6] Outsiders are often surprised by this, but the reality is that the

Table 12.1: Bluffer's guide to the difference between fraud and financial investigators

| Fraud investigator | Financial investigator |
| --- | --- |
| Skilled in a single crime type | Can investigate the financial side of any predicate crime |
| Only investigates fraud | Multi-skilled, with a working knowledge of special investigative techniques |
| Only understands criminal powers | Has a working knowledge of criminal, civil and financial investigation powers |
| Time-consuming reactive investigations | Swift proactive interventions |
| Non-transferable skill | Transferable skills |
| Generally, works in one agency | Can work in/transfer to any agency |
| Costs the organisation/state money | Raises money for the organisation/ state |

multiple skills and experiences needed to rise through police ranks do not necessarily include much (or indeed any) detective ability. For a senior officer, detective skills are a technique to deploy as one might use a forensic science examiner or a Traffic Collision specialist. The result, for the war on dirty money, is that some police supervisors on the battlefield very often do not understand how to deploy financial investigators. They typically think that financial investigators are backroom support staff sweeping up after the event, rather than undercover scouts deployed at the front line, or better still, behind enemy lines disrupting supply lines and laying ambushes. This has a damaging impact on the fight against crime and criminals because it means that cheap, effective tools are not used against them. This is because the leadership does not know how to deploy them.

The authors have had to explain to senior police leaders that financial investigators are not accountants, although it is possible for some accountants, with special aptitude and experience, to qualify as financial investigators. Indeed, although it is possible to recruit financial investigators from the public, experience shows that the cheapest route is to identify the best existing criminal detectives and enhance their skills with specialised training and experience.

## Always arrest the wife and the mother-in-law

Now that we have your attention, with this outrageous subheading, please allow us to explain this apparently sexist and perhaps even bizarre advice. From a criminal perspective it is important, indeed crucial, that money laundering works. Without money laundering, there is no point in even committing crime, something that criminologists might want to think about more earnestly. We learned in Chapter 4 that money launderers cannot really be bothered with learning all those typologies favoured by the compliance industry, but they are exercised by some important priorities. Enjoyment and control of the money are very important. Direct ownership is unwise, because even the most cumbersome legal system might be used to confiscate property kept in a convicted person's name, so other ways must be found. Enjoyment means nice real estate, nice cars, boats, and so on. These can be put in the names of legal people (companies and other entities) created for the purpose, but better still is the use of real 'innocent' people, who can enjoy your property with you. Step forward the wife and mother-in-law. This can extend to other members of the family, depending on just how much money has to be realised. From an investigator's point of view, it might be quite hard to even identify distant relatives and in-laws – surnames may be different, contact with the criminal might be confined to holidays and religious festivals. Proving the *criminal* connection of, an otherwise innocent, mother-in-law might be a serious challenge for a prosecutor. Yet time and again this line of enquiry is one that is worth pursuing at the investigation stage. Failure to investigate the nearest and dearest of wealthy criminals can result in acute embarrassment. An example, within the author's knowledge proves the point. A well-known drug dealer's wife explained how she could prove her innocence and thereby not give up her half of the marital home. She started her evidence at the confiscation hearing by commending the investigating authorities who had convicted her husband. She asserted that they had done a thorough and exemplary investigation of her husband's offences and the proceeds of his crimes and observed that in the course of this investigation they had never found grounds to arrest her, or even question her. That, she said, was proof positive that she was innocent and that there were no grounds to confiscate her half of the marital home. The judge agreed and she kept her half of the house.

It is very difficult to hide your connection to lavish wealth if you drive it, live in it, sail it or generally entertain your entourage with it. And if you do not do those things, what is the point of the crime? It follows that investigators and prosecutors need to follow the money trail. They also need to go in the right direction. The money trail *from* the crime to the criminal is likely to be hard, having been deliberately obscured by the person committing the crime, and may well go round the world. The money trail *from* the criminal is probably easier, it will go to associates, relatives, tenants, employees any of whom may be a weak link for an investigator to exploit. Because the criminal needs physical control of his or her money, the paper trail will be short and local. It will, of course, go across national frontiers, but the true control is almost certainly in the same country.

## All in this together

Twenty-one crime types have been identified as predicate to money laundering by the global standard-setter, the FATF. This includes every crime that is not exclusively motivated by politics, sex and violence and makes up the vast majority of recorded crimes. Consequently, the criminal justice systems of all countries are geared to cope with these crimes and have specialist teams to deal with many of them. What they are not geared to deal with is the money that is integral to them. This may seem surprising, but criminal justice systems are geared towards dealing with the poor. Before recent social changes, there was no need to follow the money because it had been spent, there was no need to confiscate assets because there were none to confiscate. In any case the money trail was made of paper, which was hard to track and easy to destroy. The social changes of mass drug consumption in rich countries and government corruption in poor, newly independent countries have changed the global position over the last 50 years or so. The conduit for both of these crime types were the banks, and the money trail was accounted for in their computers. Once again, Mr Keppel and innovators like him have been critical to the investigation of the world's oldest crime.

## Green shoots

Outside of the USA, the first country to tackle the proceeds of crime seriously and dramatically was the tiny Republic of Ireland, with a population at the time of just over three and a half million. In June 1996, a police officer, Jerry McCabe, was shot dead in his car while escorting a cash delivery. Three weeks later, an investigative journalist, Veronica Guerin, was assassinated while stopped at traffic lights in the capital city, Dublin. She had been reporting on the heroin barons of South Dublin. The Irish Government was shocked by the brutality of both murders. McCabe was a father of five children, Guerin had moved in the social circles of government and had represented the country at sport, her story became an eponymous film starring Cate Blanchett. The POCA was passed within weeks and the famous Criminal Asset Bureau was created a few months later in October.

The concepts underpinning the POCA spread to the nearby UK, which enacted its own POCA in 2002. The global network of asset recovery prosecutors and investigators was initiated in Dublin in 2000 after an international meeting of practitioners at the Camden Court Hotel.[7] At the heart of this dramatic turnaround was the concept of a multi-agency team investigating money laundering and asset recovery. It is commonplace for investigative agencies to share information and to form temporary joint investigation teams for a particular large or complex crime. But permanent multi-agency teams are rare. The driver for forming **permanent** multi-agency teams is an operational imperative to do so and, so far, few countries have realised that the war on dirty money **needs** multi-agency teams. The Criminal Assets Bureau was an early example; the regional Asset Recovery Teams in England and Wales (from 2004) are another. In the EU, there are Asset Recovery Offices which combine prosecutors and law enforcement, but these are a mixed bag in terms of multi-agency investigation; some are mere post boxes to other, operational teams.

The need for multi-agency teams for asset recovery requires a bit of explanation. Put simply, as soon as an asset is found to be of criminal origin (by law enforcement), it must be secured (by a prosecutor) for later confiscation (by a judge). Finding assets is not difficult, but it is specialist and necessarily covert, which normally requires prosecutorial or senior officer engagement to use special and intrusive techniques. If an asset is not secured and the perpetrator finds out that they are under investigation, then the asset will walk. This will be done immediately and urgently because criminals have great clarity of thinking when it comes to losing their assets. From the moment a criminal discovers that they are under investigation the money will be transferred or withdrawn, moveable assets will be hidden, immovable assets mortgaged, or ownership transferred. Even supposedly immoveable assets such as fitted kitchens have been ripped out and hidden. In this context, 'law enforcement' means *any* investigative body, including police, Customs, environmental, trademark, welfare, pensions, health, insurance and so on.

The fact that criminals **always** act swiftly and decisively in these circumstances means that law enforcement officials, prosecutors and judges must all act swiftly and decisively too.

Financial investigation is *always* covert, *always* urgent, and often international too. Countering the universal typology of criminals always moving threatened assets at speed, requires integrated swift working across the whole criminal justice spectrum. The only real way to achieve this is through permanent multi-agency teams. Most countries have not recognised this operational imperative and, as a result, people convicted by their courts are normally allowed, by those same courts, to keep all the money they have made from crime.

An old aphorism from the London police describes the situation before the passing of the POCA in 2002 thus: 'The constable gets his collar,[8] the prosecutor gets his conviction, the judge gets his fair trial, and the villain keeps his cash. Everybody is happy.'

## Ignorance is bliss

You may wonder why courts, so keen to take your money for traffic violations, are not so keen to take money from serious organised criminals. It is a fair question. The main reason is that no one asks them to. This is a bit simplistic, we know, but it is important to realise that courts and the people who work in them are remarkably conservative, they do not change on their own initiative. It is obvious that courts, in particular, work within a strict legal framework, so their conservatism is not surprising. When one of the authors was implementing the POCA in London, the universal opinion of criminal justice staff was that taking money from criminals was an extremely *radical* (and therefore alarming) departure from the norm. There was resistance in every criminal justice agency and at every level. Taking criminal assets is seen by most people including politicians (most politicians like to be seen as tough on crime) as a desirable thing to do. But for most criminal justice staff it was seen as impossible, risky, and a distraction. The resistance was stiffest among senior staff, especially senior police officers, judges and prosecutors who saw it, respectively, as irrelevant, unfair and risky.

It is important for policy makers, who think that depriving criminals of their assets is a good idea, to realise that the criminal justice system will resist them at every step. Policy makers often struggle to get consensus and are delighted to pass a law and then move onto the next policy without the need for an implementation plan. A good policy, after all, will succeed because it *is* a good idea and proof of this derives from the consensus that was achieved to get the legal change passed in the first place. It is a self-justifying approach that normally works. It manifestly does not work in the war on dirty money. Resistance in the ranks of the criminal justice system means that when the command is given to 'advance', nobody makes a move. Nobody takes a single step forward.

This is partly because the first laws were not very good. In the UK, the first asset recovery law, the Drug Trafficking Offenders Act of 1986, was cumbersome and largely ineffective. It was followed by a series of other statutes that tinkered with new powers but, ultimately, did not work. A *Third* report in 1998, from the Home Office working party,[9] finally alighted on the key ingredients of success, borrowing heavily from the success of the Republic of Ireland.[10] The highly effective POCA was enabled in 2003, 17 years after the first tentative steps. Even then, the success of the POCA was driven by an implementation committee which overcame resistance in the police, prosecutors and judges. The EU, meanwhile, is on its fifth Money Laundering Directive, having failed to work out why the previous directives failed. In fairness to the EU, they are in good company; most of the criminal justice systems across the world simply do not work and convicted criminals keep their profits. We know this because the FATF MERs consistently report this in their evaluations of 'immediate Outcome 8', the one about confiscating the assets of criminals.

It is worth looking at the key ingredients of the UK's highly successful POCA. We say it is highly successful because the average annual amount recovered from criminals in the ten years prior to the POCA was £15 million. In the ten years after the POCA, the same statistic hugely increased to £130 million.[11] In addition, the trajectory was steadily upwards. Year-on-year increases continued from 2003 until 2013 when the recovery rate started to plateau, although the *average* take in the years 2013–2017 was still an impressive increase to £206 million per year. Additionally, the numbers of people being touched by POCA powers increased from mere hundreds to thousands. This is important, because the war on dirty money is actually against badly behaved people, not money.

The key ingredients to the success of POCA in the UK (and Ireland) were – in order of importance – the legal power to seize and forfeit cash and the legal power to freeze assets at the start of an investigation. Previously the power was only available after the investigation had established that a crime had been committed, identified a suspect and gathered enough evidence, normally including arrest and interview to charge someone with specific offences, which was of course far too late. These two powers created the ability to tackle investigations proactively. There is, in fact, little point in reactively investigating a dynamic activity such as money laundering, the money has already gone by then. Because of the existence of a central coordinating committee, the legal powers were deployed effectively through centralised implementation, multi-agency training and centralised statistics. In Ireland, this was achieved through the multi-agency body the Criminal Assets Bureau (in the south) and the Assets Recovery Agency (in the north). In the rest of the United Kingdom, implementation was driven by a snappily named informal committee called 'Coordinated Interagency Criminal Finance Action' (CICFA).

The UK POCA changed the dynamic of the agencies conducting asset recovery. Before POCA, the Customs Service did much more than half of all asset recovery, with the remainder being done by the small National Crime Squad in connection with narcotics casework, and the even smaller Serious Fraud Office. The rest of the police forces, combined, did almost no asset recovery and did not bother keeping statistics of the little they did. Consequently, the first meeting of CICFA was chaired by a Customs official.

In the next few years, the value of asset recovery doubled every 18 months or so and the police forces matched and then overtook the Customs Service and were soon responsible for the majority of all asset recovery, more than all the other agencies put together. This was supported by a huge increase in the number of financial investigators (from 25 to nearly 400 in the Metropolitan Police in London), the vast majority of whom were deployed against local crime and worked from neighbourhood police stations, rather than Scotland Yard 'squads'. A particular effort was made to train police supervisors to minimise the problem faced by the innovative Mr Keppel.

## Last word

Because money laundering is integral to any predicate crime, *any* investigation into crime can have a parallel investigation into the money. Much of the British success was attributable to financial investigations into trivial crimes. This route was resisted in some police forces, where 'some police supervisors' took the view that financial investigators should only be deployed once substantial assets had been found. This patently absurd 'chicken and egg' position required correction from the police side of CICFA, who pointed out that substantial assets would only be found if a financial investigator was appointed. In fairness to senior officers, for as long as anyone could remember criminals had been routinely allowed to keep their wealth. The idea that criminal wealth **could** be seized and confiscated was a radical departure from the status quo.

Among the interesting realisations in the UK was the fact that before POCA large amounts of cash were routinely *found* during house searches, but they were not **seized**. This was because the police were typically unable to prove an evidential link between the cash and specific drug dealing or other crime and, therefore, had to return the cash. They learned that it was not worth seizing cash. POCA meant that they had to unlearn this long-established procedure. From an organisational point of view, the deployment of financial investigators in neighbourhood police stations was a critical success factor. It meant that officers at a house search could safely seize the cash knowing that they could give the *litigation* of the cash to a local financial investigator. They were not at risk of being left to handle such litigation themselves.

### Solutions toolbox

• The fact that circumstantial evidence is a basic and common requirement to prove money laundering needs to be widely promulgated by prosecutors familiar with such evidence to countries where it is less well understood. It is not enough to mention circumstantial evidence in the

UN Conventions without providing the tools necessary for member states to implement the Convention.

- Financial investigations and those who deploy them need to be proactive not reactive. There is no real point in starting a financial investigation after an arrest. It would be more cost effective to write that enquiry off and invest scarce resources in the proactive investigation of an active criminal.

- Police managers need a better understanding of how to deploy financial investigators. International donors, in particular, which support the technical training of financial investigators should train senior police managers and prosecutors in how they should be deploying expensively trained financial investigators.

- The 'follow the money' mantra works best in one direction. Investigators should follow the money trail from the criminal to the crime, not from the crime to the criminal. The criminal may well have covered their tracks from the crime but may struggle to hide evidence that they have given to 'innocent' relatives and other associates.

- Asset recovery teams should be permanently constituted and multi-agency.

- Parallel criminal and financial investigations should be undertaken for every predicate crime at the earliest opportunity. Waiting to deploy a financial investigator once a crime has been committed and there is evidence that assets exist, is a definition of stupidity.

## Next word

Experience has shown that money laundering investigation almost always identifies the predicate crime. In the UK, it is the police that initiate investigations and they quickly saw how money laundering investigation was integral with the vast majority of their work. This, in turn, allowed prosecutors to charge both the predicate offence and the money laundering. Put simply, if cash and drugs were found together, as they typically were, the cash was evidence of dealing and the drugs were evidence of money laundering. The prosecutor basically had two chances to prove a case. The result was that there were *hundreds of cases* of money laundering going to court.

Very quickly prosecutors became comfortable with money laundering and courts grew more and more accepting of this new-fangled indictment.

You can see, we hope, the logic of how this worked well in practice. In the next chapter, we look at circumstances where it does not work, focusing on the role of the prosecutor.

# 13

# Prosecuting money laundering

> Countries who don't have brave prosecutors and
> fearless judges will instead have plenty of thieves, many
> killers and even stupid dictators.
>
> Mehmet Murat ildan (Turkish playwright)[1]

Prosecuting money launderers is the ultimate weapon in the war
on dirty money. The enemy's ultimate weapon is to kill prosecutors
and judges, to which Mehmet Murat ildan alludes. The stakes
could not be higher. Money launderers are the criminals that
make crime pay and finding them guilty beyond reasonable doubt
would seem to be *the* ultimate goal of our army of compliance, law
enforcement and prosecution personnel. FATF evaluations devote
an entire section to ensure that: 'Money laundering offences and
activities are investigated, and offenders are prosecuted and subject
to effective, proportionate, and dissuasive sanctions.'[2]

Yet, in some ways this is the biggest red herring of the shoal
of red herrings that we discuss in this book. Finding a person
guilty of the crime of money laundering does not actually
matter. The *investigation* of money laundering at the beginning
of the process matters a lot, because it widens the scope of the
evidence being sought and the powers to find it. The effective,
proportionate and dissuasive *sanctions* at the end of the process
matter too; but in between a criminal conviction *for money
laundering* matters not very much at all, provided that they are
convicted of a crime which is capable of generating money.
The technical decision to prosecute money laundering is exactly
that, a technicality. The *investigation* determines what will be

presented to the court, so that matters, and the court *judgment* determines what happens to the criminal and the criminal asset, so that matters as well. The decision to prosecute for *money laundering* is just a choice among many that could be made along the journey.

It all comes back to Eve again, and the fact that money laundering is and always has been **integral** to the predicate offences. So long as the predicate offences are prosecuted and effective, proportionate and dissuasive sanctions are applied, then the inclusion of money laundering on the indictment does not matter very much.

So let us just set out what does matter. We suggest that the investigation of money laundering does matter. This is because a money laundering investigation looks at the circumstances of the dirty money. This wider view opens up the mind of the investigator to address the 'Five Ws and How' of the money (What, Why, When, Where and Who). This almost always identifies the predicate offences, other offenders and other crimes.[3] The fact that the investigation is into money laundering means that the resource-rich FIUs can be used both domestically and worldwide. This is an important technical point. The FIUs and those crucial STRs can **only** be used for money laundering investigations. This is because international law says so. This means that investigators of predicate offences (and those who authorise their actions) should **always** be adding 'money laundering' to the title of their international intelligence requests and to their formal International Letters of Request to foreign countries, so that they can tap into FIUs, STRs, financial analysts, financial investigators, forensic accountants and the vast sources of information that these people bring to the party. It is entirely possible to turn the current system on its head. Quite frankly, there is much to be said for the idea of predicate crimes being given first to teams of financial investigators to investigate; they could bring in subject matter experts on particular crime types, if necessary. In practical terms, this is what has happened over the last few decades in parts of Ireland and the UK. Financial investigators are better, cheaper and quicker than ordinary criminal investigators, so there may be efficiencies to be had, depending on local Criminal Procedure Codes.

## One small step for a man, one giant leap for mankind

There is a problem with investigating money laundering but not prosecuting it, and the problem is with prosecutors. In most of the world, prosecutors only authorise police to investigate when there is evidence that a crime has been committed. Now we have said throughout this book that money laundering is **integral** to each and every predicate crime, so every authorisation to investigate a predicate crime should automatically mean an authorisation to investigate the money and thereby trigger access to all the extra resources. Unfortunately, some countries have not yet adopted the 'all crimes' definition of money laundering in their criminal code and therefore **cannot** authorise money laundering unless legal thresholds of seriousness are met; others limit the class of prosecutor who has legal 'competence', so some prosecutors **cannot** do what they need to; still others do not see circumstantial evidence as justification to authorise a money laundering investigation, in effect there is no 'smoking gun' that allows them to authorise the investigation. Many prosecutors all over the world cannot initiate a money laundering case because their own laws prevent them from doing so. Frankly, it is absurd but also commonplace.

There are other problems of a more human nature. Having erected all these legal barriers to starting a prosecution, it follows that few cases are possible. This means that prosecutions are rare. Two human problems arise. In any given country one prosecutor has to be the first to authorise a money laundering case. It follows that a judge will, eventually, be the first one to make a judgment. Both people are in the national spotlight, and it is an uncomfortable place to be. No one wants to be *that* prosecutor, and no one wants to be *that* judge, so no one takes that first step. It gets worse. The result of all the legal and human barriers to starting a money laundering investigation is that, in many countries, the first case only happens when absolutely **egregious** money laundering has taken place and it simply **must** be prosecuted. Consequently, the first money laundering case that anyone in a country has ever dealt with is often a hugely complex, high-value case against an important and powerful local figure. Furthermore, the case is conducted reactively (after the event), meaning that the defendant has time to destroy evidence, move assets and hire good lawyers. The prosecution case begins from a disadvantage which is particularly acute in money laundering where covert, proactive enquiries work best, and it is already too late to deploy them. In addition, the case is vigorously defended by expensive lawyers, particularly where it is possible that defence costs can come from frozen (that is, suspect) funds. Incredible as it might seem, some countries allow the defence to be funded from suspected stolen funds. You could not make it up, really. All this puts the prosecutor and judge under enormous pressure. The stakes are high, the case takes a long time. Win or lose, no one wants to do it again. Meanwhile, the clock continues to tick, and the illicit money continues to flow.

If you thought it could not get worse, think again. In cases where a powerful figure has successfully defended themselves, they have been known to wreak their revenge. This can be career-ending for a prosecutor. Indeed, in some countries just losing your job would be seen as getting off lightly. This is an obvious danger. Less obvious, at least to those from an Anglo-Saxon legal background, is the cultural fact that in some countries prosecutors are not allowed to lose. In the Anglo-Saxon world you win some, you lose some, but you try not to lose too many. In some legal cultures the loss of a single case is damaging, the loss of a serious case could be disastrous for a career.

Finally, we started this chapter suggesting that brave prosecutors and judges are needed in this war. In addition to professional courage discussed above, there is the bravery required to carry out a difficult job in public, day after day, knowing that you might be killed just for doing it. Attacks on prosecutors and judges by the violent criminals that they routinely deal with are extremely rare. The few cases that do occur are perpetrated not by the violent unhinged madmen, but by or on behalf of the wealthy organised criminals with political connections. We discuss this further and list specific assassinations at the end of this chapter. Prosecutors and judges tackling dirty money deserve better support from the AML regime, particularly regulators, law makers and institutions. We suggest how this can be done in the 'Solutions toolbox' below. If they are not protected then 'thieves, killers and dictators' will thrive.

All of that said, there are prosecutors who are brave enough to take these cases on, but their job has been made much more difficult than it should be. If we are to win the war through prosecution, we really need to examine how to best support prosecutors. Our view is that the FATF and international development donors should look at countries where prosecution of money laundering is commonplace, understand why, and promulgate good practice through a revised Evaluation Reporting process. The AML regime puts enormous time and effort into identifying theoretical typologies that might be used by criminals and no effort at all into the real methods that can definitely be used against them. It is absurd.

## The perfect crime

Having said that the FATF are not doing enough to support money laundering investigations and prosecutions, they are also virtually silent about the most common way to bypass investigation and prosecution, and indeed, all the global money laundering prevention techniques, which is to commit the perfect crime.

The perfect crime, as we discussed in Chapter 5, is to create a legal entity, a company, partnership, or trust which acts on your behalf and can be created or disappeared at your command.

In recent years, instances of huge money laundering have been exposed. Multi-*billion*-dollar amounts have been identified as the proceeds of crime, suggesting a massive crime wave of previously unreported tax evasion and corruption. The process resembles the children's party game 'musical chairs' in which, when the music stops, the child left standing without a chair has to leave the game. In the money laundering game, however, everyone gets to keep playing. When the music stops, innocent bystanders, the shareholders who did not even know they were playing, get a massive fine. On the plus side, the fine is typically less than the bank profits made from the game, so there is no real impact on them either. The only losers are the millions of people who are the victims of crime and corruption, who have been deprived of effective public services, hospitals, education, pensions and the like, because the public purse has been stolen and laundered. Remember, money laundering is integral to the crime.

When these crimes have been exposed, hardly any people, real or legal, have been held responsible, let alone accountable. A major part of the problem is that these crimes are not being treated as crimes at all; they are not being prosecuted but regulated instead. It is true that real people involved in the money laundering scandals of recent years have resigned from jobs, and others, tragically, have suffered sudden death either at their own hand or in unexplained circumstances. But all of this is happening without involving the criminal justice system, in any real sense, at all. The criminals escape justice and the victims, ordinary people like you and me, get fewer public services. Instead of real criminal justice, weaker alternatives are sloppily proffered: regulatory fines or agreements to defer prosecution. These methods cannot and will not change the behaviour of the real people responsible, because the penalty bypasses them altogether. Even in its own terms there are multiple weaknesses in the current implementation of efforts to stem corporate crime in the UK, pointed out recently and in detail to the Serious Fraud Office Director by Transparency International and Spotlight on Corruption.[4]

## The enablers

Criminals need help to put their money in another jurisdiction. This help comes in two forms: the middlemen (typically men but there are women too) who facilitate the process: Company Formation Agents, lawyers and accountants. These are collectively known as 'enablers' and a common view among law enforcement, politicians and campaigners is that the criminal ones should be prosecuted, although they rarely are. This is because the cases would be international, quite complicated to prove and expensively defended. The second form of help comes from the official registries that record the company formation and accept the fees for formation, annual renewal and closure. These are government bodies who basically write down what they are told. They do not verify the information and enable the whole process. It is absolutely absurd. Given a straight choice between controlling wealthy private sector professionals and their own employees, it is obvious that governments should choose to control their own behaviour.

In the cases where companies have been identified as the vehicles for crime, it was obvious that they should either never have been registered or, when discovered, they should be immediately dissolved. It is, frankly, ridiculous that this does not happen as a matter of routine all over the world. In the UK, with its notoriously weak and ineffective Company House, even there, the Companies Act 2006, Section 1000, gives a power to the Companies House Registrar to strike off a company, if the registrar has reasonable cause to believe that a company is not carrying on business or in operation. However, the power is only used to regulate compliance with filling in and submitting forms, the content of the forms is never verified so the reasonable grounds are not gathered.

You may feel that we exaggerate about the army of legal persons but consider the half million International Business Companies of the British Virgin Islands. These are not allowed to 'carry on business or operate' on the islands, and there is no real way that the BVI authorities could possibly be sure of what they do even if they wanted to. We have not delved into the detail of how these legal persons hide what real people are doing, but others have, and we salute those who have brought us the Panama Papers, the Lux Leaks, The Pandora Papers and so on. Just consider *any* of the major money laundering scandals in Europe and observe that it is legal people who are committing the crimes. Europol's latest Organised Crime Threat Assessment (published in 2021) stated: 'More than 80% of the criminal networks are active in the use of legal business structures for their illegal activities.' These are legal business structures that are registered with the authorities. It is absurd.

## The case for the prosecution

We mentioned that the FATF devotes a whole section of its evaluation process to prosecuting money laundering and that this requirement has been misunderstood in many countries.[5] Apart from the abject failure of any country to routinely prosecute legal people, prosecutors are also confused about real people. Some clarification would help, and we have identified three areas of potential confusion.

The FATF mentions the need to investigate 'money laundering offences and activities'. Local experts have asked what the word 'activities' means. We think that this should be interpreted widely, to include the things that support money laundering, such as regulatory breaches (of employment or environmental law, for example) and predicate offences. Regulatory breaches, according to some legal systems or in certain circumstances, can become criminal breaches and therefore become predicate offences. It would be helpful for the FATF to be more explicit, thereby bringing extra regulatory resources and agencies into the war on dirty money and confirming the importance of predicate offences.

Stand-alone money laundering prosecutions are given a special status in the FATF Methodology, and we think that this is undeserved. Of course, we salute the heroes who prosecute and judge stand-alone money laundering offences, but the fact is that they are extremely rare, almost quirks of the system rather than a pinnacle to aspire towards. A financial investigation of dodgy money will almost always identify the predicate offence, and the easiest route for most prosecutions is a dual indictment of the predicate offence and money laundering. This also delivers the best justice, allowing the court to understand both the context of the money laundering and the scale of the predicate offending.

Finally, we found some ambiguity concerning asset recovery from money laundering. The FATF wants countries to conduct money laundering prosecutions and do asset recovery; we have found that some countries focused *only* on asset recovery from money laundering casework; they had disconnected money laundering from predicate crime. As a result, when they were preparing for the FATF evaluators they only counted their stand-alone money laundering prosecutions. They also only counted asset recovery derived from money laundering. Although the FATF text is very clear, we have found that some countries separated money laundering from predicate crimes to such an extent that they have failed to count their own success. It would help countries if the statistical requirements were much more explicit, because what gets measured gets done.

In fact, it is possible to get an image of whether money laundering is being addressed using only two statistics. One is the monetary value of the proceeds of crime confiscated, the other is the number of people subject to freezing orders. With these two numbers, collected over time, it is possible to see whether a prosecution regime is operating successfully. As it is, countries collect almost every possible statistic *except* these. The result is that there is a great deal of noise, and it is hard to tell if the battle against dirty money is being won or lost, or even if it is taking place at all. That is if anyone is really, we mean really, listening to the noise.

You can check this yourself. Next time you read about crime in the news, see if you can work out if there was any confiscation of the proceeds of crime. You will find stories about the confiscation of drugs, arms, cars that were used in crime but rarely the confiscation of any *proceeds* of crime. Similarly, you will read about the value of assets frozen, but you will not find out how many people were involved or if the money was ever confiscated. Even if you read the FATF evaluations, hardly any contain the two basic statistics; everything else, but not the ones that really matter. It is frustrating.

We completely accept and understand that the primary objective of the global AML regime is prevention. This echoes the primary objective of policing, as the 'father of modern policing', Sir Robert Peel, stated in 1829.[6] However, the Metropolitan Police found that prevention only went so far, and after a particularly embarrassing failure to prevent crime (a grisly murder, committed by a Mr Good), they founded the Detective Department in 1842. We think that the AML regime needs to accept that prevention is not enough on its own and recognise that detection and litigation need to be properly resourced, *as part of the whole regime*. Frankly, leaving the detection to woefully overstretched 'competent authorities', has manifestly failed. The continued hope that the situation might change is negligent and bordering on criminal. Something must be done.

## Solutions toolbox

- Prosecutors should authorise far more money laundering investigations. Arguably, all predicate offences should be treated as money laundering, for the simple reason that money laundering is integral to all predicate offences. In practice, opening a money laundering investigation opens up the scope of the investigation to include any assets derived from similar offending. A routine financial investigation may well identify criminal assets, other predicate offences and other offenders. It also opens access to the resource-rich FIUs and the financial sector.
- Countries should all adopt the 'all crimes' definition of money laundering. Placing artificial barriers in the way of investigators and prosecutors only helps criminals keep their assets and remain undetected. No one else gains.
- The FATF should consider revising what is published in its Evaluation Reports to promulgate good practice from evaluated countries, thereby specifically supporting the prosecution of money launderers. Countries and international development organisations need to work together on a global basis and learn from the most successful regimes.
- Courts should treat a 'legal person' who commits a crime in the same way as a real person, with the full range of practicable sanctions available within a country's criminal justice system, including the ability to delete them altogether. In particular, an officially registered legal person should be assumed to be a capable, sober adult who knew what they were doing. The practice of double indemnity for criminals using legal entities should cease.
- Company registrars should be used to strike companies off Company Registers if it is believed they do not have a genuine purpose or are not carrying on a genuine business.
- The FATF should explicitly encourage the widest interpretation of activities suitable for money laundering investigation. It should also encourage countries to count the number of persons from whom assets are seized or frozen, and the monetary value of assets confiscated following predicate crimes (including money laundering).
- The global AML regime as a whole must address the imbalance of resourcing between prevention of money laundering, investigation and litigation.

## A national shock

Sad to say, the war on dirty money has involved far too many casualties. Indeed, it is the assassination of champions of law and order that has driven the passage of laws upon which we rely to tackle dirty money.

In the USA, the assassination of former Attorney General Robert Kennedy in June 1968 was a very important factor in the passage of the Racketeering and Corrupt Organizations (RICO) Act in October of that year. The Act was enabled on 15 October 1970. Significantly for the war on dirty money, President Nixon said that the law was to "launch a total war against organized crime, and we will end this war".

From a financial perspective, the act allowed civil redress for RICO criminal violations:

> Even though RICO threatens very long prison terms for racketeers, the law's real power is its civil component. Anyone can bring a civil suit if they have been injured by a RICO violation, and if they win, receive treble damages. In the 1980s, civil lawyers attempted to fit many different claims inside of RICO.[7]

In Italy too, the effective new laws and agencies to tackle dirty money were only created after high-level assassinations. The 'Anti-Mafia Law' was approved on 13 September 1982. General-Prefect Carlo dalla Chiesa, charged with controlling the Mafia, had been assassinated ten days earlier on 3 September; the political proponent of laws to control the Mafia, Communist Party leader Pio La Torre had been assassinated earlier the same year on 30 April.[8]

In Ireland, the assassinations of police officer Jerry McCabe and journalist Veronica Guerin in separate attacks in June 1996 led directly to the passage of the Proceeds of Crime and Criminal Asset Bureau Act in June and October of that year.

The war on dirty money has to be a global war, even if it is divided into national battlefields. This is because dirty money flows to and through the weakest countries (in terms of regulation). But there is no reason to wait for assassinations in every country, we can and should learn from the countries who are scoring victories in the war. It is not necessarily easy to spot a victory in this war but, since many critics focus on the paucity of confiscated money compared to the vast sums said to be available for confiscation, the next chapter will look at confiscation.

This will include the **remarkable** conclusions reached in 2013 by the UK National Audit Office (NAO) in their report entitled 'Confiscation orders'. This report was scathing in its assessment of the very capabilities which were later lauded by the FATF in their glowing evaluation of the UK just five years later. More seriously, the NAO report was still being used as the basis for proposing legal reform by the UK Law Commission in 2021. What were they thinking?

# 14

# Snatching defeat from the jaws of victory: confiscation

Crime pays. But what is truly shocking is that criminal courts *allow* criminals they convict to keep the money. We know this because the FATF evaluates the effectiveness of countries at confiscating assets from criminals. There are four grades of 'operational effectiveness': high, substantial, moderate and low. Evaluations in the bottom half of the scale (that is, moderate or low effectiveness) indicate that 'major' or 'fundamental' improvements need to be made to law and practice. Eighty per cent of countries are in these grades. In other words, only 20% of countries bother with confiscation and, of them, just three out of 120 are 'highly effective' at confiscation.

We should clarify that this is 20% of countries evaluated, as opposed to 20% of the world by population. The top echelon includes large countries such as Russia, China and the USA. India has not yet been evaluated but we are prepared to stick our necks out and predict that they will score well in this category. Additionally, Western Europe is well represented: Italy, Spain and the UK have all scored well and we are also prepared to stick our necks out for France (still to be evaluated). The spread of countries in the top tier is uneven in other ways; several top tier countries are aligned for historical reasons with other countries. The effect of this is that when a country makes improvements that put it in the top tier, the aligned country picks up the improvements and enters the top tier as well. This seems to be the case with historically aligned countries such as Italy and San Marino; China, Taiwan and Hong Kong; the UK and Jamaica; and the USA and Israel. Notably this last pair are two of the three which attained the highest FATF grade, along with Honduras. The rest of the world, including much of that 20%, really do not do as much confiscation as they could.

Let us be crystal clear. Almost all people *convicted* in criminal courts worldwide keep the proceeds of their crimes. In 80% of countries the courts convict people of making money from crime and then allow them to keep the proceeds. Hardly any countries conduct financial investigations, and the wealthy leave court with their money intact. In every country, most criminals are never arrested for their money-making crimes. But for crime to pay even after criminals are brought to 'justice' is absurd. It is no wonder they keep committing crimes. The impact on society of this gross injustice should be hard to accept.

An added complexity is how criminals are treated in different countries. Nation states choose which *types* of criminals they pursue, and it is possible to detect hidden agendas in some of these choices. For example, it is striking that many of the Russian confiscations relate to domestic corruption cases, whereas the United Kingdom has no domestic corruption confiscations at all. *How* this strikes you will depend on your political perspective on these two countries.

Nonetheless, any criminal who is making money from crime should surely be a candidate for confiscation of the money that they have made. Confiscation seems to us to be common sense. It is counterintuitive and unjust for courts to allow criminals to keep the money.

Countries could, surely, start with the criminals who are already in their Criminal Justice 'in-tray'. So, why don't they? A common explanation for inadequate law (or practice) is a lack of political will; in other words that people (or the right people) do not care enough about this topic. Let us take a look at the kind of people who might care about this.

## Do the general public care?

What do the public make of this absence of common sense? Anecdotally, people are astonished to hear that criminal courts routinely allow convicted criminals to keep the money. They assume that confiscation is done automatically and are quite bewildered to find that this not so. But do they care? It turns out that they have rarely been asked.

Just three surveys have specifically asked the public what they think about confiscation. One was in Northern Ireland in 2005,[1] a second in England & Wales in 2009,[2] and a third in Serbia in 2011.[3] In each case the government had started to confiscate assets and wanted to find out how the policy change was being received by the public. The surveys were overwhelmingly positive towards the use of asset recovery (although the Serbian public were notably sceptical about its likely application against 'politicians and tycoons'). The UK surveys related to a newly formed 'Assets Recovery Agency' and the results are shown in Box 14.1.

---

**Box 14.1: Public opinion surveys**

**The 2005 survey in Northern Ireland found:**

• More than four fifths (83%) of those surveyed said that wealth confiscation and a prison sentence are equally important objectives in dealing with criminals.
• The majority (91%) of respondents supported the Assets Recovery Agency's power to act through civil courts to recover assets resulting from crime, even if the person has not been convicted in the criminal courts.
• More than four fifths (86%) of those surveyed agreed that 'many criminals who go to jail manage to hang on to the proceeds of crime and are able to live a wealthy lifestyle when their prison sentence is over'.

**The 2009 survey in England & Wales found:**

• Despite relatively low levels of knowledge about asset recovery, respondents' views were generally very positive: 86% of respondents supported it and over 50% felt it was an effective or very effective crime deterrent.
• Public opinion of the police might be improved if awareness of the successful use of asset recovery powers is increased.
• Asset recovery was viewed by respondents as an effective crime reduction technique. It came third after more police on the streets and longer prison sentences. But, importantly, the more they knew about asset recovery, the more of a deterrent they thought it was.

---

## Do the police care?

The fact that very few countries confiscate assets is, to a very large extent, caused by the police failing to investigate the finances of criminals. It is obvious that a court cannot confiscate the proceeds of crime if it has no evidence about such proceeds. The police will investigate things if they are asked to do so by a court, or by a prosecutor, but this does not happen. They may, additionally, be *unable* to do so because they lack legal powers, investigative tools or training, but that is a different issue.

You might ask why the police do not lobby for such an obvious deterrent to crime, but it is a much bigger proposal than you might think. A police force that has never experienced a successful confiscation regime cannot really imagine how it is done. Policing is very parochial, limited to national frontiers and, even if they did look at neighbouring countries, they are unlikely to find an example to follow. Four out of five countries do not have effective confiscation regimes. International policing organisations such as Interpol or Europol are largely engaged in helping national police forces work with each other, rather than innovating *how* they work. Similarly, international training organisations, such as the European Union Police College (CEPOL) train police in *how* to use existing powers, rather than lobbying for new ones.

Confiscating assets is an element of crime fighting, itself a surprisingly niche activity within the police. The police have a wide variety of responsibilities: public disorder, disaster recovery, sex crime, traffic control, domestic and other violence, alcohol, or firearms licensing and so on. Policing is often the service of last resort for health crises, particularly mental health. Therefore, *acquisitive* crime is not the top priority that people assume it is, so neither is confiscation. Specialist units addressing tax and Customs evasion, corruption and organised crime are more likely to want confiscation, but their specialist nature means that they lack popular support and thus political clout.

## Do prosecutors and courts care?

Prosecutors and judges, when asked to explain why confiscation orders are not made in their countries, simply state that the evidence is not available to prosecute the proceeds of crime nor to make an adjudication. It is, for them, a chicken and egg problem. The fact that in many countries it is the prosecutor who directs the investigation is side-stepped. Prosecutors the world over are overworked and not looking for extra responsibilities, so for them, the efficacy of confiscation to address crime is a political issue not a legal one.

## Do governments care?

Ronald Reagan's observation about his fellow politicians remains true: "If you can't make them see the light, make them feel the heat." We have referred elsewhere to tragic political assassinations that were a trigger for confiscation legislation in the USA, Ireland and Italy, but surely there must be a better way to drive policy, than this drastic option? Confiscation remains an afterthought in the world of crime fighting. This remains true, despite public opinion, despite the example of successful confiscation regimes and despite the FATF's Recommendations. Perhaps this book will help galvanise opinion? We hope so.

## Do criminals care?

Surprisingly, there is almost no academic research into this vital topic. The global war on dirty money is based on the idea that successfully waging it will alter criminal behaviour and reduce crime. Many investigators and prosecutors can cite their own experience that it works. The public also, when asked, think it is likely to work. But we have never asked criminals what they think nor researched their behaviour after assets are seized or confiscated. Importantly we do not know if different types of asset recovery are more efficacious than others or, indeed, whether any of it works. This seems absurd. Globally we are spending US$210 billion based on some anecdotes. We think that we should divert some of this money to fund proper research into what criminals think and to formally examine apparently worthwhile activity to see whether it worked as intended. It seems far more likely to us that an activity specifically aimed at the motive for committing crime will have more effect on crime than incarcerating someone after a crime has been committed and allowing them to keep the proceeds.

We also think that the vicious circle of poverty, crime, imprisonment, release without prospects, and further crime could be transformed into a virtuous circle of crime, the recovery of the proceeds of crime, reinvestment in the community and anti-crime agencies to prevent further crime. We are not alone in thinking this; many countries have begun to reuse confiscated assets for the public good.[4]

## The case for confiscation

Confiscation means victory in the war on dirty money. It is the moment when the money made through crimes against individuals and society at large is recaptured. There is the opportunity to compensate the victims or reuse confiscated assets for the public good. We could publicly celebrate that crime does not pay; we could assuage the harm from crime by disbursing the money to the communities that have been harmed. It is curious that we do not.

Perhaps the victories are too few and too small. Sometimes victory is hard to identify. Our governments are secretive about this topic, for reasons which are unclear. Our mainstream media are quick to criticise and obsessed with bad news. The successful confiscation of criminal assets does not meet their criteria. Perhaps this explains why the publication of criminal justice agencies' success in the war on dirty money is so hard to find. A browse through the latest press releases of Interpol, Europol, the US Federal Bureau of Investigation, the UK National Crime Agency and any other official police website will reveal seizures of drugs, contraband and guns. You will also read of arrests and prison sentences. Occasionally cash is seized, but its confiscation, or the confiscation of real estate, investments and serious money is rarely mentioned. The global media follows the same pattern. When they do mention asset recovery, journalists frequently get important technical details wrong, often conflating seizure with confiscation, even though these are events often separated by four or five years of litigation. The confiscation of cash is the nearest the public get to hear about the confiscation of the proceeds of crime.[5] Unless they read this book, which is why we wrote it.

This is to be contrasted with the imposition of huge fines by regulators on banks, which are trumpeted on the front page.

These fines are often meaningless, because the bad behaviour being punished was the responsibility of former executive staff, but the fine is imposed on current shareholders. Consequently, these fines do not, indeed cannot, influence the relevant bad behaviour. Their main, perhaps only purpose is to fund regulators, which is perhaps why they are so celebrated.

## What is confiscation?

Although there is a lot of media reporting about crime, criminal fortunes, and portrayals of wealthy criminals, there is not much about confiscation. There are some academic experts but precious few. Professor Michael Levi and Lisa Osofski's ground-breaking empirical study of confiscation remains one of the very few to look at a national regime holistically, and that dates, literally, from the previous millennium.[6] Dr Ron Pol in New Zealand regularly laments the enormous gap between the amount that could be confiscated globally and that which is. The Universities of Trento, Bristol and Maryland regularly study aspects of confiscation (and there are many others) but, frankly, given that over US$210 billion is spent each year on trying to prevent dirty money entering the financial system one might expect more discussion on *why* so little is recovered.

## How does confiscation happen?

In the previous chapter, we explained that between the investigation and the final confiscation of assets, there has to be a successful prosecution of a crime. This is still true in many countries but in others criminal confiscation has moved on. In some countries cash can be confiscated because it is *probably* dodgy, in others real estate and serious wealth can be confiscated *without anyone* being prosecuted or even arrested. This is because the law is catching up with societal change and technology.

There is a good understanding among the public that crime pays. This is partly helped by a healthy human scepticism of the phrase 'Crime doesn't pay'. The UN Conventions against Narcotics, Corruption and Transnational Organised Crime (starting in 1988) and the consequent changes in legislation to *allow* confiscation, have highlighted that not enough confiscation is going on. At the same time journalists started to report the confiscation of assets. Films and TV started to show that crime paid. Perversely, before confiscation legislation there was no discussion. Those in the criminal justice system never thought about getting the money back, and the rest of the population (based on dozens of conversations with the authors) naturally assumed that getting the money back was the first thing the court did. Quite simply, nobody gave it a thought. Absurd, but true.

The efforts to bolt confiscation onto the criminal justice system have met with a simple ineluctable truth. It is impossible to prove beyond all reasonable doubt that a particular asset came from a particular source of money. Consider, if you will, stealing a US$10 bill and putting it in your wallet, with other such bills that you got from the bank where your legitimate income is received. Then buy something. If you buy the thing with the stolen bill, then it becomes the proceeds of your earlier theft. You do not know which bill was used. Nobody knows, no prosecutor could prove anything, because the only witness is you and you yourself do not know. This simple example can be extrapolated as far as you like. Once even a small amount of money is mixed in a wallet, a bank account or real estate it cannot be found. The only legal solution to this difficulty is for the whole amount to be considered as tainted. The stolen money taints the rest; a kind of financial corollary to the well-understood legal term 'fruit of the poisoned tree', meaning that illegally obtained evidence cannot be used, however relevant or true. But this only works if you rewrite the law to say that this is the case, and most countries have not done this.

Money is 'fungible', a lovely-sounding word from the study of economics meaning interchangeable. This fungibility is what makes the modern litigation of the proceeds of crime possible. Prosecutors in most countries still struggle with the old law, but some countries have side-stepped the problem altogether by providing alternative legal weaponry.

There is now a plethora of legal routes to recover the proceeds of crime. So many that it is hard for a non-expert to know what is happening, especially at a global level, because each *national* criminal procedure is unique. It is perhaps helpful to imagine the prosecution of money laundering as one of a selection of weapons in the armoury. The legal weaponry in some countries, outside of prosecuting a specific crime, is truly awesome and getting more powerful all the time. There are now so many diverse weapons in the war on dirty money that we need a catalogue just to describe them.

We touched on this in Chapter 2, setting out the jargon that describes the various legal procedures available. We try in this chapter to make sense of this legal weaponry in terms of the arsenal of weapons available to each country. Remember, each country can only use its own framework of laws, its own arsenal.

## Different levels of confiscation

Confiscation[7] is a type of asset recovery that happens after conviction for a crime, but there are other legal routes such as cash forfeiture and non-conviction-based confiscation. We explore what this means in the following section. National asset recovery regimes can be defined by their legal limitations. This becomes important when countries are trying to cooperate, because regimes operating at a basic level cannot cooperate except at their own level. Advanced regimes are therefore limited when trying to recover assets abroad, from countries with more basic frameworks.

Below, four different *levels* of asset recovery *regime* are described. Other experts have suggested ways to categorise asset recovery levels,[8] but none have been accepted by the global community. We think that it would help the world if the global standard-setter – the FATF – considered adopting a methodology for evaluating the effectiveness of confiscation according to the *regime levels*.

## Level 0

The lowest level, the 'ground zero' of asset recovery, is where the evidence submitted in a criminal case has monetary value and the court decides to confiscate it. All the world's criminal justice systems have effective laws and procedures to confiscate such evidence as a matter of routine. There are just two categories, namely *instruments* used to commit the crime and the *object* of the crime itself. For example, asset recovery from a recent bank robbery might include the gun and the getaway car used as *instruments* to commit the crime, while the cash that was stolen was the *object* of the crime. Assets from street drug dealing include the drugs and cash typically found on the defendant upon arrest.

## Level 1

The next level is the recovery of the ***proceeds of a specific crime*** after conviction. For example, tangible assets such as cars or jewellery that have been purchased with the cash gained from a robbery or drug dealing. This is usually extremely difficult to prove (as discussed above), but there are some cases where the evidential connection can be made. Where the money has been used to buy non-tangible goods or everyday expenses, many jurisdictions can recover the value of the proceeds of the crime. Few countries, however, do the investigations necessary to enable asset recovery. It is simply not a priority for most justice systems.

## Level 2

This level is the recovery of the ***proceeds of multiple crimes***, not all of which have been proved. The most obvious example would be the conviction of a wealthy career drug dealer, who is found to be responsible for years of individual drug sales too numerous to count. This is still conviction-based asset recovery, but it allows a court to make assumptions based on the type of crime committed.

In the UK, for example, Section 75 of the POCA defines 'being a criminal',[9] and if the criteria are met, the court can assume that all the defendant's assets are the proceeds of crime, without specifying which crimes. This pragmatic approach was developed because of the difficulty of connecting crimes to particular assets in court. In other jurisdictions, this level is achieved by prosecuting people for the crime of 'Unjustified Wealth'. This level has been routinely achieved in the UK, but rarely elsewhere.

## Level 3

The highest level is **non-conviction-based asset recovery (NCB)**. The FATF glossary states: ' "Non-conviction-based confiscation" means confiscation through judicial procedures related to a criminal offence for which a criminal conviction is not required.'

Examples include asset recovery in civil courts (also known as 'civil recovery'), administrative cash forfeiture at frontiers and litigation against deceased or absconded criminals. These are explained below and there is a handy summary in Table 14.1.

**Civil recovery** in common law jurisdictions is conducted against serious organised criminals by specialist agencies such as the Criminal Asset Bureau in Ireland or the Asset Recovery Agency in the UK (whose functions and staff were absorbed into the National Crime Agency). The term derives from the fact that litigation takes place in the civil (as opposed to criminal) courts. Specialist legislation is required. This legislation has frequently, but wrongly, been described as 'reversing the burden of proof'. The standard is not reversed, the burden still rests with the competent authorities to prove their accusation, but the *standard* of proof

**Table 14.1:** Proposed levels of asset recovery

| Level | Category | Legislation |
|---|---|---|
| 0 | Conviction-based asset recovery of the instrumentalities used in, or the object of a specific crime or crimes | Available worldwide and routinely applied. |
| 1 | Conviction-based asset recovery of the proceeds of a specific crime or crimes | Available worldwide but 80% of jurisdictions do not use this power, because it is difficult to prove and because no financial investigation is done. |
| 2 | Conviction-based asset recovery of the proceeds of multiple unspecified crimes | 1. Variously called 'extended' or 'enhanced' confiscation applied to specified crime *types*.<br>2. Unexplained wealth *crimes*, these still need to be prosecuted. |
| 3 | Non-conviction-based (NCB) asset recovery of multiple unspecified crimes | Cash forfeiture powers exist at most frontiers worldwide but are seldom used, normally because Customs agencies often have no detective capability. The NCB powers are relatively new globally and seldom used, the main exception being the use of cash forfeiture and (to a lesser extent, civil recovery) in the USA, UK and Ireland. |

needed is lower. They do not need to show that the assets are the proceeds of crime 'beyond all reasonable doubt', but merely on the 'balance of probabilities', or 'probably the proceeds of crime' as normal people would say.

**Administrative cash forfeiture** is commonplace globally and describes a power to seize and forfeit cash which has been found by Customs or frontier police and not been declared by the holder. This power exists *within the frontiers* of the UK and Ireland and may have been an important catalyst for asset recovery success in those jurisdictions. The discovery of very large amounts of cash in the course of exercising criminal search powers has allowed courts to draw a common-sense inference from the circumstances. The absence of a plausible explanation allows administrative forfeiture.

**Other administrative forfeiture.** In addition to cash at the frontier, many countries require elected or civil service public officials to complete declarations of wealth before, during and upon leaving public office. Sanctions for a false declaration can include forfeiture.

## Tax penalties

Some countries can impose a tax settlement that is punitive if a taxpayer has failed to pay their tax as required. The additional sums can be much more than the original tax owed and thereby exceed rates of 100%, making them specifically punitive. The famous Irish Criminal Assets Bureau extracted more money using its tax powers than by its civil recovery powers. Indeed, *criminal* confiscation in the Republic of Ireland after prosecution in the criminal courts has historically been low.

**Litigation against criminals who cannot be convicted** is possible in most jurisdictions. Even civil law jurisdictions can litigate criminal assets even though the owners are deceased, unfit for trial through illness or have absconded.[10]

## Levels of asset recovery: a summary

It is important to understand that Levels 2 and 3 of asset recovery are ***necessary*** because the lower levels are not really operationally effective against dirty money. Level 0 does not even include the

***proceeds*** of crime at all, and Level 1 is virtually useless because the evidence so rarely exists. The levels are also cumulative; as the regimes advance, they retain the previous legal powers and add new capabilities.

## The strange case of the UK National Audit Office

As we noted above, governments are often secretive about asset recovery. This is understandable, since less than 20% of them have 'operationally effective' asset recovery regimes. One of few to be lauded by the FATF and graded as Substantively Effective' is the United Kingdom. The FATF evaluation in 2018 stated:

> The UK recognises the importance of asset recovery and law enforcement agencies consistently pursue civil and criminal confiscation as a policy objective. This finding is based on a review of law enforcement and government policies, strategies, and guidance on confiscation and asset recovery; discussions with law enforcement officials and prosecutors; and case studies illustrating the UK's commitment to confiscation.

Until 2003 the UK had a practically non-existent asset recovery regime, with convicted criminals routinely keeping the proceeds of their crimes. Despite efforts to bolster the law following a failed drugs case in the 1980s,[11] the repeated efforts to improve legislation just did not work as expected. Then the POCA, 2002, transformed the asset recovery process. In the first year of operation the amount recovered went up by over half, and for the next *ten consecutive years*, the UK asset recovery regime broke the previous year's record. The number of criminals and their associates deprived of their ill-gotten gains, once measured in dozens, came to be counted in thousands. In the decade after 2003, £1.2 billion was taken from criminals and associates, in the previous decade it had been just £0.15 billion. A brand new profession of Accredited Financial Investigators was created – the number of accredited financial investigators in London's Metropolitan Police alone went from 25 to nearly

400. Regional Asset Recovery Teams were established in half the country and, despite the public spending cuts precipitated by the economic crash in 2008, the regional network was *expanded* to cover the rest. The Assets Recovery Agency in Northern Ireland was praised in the same way as its more famous equivalent in the Republic of Ireland – the Criminal Assets Bureau. The UK regime was transformed and duly celebrated by the FATF. In between, however, something odd happened.

In 2013, after ten successive years of success, the UK NAO reviewed the *confiscation* regime. We note that confiscation is a subset of asset recovery, but the NAO report's very first sentence asserted, without any evidence, that: 'Confiscation orders are the main way through which the government carries out its policy to deprive criminals of the proceeds of their crimes.' The NAO then ignored the year-on-year success of the regime and failed to conduct any sort of 'before and after' assessment of the POCA. Instead, it simply concluded it was 'not working well enough' and was 'not value for money'.[12] This latter finding was reached despite the NAO's own calculation that the regime turned a 33% profit and the fact that the rest of the criminal justice regime made a total loss (of around £12 billion per year). The report was a peculiarly British act of self-harm.

## The case for global reform

The UK's NAO report is strong evidence against the idea that national governments can be trusted with the global war on dirty money. After all, if a national regime cannot even recognise its own *outstanding* success, how can other regimes learn of good practice? The UK has the highest *level* of asset recovery regime, able to deploy a substantial variety of legal powers and an overall regime rated as one of the best in the world by the FATF. Yet its own government fails to realise, celebrate and support it. Powerful legislation has been undermined by weak resourcing of the relevant agencies. A more global approach is needed and perhaps a new philosophy of how asset recovery fits into the war on dirty money.

We offer a different way of looking at asset recovery. We suggest that money laundering is integral to every predicate crime. This is how criminals view it and we agree; there is no point in doing the crime unless you get to keep and enjoy the money. In this sense, the total of predicate crime *equals* the total of money laundering, no more and no less. This agrees with the concept of parallel investigation promulgated by the FATF, where the criminal investigation has equal parallel status with the financial investigation of the assets. We want to take this one step further and suggest that the proceeds of crime equate to both predicate crime and money laundering. They are just three different ways of describing the same phenomenon, as any one of these categories rise or fall the others do too, in equal measure:

$$\frac{\text{Predicate}}{\text{crime}} = \frac{\text{Money}}{\text{laundering}} = \frac{\text{Proceeds}}{\text{of crime}}$$

The significance of this idea is that money laundering is a way of evaluating crime and that asset recovery of the proceeds of crime is a way of controlling it. The *asset recovery* of the proceeds of crime should have much greater importance in the war on crime and dirty money.

This proposition also agrees with 83% of the Northern Irish public, who (when they were finally asked) thought that 'wealth confiscation and a prison sentence are equally important objectives'. Our current approach to crime is driven by incarceration as the primary deterrent, but we suggest that, in the modern world, asset recovery is at least as important. We accept, of course, that the majority of the money made from crime is spent on living expenses (much like legitimate income), but whatever is left is capable of being recovered. The executive preamble to the UK POCA had this to say:

> Leaving illegal assets in the hands of criminals damages society. First, these assets can be used to fund further criminal activity, leading to a cycle of crime that plagues communities. Second, arrest and conviction alone are not enough to clamp down on crime; they leave criminals free to return to their illegal enterprises, or even to continue their 'businesses' from prison. And third, it simply is not right in modern Britain that millions of law-abiding people work hard to earn a

living, whilst a few live handsomely off the profits of crime. The undeserved trappings of success enjoyed by criminals are an affront to the hard-working majority.[13]

Asset recovery is the ultimate measure of our success in the war on dirty money and by that measure, according to Dr Ron Pol's research, we are losing big time.

## This needs more work

The simple comparison between the amount being made from crime and the amount recovered shows that there is a mountain to climb. Dr Pol's estimate for the highly successful British regime suggests a recovery rate of just 0.1%.[14] He cites the opinion that, in the UK, 'if the system overall is so badly broken, then mere tinkering and tuning is worse than useless'.[15]

We do not dispute the research, but we do query the conclusion. The evidence of public opinion and the view of financial investigators, prosecutors and policy makers is that asset recovery is *likely* to have an impact on criminal behaviour. We think that the gap between these two positions can be, at least partially, bridged by considering the *nature* of the recovery, rather than the numerical disparity. Confiscation orders after conviction are made in court years after financial investigations were started, the *enforcement* of confiscation orders happens even later. Individual criminals have had years to get used to the idea of losing the money, the impact on a person's behaviour of a judge imposing a confiscation order is likely to be negligible.

What matters is the *seizure and freezing* of assets at the start of the confiscation process. There is almost no research at all on the impact of seizing assets; much of which is cash. Almost a quarter of assets confiscated each year in Britain's (largely cashless) society is of folding money, an astonishing £55 million,[16] forfeited from 3,500 individuals.[17] For each individual, this is an immediate and substantial loss of the proceeds of crime, without warning and rarely returned, yet its impact is unknown. Imagine for a moment that you are the courier for a serious organised criminal and the police have just seized and confiscated the cash you were transporting. On a scale of one to ten for the gravity of the situation, we just hit ten, didn't we? We think that the impact of seizing or freezing vehicles, real estate and bank balances may also be serious. We do not know, there is no research at all on this crucial topic. Surely some of the US$210 billion spent on preventing money laundering every year could be spared to find out.

## Solutions toolbox

- The FATF's current New Methodology for evaluating the effectiveness of confiscation helps a single country to improve between evaluations. The process is clear and transparent. However, that effectiveness can only be improved within a country's own legal framework. The framework itself is not judged against a global standard, because no standard exists. Its ability to cooperate with another country's legal regime is also not judged, because there is no comparative standard for regimes.
- By adopting a simple and comparable standard based on an ideal legal framework, the FATF would be able to measure effectiveness against that standard. The standard would also clarify a regime's ability to cooperate with other regimes. Any two regimes at different levels can only cooperate at the lower of the two levels, that is, a high-level regime and a moderate-level regime can only cooperate at the moderate level. The higher-level regime cannot deploy its true strength in the battle against dirty money. Ultimately, this means that criminals keep their money in weak confiscation regimes, fatally undermining the global effort to fight crime.
- This chapter sets out a way to define a confiscation regime simply and consistently by four standard levels of what a legal framework can achieve. Adopting these standard levels into the FATF Methodology would bring added consistency to the evaluation process. It would also create a meaningful way to assess international cooperation in this vital area.
- The confiscation of the proceeds of crime should be given much more prominence than confiscating the instrumentalities of crime. Indeed, perhaps the basic ability to recover instrumentalities and the object that has been stolen should be disregarded altogether in FATF evaluations.

- In the world of asset recovery 'what you seize is what you get'. Much greater emphasis should be applied to assets being legally frozen or seized at the start of the criminal investigation process to limit criminals' opportunity to avoid true justice.
- Finally, more empirical research is required on the impact of asset recovery on the behaviour of existing criminals, on public confidence in government agencies and asset recovery's ability to deter predicate offending. This should include research into different types of asset recovery and different predicate crimes.

## A shock to the global system

If asset recovery and confiscation are the poor relations in the war on dirty money, under-researched, under-valued and given up, by some, as a lost cause, then the next chapter is a true contrast.

In 2001, the world was rocked by the tragic events of 9/11. The world of AML was suddenly thrust into the limelight as the terrorist attack on that day suddenly focused us all on the relationship between crime and money.

# 15

# Countering the financing of terrorism: money laundering in reverse

> Are they relatives ... ? No, they are not even from the same planet.
>
> The authors

The comfortable world of AML was pottering along in a backwater of global public policy when 9/11 suddenly turned that world upside down. The attack on the World Trade Center in New York had clearly been planned for months if not years and it had been *financed*. It was clear to everyone that there was a link between the crime and the money, but what was it and what could be done about it?

Financial intelligence could have flagged up foreign nationals taking flying lessons. Financial links to previous known suspects and previous attacks could have been better harvested and passed to law enforcement agencies. But the attack, its precursors (in East Africa) and its suspects' movements had been tracked all across the world from Malaysia to Yemen and from Pakistan to California. A global approach was needed to harness such information. A global system already existed to identify finances which were the proceeds of crime after the event, so identifying finances before a criminal event was sort of similar. The same players were involved: banks and financial investigators. The same techniques would be used: financial analysis to detect unusual transactions, the freezing of assets pending investigation. The same preventative methods could be deployed: compliance with Recommendations likely to assist with identifying suspect people and entities. It was just like AML, only in reverse, pre-facto not post-facto.

Of course, terrorism was not new, but the idea of addressing terrorism through finance was relatively new. Two years before, in 1999, the United Nations had agreed a 'Convention for the suppression of the financing of terrorism'. The UN had failed to agree on a definition of terrorism, and we are not going to attempt to do so here. The Convention text referred to previously agreed conventions relating to terrorist-type crimes: bombings, hostage taking and the hijacking of aircraft and ships. For our purposes, in this book on dirty money, the key points are that terrorism is widespread around the world, some of the financing is dirty money derived from crime and the main technique to tackle it is closely linked to the war on dirty money. The fact that the 9/11 attacks were terrorist attacks on the Western world and the response was a kick-start to global financial compliance to counter crime is reason enough to explore the topic.

## The global war on terror

The Western world is currently fixated by what it calls Islamic terrorism, but separatist terrorism in Europe, specifically in Ireland and Spain, has a long history. Many countries across the world have their own separatist issues, which can manifest as terror attacks intended to alter government policy towards minorities, who feel otherwise ignored or persecuted. There is also terrorism that is less easy to categorise or even understand; consider the anarchist terrorists in 1960s' Italy and Germany, the sarin attacks in Japan in 1995 or Somali pirate hijackings which were a response, essentially, to economic deprivation of inshore fishermen. Terrorism against civilian targets has been a global phenomenon for well over a hundred years and looks as if it is here to stay, but the use of financial intelligence to combat it is relatively recent.

This book is concerned with the financing of terrorism and, in particular, the relationship between AML and Combating the Financing of Terrorism, commonly known by the acronym 'AML/CFT'. The well-known acronym is used by hundreds of thousands of people as part of a huge effort to comply with Recommendations to 'do' AML and CFT. Following the 9/11 attacks, the formal link from CFT to AML was made as swiftly as possible. Within three weeks an extraordinary plenary meeting of the FATF, held on 29–30 September 2001, agreed to come up with guidance for financial institutions. This was issued in April 2002 and the FATF added to its core business (of evaluating global compliance with its 40 Recommendations) an additional nine *Special* Recommendations. We should probably note that two years before 9/11 the link between the UN Convention in 1999 and AML was **not** made by the FATF. We think that this is an important point. A repeating feature of the war on dirty money is that activity is often driven forward by extreme political events and, in between those events, the progress in the war is quite static. That is not to say that nothing is happening, it is just less easy to see. In fact, in the years before 9/11 the competent authorities and the FATF had been making steady progress. When the war on terror was launched by US President Bush in a speech to both houses on 21 September 2001, the FATF membership was well able to respond to his call to "starve the terrorists of funding", and its global reach meant it was also well placed to respond in all of the 80 nations whose citizens "died with our own".[1]

## From AML to CFT

The first efforts to tackle drug finance in the UK had created the 'Drug Desks' – small teams of investigators with rudimentary training in finance were created in 1989 to work alongside police drug enforcement teams. By the mid-1990s it was realised that financial intelligence could be used – and was used – to solve murders, sex crimes and indeed any crime. It was a way to find out from a desktop what was in a known suspect's wallet. From an investigative perspective, this is an *incredibly* useful way to connect people to places, to events or to other people. *Any* crime could be approached in this way. The financial intelligence development officer courses were a revelation for the detectives who attended them from 1997 onwards. The organisation (London's Metropolitan Police Service) was less quick on the uptake, but the groundwork to create and develop courses, train trainers and establish operational expertise was done, in a way, despite the leadership not because of it. This was very useful indeed when the need arose to gear up capacity both for the new war on terror launched after the 2001 attacks and the new ability to confiscate criminal assets created by the POCA, 2002. The Met Police was able to call on a large reserve of trained people as soon as the POCA came into force, long before the formal training was designed, and later delivered, by the new Assets Recovery Agency.

This is an important feature of the war on dirty money; it is the practitioners who have driven the 'operational effectiveness' in most countries. The UK was far from being alone. In 2000, practitioners from all over Europe and North America gathered in the Camden Court Hotel, Dublin and created the idea of an informal network designed to make international asset recovery work, despite the barriers created by national governments at their frontiers. The practitioners named the new idea after the hotel they stayed in: the 'Camden Asset Recovery Interagency Network' (CARIN). Since then, this practitioner network has multiplied across the world, via regional networks modelled on the 'CARIN' original, made by practitioners for practitioners.[2] As ever with the war on dirty money, the leadership was typically following not leading, but it did support a formal secretariat for CARIN, which is still based at Europol two decades later.

## A new front in the war on dirty money

The result of this practitioner-led initiative for the UK was that trained 'financial intelligence officers' already existed in the 1990s. They had already been deployed against all sorts of crimes including terrorism, so when the kick-start of 9/11 happened there were plenty of human resources available to deploy. This was because it was already understood that information sharing with the financial sector could be used against any crime, and terrorism is a crime. It was also understood that the very best detectives could be quickly trained as financial investigators and these officers quickly found that financial intelligence was a very versatile and operationally satisfying tool to use against criminals. A new profession was being born and the war on terror provided a well-resourced opportunity for its worth to be demonstrated. Many far-sighted officers could see that the new profession would open up new career opportunities that included the opportunity to travel, transfer and progress in different agencies or move over into the financial sector. At the time, London's Metropolitan Police had national responsibility for counterterrorism, and it had already formed a small Financial Investigation and Special Access Centre, as part of Special Branch for this purpose.[3]

The legislation was catching up. The UK Terrorism Act, passed in the summer of 2000, created an offence – to fund-raise for terrorism – a specific objective for financial investigators to work towards. The events of 9/11 and the fear of a repeat attack increased management interest in financial investigation and the Special Branch unit multiplied in size and became the National Terrorist Financial Investigation Unit – the teams that were needed to deploy against the new threat. Entirely coincidentally, the POCA in 2003 gave an equal if not bigger boost, to financial investigation, as the sudden ability to really tackle organised crime became a reality and new opportunities for operational effectiveness became possible.

## An unhappy marriage

The superficial similarities between AML and CFT around staff, techniques and general purpose made the FATF decision to take on CFT understandable; a marriage of convenience, if you will, but not a happy one. From an operational perspective, there is very little coordination between units investigating the proceeds of crime and units investigating the financing of terrorism. There are several reasons for this. One is a matter of priority, the sudden devastating harm to the public of a terrorist attack trumps every other 'predicate' crime on the FATF list. One might argue that some of the crimes against the environment are more harmful in the long term or that the scourge of tax evasion is more damaging to the fabric of society, but the operational reality is that even a small terrorist attack will take up every available leadership and investigative resource. Second, terrorism is often a matter of national security and, until the contrary is proved, a terrorist incident is seen as an attack on the government and consequently all its resources will be made available to respond. With the national security designation comes a degree of secrecy. The need to control information for operational reasons necessitates vetted staff, secure private communications and media control. While this is obvious against the backdrop of an actual attack, this reality means that all counterterrorism teams operate in this way all of the time. This means that counterterrorism does not, in fact, mix with countering crime. CFT and AML do not, in fact, work together but side by side or indeed, just nearby. If you wanted some evidence of this operational separation, the contemporaneous investigation of the events leading up to 9/11 itself provide ample evidence. The different approaches of the Central Intelligence Agency and the Federal Bureau of Investigation led to catastrophic failure. This is dramatically portrayed in the TV series *The Looming Tower* and is the subject of more forensic analysis in the damning 9/11 Commission Report.[4]

The separation of the AML and CFT investigations begins at the beginning, with how SARs are handled. These are the building blocks for almost all AML/CFT investigations, and the reality is that most FIUs routinely sift out the ones believed to relate to terrorism for dissemination to the appropriate counterterrorism unit. Only after that process does the remainder get looked at for its relevance to other predicate crime.

The AML/CFT investigations begin separately and stay separate. It is true that initial training will be the same, but thereafter the whole process is operationally separate, done by different teams, managed by different managers. The two investigations only join together where the terrorism is funded by crime. This is not as often as you might think.

## One man's terrorist is another man's freedom fighter

At a global level, the war on terror (and therefore the war on countering terrorist finance) has a clear leader. The United States produces annual 'Country reports on terrorism' and the latest one describes itself thus: 'Amid this diverse and dynamic threat landscape, the United States continued its long-standing role as the world's counterterrorism leader, taking decisive action to combat these threats and rallying its allies and partners to contribute to the fight.'

There are some international terror organisations that justify the global approach, in the sense that they would be difficult to tackle by a single country. Examples include the Haqqani Network[5] and the Islamic State of Iraq and the Levant.[6] This type of international organisation is difficult for one country to address. This is especially so in countries where the organisation enjoys a – more or less – supportive environment because of the resident community. The national authorities there are inevitably compromised in these circumstances. In other countries, these organisations are helped by their ability to register anonymously owned entities which can, in turn, facilitate the international movement of assets and people for terrorist purposes. In effect, countries that allow anonymously owned entities to be registered are providing a more or less supportive environment; the national authorities there are inevitably compromised in these circumstances.

The US 'Country reports on terrorism' confirms that the battlefield of terrorist finance is really fought country by country. We think that it is much like the war on dirty money in this respect. Furthermore, the closer you look at each country, the more confusing the battleground appears. In relation to terrorism emanating from separatist communities they frequently perceive that they are economically disadvantaged by the government from which they wish to separate. It is a chicken and egg situation. Economically active community members may have limited opportunities in the legal economy. Informal employment which is unregulated and untaxed is more likely to blur with activities that are criminal. The government, already hostile to its separate community, may well choose to act against such criminality. It is easy to see how things can get confused and then out of control. Where is the line between businesses and the diaspora contributing to 'the cause' and extortion in support of terrorism? In an informal economy, it may be hard to tell, particularly when the information in the public domain has been gathered by the government's own security forces.

The main difficulty connecting AML to CFT is that terror attacks are quite cheap; three quarters of attacks analysed in Europe cost under US$10,000.[7] The weapons can include stolen vehicles, which are free, and articles which are legitimate and cheap, such as agricultural fertiliser. Some countries take the view that countering terrorist finance only includes the money spent on attacks, which blunts the efficacy of CFT when 'the operational costs of individual terrorist attacks may be rather low, the costs of sustaining a terrorist organization are not. It has been suggested that only around ten per cent of terrorism financing are devoted to the execution of operations.'[8] 'Sustaining a terrorist organisation' is not dissimilar to sustaining a criminal organisation or indeed any informal organisation. The real costs are just those to sustain people – accommodation and living expenses. The sources of these are frequently 'normal', derived from wages or welfare. Terrorists are sustained by belief not money, they are generally cheap to run. A study of 40 jihadi terror cells in Europe concluded that 73% of them 'generated income from legal sources, and the most common income source was the salaries and savings of cell members'.[9]

The war on terror stemming from 9/11 had some of the characteristics of a culture clash rather than a war. *Hawala* banking was implicated as a possible vehicle for terrorist finance and *Zakat* was also portrayed as a possible disguise for supporting terror. Neither was made illegal though, for the excellent reason that they serve a public good. Hawala banking provides a community-based way to transfer money abroad based on trust. It does the same as international banking or Western-style Money Transmitters; the difference is that it is very cheap and because it is based on community trust, requires minimal external regulation. Hawala is extensively used by poor Islamic migratory workers who choose not to use expensive methods to send money home. It could easily be viewed as a threat by the Western financial sector. Meanwhile, '*Zakat* (giving to the poor) in Islam is not an arbitrary charity nor a supererogatory donation handed out according to each benefactor's wish. On the contrary, it is an obligatory *fard* (an act decreed by God Himself, Senturk, 2007)'.[10]

The clash has had an unfortunate, unintended consequence: 'There has been a noted decrease in the fundraising income of legitimate Islamic NGOs since the 9/11 attacks. ... It is ironic that attempts to close down or control formal NGOs have had precisely the opposite effect by forcing charitable giving into less regulated channels.'[11]

## State-sponsored terrorism

We are not all in this together, however. Some countries are chasing the finances of people and entities and other countries are refusing to help them. Some countries, notably Iran and Syria, have been publicly accused by the USA and its allies of actually sponsoring terrorism. Hiding in the shadows are some small countries allowing anonymously owned entities to be registered, thereby facilitating terrorism. We even have governments that will not act against another country even though it believes that it is sponsoring terrorism, but does allow individuals to take such action. This last example sounds bizarre but in 2012 Canada passed the Justice for Victims of Terrorism Act, whereby individual victims of terrorism could claim the assets of designated state sponsors of terrorism. Using this law, individuals successfully sued Iran and in 2021 enforced the sale of Can$28 million worth of real estate in Ottawa and Montreal.[12] The case was based on the idea that because Iran had been declared a 'designated' state by Canada (along with Syria) and it had sponsored Hamas and Hezbollah, victims of those two organisations could sue Iran. This feels like Canada passing government responsibility to individuals, but it is not dissimilar in concept to the US government allowing individuals to sue criminals under the Racketeer Influenced and Corrupt Organisations law of 1970.

We also have governments that use CFT legislation for purposes that look more like political gain than crime prevention. In September 2018, Egypt used CFT legislation to:

> seize assets belonging to 1,589 Muslim Brotherhood supporters or alleged sympathizers, as well as 118 companies, 1,133 NGOs, 104 schools, 69 hospitals, and 33 websites and TV channels with alleged ties to the banned organization. These confiscated assets—as much as 60 billion Egyptian pounds ($3.4 billion) according to some reports—were transferred directly to the Egyptian Treasury.[13]

### Sanction, what sanction?

A major part of the war on terror at a global level is the ability to freeze the assets of people and entities using the UNSCR 1373 which criminalised the financing of terrorism, enabled the freezing of assets, improved mutual legal assistance between countries and the use of Suspicious Activity Reporting (by the financial sector to law enforcement). The Resolution, passed in 2001, sounds tough:

All States shall:

(a) Prevent and suppress the financing of terrorist acts;
(b) Criminalize the wilful provision or collection, by any means, directly or indirectly, of funds ... used, in order to carry out terrorist acts;
(c) Freeze without delay funds ... of persons who commit, or attempt to commit, terrorist acts ... of entities owned or controlled directly or indirectly, etc.

To give the reader an idea of scale, at the time of writing, 289 individuals and 89 entities were listed. The effect of the listing enables, indeed requires, that financial institutions notify the local FIU so that it can freeze assets of customers on the list.

There are some issues, however. The UNSCR allows countries to call on the help of other countries to freeze assets, but this can be refused. For example, the Indian Ministry of Home Affairs continues to freeze the assets of Kashmiri and Sikh terrorist groups, but there is nothing it can do to ensure that these entities' assets are frozen in Pakistan.

There is also an imbalance of resources being applied nationally:

Whereas the US Treasury Office of Foreign Assets Control has more than 100 staff working full time on implementation of financial sanctions, the Bank of England had a staff of about seven, the French Ministry of Finance has two people working part-time, the German Bundesbank had one, and the European Commission in Brussels had only one person and a half-time assistant (Greenberg).[14]

Finally, there is the issue of implementation, the actual freezing of any assets. To explore this the UN conducted a comprehensive review in 2008 of the implementation of the Resolution.[15] The survey was global and assessed the legislation, the implementation of CFT, border control, domestic security and law enforcement agencies and international cooperation.

The report summarises the first seven years of effort: 'Over recent years, States have introduced a vast array of legal provisions and policies, established dozens of institutions and trained thousands of officials worldwide in measures aimed at combating terrorist financing. However, effective implementation remains elusive.'

The report lacks *any* statistics about the actual freezing of assets, still less their confiscation.

As an example of the sanctions regime, consider the UK. The FATF has evaluated the operational effectiveness of the sanctions regime in around 120 countries and the UK is one of just three countries regarded by the FATF as 'highly effective' at CFT, along with the USA and Israel.[16] The UK's CFT regime used to be independently reviewed by a senior lawyer. In his last report, published in 2015, David Anderson QC remarked that 'the figures for assets frozen are remarkably low', although they were in fact consistent with the previous three years, with a median figure of around £100,000.[17] There were no figures for confiscation. The regime is not currently subject to specific review; Mr Anderson's work is, presumably, considered done.

In the war on terrorism the CFT regime is important in terms of financial intelligence to identify terrorists and their supporters. This activity involves thousands, perhaps tens of thousands, of people worldwide and their efforts have undoubtedly prevented terrible crimes, disrupted financial support and acted as a significant deterrent. Financial investigation is also one of the few ways to tackle this crime, being far cheaper, quicker and better than other methods of tackling organised crime, as we have remarked before.

This book, however, is about the war on dirty money and the fact is that terrorism does not cost very much and does not generate any dirty money. Consequently, in the war on dirty money, CFT is an outlier, almost a fringe activity. It has, however, made one very significant contribution to our understanding of AML.

As a result of 9/11, CFT shone a sudden light on the policy backwater that is AML, and this is important. Over the last 20 years since those terrible events, we can look at the war on dirty money through the prism of CFT. We can observe that for terrorism, one of the most important crime priorities on the planet, criminal justice, particularly international justice, is once again, woefully lacking.

## Solutions toolbox

- On balance, CFT brings a benefit to the war on dirty money. The utility of CFT against terrorism provides a shining example of how the same investigative techniques, applied with more resources, could be so much more successful against crime than they are now.
- The continuing presence of CFT shines a light on its impoverished partner AML. The grossly inadequate resources available for fighting crime compared to the limitless resources spent combating terrorism are a persistent and useful reminder of the inequality in the overall system.
- For this reason, we think that the AML/CFT marriage should continue and be celebrated.

To try to counter this shortfall, the FATF has, since 2012, tried to encourage countries to conduct NRAs for AML/CFT within the realm of national security. Let us see how they are doing.

# 16

# National security vs the threat of money laundering

> It is difficult to get a man to understand something when his salary depends upon him not understanding it.
>
> Upton Sinclair – candidate for Governor of California 1935[1]

If Ben Bradlee, an editor at the *Washington Post* during the US Watergate scandal was right when he said, 'It is my experience that most claims of national security are part of a campaign to avoid telling the truth', then discussing money laundering as a threat to national security needs to be included in this book.

Bradlee's statement suggests by attributing national security to any topic, it then becomes too sensitive to discuss openly in public. Any such move then to resolve it must require sensitive management and coordination at the highest levels of government administration. So, does this now mean telling the truth about money laundering is so awful that it has to be attributed as a threat to national security to protect us? Yet is money laundering really a threat to national security? Maybe it once was, but with such vast amounts of 'dirty money' now in circulation, has the threat simply gone away? Has the threat dispersed to such a point that it is hard to pinpoint where the actual threat to national security is now coming from?

With the lack of tangible knowledge on money laundering as it is happening today, as discussed in Chapter 3, it is still easy to believe money laundering has a significant bearing on national economies. This is regardless of it being attributed as a customary practice of most serious crimes. Nevertheless, attributing money laundering to national security seems to be all too easy for the policy writers, government officials and those who navigate the direction of AML/CFT compliance regimes.

Of course, there are many definitions of national security, each one we suggest relating back to the reasons by which it was created. Still, it is possible to generically determine national security as 'a nation state's ability to protect or defend its people'. So where then is the evidence that money laundering is a threat to national security? Is it with suggestions like those of the IMF who have estimated money laundering comprises approximately 2–5% of the world's gross domestic product (GDP) each year, or approximately US$1.74–US$4.35 trillion in 2019? Or is it because there is little distinction as to the effect money laundering can have on individual states, or its ability to cause unfair distribution of wealth? After all, these are problems which apparently have disastrous consequences for a state's economy and the well-being of its citizens.

Suggestions that money laundering is such a fundamental problem can also go as far as saying that the reputation of a state can drastically decline if there is suspicion of secrecy and corruption, meaning foreign investment can also waver. Equally, money laundering can be considered a threat because it takes funds out of the economy, increasing pressure on legitimate businesses and individuals. It is also suggested that money laundering diverts funds that would otherwise be used to support social services. So, perhaps the lack of clarity and assorted reasons are why we still have no clear idea about the amount of illicit funds continually slipping past the efforts of law enforcement, regulators and the private sector. Equally, all this confusion could be the result of secretly acknowledging that the threat of money laundering is still difficult to prove.

Money laundering sits on the shoulders of organised crime, which for a long time has sat alongside terrorism as another familiar threat to national security. Yet, by attributing money laundering to organised crime, policy makers have assigned them as equal threats, thus bypassing the need for individual reasoning. We feel it is perhaps the 'organised' in organised crime that gives greater credibility to the threat posed by money laundering on a nation state. In doing so, it allows nations to then deploy an 'organised' response of continually creating AML/CFT legislation, policies and risk assessments.

Take a dispassionate attitude to the statements provided by policy makers and pundits and you will realise dirty money is, in fact, everywhere. Essentially, dirty money is changing economies, altering political power and allowing the rich to get richer. Much of it can be sourced through appalling scenarios involving human trafficking and quieter activities such as fake commodities, environmental crimes and slavery, but equally through tax evasion and corruption. Yet, since we know where dirty money typically comes from, it is also possible to separate the frequently bundled together crime types into *organised crime type crimes* and *the behaviours of wealthy individuals and corporations*. However, what is still absent from all the discussions that take place is *how* money laundering as a specific crime is exclusively a threat to national security.[2] What seems to have happened is that money laundering, through its links to organised crime, has been thrown into the mix of problems too hard to tackle head on.

Despite the lack of clarity, perhaps money laundering is a threat to national security in some other way. Or, as we believe, unfortunately inferences were drawn too quickly as to the magnitude of the problem of money laundering, and they have stuck with us ever since. This suggests that, today, there is no appetite to challenge existing perspectives because, in doing so, the solutions may need a firmer national response. We know terrorism and organised crime are inextricably linked since terrorists can use illegal activities to fund their endeavours. While this may be factually correct and supported by case study examples, the evidence behind many of these assessments is based on a nexus which is not always critically examined in detail. The problem has now arisen that money laundering is simply just another egg in the basket called *national security*. Yet it is the guilty by association with the other eggs in the basket – terrorism, organised crime, the financing of nuclear proliferation and threats from state-sponsored attacks on corporate or national infrastructures – that causes the greatest worry.

## Complicating simplicity

Guilty by association it may appear to be, but has money laundering had a fair trial? Perhaps many will immediately say 'of course' referring back to government policy and risk documents insinuating money laundering is a threat to national security and suggesting, "Well why wouldn't it be? It's obvious it is". Whatever the justifications given, advocates for money laundering are unlikely to see a retrial anytime soon. The main reason for this is that by attributing national security to the problem of money laundering, there is then stronger reasoning for what follows – whether this be more legislation, widespread policies or technical solutions.

The novel measures for determining money laundering values, either nationally as a percentage of GDP or internationally as a figure of illicit financial movement, are, as we recognise, frequently mentioned. Equally, proceeds of crime figures can be added to promote AML/CFT priorities. Yet these amounts are typically only used to justify the policies, recommendations and legislative requirements now focusing on money laundering. What they fail to do, is describe a picture of money laundering in today's world. Equally, the figures and reasonings provide almost no scope to refute the idea that money laundering is a complex, technical and hard to comprehend problem. While we acknowledge an oversimplification of money laundering could cause some to cough and splutter and others to loudly shout obscenities at such an inkling, there is a need to do so. If the act of money laundering really is a threat to national security, then understanding money laundering in its simplest form needs to first take place. If this can be done, we may just see it is in the initial crime types where the threat to national security originates and thus remains.

Whether it is the vulnerability of a country at attracting illicit proceeds or a lawless environment, the seriousness of money laundering as a stand-alone activity largely appears to be ignored. Is this why there is less of a direct and level-headed approach to the problem in some countries? Why particular countries are more susceptible to money laundering is also rarely considered. The result of this is a generic assessment that fails to help tackle the problem of money laundering at the front line. We also think this is because composite indicators, those statistical tools which could enable researchers to describe money laundering quantitatively through its measurable components, remain woefully absent. There is also scarcity of evidence to support the argument that due to globalisation and technology, illicit money could move everywhere. Nor do we have evidence as to whether countries with high money laundering vulnerabilities really do attract foreign (or external) money laundering threats. All these factors help to muddy the waters as to whether money laundering is a threat to 'a nation state's ability to protect or defend its people'.

Is it therefore possible that there are actually benefits to having the problem of money laundering to contend with? We are not suggesting money laundering is allowed to take place, nor are we suggesting it is wilfully ignored. What we are questioning is why there is less interest in understanding money laundering than there is towards creating AML/CFT compliance solutions. It could be as Upton Sinclair – a then candidate for Governor of California 1935 – said, "It is difficult to get a man to understand something when his salary depends upon him not understanding it". Although the evidence is there, money laundering is never considered as simply a series of *transfers and purchases* throughout the purge of IT solutions now flooding the AML/CFT compliance markets worldwide. Instead, to support these profitable activities, money laundering is always catalogued into intimidating, cumbersome and mystifying typology reports. The mystique surrounding money laundering then helps to link it back to a threat to national security.

Even if money laundering is a threat to national security – it is unlikely to be a national security threat of every country. With cultural, social, and even criminal differences among 200 countries, any such universal statement is difficult to imagine. Add in the differences in flows of illicit funds and no two countries can be judged as being comparable. Yet by complicating money laundering to the extent of attributing it to national security makes the idea of preventing money laundering a whole lot easier to argue for. The obligation is simply for every country to follow the FATF's standards in full, no matter their individual status – something expressed by David Lewis (former Executive Director of the FATF) in March 2021 when he said, '[I]f everyone implemented the standards we already have, then we'd all be doing much better'.[3] However, should there also be a stronger focus on *to whom, why, how* and *when* the threat is truly relevant? If, just for a moment, the threat was universal, surely the origins and movement of the illicit funds would have an influence? What then would the consequences be and to whom?

So, is it then possible that the process of money laundering is a threat to national security only if the wealth is 'used' where it was generated? Or is the threat bigger for a country where illicit funds are moved through, moved to, or used to support further criminal activities – as opposed to being used for purchasing real estate. Is this why the FATF NRA process advocates adoption of the FATF's Recommendations (the 40 tick-boxes) rather than understanding the environment in which they must be implemented? As a national obligation, the NRA process, even though it is not unanimously implemented, purposely adopts the material provided by the FATF.

Once again, if money laundering is a threat, then how should countries gauge its scale? The issue is not the threat of money laundering as a 'value', as we know these are simply guesstimates, sometimes educated, sometimes chosen figures to express increased severity of the problem to support a policy creation. What we are not told is just how big the money laundering egg is and how it relates in size to the other eggs in the national security basket. It seems to be a case of 'it's in the basket, nothing more to discuss'.

Worryingly, this very lack of clarity and an overcomplication of money laundering practices may then be part of the sustained appeal by advocates for AML/CFT compliance solutions. Does, as the late Steve Jobs (co-founder of Apple Inc.) was once quoted as saying, "If you define the problem correctly, you almost have the solution" ring truer in this instance than many would prefer to acknowledge? Perhaps yes, but the appeal of AML/CFT may also sit comfortably with many politicians. This may be the reason why there have been few attempts to examine what the issues really are or to finally define the actual problems. Keeping the issues broad, choosing not to determine specific threats no doubt reduces the likelihood of questions on topics which would normally expect to have evidence supporting them. Consequently, general statements can lessen any potential accusations of failure being addressed towards sectors, people and policies. Linking national security to money laundering has become a way of saying 'it's important and that something is being done about it'. Yet no one can say what or even why because it is now a state secret – albeit disproven.

## Simply servants to a policy

The AML/CFT policy in many countries is not unique, nor is it dissimilar to other policies. All it does is follow or more appropriately replicate the FATF's global wishes via the 40 Recommendations. Associating money laundering to national security then provides more emphasis on the AML/CFT obligations at the state, sector and business levels. What this then means is that national AML/CFT policies become more justifiable and predictable, in the same way sheep behave in fields. When one sheep runs (for what appears to be no apparent reason) all others follow. Yet those that follow most likely have no idea why they are running. Perhaps then countries need to start questioning why they aimlessly react and follow the rules set by others year after year. A scenario we call 'the power of the sheep'.

Go back to 2012, when the FATF declared that countries must demonstrate knowledge of the distribution of risks within their jurisdiction. Despite no mention of an NRA until the following year, the release of the FATF NRA guidance document has since been instrumental in adding the national security context. The guidance explained that 'ML and TF activity also causes damage to a country's national security and reputation and has both direct and indirect impact on a nation's economy'. The guidance also listed a series of examples of consequences of money laundering from a 2006 resource. Yet, despite the ten-year period between 2003 and 2013 when there was no specific requirement for an NRA, the guidance managed to provide enough evidence to still push the FATF recommendations within many states' domestic policy. It seemed right then, that the box was then ticked, meaning there needed to be no more questions, no more queries and no excuses found. Money laundering was, from this point onwards, simply a threat to national security and no one thought or dared to question it.

Yet, these same NRAs now depict many concepts. Most lack clear operationalisation details, instead repeating the FATF's guidance definitions and going nowhere near mentioning just *how* threats might be measured. Most NRAs rely on one or two data sources at best, are generally analytically weak and do not explain the method used to actually form the NRA. It appears that these

NRAs are produced as a 'box-checking' exercise – something required by the FATF during Mutual Evaluations. Perhaps this is the real intention. After all, the guidance by the FATF is extremely generic in comparison with the highly prescriptive nature of other FATF documents.

Surely, if a problem existed time and again, the FATF would, by now, have sought to quickly develop a stronger NRA Methodology that would coincide with money laundering's apparent threat to national security. This would be quite different from allowing the NRA to be only an evaluation of the likelihood of money laundering – not an assessment of the consequences. In reality, it seems the current process is all too convenient. The process shows a future in which idle comparison that conveniently fits an argument is now the ideal scenario. If no one dares to question the statements being given about money laundering and national security, then there is clearly no problem. If there is no problem, no one is required to do anything about it.

This process is similar to the addition of 'organic' on labels for vegetables that took many Western countries by storm in the early 2000s. Not only did it suggest superiority of the items, but it also meant you could charge a higher fee. Whether the cost aspect is now for a so-called AML/CFT solution, a consultancy service, a justification for national obligations to be followed, or the fines which follow a failure to comply, the cost has increased. In this case, caused by simply adding 'national security' to anything linked to AML/CFT compliance. Yet, the addition of national security to purposefully bolster policy development on the problem of money laundering and, equally, terrorism financing, is perhaps nothing more than a mischievous ploy. It has formulated a way to add validity, not necessarily provide a tastier, healthier offering which is easier to consume.

We think the adding of money laundering to the national security basket has been a mistake. It is not the illicit funds that have caused the threats to national security, but the predicate offences. If a country has a high rate of predicate crime, then money laundering, as an integral feature of that offending, can easily be explained as a security risk to the country and its people. Where the country is exporting dirty money from drug production (Afghanistan and Colombia as popular examples) or importing money from, say, corruption (UK), the import/export comes at a social cost.

We think this misalignment of the threat is a problem and wonder why this has been too hard to understand or consider in this context. What we are sure has happened, is that the FATF were the first to stand up and say, 'We will take it from here'. The FATF grabbed the entire money laundering problem by 'the scruff of its neck' and marched forward, proposing it as a threat to national security. This worked – it caught the attention of those that needed to sit up and listen. The FATF was then able to make people believe that money laundering was a fundamental problem, not a stand-alone issue. Unfortunately, the wool has well and truly been pulled over the eyes of so many, because from the start no one sought to question the supposed facts; especially where the threat was actually coming from. Was it money laundering or drug use? From then on, state-controlled policy writers have followed the directions of the FATF like lost sheep, largely ignoring the true implications of the predicate offences on a nation's actual security.

## Crime as a benefit

Consider for a moment the notion that crime may be a notable source of benefit to a state and its leaders. It may then come as little surprise that ministers of finance may be willing to welcome FDI without AML/CFT checks. After all, money, no matter where it comes from, can typically be of significant benefit to the recipient. This is not necessarily a case of turning a blind eye, but globally it is known that financial institutions like liquid capital and investment in profitable enterprises. Financial institutions would then be "shocked, shocked I tell you", in the style of Captain Renault (in the film Casablanca) to learn that crime is also a notable source of these benefits, hence why crime may not be such a terrible thing to all.

Seemingly, money still makes the world go round. Yet a question which could then follow to evoke clarity is 'does dirty money make the world spin faster, slower, or simply ensure money remains the catalyst for corruption, greed and huge wealth division across almost all societies?'. One may point out that dirty money, once in the legitimate financial system makes no difference, raises fewer eyebrows as it is merely just more money hidden among all the other money. With so much dirty money now flowing round the world, any idea of singling out the dirty money that is being laundered while confirming it as a specific national security threat is near impossible.

## Ignoring any opportunity

The authors do not doubt that stopping money laundering would save lives. The evidence is plain to see and even repeated indirectly time and again in NRAs, soft and hard policy documents and court proceedings – some of which have been spawned over 30 years. Yet the worrisome point needing to be made here, is that few seek to identify whether the time has also come to stop, reassess and clarify from the ground up to see if what is taking place is working. Perhaps this is not done for fear of being ostracised or ridiculed. After all, willingly standing in the path of an avalanche is unlikely to alter its direction no matter how strong you may feel. We believe the power of the avalanche – the huge force that for many decades has chosen to tackle money laundering – is still too strong to stop. But that does not mean we should give up trying to at least divert it to where we can better manage it.

So, while money laundering may appear on the surface to have the power to damage financial sector reputations, reduce FDI and increase corruption and bribery, beneath the hype, the arguments lack credibility. It is not uncommon for the arguments to be supported by stories of illicit finance, the magnitude and volume linked to large-scale money laundering scandals within the context of national security.[4] Yet, dig a little deeper and what is usually absent is the acceptance that money laundering can never be singled out. We agree money laundering is a problem – but what we struggle to comprehend is how it is the existential global threat we are so often encouraged to believe.

Of course, in many Western-type democracies there is little concern to national security because of issues from money laundering. If there had been, the focus would surely have been a lot stronger on doing more to prevent and investigate it. Perhaps a notion would have come about that it would have been best to tackle the causes of money laundering, those annoying predicate crimes, in the same way, so as to not allow an avalanche to suddenly occur and destroy all that sits in its path. Or simply, it would have been best to introduce measures to stop it from becoming a threat in the first place.

Adding national security to the issue has possibly become the ideal alibi for the failures over the last 30 years. We think now is surely the time to hand over the evidence or drop the severity surrounding money laundering and instead do something meaningful to control and stop it. A new focus is required – a focus on the crimes which are the real threat to national security. Money laundering is simply an enabler of other threats, not in itself a threat to national security.

## Solutions toolbox

- It is time that money laundering, despite the role it plays in furthering criminal behaviours, is no longer heavily associated with threats to national security. Of course, money laundering can have critically influential consequences on a nation state but, as a single activity, money laundering alone is not the issue. After all, money laundering is a series of transfers and purchases, it is the crime which generates the funds in the first place that presents the greatest threat to a state's population.
- Illicit finance should replace money laundering as a threat. 'Illicit finance' takes into consideration all illicitly sourced wealth, not just that resulting from a predicate offence. A play on words admittedly when taking the 'all crimes' definition into consideration. But 'illicit finance' can be better utilised for also emphasising tax evasion alongside more notable crimes such as human trafficking.
- If money laundering must be categorised as a threat to national security, then there needs to be (1) more empirical evidence and (2) evidence as to how it is being tackled. It is no longer appropriate to say it is a threat and that we cannot say too much about how the threat is being managed because it is a state secret. Transparency will improve all efforts focused on reducing money laundering.

While there appears to be a total lack of understanding, if there was ever a solid reason as to why we must tackle money laundering, adding a national security threat association to it would almost certainly be the best outcome. But what if the threats are not the money generated by crime, but instead the money which is not captured by tax systems which damage a nation's economy? Setting aside the obvious threat from terrorism financing when making such a proposition, in the next chapter we will explore this idea more and, in doing so, explain just what the difference between tax avoidance and tax evasion is.

# 17

# Tax avoidance vs tax evasion

Our relationship with tax is complex. We all pay some tax, but we avoid doing so unnecessarily, if we can. National tax authorities devise taxes which are hard to avoid, so we use the word 'avoidance' to describe lawful ways to limit our liability to pay tax, but we say 'evasion' when we are describing the crime of lying to the tax authorities to escape proper tax payment. We use sporting terminology to describe this cat and mouse situation whether it is avoidance or evasion; we say tax 'dodgers' or tax 'cheats'. The word dodge suggests something clever, artful, something we can even approve of; we do not say tax 'criminals'. This is perhaps because, as an ordinary citizen it is hard to say if someone else is avoiding or evading tax. The topic is so complex we rely on the national authorities to make a finding on a case-by-case basis. National tax authorities are generally well equipped with laws and procedures to identify tax evasion within national frontiers.

Globalisation has created the phenomenon of international tax evasion. While this may always have been a problem, the scale of it now has earned a place in this book. The war on dirty money includes a vast amount of unpaid tax, which would have been paid to national treasuries in the past.

Campaigning organisation, the Tax Justice Network, estimates that countries are losing US$483 billion in tax a year to global tax abuse, US$312 billion of this tax loss is due to cross-border corporate tax abuse by multinational corporations and US$171 billion is due to offshore tax abuse by wealthy individuals.[1] They recommend transferring tax convention responsibility from the

Organisation for Economic Cooperation and Development to the UN, and the imposition of an Excess Profit Tax and a Wealth Tax.

The result of this lost tax revenue is catastrophic. Whole populations are deprived of public services – such as hospitals, schools, law and order, old age pensions and welfare support – because the tax revenue that would pay for these has not been paid. The lost tax – US$483 billion – should be added to the cost of attempting to prevent it from entering the international financial system – another US$210 billion. This because it is clear that the lost tax has entered the financial system and that it has been spent on something other than public services. A waste of US$693 billion, and rising, every year. Yet although national tax evasion is a serious crime, *international* tax evasion is not a crime at all. We think it should be a crime and treating it as a crime could be done just by looking at it in a different way. But first, how did we get to this absurd position?

Apart from extremists who think that any tax is theft by the government, the rest of us accept that tax is necessary to buy things that a nation needs: defence against enemies, justice for victims, welfare for the needy, education for the young and so on. Tax is collected by national governments, and it pays for a nation's common good. This has been true since the beginning of recorded tax history (on clay tablets 6,000 years ago in Iraq). Generally, it has been based on a percentage of land or the produce from land. The collection and disbursement of tax revenue has, until relatively recently, been tied to national geography. Historically tax has been calculated on the wealth and/or income attributed to an individual and their perceived ability to pay, and has been imposed by that individual's national government. It is only in the last hundred years or so that we have started to tax companies. More recently still, we have been faced with the reality of multinational companies. While an individual can only legally avoid tax in one country; a multinational company can be seen as an individual that can split itself between two or more countries, thus allowing legal tax avoidance in each country. It is legal and therefore not tax evasion, but we think it could be a different crime.

From a dirty money perspective, the avoidance of tax owed is legal but the evasion of tax owed is illegal. We have earlier established that dirty money is the proceeds of a crime, so a criminal has to commit a crime to make dirty money – the proceeds of crime. Tax is different in the sense that clean money becomes dirty, at the point when it is due to be paid as tax and the payment has, illegally, not been made. The crime is by omission rather than active commission. The tax authorities try to collect the money when it is due, but tax collectors are bean counters not law enforcement officers. Tax collection has always been subject to a cost/benefit calculation. Tax agencies do not want to pursue people without the ability to pay or waste effort pursuing money that is expensive to collect. Tax agencies are judged on the *net* income they collect. This cultural approach works for the general public. Our national approach to tax is based on collection, not enforcement, and so we approach international tax in the same way. The authors think that this is the wrong approach.

This 'tax by consent' approach totally fails against criminals. In the war on dirty money, criminals want to keep their ill-gotten gains, whether they are street robbers or tax evaders. The authorities need to be clear about the difference between avoiders and evaders and to treat them differently. Clean money should be taxed, dirty money should be confiscated. To expand on this idea a bit more, a proportion of clean money should be taxed in an agreed and agreeable way; dirty money cannot be taxed without condoning the crime, so dirty money *has* to be confiscated. There is a moral line between tax avoidance and tax evasion. The true *cost* of confiscation is the price society must pay for fairness and justice and should be categorised in the same way as the cost of a murder investigation or the cost of incarcerating a dangerous offender. All too often, confiscation is regarded as a type of tax, but confiscation is very different from tax. If tax is the price of a civilised society, then confiscation is the price of a crime-free society.

## Avoidance

Taxpayers sometimes try to avoid tax. In ancient times, tax policy makers taxed things that were hard to disguise, such as death and land ownership. Medieval tax avoiders built overhanging upper stories because the tax was calculated on the ground floor area. A few hundred years later, European tax avoiders blocked up their windows to avoid the taxman. This was not to hide from officials, but to reduce the numbers of windows that they counted towards the tax assessment. The rate was sixpence per window for up to ten windows and ninepence for each extra window (an interestingly progressive rate). The British window tax lasted from 1696 to 1851, while the French equivalent was not abolished until 1926. Today's inheritance tax in the UK can be avoided by giving away wealth and then not dying for seven years; this is when gaming the system becomes a dice with death. By far the most common way to try to avoid tax these days is to claim that the thing being taxed is something else, that pays a lower rate of tax. Thus, an individual might claim that income from work was actually a gift; the purchase of boots solely for work might be tax deductible unless they are also used for a walking holiday. The validity of the claim in each case will determine whether it is classed as avoidance or evasion. This gaming of the system is akin to sport. Often the line is crossed into crime, for example paying a tradesperson a cash-discounted price in the expectation that the tradesperson will not declare this as taxable income is, in effect, a conspiracy to evade tax and split the proceeds between the tradesperson and the customer. This kind of behaviour can be controlled in a single country by an efficient tax collection agency able to impose meaningful penalties. In general, this phenomenon is so well known that it has a name, the 'tax gap', the gap between what should have been collected and what was collected. The phenomenon is managed by the tax authorities, and although they do have criminal powers they are seldom used. The gap is considered manageable without recourse to law enforcement and the courts.

## Evasion

The evasion of tax on a sustained basis within a country is quite hard to do. Sooner or later the tax authorities will connect the dots and tax you. This is so well understood that it features in quotable quotes attributed to such luminaries as Benjamin Franklin: "In this world nothing can be said to be certain, except death and taxes" and Mark Twain: "What is the difference between a taxidermist and a tax collector? The taxidermist takes only your skin". Our point here is that national tax systems mostly work; if they do not, then the problem is probably corruption of the tax system rather than the system itself.

## Tax crimes

The evasion of tax due is not the only kind of tax crime. Organised criminals have worked out how to dupe the tax authorities into giving them refunds of tax that was never paid in the first place. This kind of organised crime has attracted much less publicity than the sums involved merit. This is partly because these tax crimes have been badly described. For clarity, the following terms are all the same thing: carousel fraud, Value Added Tax fraud and 'missing trader' fraud. These are all crimes directly against the tax authorities; this is not a loss of taxes that *should* have been paid but tax that is collected from legitimate taxpayers and then *given* to organised criminals *by* the tax authorities because they have been duped into thinking a refund is due. Needless to say, the process is quite involved and complex, but it hinges on the simple fact that tax authorities are required by governments to support businesses by issuing prompt refunds. It is fair to say that the sums involved are so huge that businesses would collapse if genuine refunds of this scale were needed. But the awkward truth is that they are not refunds at all and the tax authorities get scammed in this way all the time. The organised crime gains from this type of crime, in the European Union, is an incredible €60 billion every year, and substantial transfers of billions of euros have been made by all the tax authorities in the EU since at least the mid-1990s.[2] There is an argument that such frauds against the tax authorities should be investigated by a different and independent authority. The fact that the tax authorities are **regularly** deceived makes them at least partially complicit. They are clearly not doing enough to prevent crime, and crime prevention specialists should be called in. Additionally, the tax agency culture of collection works against effective investigation; a cost/benefit approach weakens the investigative resolve. Value for money and efficiency are still required but a cost/benefit philosophy is a distraction from the ruthless focus needed to tackle serious organised criminals. Finally, the narrow experience of tax investigators means that they simply lack the lateral-thinking knowledge of experienced financial investigators. As ever in the war on dirty money, the traditional direct frontal assault fails; investigators need to infiltrate, to find the weak link, to go round the outside, to find the different approach that is needed on a case-by-case basis.

Carousel fraud is not the only way to fool the tax authorities. A similar type of fraud, also involving false tax refunds, handed an estimated €55 billion to organised criminals (€31.8 billion in Germany, €17 billion in France, €4.5 billion in Italy and €1.7 billion in Denmark).[3] The CumEx scandal is so-called because it relates to trading shares which are either valued with (Cum) or without (Ex) the annual dividend. The tax authorities were deceived into paying unwarranted tax refunds by traders hiding the true tax liability in complex, massive and repeated trades. Although designed in London, these false trades started in Germany in the 1990s but were committed in multiple European stock exchanges over many years. Significant criminal trials began in Germany in 2019 and it seems likely that they will run and run. These tax refund cases are such huge amounts of dirty money they deserve a place in this book.

You will note that these offences have been continuing, more or less unchecked, for decades. There is a strong case to review how they are addressed.

## 'Show me the money'

> There is not a crime, there is not a dodge, there is not a trick, there is not a swindle, there is not a vice which does not live by secrecy.
>
> Joseph Pulitzer[4]

There is a widespread belief that 'les paradis fiscaux', as the French so lyrically describe tax havens, are awash with dirty money. It is true that expensive yachts and isolated luxury villas in the Caribbean suggest wealth, but a glance at real estate prices and the cityscapes of London and New York tells us all that the money is in big cities not small islands. It may be that some of the dirty money is in cash or in banks, but any competent adviser – whether dealing in dirty or clean money – will only recommend cash media for short-term holding and transfers. The money is converted into assets such as sumptuous real estate and luxury goods or spent on school fees, city lifestyles and influence that protects the criminals from scrutiny. Otherwise, what would be the point of having dirty money? One of the first cases the author came across was a fraudster who rented a modest house in London. The house was owned by a series of offshore companies, which were painstakingly uncovered by the financial investigator. This mechanism was intended to frustrate confiscation in the long run but more immediately to *avoid* property transfer tax and *evade* income tax (on the rent) and inheritance or capital gains tax on the asset. The ultimate beneficial owner of all the companies and the house, was, of course, the criminal who lived in it. It is *normal* for criminals to keep their assets where they can see them; they just pretend to be offshore. It is a distraction to look offshore. If the public, the media and even the authorities are looking offshore then they will not see the results of tax evasion all around them in their own cities and suburbs. For criminals, that is the point of offshore, not so much the tax savings, although they do help offset the administration costs, but the **secrecy** *that* enables them to hide in plain sight.

This book is about tackling dirty money and it seems that the national competent authorities are being outmanoeuvred by international secrecy, specifically the true ownership of foreign companies. The competent authorities are adept at getting information for enquiries in their own country, but it is much more difficult to make enquiries abroad (despite the best efforts of the CARIN and the like). But some simple anti-secrecy provisions could change everything for every country. It seems incredible to us that a public authority can do any kind of business with an offshore entity without knowing who they are dealing with. There is an obvious risk that the offshore entity could be secretly owned by an official working at, or even directing, the public authority. Public officials could easily be secretly signing off contracts for themselves, relatives, friends, political donors and so on. This corruption risk is obvious, significant and unconscionable. Public authorities should be acting on this right now. If you were in doubt about the importance of secrecy in public contracting, we hope that the recent COVID-19 procurement scandals across the world have helped make this *long-standing problem* crystal clear.

Why not have a law that requires a company in a financial relationship with a public authority to declare its ultimate beneficial owner before any new (or further) business can be transacted? Due diligence by the public authority is not enough – and is a needless public expense – the offshore entity should declare and prove its true ownership under pain of criminal liability. Furthermore, it should be a criminal offence by the authority to receive money without knowing whose it is. This may seem rather dramatic, but it is only fair that criminal liability in order to protect us all, is shared between the procurer and the procured. Secrecy about your personal business is fine, but if you want to do business with the public purse, we all need to know who you are. Secrecy comes at a price and that price is transparency when it is needed. The current situation is absurd and untenable.

The Liechtenstein tax leak (2008) and about half a dozen similar leaks culminating in the Pandora Papers (2021) have demonstrated the dangers of secrecy, as detailed by Oliver Bullough in his book *Moneyland*.[5] This useful term describes not a specific place but a construct of laws that protect the wealthy from scrutiny. The tax evasion, political financing and immoral behaviour that has been revealed by investigative journalists have undermined confidence in political leaders whose private behaviour has contrasted with their public pronouncements. Some have said that this is undermining democracy in the Western world.

An important assumption in the West is that so much secret money is flowing in, that it is materially inflating property prices. It is said that foreigners are buying up so much real estate that local young people cannot buy even a one-bedroom apartment in any major European, North American or Australian city. But what if the foreigners were not foreign at all, but domestic tax-evading criminals? To us this seems not only possible but probable; we urgently need to follow Joe Pulitzer's wisdom and make *unwarranted* financial secrecy illegal.

## The British Empire

This is intended as a global book, but we cannot really talk about the war on dirty money without mentioning the British Empire. Our journey to the present day, when international illicit finance is effectively uncontrolled in any real sense, would be incomplete without talking about the empire. By 1961 most of this empire, which had included a quarter of the world's land and a quarter of its people, had been given, more or less willingly, independence. The remnants of it were a few islands which were not profitable for the UK and yet did not want independence.

In an effort to divest itself of loss-making colonies, London encouraged its Caribbean islands to provide financial services. London had the expertise to establish such enterprises and it could be done with minimal investment. This effort coincided with the creation of UK Corporation Tax in 1965, extending tax beyond real people to companies. The rest, as they say, is history. The expansion of the post-colonial investment in tax havens is well documented as wealthy white colonists sent their money to safety. There is an irony that the new leaders who took over did the same. This tradition from the 1960s and 1970s has continued to the present day. According to Professor Frank Vogl, co-founder of Transparency International:

> The kleptocrats need the enablers because they constantly strive to keep their personal wealth in international, mostly western investment assets. They export their funds because they do not trust their own laws and their wealth could be in jeopardy if they lose their power. They have far greater faith in the integrity of western courts. They move their funds into our markets because, thanks to the skills of the enablers and the insufficiently effective western AML laws and regulations, they can.[6]

What is surprising, is the acceptance by populations of the extraction of this wealth into secret places. This does obvious damage to the common good in both rich and poor countries and yet it has been not only tolerated but literally applauded by enthusiastic audiences of Hollywood movies, which have promoted the glamour of tax evasion for generations (see Chapter 5): "Every society gets the kind of criminal it deserves. What is equally true is that every community gets the kind of law enforcement it insists on" (Robert Kennedy).

## International tax evasion

The traditional claim by those who support the existence of tax havens is that 'it is all legal', which is true of anything, up until the end of the first test case that decides that it is not legal after all. A great deal has been written about how multinational companies manipulate their accounts so that something called 'profit', which is earned in one country, is taxed in another, where the liability for tax is lower (sometimes nil). These intracompany mechanisms to reduce operating profit and shift the money to the low-tax country include expensive loans; charging for the use of a copyright; executive remuneration via shares and similar intracompany transfers. The list of clever mechanisms is, in fact, endless, because as soon as one loophole is closed by the tax authorities another opens. The current drive by tax justice activists is to impose 'country-by-country' reporting. One can only imagine how long that would take to agree and implement. A more direct approach would be to improve accounting standards. There is already a standard to prevent accountants recording something which has no commercial purpose, it may be possible to create a standard requiring accountants not to record an entry in one country if its sole purpose is to manipulate tax liability in another. No doubt a workshop of tax accountants could be divided into groups to work out how to impose this, how to prevent its imposition, how to get around it once imposed and how to maximise their fees for advising about it.

The current problem in the war on dirty money is that national tax authorities have not worked out how to effectively address the twin phenomena of multinational companies (which are a single entity for profit purposes but several entities for tax purposes) and independent countries competing for revenue from those companies. Revenue from companies to national treasuries is not just corporation tax. The British Virgin Islands gains significant revenue from company registration fees, Ireland gets significant investment and employment by hosting multinational companies' headquarters. International tax collection from companies is complicated, but there is a war on dirty money going on, so let us put things on a more wartime footing.

We have pointed out that multinational companies are exploiting national tax authorities, effectively making them into rivals to attract some tax even if it is heavily discounted. This has been called a 'race to the bottom' in terms of tax rates (and tax revenue). We have pointed out a few ways that this is done. Fundamentally, why is it that multinational companies do not adjust their profit by these intracompany transfers in a single country? One answer is that the tax authorities would not let them get away with it and they would be taxed, but there is another answer that opens up an intriguing possibility.

We started this chapter by suggesting that because national tax evasion is a crime, international tax evasion should be a crime too. Many of the multinational corporate schemes used, if done in one country, would be money laundering and tax evasion crimes in that country. The fact that the schemes are not structured in one country is because they would not work for tax purposes. The possible criminal nature of these schemes is not actively considered because it is a theoretical, and therefore untested, notion. We think it should be tested.

We suggest that multiple nations could look again at some of these multinational schemes. We all accept that these are legal schemes in their respective countries, according to tax law. But would they be legal when viewed through the lens of tax evasion and money laundering? We suggest that a different type of expert would reach a different type of conclusion. Criminal financial investigation of some of these complex corporate structures may conclude that there is a case to answer.

At a national level, there is a money laundering typology which perhaps illustrates the conflict between tax collection and criminal confiscation. It is known that some criminals promptly pay their taxes (including back taxes) when they suspect that they are under criminal investigation. Early tax payment is a way to thwart confiscation of 100% of criminal assets in favour of losing a small proportion of those assets to meet the tax bill. Paying tax on a portion of income that has been derived from crime, has the effect of legitimising it. This is because any subsequent effort to confiscate the money would require the prosecution to call the tax staff as witnesses for accepting taxes on the proceeds of crime. This would be awkward and embarrassing, to say the least. In fact, knowingly receiving the proceeds of crime in taxes could be more than embarrassing, it could be a crime committed by the tax authorities. Money laundering is defined as knowingly receiving the proceeds of crime, which may include 'should have known'. Most tax authorities do not have the ability to avoid this specific problem. They lack the necessary access to data, skills, training and legal powers. A significant shift in agency culture is needed. In the war on dirty money, we need much better interagency cooperation between tax and police, of a sort that is often absent from national infrastructures.

We argue that international tax should be looked at in a different way. We need different people to look at the problem. The failure of multinational companies to pay proper national taxes is viewed as an insoluble, complex issue like a modern-day Gordian Knot. International experts – tax justice accountants, revenue collectors and government lawyers – are trying to untie it. They are developing entirely reasonable solutions based on their expertise in their respective fields.

Alexander the Great had none of their attributes, which is why he solved the Gordian Knot by simply cutting it with his sword. In the war on dirty money, we need a warrior to cut through the secrecy that is at the core of this problem. We need someone to say that international tax evasion is a crime and start arresting people.

### Solutions toolbox

- The tax arrangements of multinational companies should be reviewed by international criminal experts, perhaps in a multi-agency setting to maximise diverse expertise.
- National tax authorities should routinely and proactively share information with police and prosecutors, not merely on a case-by-case basis, but as part of a strategic approach to dirty money.
- There is an argument that long-standing types of tax crime should be investigated by different non-tax authorities to see if a different approach is more effective. The French, for example, have mandated that any tax demand, above certain monetary and penalty criteria, must be referred to the prosecutor for investigation.
- Financial investigations should routinely by done by multi-agency teams to avoid single agency narrow thinking and widen the knowledge base.

There is a strong argument to promote the profession of public-sector financial investigator that was created by the UK in 2003 (this was later identified as good practice for promulgation across the EU).

## Conclusion

In this chapter we have asserted that an efficient national tax authority can collect tax adequately in any particular country unless the system itself is corrupted. What if it is corrupted? How does this happen and what can be done? Read on, into the rotten State of Denmark.

# 18

# Corruption: where did all the good apples go?

In the corrupted currents of this world, offence's gilded hand may shove by Justice, and oft is seen, the wicked prize itself buys out the law.

Shakespeare, *Hamlet*, Act 3, Scene 3

Shakespeare suggests that the offender's bag of gold may subvert justice and the law, and, in this chapter, we explore the modern-day crime that not only subverts the 'rotten State of Denmark' but the whole world. At one level, corruption is just an important crime type in the global war on dirty money, but at another it enables many other types of crime, so its importance is amplified. Curiously, it remains undefined. The United Nations Convention against Corruption (2003) has clear definitions of dirty money (the result of corruption offences) and clear definitions of anti-corruption techniques (such as freezing and confiscation), but corruption itself remains elusive. We favour the Transparency International definition of 'the abuse of entrusted power for private gain',[1] but who are we? At the time of writing, eminent university Professors of Corruption – Rothstein (Gothenburg), Stephenson (Harvard) and Barrington (Sussex) – were having a public set-to over whether anti-corruption efforts were measurable or even working at all, via the excellent Global Anti-Corruption Blog, which we commend to those interested in corruption. We make no comment on this debate; we simply observe that it is lively, widespread and unresolved.

Our focus is on dirty money and that means crime. Remember, money laundering depends on a crime being committed. No crime, no laundering. The trouble is that some world leaders are directly involved in corruption, which makes it very difficult for the prosecutors, whom they appoint, promote and pay, to prosecute them for their corruption crimes. Without prosecutors prepared to prosecute corruption, it can appear that there is no corruption in *any* given country. Victims do not usually come forward to allege corruption by the political leadership, it is too dangerous, and, in that sense, corruption is a victimless crime. The victims of grand corruption are the people of the country whose leaders are helping themselves to the national wealth. The prosecutors do not prosecute, and the police do not record the crime, there are no official statistics. Our knowledge of grand corruption is reliant on brave journalists, brave whistle-blowers and NGOs. Our statistical knowledge is so poor that little, if anything, can be relied upon to quantify our understanding. A recent study of commonly quoted corruption statistics decided that *none* were credible.[2] The study identified 71 global statistics and whittled them down to the most important top ten "selected corruption statistics that have appeared prominently in speeches, fact sheets, issue briefs, and similar documents from major organisations." This included, for example, an oft-cited global statistic of US$2.6 trillion being corruptly stolen or embezzled each year. The research concluded that the statistic was unfounded, it "appears to reflect a misinterpretation or misrepresentation of a statistic on a related but distinct matter in a 2018 speech by the UN secretary-general".

The difficulty is compounded by a lack of transparency. The main anti-corruption NGO, Transparency International, has been flagging this up since its inception in 1993; it has since formed chapters all over the world who contribute to the CPI. Faced with the difficulty of measuring prosecutions, Transparency International went with *perceptions* of corruption. The CPI has been criticised for flagging up poor countries as being corrupt and rich countries as being not corrupt. This is partly because the populations of rich countries do not perceive corruption in the same way as populations in poor countries. Another factor is that the CPI is composed of a basket of measures typically created by experts. The fact that these people have experience and knowledge creates a tendency for their perception of their immediate surroundings not to change. We fully recognise this problem, we also think that change in the war on dirty money often moves at a glacial pace, which is why we have often cited evidence which can be years old. We have used it because it is still valid. However, changes do happen, for example the recent successes of the Kenya Ethics and Anticorruption Commission and the firing of the entire Republic of Georgia Traffic Police back in 2003. All of that said, the CPI tends to give a picture of the world as a static place, and it would be good if it could somehow capture emerging trends and include enforcement data. In particular the insidious connection between grand and petty corruption deserves more attention. This is because, while both rich and poor countries are probably affected by 'grand' corruption to some degree; the daily lives of the populations in poor countries are impacted by something dubbed 'petty' corruption.

## Grand and petty corruption

So far, we have only talked about 'grand' corruption by country leaders. This should be understood in the broadest sense, to include political leaders, senior officials and their families. Below this we have some different kinds of corruption which are variously described as 'endemic', 'petty' or 'institutionalised', meaning that so many people within an institution or sector are behaving corruptly that the whole institution or sector is corrupt. For ordinary people, petty corruption manifests itself as facing unofficial payments to get a service from a public provider that should be free, or to avoid it being refused or delayed. This may include life-saving medical treatment, so we should treat the use of the term 'petty' with some contempt. This kind of corruption blights the lives of millions on a regular and direct basis.

The most obvious way to perceive corruption as an ordinary citizen is the behaviour of police officers in charge of traffic who, in many countries, routinely administer on-the-spot fines and pocket the money. This is not necessarily a discreet one-on-one transaction but can be a very public extraction of money from private taxis and buses (a frequent phenomenon in poor countries in the absence of public transport). The police fines are obviously passed on to passengers and paid by all except the richest members of society. In much of western Europe this practice does not happen, because it has been eradicated over recent decades, but the practice persists in parts of eastern Europe, Africa, Asia and South America. The connection between a country's president (and leadership colleagues) helping themselves to a nation's wealth and the traffic cops helping themselves to the cash of passing motorists deserves more attention. The president and the cop are both in positions of 'entrusted power' which they are abusing. More specifically, the cop is in uniform, a uniform entrusted to him, ultimately, by the president. The corrupt traffic cop is, more than anything else, a symbol of a president's corrupt practices. Tackling the corrupt traffic cop seems like common sense, since it is obvious that corrupt traffic cops can be controlled. It is hard to think of an easier target for anti-corruption officers than the traffic police. The offence takes place in public, in uniform, against a member of the public that the cop does not know, often in broad daylight. Substituting an undercover cop for the member of the public, covert surveillance, turning victims into witnesses and the financial investigation of officers are all obvious avenues to address this commonplace scourge. The existence of traffic cops on the take is an institutional *choice*. The question is why is nothing done against such a simple and solvable crime?

## Noble cause corruption

But first, we need to describe another form of corruption that afflicts the police specifically; the malaise of 'noble cause' corruption. One of this book's authors was in Africa a few years ago and the local daily paper front page had four photographs of an armed police stop of alleged armed robbers taken by a passer-by. The first photo had men standing by a car, hands-up held at gunpoint. The second photo had them getting down on their knees. In the third, they were lying down looking up at their captors and in the fourth they were dead, apparently executed by the police. It was shocking. This is an extreme example of a phenomenon that is all too common in many parts of the world, perhaps everywhere, to some extent. This is the practice of police meting out summary justice to those they believe to be criminals. This is done because the police believe, rightly or wrongly, that the criminal justice system will fail to deliver the justice that the police want. This problem may be mild or serious; a cuff around the ear to a misbehaving youth is quite different from a summary execution, but both **matter** to some degree because they undermine the courts which should deliver justice. Perhaps, more accurately, the existence of police noble cause corruption exposes the ineffectiveness of the justice delivered by courts. If we were searching for a definition of corruption perhaps it is that corruption is the opposite of justice. Each concept is difficult to define, but you know each one when you see it.

In terms of perceptions of corruption, addressing 'noble cause' corruption is a crucial prerequisite to justice. If a country's police perceive that their own justice system will not deliver justice because it is corrupted, then this issue must be tackled before other anti-corruption measures can be attempted. Noble cause corruption and traffic police corruption are both visible symptoms of a much deeper sickness within a national justice system. The former can be addressed by improving the courts, so that the latter symptom, the traffic cop, can then be addressed.

The reason that nothing is done to stop the traffic cops on the take is that the supervisors get a cut, and the managers too, all the way up to the top of the organisation. Traffic cops on the take are *always* just the tip of the police corruption iceberg. That is the only possible reason for them being allowed to carry on. This is based on the simple fact that policing is much the same the world over, done by the same sort of people in much the same way. Failing to understand this simple fact has undermined the global fight against corruption. The issue with traffic cops on the take is that they are not policing at all, just criminals in uniform employed by a criminal organisation. One solution is to fire them all. This was actually done in the Republic of Georgia in 2003. A new government recognised that the traffic police were the symbol of corruption and, after anxious internal debate, fired all 16,000 of them. There was a worry that traffic safety would be compromised but in fact after the mass sackings, 'many observers believe that the roads were actually safer'.[3] Over subsequent years crime fell by half, armed robbery by 80%. Encouragingly, this radical move had some sustainability, seven years on:

> A 2010 survey indicates that only 1 percent of Georgia's population reported having paid a bribe to the road police (World Bank and EBRD 2011). Comparable numbers were 30 percent in the former Soviet Union countries, 7 percent in the new member states of the European Union (EU), and zero in selected EU members (France, Germany, Italy, Sweden, the United Kingdom).

The public face of modern police corruption is exemplified by a recent Russian case. Traffic police Colonel, Aleksey Safonov, who had publicly condemned bribe-taking by police officers was found, on his arrest, to have corruptly obtained lavish wealth including a golden toilet,[4] apparently the go-to choice for Russia's elite. He and over 30 of his officers were accused of taking a US$250,000 bribe.

The reason that police corruption is so important in the war on dirty money is that the normalisation of corrupt police on the public road allows endemic corruption to exist everywhere else. Corrupt traffic police are a symbol of a lawless society. If the traffic police are corrupt, what would be the point in calling their colleagues to deal with teachers selling exam results or doctors treating bribe-payers ahead of other patients? If the police cannot deal with their own corrupt officers, how can they possibly be looked upon to deal with other corrupt professionals? This is aside from the issue of dealing with grand corruption, which is obviously quite beyond the capability of such a police force. Pause for thought though. If you were a corrupt president (or state governor) surely you would *ensure* that your police were under-resourced, undermined and, hopefully, fully corrupt. Then you are safe. The relationship of the bent traffic cop by the side of the road and the corrupt president in his palace is symbiotic.

An answer to the existence of corrupt police is to try to side-step them and create a separate anti-corruption body.

## The rise of Anti-Corruption Commissions

The global approach to anti-corruption has been to assume that the police are beyond reform and to set up an independent anti-corruption investigation body, as suggested by Article 36 of the UN Convention Against Corruption. In practice, this is modelled on two Anti-Corruption Commissions (ACCs) which have been perceived as successful, in Hong Kong and Singapore. It should be said that the anti-corruption drive comes from the rich countries and is led by development aid. Setting up an independent body has several advantages from a donor perspective. It is quick and visible, with a new building, new staff, marketing and activity all achievable in a few years. It is the opposite of a long-term effort to reform a police force, which will, out of necessity, be working with existing organisational structures (and therefore constraints).

The problem with ACCs, from the perspective of the war on dirty money, is that they are often a solution for a different problem from tackling corruption through prosecution and/or asset recovery. Reasons for establishing ACCs include pressure from 'multi- and bilateral donors (including as a condition for donating); a fast-growing anti-corruption industry (which regards ACCs as an appealing consultancy product); and [political] incumbents under domestic and international pressure, desperate to obtain reputational gains'.[5]

Consequently, the typical ACC does not recover the proceeds of corruption. They are engaged in awareness-raising, prevention campaigns and education. Some ACCs do attempt investigations, but few are successful. This is partly because they are bolted-on to the local criminal justice system. Their investigations may be fed into a corrupt prosecution system or heard by corrupt judges. In an effort to avoid experienced but suspect investigators, they may recruit 'clean skins', choosing bright young graduates in the hope that youth and enthusiasm may triumph over age and experience. There are multiple issues.

There are some isolated success stories. In the Balkans, the Croatian ACC (the local acronym is PNUSKOK) has had success in recovering dirty money over the years. More recently the Kenyan Ethics and Anti-Corruption Commission has managed several post-conviction confiscations, and notable amounts of stolen assets including land and buildings have been restored to communities. But these two examples are the exception, not the rule.

## Can the police ever be reformed?

The working assumption that the police are beyond redemption seems a surprising conclusion given the evidence available to the rich countries who are donating the anti-corruption expertise and resources. A great deal of time and effort is devoted by rich donors to finding examples in the developing world of anti-corruption success, as if police corruption has never existed in the rich world. Earlier in this chapter we noted the finding of the World Bank that traffic bribes in France, Germany, Italy, Sweden and the United Kingdom were reported as *zero*. All of these countries have eradicated this form of corruption in their own police forces within living memory, and these are the very same countries providing anti-corruption support. What is it that prevents them from applying their own successful solutions to the countries they want to help? It may be that the solutions to police corruption in rich countries are not transferable, but this seems unlikely to us. We think that it is more likely that generic solutions to common problems just need a little local adaptation. We accept that every country has to find its own unique solution, but it seems likely that tried and tested solutions are worth a try, ahead of experimentation.

We speculate that the rich world expertise in police reform comes within the security and defence sector and that sector is dominated by the military and by uniform (often junior) police officers. The investigation and intelligence arm of policing has simply not been asked to assist with the problem of police corruption. Furthermore, the invasive nature of police corruption, infecting everything in a police force from top to bottom, has simply not been given the priority it deserves. The result is that police reform is delivered through technical training courses, short-term mentoring and the provision of equipment. Any anti-corruption element of this short-term, peripheral assistance is consistently undermined by a failure to tackle fundamental management issues around recruitment, pay, promotion and supervision. In addition, police development programmes tend to have absurdly small lifespans, only five years or even less. Given that the lifespan of a single criminal corruption investigation and prosecution is often more than five years, police reform programmes often fail to address long-term issues like corruption. They are also poorly coordinated between donors; duplication and waste are common. Asset recovery and anti-corruption have some similarities. Both require fundamental change to culture, the most difficult of all changes to achieve. One of this book's authors was recently asked to review all the donor-funded asset recovery reports for a single country. There had been 18 reports on this single topic in this country over a single decade, starting with the author's own report. All 18 were actually surprisingly good quality and contained useful (albeit rather repetitive) recommendations. There had, however, been a failure of implementation; an often repeated and ignored recommendation was to set up a coordinating implementation committee. There lies the problem; a coordinating committee would actually focus on the problem, and it is easier to just appoint an anti-corruption 'champion' or an ACC to deflect attention from institutions needing true reform.

## International bribery

Another way to avoid reforming the local 'assumed-to-be-corrupt' police is to try to side-step them and get foreign police to run international bribery cases with the token assistance of local officers. If traffic police corruption is easy for anti-corruption officers to tackle, then international bribery to get contracts is probably even easier (if the right infrastructure existed). There is documentation to examine, governance to see, obvious red flags which are well known. But, once again, no one is really looking. More importantly, even if an investigation provides evidence, there is nowhere to prosecute a case. More precisely, because the offence is normally committed in at least two countries and often many more, there is no single court to bring the case. The perpetrators, witnesses and documents all provide evidence for everywhere and thus, as it turns out, nowhere.

A common claim is that rich companies bribe officials to get government contracts. This has been described as demand and supply side corruption, with the corrupt official being on the demand side. This construct lays the blame with the poor country's government for demanding that companies conform to their corrupt practices if they want the contract. Criminal justice does not see it this way; the law says both parties are equally culpable.

It may be easier to understand this type of corruption by describing a typical example. It is a real example. There are three criminals: A, B and C. A pays a bribe to C, using an intermediary called B. The contract is worth US$110 million of which the bribe is US$10 million. To avoid prosecution and confiscation A, B and C all use companies to commit the crimes so that they can enjoy the double indemnity that this provides (see Chapter 12 on prosecution).

This is how it works. We start with Criminal A, a real person, a director of a large company in a rich country. He is powerful in the company and can sign off payments and make major strategic decisions. At the specific times when he is doing this, the company is effectively his, he has 'entrusted power' which he is abusing for the gain of all shareholders and recipients of performance-based bonuses, from which he and others will benefit. The company is his for the purpose of the contract, so we will call it Company A. Criminal A recruits a real person, Criminal B, and creates a subsidiary company, Company B, which will run things in the poor country. Criminal C is a career civil servant in the poor country who directs an agency which is part of the Ministry of Interior. C creates Company C for himself, safely offshore. He will collect the bribe in the poor country in cash and pay it to Company C.

That is the structure that was actually used in real life. This is as simple as it could be. Simplicity reduces costs, but complexity reduces the risk of law enforcement discovery and successful prosecution. The sad truth is that even slight complexity will confound most criminal justice systems, which are profoundly under-resourced.

The operation works like this. A, B and C agree a deal in advance. Their respective companies will provide the cover for the bribe and the excessive profit that makes it all worthwhile. To comply with transparency rules a tender is published to deliver something to the poor country's Ministry of the Interior. In this case it is a computer system. The system will be delivered across the country involving local trainers and expensive equipment which will need to be guarded. Company A wins the tender and its subsidiary, Company B will deliver the system. It is no longer possible to show the bribe in the accounts (there was a rule change in the 1970s to stop this) so it has to be disguised as something else. To do this, Company B hires extra trainers and guards who do not actually exist. Their pay, in cash, is actually collected in person by C, who pays it into his Company C account disguised as 'consultancy fees'.

That is it, three people and three companies. The companies will exist for the life of the contract and then they will be dissolved, taking their evidence with them. You may wonder if it is really possible to carry large amounts of cash on a plane and pay it into a bank offshore without declaring it. The UK National Crime Agency convicted two men in 2018 for money laundering. Their method was to fly from the UK to Dubai with dodgy cash. One was arrested at a UK airport with four suitcases packed with £1.5 million in denominations of £20 and £50. The investigation showed that:

> Between 2017 and 2018, the two men made nearly 200 return flights with both frequently travelling out with a significantly greater weight of luggage than they returned with. NCA [National Crime Agency] investigators estimate that Fahad [the second man] left the UK with an extra 379 kilos over the offending period, which would equate to around £5 million in cash.[6]

This is about as simple as it gets, but this is very hard to prosecute. The main issue is that it is one crime committed in three countries (money laundering is integral to the original predicate crime of bribery). A is in the rich country, B and C are in the poor country and the money is in an offshore country. Prosecutions happen in countries, there is no international place in which to prosecute this single, simple crime and there really should be.

In lieu of a simple solution like an international court for simple corruption, the countries involved have to agree what to do. For clarity, the bribery took place in the rich country and the poor country, and the money laundering is in the offshore country. It may be possible to agree that one country will prosecute, and the other countries will assist their prosecution, but who will pay for this to happen? Every participant is an offender (and a witness) in every other country. The other complication is that at the beginning of the investigation none of the above is known, it all has to be unravelled and put back together for the court – wherever that may be. Meanwhile the money has to be found and seized – wherever that may be. In order to capture the money, this will have to be frozen immediately at the start of the investigation, or it will disappear, so the agreement to prosecute, the agreement to fund, the decision to freeze, the exchange of information that underpins everything, all have to be done in double-quick time. Incredibly this has actually been done successfully, **despite** the United Nations, national governments, the financial sector and the FATF. We know this because the World Bank's StAR database has recorded and published all the cases. There have been fewer than 90 (see Chapter 5).

## Persons to blame

You will note that we have blamed the United Nations, national governments, the financial sector and the FATF. We know that this is unfair. We selected these culprits because they are the only bodies who have **tried** to fix the problem **and** actually have the power to do so. They just have not done enough, and we exhort them to do more.

In particular, we suggest a different approach based on tackling corruption via dirty money. We also suggest changing the balance between prevention and enforcement to provide far more resources for criminal justice at a national level and a focus on police corruption. More resources for justice will help address 'noble cause' corruption and clear the field for tackling police corruption proper. Addressing police corruption is a quick win because it is easy to identify and there are many examples, particularly in Europe, on how to address it. Furthermore, police corruption causes the most harm to the general public and tackling it is a key mechanism to reduce many, if not all, *types* of crime. A corrupt police force is worse than useless and a complete waste of money. How do you tell if a country is corrupt? Ask the public about the existence of corrupt traffic cops. It really is that simple and it is, we say, relatively simple to fix.

Is it really possible to solve police corruption without solving grand corruption, first? Of course it is. That is what rich countries have already done, for decades. We do not suggest that this is deliberate, by the way, we think that where endemic corruption exists, rich country observers conclude that 'even the police are corrupt'. We think that this is the wrong conclusion; if the police are corrupted that means that everybody else **can be** corrupt. It is simple really, the public will not report corruption of any sort to a corrupt police force because it would not investigate and the public, correctly, perceive this to be so.

### Solutions toolbox

- Grand and petty corruption are symbiotic evils and petty corruption is both more immediately harmful to more people and easier to fix. We therefore suggest that countries and international donors should focus on petty corruption as a solvable problem, starting with the police. Police corruption itself is split between 'noble cause' corruption and petty corruption; both must be addressed.
- The approach of setting up ACCs should be recognised as short-term and superficial. A better use of international resources would be to focus on eradicating corrupt traffic police, which should be recognised as a key symptom of endemic police corruption. Once the police are in a position to investigate corruption in other sectors, they should be properly equipped and resourced to do so.
- The Corruption Perceptions Index produced by Transparency International is recognised as valuable and the authors hope that police corruption, as a key indicator of endemic corruption, can be given some space in the methodology of the CPI.

## Conclusion

In the war on dirty money, the frontal assault on grand corruption has demonstrably failed for decades. We would certainly suggest that big cases should continue to be brought, because the corruption at their core has already happened and will continue to happen. Justice should be done, or at least attempted.

However, we think donors could do more to address corruption, in their own interests. A few years ago, donors started to recognise that corruption was eroding their efforts and they set about including due diligence and corruption prevention techniques in their financial disbursements. This was an important difference in donor thinking and we commend it. We suggest another change of a similar sort. Instead of giving up on the police as a lost cause, donors should re-double their efforts. First, this will benefit the poorest in society, who always bear the brunt of bad police behaviour. Second, it might just make a difference to the grand corruption by undermining and outflanking corrupt actors rather than attempting the set-piece frontal assaults which do not seem to work. Poor people in poor countries deserve a chance of living without endemic 'petty' corruption, just like poor people in rich countries. Donors need to face up to the political elites with whom they have to work and be less generous if 'the political elite appear reluctant to create a democratic and independent police force that they are then, by definition, unable to manipulate and that may even investigate the corrupt activities of these elites themselves'.[7]

# 19

# AML/CFT supervision or tick-list observers?

> More often than not the [supervisors] are asleep, but
> still, they seem to always keep one eye open.
>
> Anon

The battle to defeat money laundering has highlighted a game of 'cat and mouse' taking place. In doing so, two critical players are clearly defined: the supervisors, or regulatory authorities (the cats) and the opposition – the reporting entities (the mice).

In terms of costs for all this, they are significant for both players. Globally, we have witnessed an extraordinary growth in efforts to control money laundering and it seems the costs are not due to lessen anytime soon. Associated costs have largely been driven by the FATF and through a desire by countries to pass the FATF-created, controlled, partially administered, and unevenly applied MER. Like the pull of gravity, the reality of the problem of AML/CFT lies predominantly with those at the bottom. It is here where most are left scrambling to adhere to costly regulatory obligations while following guidance on a problem, perhaps equally as old as they are. It is here too where money is thrown in the billions at problems to make them appear no longer a problem.

The fallout from this AML/CFT scenario has been the creation of a distinct 'us and them' position. On one side of the battlefield, as we will call it, is the supervisor or regulatory authority. On the other side, hunkering down behind makeshift defences, are the reporting entities – most too scared to raise their head above the parapet even to surrender. This situation has created a global scenario that has thrown genuine partnership working out of the window. It has created an opportunity to openly punish entities for regulatory failures. The fear of huge fines and subsequent reputational harm – not always for allowing money laundering to take place – has forced some entities into a spin while others have simply accepted punishments as a cost of doing business.

Whether called 'supervision' or 'regulatory oversight', the rules of the game have by now been carved into stone. Governed by the FATF but equally controlled by the wealthiest countries, the rules, whether perceived as good or bad, have created businesses, authorities and agencies intent on supporting AML/CFT efforts. However, it is clear from the scale of money laundering as a problem today, the intent has not delivered anything spectacular. What we think the intent has delivered, is an extremely expensive 'regulatory new world order'. We knew this would eventually be the case, since the FATF had identified in Recommendation 1: 'countries should designate an authority or mechanism to coordinate actions to assess risks, and apply resources, aimed at ensuring the risks are mitigated effectively.'[1] We just didn't see it becoming such a distraction for the original war on dirty money.

## Just playing the game

As with most activities, after 30 years of 'cavorting about', it would be expected that the rules would be clear for all players to conform to. Not quite, so it seems, with AML/CFT compliance. Regulated reporting entities, such as financial institutions, 'gate keeper' professionals and other sectors captured by AML/CFT legislation have obviously chosen, and why not, to play by their own rules. This is something that has intensified across the globe through differing levels of aptitude towards adopting the FATF's recommendations and a scenario in which entities have been lumbered with obligations far beyond their initial (intended) preventative scope. All this has taken place on top of the need to manage increasing numbers of transactions and customer databases as the global population has 'moved online'. So, whether it is intentional, ignorance or outright mischievousness, the level of conformity naturally varies across sectors and AML/CFT regimes.

Supervisors, of course, do play a key role in preventing money laundering – or so they have us believe. Perhaps their role is more important than many realise. This requirement to oversee the front line against money laundering and terrorism financing – largely the financial institutions – is one such critical role. It is these same financial institutions which have borne the brunt of the FATF's recommendations for the longest time, 'presumed to be the sonic screwdriver solution to any ill that has a financial connection (which is most of them)' according to Tom Keatinge at RUSI in London.[2] Still, we now see a growing number of entities being brought into the fold to implement checks and report suspicious activity. Even so, what is the point in having rules if they can be ignored?

Bring forward, then, the supervisor of AML/CFT reporting entities. In the UK as an example, the Treasury Department uses the Office for Professional Body AML Supervision (OPBAS). The critical point to make here is that OPBAS are not direct supervisors of entities, but supervisor of the supervisors – all 27 of them. We see this model offering an opportunity to shift responsibility for monitoring money laundering compliance activities to the 27 individual entities. By outsourcing responsibility for managing AML/CFT compliance, the obligations and liability, OPBAS automatically becomes an oversight agent, dissipating its supervisory control. This arrangement clearly adds another level of separation that, in turn, reduces the likelihood of anything constructive coming forward to further support UK AML/CFT efforts. Despite the risk, the 27 Professional Body Supervisors now pay OPBAS for the privilege of managing the nation's AML/CFT risks – a scenario that may not seem ideal for centralising the entire supervisory landscape to strengthen a nation's efforts. Nevertheless, it is a clever intention, particularly for a country with a capital city considered to be the money laundering capital of the world, a leading member of the FATF and the proud recipient of an amazing MER assessment.[3]

New moves across Europe to supervise AML/CFT compliance are under way. But, for many, the 'possible results' are not worth holding their breath for. Regarded as the supervisor of the riskiest, the new EU AMLA (or AML Authority) will take some time to go live; estimated to happen in 2026. By then we may know whether the AMLA will become just another layer in the layering of AML/CFT compliance and supervision, or a real force to control the unruly. The self-proclaimed cynics will tell you this is just another level of bureaucracy, a smoke screen, and a diversion from making any traction towards dealing with the consequences of money laundering. Still, no one ever mentions focusing on the predicate crimes or whether the cynics may be correct. Instead, the focus is always on reviewing compliance and introducing more compliance to somehow overcome any anxiety by the public. The AMLA, the 250 employees of which will annually cost the EU upwards of €45 million, will eventually take over from the EBA. In the meantime, with no light at the end of the tunnel, the EBA will continue in its work, no doubt feeling somewhat betrayed and intimidated by those who know it will soon be leaving the party.

Key to the likely failure that may come, is just how the AMLA will focus solely on the financial industry, thus ignoring the idea that the financial industry is not really the sonic screwdriver for AML/CFT. Although the most vulnerable sector to money laundering and terrorism financing and the largest across Europe, it is not the only sector capable of allowing *transactions and purchases* for the purpose of money laundering. Worryingly, the AMLA also seems to be positioned far too close to the EU's strategy of applying bigger, stronger and longer solutions to problems that initial solutions were struggling to tackle. Will this then create yet another intra-national body funded by the taxpayer to simulate a smaller regional version of the FATF? Will it become a body that simply introduces brazen policy changes and patrols member states looking to identify those which need to be *named and shamed*?

Still, any rolling of eyes or sighing with disbelief about the future AMLA does not need to stop there. There is also the strong disbelief that the AMLA – the new watchdog – will have the power to take over the supervision of specific cases when national authorities apparently fail to do their jobs properly. Will this lead to another option for punishing those not playing by the rules, or as a means to assert political pressure on the weak? Of course, as with most developments of such geographical spread in authority, only as time passes will we know the answers. But, if results to date are anything to go by, especially those involving the UK and US, then imprisonment rates of convicted bankers, CEOs and money laundering experts will be unlikely to increase.

## Is supervision so far effective?

Any reduction in AML/CFT compliance failures is, we think, a long way off. Even so, businesses are spending billions of dollars attempting to achieve what is seemingly impossible. And all this is happening while managing costly processes, procedures and activities which can, at best, be described as a waste of time. Where then is the motivation for all those involved in AML/CFT compliance to keep engaged and doing the right thing?

Nevertheless, supervisory efforts are still one of the most critical key performance indicators (KPIs) of the national compliance regime – meaning their results indicate integrity in a national system of convenience. Granted, this is an outdated and no longer entirely appropriate system, but still it is a system intentionally designed to keep the troops in line – worldwide and countrywide. While it may not always be as prominent as the drill sergeant on a parade ground with a true voice of authority (and integrity), the supervisor is meant to question ALL entities not meeting the compliance expectations placed upon them.

Yet, success of supervision is not always apparent beyond the headlines. Nor are the results indicative as to whether any AML/CFT compliance regime is really working. Supervisors can easily choose to ignore the need to comprehend the granular impact of change, or how the cost of complying with AML/CFT regulations can, for some businesses, be extremely disproportionate to their size and their level of risk. Perhaps it is a lack of training that is to blame, despite the FATF establishing a training centre in South Korea to push its own thinking and fixed approach to audiences far and wide. Yet an unwillingness of supervisory staff to also challenge the many orthodoxies that now exist in the FATF approach, suggests this training is simply 'more of the same'.

As the many AML/CFT compliance processes continue, we see that a lack of understanding on the fundamentals of what supervisors are supposed to be doing is causing dismay among many concerned parties. Bring into the mix the close relationships with large consultancy firms and compliance advisory groups, and the role of supervisor moves from drill sergeant to counsellor, confidante and best friend willing to wear rose-tinted glasses.

In the same way that the FATF's international naming and shaming process exists, national instances can also be present. Whether these are usually in the lead up to a MER, the authors have not sought to clarify. What the authors have seen is how *victims* can be the smaller entities unable and too hesitant to question the rules which they have been instructed to follow. With AML supervision, catching a single fish with a single hook has been more appropriate than catching many fish with a net. Still, it is the results of such 'small catches' that help to determine success against the unwritten supervisory KPI that is both unworkable at preventing money laundering and terrorism financing as it is an indicator of strong supervisory performance. Selecting 'the small, weak entities' alongside the odd 'big fish' in essence does little to evidence exceptional performance of a national supervisor. Yet nobody dare raise this obvious issue. Nor does it ensure compliance of all others. It is true, certain situations may send an immediate message that failures at any level will be tolerated, but think about the last time you heard of an entity closing its doors for the final time after supervisory action was taken. If this is the most effective means to supervision, then it is clear that most entities, when found to have an AML/CFT compliance failure, will ride out the inevitable storm which follows. Financial penalties, no matter how big, are clearly insufficient at stemming the problems of AML/CFT failures. So perhaps, it is worth considering whether now is the time to stem the tide and remove operating licences.

Should you still be sceptical as to the purpose behind the efforts of AML/CFT supervisors, take a moment to consider the events in Denmark and Estonia with Danske Bank.[4] It is difficult to pinpoint exactly when national supervisors were asleep and unable to see the problems that were unfolding into huge historical compliance failures. Equally there are the events in Germany, where there are still serious failures occurring which the Federal Audit Office has pointed out by stating: 'there is no effective money laundering supervision'.[5] In Germany, many such failures are occurring outside of the financial sector, in real estate transactions, in the car trade and the art market, where the German federal government is already expecting a volume of up to €30 billion to be laundered annually. These vulnerabilities in German money laundering supervision were perhaps brought to light by the single Wirecard case involving an investigation into money laundering fraud, balance falsification and market manipulation which industry commentators and politicians have since criticised as a hands-off approach by supervisors. In this instance, the supervisor missed opportunities to spot the problems that were taking place at Wirecard, neither looking to hook a single fish nor deploy the more appropriate net to Germany's riskiest sectors.

## Downward trend

It seems somewhat obvious that the entire AML/CFT process should then be mandated to pass messages and obligations downwards. With details dictated by the FATF acting as the puppet for the wealthiest countries, it is then the national supervisors who need to use this same information to inform the industries which they regulate. Even with the material outlined in sector risk assessments, copied and pasted by the FIUs, the industries below are only ever driven by one thing – profit. The conventional thinker is winning as no one wants to even suggest something is amiss.

So, perhaps the most incomprehensible issue here is just who decides what the FATF dictates to be relevant all the way down to the ground level in each country? It seems few are choosing to question the relevance of what the FATF determines to be necessary in a specific country. Is this a case of many sheep following a single sheep without what many would see as obligatory reasoning? It may certainly be obvious there is a need to introduce certain measures to prevent money laundering and terrorism financing, but *how* and *why* are the FATF recommendations always so *right for the job* over and above the previous consultations between members which led to its creation? With the authors having consulted internationally on this very point, questions have been raised time and again as to why the FATF obligations are so rigid. The answer to this question can sometimes be difficult to justify – perhaps because cultural, legislative and procedural differences across FATF member countries are not always well understood.

This raises another important question: 'Why are supervisors not raising their own country's issues with greater vigour?' Is it perhaps a similar case to why many of us never questioned our teachers at school, because if the school had a good record for exam passes, then there was no reason to think they were perhaps wrong in what they were teaching us? But with so many AML/CFT failures globally, is now the time for supervisors to instead supervise what is before them, rather than rigidly follow the global consensus originally developed to serve other purposes? After all, the supervisor is both guardian of the obligations and mentor to all reporting entities. If they see something that does not align nationally, the obligation must be on the AML/CFT supervisor to take responsibility, speak up and do what is right. We know the FATF recommendations are just that – recommendations – but does evidence exist that not following them leads to a positive outcome?

Then there is the question: 'Just how often are supervisors looking for regulatory failures?' Ironically, it may be a case, as already alluded to, that failures could be identified in the lead up to a MER for the purpose of evidencing proficient and effective supervision. Or perhaps they arise when susceptible sectors have been again identified as FATF priorities. Or are they identified at the same time political and business pressures increase, thus forcing a stronger stance against those who may be offering more cost-effective solutions in the financial industries markets? From our understanding, it appears there is still no real understanding as to the timing or as to how supervision is best undertaken across all reporting entities. Supervisors worldwide seem to adopt an approach that works for them. There is clearly a lack of direction and yet still an obligation to bring forward sacrificial entities as evidence of a tough AML/CFT supervisory regime when the need arises. Needless to say, this is unlikely to serve well in the long term.

While this mismatched logic of supervision continues, it seems the supervisors continue to justify their actions based on assurances of many like-minded fools who set the landscape for them to roam across. This almost inevitable situation now before us has created a 'merry-go-round' that no one can stop. It is a costly and fruitless 'merry-go-round' where the only hope is that as it speeds up it will finally break apart. In doing so, we see then the opportunity for an entirely new and fair regime where there are no intentional victims.

## Is the writing already on the wall?

Is what we now see a case of 'do as I say, not as I do' or something a little more sinister? With integrity needing to be at the heart of any AML/CFT supervisory regime, then the supervisory regime should be able to demonstrate it is not simply seeking a return on any of its investment. Tough new measures and the cracking down on certain sectors only, promise progress at preventing money laundering and, to a lesser extent, terrorism financing. Yet, with unimaginative regulators combining common narratives alongside a constant stream of self-reinforcing, it is difficult to see how individuals who facilitate financial crime will be prosecuted anytime soon. What will likely continue for many years is the frequent fining of entities for failures that have little influence on other entities' commitment to AML/CFT compliance nor their own at preventing money laundering. The threat of law enforcement action against a law firm for AML/CFT compliance failures is only ever used as a scare tactic by the compliance consultants and salespeople of software solutions seeking to deliver so-called solutions. In reality, the chances of this happening seem worryingly low. A compliance failure by others may be the topic of discussion over the pouring of coffee in the communal kitchen, but a thorough review of the entire AML/CFT compliance regime within most unscathed organisations is almost certainly never going to be a reaction to write home about. Profit comes first and, in most cases, AML/CFT compliance can be put to one side until the need arises for it to be addressed.

Similarly, failures can reflect very badly on supervisors on the international stage. Perhaps this is why whistle-blowers are feared not only by their own organisation but also by those having supervisory obligations to ensure AML/CFT compliance requirements are met. Whistle-blowers can cause fingers to be pointed at supervisors. And supervisors we expect will not like this.

Fines may serve to raise immediate attention and inform outsiders as to just how critical the work of a supervisor is, but the world has become desensitised and even dismissive to such large fines for AML/CFT compliance failures. Many such figures can be overshadowed by a possible and scary scenario of 'supervision for profit'. And, like 'policing for profit' (discussed in Chapter 8), both practices raise questions as to whether they are self-serving and ineffective – not necessarily unethical – practices hiding behind the preventative approach to tackling money laundering. The authors argue that it is a relatively easy task picking up the pieces of poor compliance and then profiting from it – rather than employing targeted, even information-led and meaningful actions to support entities throughout. Consequently, this may be why no one seemingly ever wishes to 'put their head above the parapet' and raise any issues. Hence the fear too from whistle-blowers. Even if whistleblowing is to be encouraged – which there is little evidence of – the consequences of being reviewed by the AML/CFT supervisor is unlikely to lead to anything remotely positive.

Still, some national AML/CFT supervisors can appear to be in control, determining the rules and setting expectations. But the unfortunate reality is, they are merely a single piece in a much larger, complicated, and sometimes unknown jigsaw. Acting primarily for the intentions of the FATF, supervisors also take their directions from within political confines. It is the *supervision for profit* premise that perhaps creates the biggest worry for anyone looking at the failures of AML/CFT compliance from afar.

Take, for example, the UK's FCA. The FCA is funded by the banks and yet responsible for oversight of their actions. What that means is the FCA is policing its paymasters. This is an almost incomprehensible situation, yet an approach credited by some as 'a force to be reckoned with' when the FCA acted against NatWest Bank. Yet, in real terms, this particular action had the same effect as a wet marshmallow on a plate, recounts Ian Ross, a financial crime risk & training professional in the UK on an online forum highlighting how the criminal prosecution which will follow will unlikely see anyone standing in front of a judge for sentencing.[6]

The harsh reality is that the financial crime (FinCrime) industry has been motivated by a 'box-ticking' culture rather than a desire to stop money laundering and terrorism financing. It is true, reporting entities do try to play nicely with their AML/CFT supervisor, but what is happening below the surface is most worrying. Here supervisors serve the political intentions of those with control – their paymasters – rather than focusing on preventing money laundering and terrorism financing outside of the FATF obligations, which many will know are not working. Is there really evidence that the supervisors have made any positive changes to the entire AML/CFT compliance regime – anywhere? We are not sure, because after all, helping entities to know why they must be compliant, is very different from thoroughly checking they are *all* meeting their AML/CFT obligations.

Since the AML/CFT supervision process is seldom questioned, entities just prove compliance rather than achieve better outcomes for preventing money laundering and terrorism financing. Unfortunately, at present, no one genuinely cares that there is a major gap despite the publications, the press releases and on-stage presentations at conferences. By conferences we mean those events where people with similar interests meet to advance common agendas and shape AML practices and behaviours. We think the reason for this is that there is still a lot more to be gained under the current circumstances of poor supervision practices. Does this then mean we first need to consider whether the intentions of the AML/CFT supervisors are correct and aligned to the purpose for which they were created? We certainly think so.

## Accepting responsibility

Is this really the best supervisory situation we can be in after 30 years of AML/CFT effort? Perhaps it is easy to quickly argue all is fine, since there is no point in arguing for change while the spending of billions of dollars ticking boxes is the 'new normal' across a growing number of business types. Yet globally, we have an AML/CFT regime that is no firmer nor more appropriate than it was on day one. Therefore, can more be done at a country level? After all, if supervisors are going to supervise AML/CFT regulated entities – then they must at least do it right, and not be seen to play games with entities to prove dominance, while still choosing to hide in the shadows of the much larger controlling figures such as the FATF, political masters and large or prominent institutions.

The time to rethink compliance, we suggest, is now. Still, this is an obligation which in practice will never be entirely straightforward. It is clear, just from the progress to date, that very few want to risk their career. Equally, it seems few politicians have any interest in making the necessary changes, despite evolutionary change usually coming from a state's own leadership.

Whether the AMLA, the EU's pending main body with a direct supervisory role over large financial institutions, is a solution of sorts, will not be known until long after 2026. What the FATF, money laundering and terrorism financing will then look like is anyone's guess. Sadly, it is unlikely, based on the developments so far, that someone will have taken the time to also look carefully at the activities to date. Instead, most will remain pleasantly distracted like the children who followed the Pied Piper. What is also known, is that by 2026 opportunities will have been missed countless times to detect those entities allowing money laundering and terrorism financing to take place.

If the AMLA solution of a single rulebook with which everyone must comply, or the standardised approach for bank regulation across the EU, are to prove worthwhile, or at least viable, the integrity behind supervision and associated activities will need to be a whole lot stronger than it currently appears to be. To date the supervision has not manifested into anything more than a criticism of the EBA, which – having held this responsibility since 1 January 2011 – has failed to hold national regulators accountable for sleeping on the job.[7] The AMLA will therefore look to repair the reputational damage that the EU has endured over the recent years due to various money laundering scandals. Although the EBA could have received increased scope, negating the need for the AMLA, debates which will no doubt continue for some time to come, the EBA was known to lack independence from all EU countries. The problem this caused was an inability to hold entities to account. Perhaps this is why it needed to go, but equally we suspect some would have preferred it remained.

Even if AMLA's Board will not be formed of representatives from EU member states (to guard against influencing investigations and punishments), it will be interesting to see just how many of the financial institutions in the Wolfsberg Group will at some point make it onto the AMLA's monitoring list. Will it be a token few who also face little punishment? Could it be nearly all of them (unlikely) or will it just be the obligatory sacrificial entity that political influence may have been instrumental in selecting?

Of course, we recognise it is easier to criticise than it is to build innovative options from the ground up. But we see it as a state's responsibility to ensure its efforts are worthy of the expense and the time of so many. Only by creating purpose-driven and truly open partnerships can we begin to define those places where money launderers and terrorism financers operate. Most of which, despite the sale brochures, are beyond the reaches of current technology solutions.

We could consider exchanging followership of the FATF, to instead deliver leadership for the people of the state. Admittedly a bold option, but an option able to help drive effectiveness of measures assigned to the problems and informed by basic principles from the FATF. However, this would first require raising the standards of a nation's supervisory bodies rather than simply waiting for the FATF to find evidence, compile and disseminate guidance notes and obligations, because by then, the train has already left the station. Meeting the train as it arrives in the station is critical and the FATF struggles to always do this. To be successful, supervisors must at least be dealing today with the issues entities have been grappling with for some time and predicting those problems of the future. We must remember a list of red flags in 12 or 24-months, outlined in basic guidance documents, does very little to support compliance with AML/CFT regulations.

We also believe financial institutions in particular are over-regulated, with intense expectations to function as investigators, spies and agents of the state. All this pressure has occurred while other sector professionals – such as lawyers, accountants, and real estate agents have been able to skip even the most basic of risk-based expectations outlined by the FATF. Supervisors must be seen to collaborate at an equal level if things are to change for the better. This means, we suggest, taking responsibility and answering questions from the entities for which they have responsibility, not simply acting as the national AML/CFT bully.

It can no longer be acceptable to expect an entity to follow ineffective rules, and for them to then be fined for not entirely following those rules which, in practice, do not work. Maybe, just maybe, in Europe this could be where the AMLA will serve as a solution; as a chance, some would suggest, for creating harmonisation of the EU's AML/CFT obligations, improving cross-border information sharing and coordinating the EU's supervisory approach. Or will it, and it is very possible, just simply act as a way to whitewash bygone failures?

## Solutions toolbox

- Supervisors need to be firmer, and accountability needs to be called into question. But it is not only the accountability within entities which are failing to meet their AML/CFT compliance obligations that needs to receive greater attention, but also the accountability within AML/CFT supervisors themselves. Supervisors can no longer be 'a law unto oneself' lacking transparency of their regulatory enforcement.
- The global AML scene is led and influenced by supervisors focused more on directives, policies and subsequent tick-boxes, than outcomes. Supervisors need to take a state-led focus on the 'real outcomes' needed and work backwards to ensure they are more effective than the international and uniformly backed guidelines and directives.
- Supervisors need to act ethically and with integrity and oversight. It is not always true that AML supervisors are working to the same standards as those in AML/CFT practices. In the same way that we are expecting CEOs to take account of their AML/CFT obligations within their businesses, those leading AML/CFT supervisors must have the same height to fall when things are found to be wrong.
- Supervisors need to address technology options. The FATF are seeking to understand more how technology can assist. With supervisors asking a lot from entities, they too are looking into technology options. But, as we discussed in Chapter 9, there are some issues with this fast adoption of AML/CFT solutions. Still technology will be part of the future of AML/CFT compliance, so supervisors need to understand their technology obligations – not as a means to trip up entities, but rather to support them to manage their AML/CFT obligations. And if the responsibility sits with supervisors, it equally sits with governments to utilise technology to catch more sophisticated forms of wrongdoing. The FATF requires national

governments to demonstrate an understanding of the distribution of money laundering risks across different sectors of the financial system. This is the foundation for effective control of money laundering under the risk-based approach called for by the FATF. Hence, supervisors of AML/CFT regulations need also to apply their supervision on a risk basis and be able to evidence this in an open forum. The cannot hide behind their supervisory/audit role.

• Supervisors need to recognise and capitalise on the importance of setting strong leadership when it comes to energising the reporting entities to undertake the weird and wonderful array of AML/CFT obligations. We can quibble about the effectiveness of government standings on the problems, but it is the supervisors that hold the closest leadership responsibility to the reporting entities – not timely words of almost certain inaction from sporadically elected political puppets.

With punishments acting as the primary performance indicators for some AML/CFT supervisors, it is likely that the current model is set to play out for many more years. In the next and concluding chapter, we look to what extent punishments are necessary and to whether any good comes from them. Who really pays for the fines imposed on businesses that fail to meet AML/CFT compliance obligations, and who really benefits from the 'supervision for profit' model?

# Punishing AML/CFT failures or raising government funds?

AML/CFT supervision for profit.

The authors

Today there is little opportunity to ignore the policies, ideas, behaviours, software solutions and the rigorous AML/CFT compliance 'tick-boxes' which exist to fight money laundering. Most of this effort is governed by the FATF. Punishments, some would argue, are critical to all this effort; they act as a consequence for poor attitude and behaviour. Yet it is difficult to now find a major financial institution that has not breached money laundering regulations somewhere in the world.

Danske Bank and Nordea in Denmark, HSBC and Standard Chartered in the UK, Deutsche Bank and UBS, Credit Suisse, and HSBC North America – along with many more – have all had to answer to offences relating to AML/CFT compliance failures. A report in 2021 by consulting firm Kroll found fines for AML failings by regulated institutions were five times higher in 2020 than 2019, totalling USD$2.2 billion. Widespread media coverage has ensured we all know this, as well as how Europe has now overtaken the US and Asia in terms of enforcement. More than half of the fines in 2021 came from the Netherlands. This was of course due to Dutch lender ABN Amro, which reached a €480 million settlement with prosecutors after being accused of violating AML laws 'for a number of years and on a structural basis'.[1] You could think these businesses are simply not learning from their own mistakes and those of others. Do they perhaps no longer consider AML/CFT compliance a worthwhile exercise?

Whatever the reason for the failures, what seemingly follows *the slap on the wrist* is the generic statement incorporating responses such as 'we are taking our legal obligations very seriously', 'we have now worked hard to build a robust compliance programme' and 'we are fully committed to undertaking our obligations'. Whether genuine or not, the punishments seem only to be increasing in value as time passes by. All the while the customer continues to pay. The idea of being sorry has, perhaps, become meaningless. All too often the corporate memory simply defaults to bygone activities.

It is at this point, the authors take caution with what we say, but the reasons why these failures happen suggest why the war on dirty money has so far been lost. The lack of interest or knowledge, ignorance and perhaps even wilful blindness? Although for wilful blindness you need to act against the knowledge you have and, with such poor knowledge in circulation, this we are sure raises many concerns. Even unintentional blindness or the growing problem of dealing with the 'unknown knowns' or those dirty little secrets that no one wants to talk about – although everyone knows they are there – can be included. Yet, because it is always someone else's money that covers the costs of failure, it leaves those with ultimate responsibility an opportunity to still go home at the end of the day.

## Fines and settlements

Fines and then the obligatory payment to make a problem go away – a settlement – are what we generally recognise as the punishments being handed out for AML/CFT regulatory failures. Unlike vehicle speeding enforcement fines in many Western countries, there are generally no set figures aligned to the offences of AML/CFT compliance failures. Since it is also possible to make the problem of a compliance failure go away by way of a settlement payment, it seems settlements work out perfectly for both sides when the need arises. Fines can be symbolic to the level of failure, but making a problem disappear a whole lot quicker has, you would think, become the more favourable choice.

We kid you not, but compliance failures allow the supervisor to recoup monetary value almost certainly exceeding that spent assessing the actual failures. Is this a brilliant business strategy, or simply a problem in itself? Whether it is the entity who is considered to be laundering illicit funds or trying to finance terrorism, or the individual (the customer) who first initiates the transfer and purchase that in the end is responsible, fines, and especially settlements, are staying on the table for some time to come. We need to remember in possible defence of reporting entities, that despite their obvious failings, it is almost impossible for an entity to detect all wrongdoing among millions of customers. Not an excuse, but consider for a moment, if we are punishing failures with fines, is this perhaps why accepting failures and regulatory punishments are aspects of business practice now being tolerated? Are reporting entities, despite their apparent best efforts, accepting failure? Have supervisors recognised this and come to see a bright profitable future ahead?

## Impressive results!

Despite years of regulatory punishments, it is hard to fathom how these regulatory failures keep happening. All reporting entities are obliged to do the same, but we recognise, as so many others will, that consistency is elusive across so many entities and sectors. Other than major financial institutions, most businesses would not cope with receiving such large financial punishments. Yet major financial institutions continue to accept the AML/CFT turmoil without expressing any obvious frustration. Even when someone else is responsible for paying fines and settlements – namely the customer – having failures plastered across media headlines is surely bad for business. So where has it all gone so wrong and why do the supervisors seem to always win?

Fines imposed do indicate AML/CFT regulators are doing what is expected of them – cracking down on inadequate AML/CFT controls. Yet is it becoming far easier to hand out a fine than reflect on one's own failures of supervision? Are we actually in the midst of a system in which 'quantity not quality' is leading to so little inaction in punishing AML/CFT failures above any financial penalty? While most punishments can reflect the severity of the failure, in the case of AML/CFT regulatory failures, there is no real punishment, no actual deterrent, just a game of *tit for tat* being played out. Very few people are ever held to account – we recognise this. When a sacrificial scapegoat is identified, a golden handshake and an exit from the rear of the building is what usually follows. The authors know this because they have purposefully spoken with such scapegoats who, they themselves know, fell from grace simply because they were willing to be pushed.

Despite the possibility of reputational damage – something so frequently affixed to punishments for AML/CFT compliance failures – are failures then happening time and again? Well, the truth is, reputations are rarely damaged through the process of handing out fines. Few people are ever required to publicly admit fault, be blamed and fall from grace unwillingly. While, it is true, smaller businesses and entities would most likely fall foul of negative publicity across regions and local communities, larger financial institutions typically remain unscathed. You perhaps then have to wonder, are the fines too small, are the fines irrelevant as a punishment? Something is certainly amiss.

Even when wrongdoing is uncovered, financial institutions just continue to exchange customers as they move from one institution to the next in search of more favourable interest rates and more appealing customer benefits. Financial institutions, it could be said, are dismissive of the belief customers will leave even after an AML/CFT compliance failure results in a media storm. This is despite links to crimes such as child exploitation and terrorism, as in the case of Westpac Bank in Australia.[2] It could also be argued that nowhere else exists for these customers to go.

If insanity 'is doing the same thing over and over again and expecting different results',[3] then three decades of money laundering regulation suggest medical attention is urgently required. Yet in this case, the quote highlights the ingenuity of the financial system to hide among such repetitive actions, knowing there will be no change – instead, just minor inconveniences along the way. It goes without saying there may be fines, even settlements to manage but from what is happening, it is plausible to suggest they are of little interest. The need to front the media, apologise and move funds from Peter (the financial institution) to pay Paul (the supervisor) has become another aspect in managing a business in the 21st century. But do these practices equate to a cover up or are they just the result of an inadequate process that has been allowed to creep slowly into societies, business communities and government policies across the globe? We think this whole situation needs to be questioned because supervisors have become distracted by the rewards, instead of the ramifications of failures of AML/CFT compliance.

## A simple cost of doing business

For years, speed humps, or 'sleeping policemen' have been introduced by road engineers in many countries to encourage drivers to slow down. They impede traffic flow, especially when combined with bollards and traffic islands. These impediments can have disastrous consequences for drivers not attuned to how concrete bollards can be extremely unforgiving when collided with. Such practices serve a purpose, in the same way AML/CFT regulations are thought to prevent money laundering and terrorism financing. They act to prevent the money launderer and terrorism financer from moving their funds by adding in restrictions and obstacles within those entities deemed capable of facilitating transfers and purchases. Sometimes there can be an unfortunate collision, the result of which can be the submission of a SAR or, equally, regulatory enforcement action.

For the regulated entities and their customers, these restrictions and obstacles are now, so it seems, embedded and part of daily business practices. In the same way that a motorist may begrudgingly accept scratching a wing mirror or wheel on a traffic island as they navigate new traffic flow obstacles too fast. Large financial entities in particular are seeing fines and settlements as simply a cost of doing business. A cost that can be absorbed – even when it means their own vehicle is damaged.

Consider the case of the large financial institution as an equation when considering AML/CFT compliance failures and the reality of this argument becomes clearer:

$$\text{'Profit from trading' less 'compliance spend'} = \text{more than 'any regulatory fine'}$$

While we suggest the situation as a simple equation, perhaps too simple, we wish to raise the point that it is only a cost of business *if* the entity is found to be failing in their compliance obligations. It is possible to believe that as long as the business is profitable after all costs and fines are paid there is less chance of the business ever collapsing.

Understandably, it would not be the ideal situation for any government to have businesses failing, yet putting large financial entities out of business would provide a stern warning to others on a global stage. It would also, and this is where an alarm bell may start ringing, reduce the amount received in fines and settlements by supervisors. This is a notion that is clearly never going to sit comfortably with those in charge, even if the drastic change necessary is staring them in the face.

Still, if there is ever the need to evidence the statement, we feel HSBC's actions provide the perfect example. In 2012, a USD$1.9 billion settlement was made by the London-based bank HSBC[4] following claims it facilitated money laundering and financial transfers for corrupt officials, terrorists and drug cartels through its US subsidiary. This figure, at the time, equalled 11% of HSBC's USD$16.8 billion in global profit during 2011. A drop in the ocean some might suggest.

## Clicking of handcuffs in the boardroom

With all that has gone before – the increasing level and values of fines, the huge value settlements – why then are there so few prosecutions? While previous fines may have appeared extreme, the message seems always to be weakened by an underwritten clause from the regulator of 'we are not alleging [they] have allowed or enabled money laundering or the financing of terrorism to take place'. We cannot believe the answer to future failures can be more fines. Nor do we see settlements and the recruitment of more compliance personnel as a solution for the failures which will undoubtedly continue. Equally, nor can it be the spending of yet more company funds on compliance tools and so-called IT solutions that, in the end, only deflect interest in a problem elsewhere.

Instead, we think business leaders and the public need to hear the reassuring sound of handcuffs clicking tight in the boardroom, and all the way down the chain of command. The time has come to remove the legal defences that allow for arguing a lack of knowledge or criminal intent by CEOs. We also need to end the opportunities to hide behind collective decision making. If we could introduce a version of the Sarbanes-Oxley accounting law in the US, passed after the Enron and Worldcom scandals to force managers to take responsibility by signing off on financial reports, then AML/CFT compliance would change overnight. Taking a compliance failure to the boardroom immediately brings about a whole new dimension to the issue of AML/CFT compliance. We know punishments of late are usually attributed to the customer fronting up the fee, so why not flip the option for punishment on its head once and for all and see how hard the failures become for the supervisors to find.

As the authors, we see that unless 'profit from trading' becomes less than 'a regulatory fine' or fines are accompanied with obligatory criminal prosecution and prison time, the entire process will continue as a 'supervision for profit'. We agree, it can sometimes appear that supervisors are getting close to the door of the boardroom, so much so that those inside could at last be starting to alter their stance on understanding their liabilities. Increased AML/CFT governance training and suggestions of taking responsibility are a step in the right direction. But of course, the sceptics among us will presume this to be those at the top just finding ways to protect themselves more adequately from the possibility of prosecution. Whether this is as close as we get to the boardroom, largely depends on whether the loopholes are closed by the supervisors. Equally, we need laws detailing what is essentially a corporate social responsibility for preventing money laundering and terrorism financing.

The possibility of holding to account those responsible for AML/CFT compliance failures is difficult – we understand this. Still, we feel prosecutors need to start seeking indictments without hiding behind the difficulties of proving intent in white-collar crime cases. A greater focus is needed on proving a breach of conduct and any intentions to break the law. The former may be easy; the latter much harder, but without it, money laundering and terrorism financing are crimes of little consequence for many. If this is not viable, then another solution needs to be found.

Of course, we must not forget the law in most countries is typically quite clear – in that any wrongdoing needs to be proven, not simply assumed. It would be ignorant of us to assume those responsible could be thrown in jail because of a public outcry. Still, if Danish prosecutors are giving up investigating Danske Bank's ex-CEO, Thomas Borgen, despite the bank's US$200 billion Estonian money laundering scandal, then there are far too many 'get out of jail cards' floating about. Or at least we hope it was difficulties in proving guilt was the real reason. But for many, the niggling voice in their head is saying that these entities just still seem 'too big to face the music' and 'too big and important to ever fail'. Is this why entry to the boardroom will never actually happen? Sometimes we might find those inside are 'too big to jail' despite the publicity.[5]

## Unsurprising failures

Is it possible that the AML/CFT regulatory system is so terribly designed that compliance failures are inevitable? We recognise it may not be a specific case of 'set up to inevitably fail', but it could be. There is little doubt there are too few 'unsurprising failures' from which supervisors receive (but not personally) huge monetary rewards through fines and settlements. Although perhaps a very cynical or naive perspective, we feel it must be obvious by now that money is simply being taken from Peter (the reporting entity) to pay Paul (the regulator), thus not delivering the initial intentions of AML/CFT. What we see existing is a process permitted and even encouraged to happen again and again. There are simply no relevant preventative activities from the administering of fines – as fines can be anticipated and almost prepared for. It is clear the element of surprise has gone but the benefits of reward are still well and truly here.

If, and it is a big concern should it be, entities are being *set up to inevitably fail* in their AML/CFT compliance obligations, then the light ahead is a train coming towards us in the tunnel. Money laundering and terrorism financing will be that train. We strongly suggest the need to step back and look at what happens when AML/CFT supervisors also decide not to provide sufficient guidance to high-risk sectors to support their risk-based assessment process. We agree, as a single failure this may not raise too many initial concerns but consider the move a short while later, when an entity is questioned about their approach and found in the supervisor's opinion to have an unsatisfactory risk-based model. From this, questions should arise as to what game is being played by the supervisor. We already know the FATF introduced a risk-based approach which is **subjective**, meaning there is **no definitive right or wrong answer**. So why then can a supervisor decide not to agree with the assessment made by the entity and not provide reasoning behind their own judgement before handing out the fine? Does this sound ethical, particularly when the process accepts there will be mistakes? We do not think so, but since there is no effort being taken to put a stop to this vicious circle of poor guidance, compliance failure, then fine, we feel the war on dirty money needs a rethink a long way back from the battlelines.

## Correcting the obvious wrong

The apparent *supervision for profit* model is clearly doing less harm than good. Few fear the fines, many welcome discussions for a settlement and few, it seems, succumb to the apparent problem of reputational damage. A *sorry statement* it seems will now suffice. The current system of AML/CFT supervision allows fish to be plucked from a barrel while the same system continues to feed them in the hope they multiply. It is clear to us, and we hope to readers that the entire AML/CFT regime needs an overhaul.

If an overhaul is to happen, there first needs to be a review of AML/CFT compliance practices in conjunction with a review of the punishment regime. We already know the consequences of a compliance failure are inadequate, but choosing to outsource to contractors in order to manage compliance failures simply equates to washing your hands of the problem.

As it now stands, it is actually possible there is a general unwillingness to refute accusations of AML/CFT failures while the punishments are manageable. Is it equally possible the scenario playing out right before us allows both the entities and the supervisors to be a winner no matter the outcome? We agree, neither side may wish to be the outright winner, but if fines are seen as a performance success while the profit from AML/CFT compliance failures remains larger than the fine, we could have two very smug players.

Even so, it seems the realisation that punishments no longer fit the crime is still some way off. It is unclear by what we have seen, exactly when we will see those who hold ultimate responsibility being held accountable for AML/CFT compliance failures. It is not ridiculous to think fines levied could also be used to support investigations and develop IT systems to support law enforcement. Fines could also be used to increase analysis capabilities and bring together experts from academia, NGOs and private sector organisations to focus the effort towards preventing and detecting money laundering. Yet, these options are not yet the intention of the apparent game being played out. Whatever happens, fines need to be used for the right reasons if there is to be any truth in the notion that we are waging a war on dirty money.

So, whatever the future turns out to be, the problem of punishment brings us right back to where we started this book – global standards and the risk-based approach. Although attempts to hold senior management responsible for their actions, and inactions has led to widespread coverage, most are unable and unwilling to deliver real improvements. Maybe, just maybe, it is time to recognise that the entire system we are punishing people for is also 'no longer fit for purpose'. Fines are a consequence, not any form of fixing what is clearly broken. They contribute nothing towards creating a long-term strategy that eliminates AML/CFT failures and breaches.

Like it or not, ignoring the issue is not going to work; failures are happening all of the time. Long after 2026 we could see some positive results as the AMLA sets in place a requirement for banks to specify one member of their management Board to hold responsibility for their entities' AML/CFT programme. Perhaps this will make at least one person accountable, in reality – maybe not. But at least it will on paper, and those who suggested it will know they have tried to do something good. Whether this person will end up in prison following a compliance failure, again only time will tell. Still, if US compliance examples are anything to go by, with Europe and UK not too far behind in its examples, employees receiving even a conviction for money laundering will likely be extremely rare.[6]

Oddly for the most part, it is worth remembering as a final closing comment that fines are typically for compliance failures not for actual money laundering and terrorism financing. So, no matter how we punish, what we punish for and how much of a discomfort the punishment seems to deliver, what is seemingly inevitable is that we can expect to see large fines continue well into the future, as the problem of money laundering gets a whole lot worse. That is unless before we do anything else, we first assess whether what we are doing is effective.

## Solutions toolbox

• Fines may once have been an effective deterrent. But when it is not your money, why would the value needing to be paid be of concern? Fining entities for AML/CFT compliance failures needs to be replaced because the bigger banks probably set aside provisions in anticipation of this. Whether by criminal prosecutions, withdrawal of trading licences, mandatory closure of the entire business, suspension of international transfers and cross-border banking embargoes for a certain period, something new, personal and hard hitting needs to reinvigorate the punishment schedule. That is unless 'not so dirty money' is more acceptable as a payment than 'dirty money' linked to crime.

• There needs to be greater transparency of the fines. Both the setting of fine amounts and the use of such fines once collected. Perhaps even transparency from the businesses fined as to where the money is coming from. This would inevitably un-nerve many who have simply played the moving money from Peter (the reporting entity) to pay Paul (the supervisor/regulator) game for far too long.

• These figures of large fines are helpful for one thing, drawing attention to the need to make change to reach the desired goal of stopping money laundering. Firefighting the current workload of compliance expectations needs to stop, as clearly the fines, no matter how big, are not acting as a deterrent or pulling entities into line with the expectations placed upon them.

• There is now a need to make punishments just that, a punishment. If the *mens rea* or *guilty mind* can be proven, then there needs to be personal punishment, not an organisational fine. For this to happen someone with experience as the role of auditor/investigator will need to work out who is not telling the truth. Difficult, but possible.

- Alongside punishments we also need to start handing out rewards. If there is evidence of satisfactory performance, compliance, and so on, then rewards must be available, although the criteria would need to be far stronger than those used to punish for clear AML/CFT regulatory failures. And the question then arises, what would a reward look like? A public notification that an entity has complied, perhaps.

- The Sarbanes-Oxley accounting law in the US passed after the Enron and Worldcom scandals – which forces managers to take responsibility for their books by signing off on financial reports – needs to be replicated for AML/CFT compliance.

- As the foundation for an AML/CFT programme, the risk assessment holds significant weight in guiding the direction of the AML/CFT policies and procedures which follow. Yet, does the risk assessment, the result or outcome of the FATF 'risk-based approach' to AML/CFT actually go far enough? Instead of searching anxiously for all risks to justify what then follows, could the focus be more towards capturing uncertainty? Or as a very minimum, a formal recognition that the obvious risks are not where the money launderer is making the greatest headway.

It is about time we changed the conversation and stopped adding funds to the supervisors' bank accounts even if the ultimate intention is to pressure others to also bring their AML/CFT standards to a more respectable level. Still, it is the 'will' to change, improve and implement that outweighs the 'normal way' things need to be done. But now is the time to also wrap up this book and bring together those points which can make the future a little more positive for those of us that want to see some changes made to what is AML/CFT. A good place to start is setting out an ideal future landscape.

# 21

# A future landscape

## What happens if we win the war?

During a previous global war, the Second World War, an academic turned temporary civil servant in the British government, William Beveridge, tried to imagine a different post-war world. The Beveridge Report was published in 1942 and after the war became the basis of what is now known as the 'Welfare State'. The publication of the Beveridge Report was initially delayed because the British minister of finance considered that it involved "an impracticable financial commitment".[1] At the time, the financial cost of the Second World War was crippling for Britain (and many other countries). Nonetheless, the policy went ahead and changed the lives of tens of millions of British people for the better in the post-war period. Beveridge identified five Giant Evils which he thought should be addressed: *Ignorance, Want, Squalor, Idleness and Disease.*

These evils still stalk the world, now adversely affecting the lives of not millions but billions of people. This chapter imagines how a victory over dirty money would free up the resources to change the world. These resources could make a real difference. The amount of lost tax, for example, converted into dirty money each year, is estimated at US$483 billion.

## Where prevention fails enforcement should follow

The prevention part of the current War on Dirty Money costs an additional US$210 billion,[2] and the cost keeps rising. This could be described as 'an impracticable financial commitment'.

Against this background our proposals for winning the war through enforcement seem absurdly cheap. This US$210 billion is currently spent on trying, but unfortunately failing, to prevent dirty money from entering the global financial system. Of the hundreds of thousands of people engaged in this prevention effort, almost all of them in the private sector, are failing to receive the support they deserve from governments. We recognise that prevention is better than enforcement, but it is our view that criminal enforcement has not yet been achieved or, we argue, even been seriously attempted. That is not to downplay the *effort* of the few people engaged in enforcement against dirty money; they are doing what they can. They are just absurdly few in number, generally underpaid relative to private sector compliance staff, and under-supported by their own colleagues in criminal justice.

This lack of support, we think, arises from a major mis-understanding about the nature of 'money laundering', 'financial' or 'economic' crime which have been pigeon-holed as 'specialist' activities when they are, in fact, integral and commonplace in a general crime wave that could be called 'acquisitive' or 'greed' crime. We recognise the importance of specialist skills but argue that acquisitive and greed criminals are all vulnerable to financial investigation and asset recovery when supported by financial intelligence provided by a huge, largely untapped resource, in the form of private sector compliance personnel, equipment and software.

Different crime types (corruption, environmental crime, fraud, robbery, tax evasion, and so on) can all be tackled by the relevant subject matter experts, but it is the use of financial intelligence, investigation and asset recovery, far from being a specialism, which needs to be commonly applied. This requires applying an age-old adage 'to catch a thief you have to think like one' to a modern world awash with computer-enabled financial information and a modern criminal code that includes a flexible and generic crime called money laundering. Criminals think of ways to acquire and spend money; to succeed against them we should apply financial tools. We think that this could change the current 'whack-a-mole' problem, whereby scarce specialist subject matter experts concentrate on a crime type, succeed in suppressing it only to find that criminals have been displaced to another crime type.

The forces of law enforcement are forever playing catch-up. If the strategy is nudged towards being tough on the main cause of crime, by making crime not pay, then law enforcement is always on the front foot. If dirty money is always the target, then criminals are always on the run.

We think that both the army engaged in prevention and the little battalion of enforcers deserve some justice, and our proposal is simply to give criminal enforcement a chance. To be clear, we encourage prevention and the need for stronger analysis, and this should always support arresting and prosecuting criminals and confiscating their money. Where this is difficult, we recommend litigating criminal money and, if that fails, we favour punitive taxation. This hierarchy of options, incidentally, is reflected in the POCAs of Ireland (1997) and the UK (2002), so it is not an original idea.

## Building on the FATF success

As a policy option, enforcement through financial investigation and asset recovery has a firm infrastructure to build upon. At a national level, in most countries, the legal and organisational infrastructure is largely in place and so is the expertise. This infrastructure has been nurtured or created over three decades by the efforts of the FATF – meaning it now falls to the FATF to make this infrastructure deliver. The main problem is that the infrastructure is run by very, very few people and it is not supported by a logical framework based on research. It has just evolved organically. We find this surprising, given its utility. Generally, financial investigation is a net contributor to the rest of criminal justice in terms of the intelligence contribution and its evidential product. The cost of running the asset recovery process is negligible; and in the few places where asset recovery is routinely done, the value recovered comfortably exceeds the cost of the resources needed to do the work. As far as we can work out, asset recovery raises morale, reduces crime and is better, quicker and cheaper than traditional investigation methods. The lay reader may then wonder why criminal justice systems do not invest in all the benefits offered by financial investigation and asset recovery. We wonder about this too.

For the most part, people in criminal enforcement do not embrace change or think about the bigger global picture. Also, because financial investigation has been pigeon-holed as a specialist subject, strategic awareness of its potential is rare. If strategists did want to find out what financial investigation and asset recovery could do for them, there are very few books available in which to find the answers. That is why we wrote this one.

## Understanding the problem

At the moment, the criminal enforcement war against dirty money is being fought separately, country by country. About 200 unconnected battlefields. The criminal law is written and executed exclusively at a national level. This makes it hard to do and even harder to then see through the fog of war to view what is going on at a global level. Meanwhile the focus of criminal money, and those who have it, is to dodge the battlefield altogether. Some writers have identified where the battle should be engaged. Author, journalist and investigator Nicolas Shaxson identified what he called 'Treasure Islands', where the wealthy hide the information about their money. More recently, Author Oliver Bullough invented the concept of 'Moneyland'. We think that both concepts are worthy of more examination – as places to conduct the next phase on the war on dirty money. Moneyland is not a particular country or even a collection of countries, but is a legal construct, a flexible ever-changing, ever-moving international place, shrouded in clouds, veil and blankets of secrecy. People do not live in Moneyland, but it is full of vital information about their money.

This might seem a difficult place to fight a battle, never mind a war, but there are many vulnerabilities we simply cannot ignore. It is a legal construct and ultimately national law can penetrate and overcome it. Incredibly good laws exist, the superlative POCAs of Ireland and the United Kingdom contain excellent powers to seize and forfeit cash and the only statutory definition of 'being a criminal' exists in Section 75 of the UK version. The power of Section 75 is that it triggers 'assumptions' about the criminal origin of assets that enable asset recovery. Many other countries have legislation aimed at the same objective but use different legal constructs. Such examples include the crime of Unexplained Wealth in France or anti-Mafia laws allowing enhanced confiscation in Italy. Later tweaks to the British POCA have since extended cash seizure to bank balances and improved the legal ability to confiscate assets without a person being convicted of a crime.

Criminal money is already litigated and has been for years, and cash forfeiture laws have been styled with this in mind. These cases are listed against the money and would be named, for example in the USA, 'The People versus US$1,234,567'. Or in the UK, 'The Chief Constable versus £1,234,567'. The criminal offence of money laundering, originally created in 1988 by UN Convention, thankfully had international litigation in mind: *If a person transfers the proceeds of a crime to another person, who knows it is the proceeds of crime, then both people simultaneously commit the crime.* If the transfer happens across a national frontier, then each commits a crime in the respective country at the same time. Yet we see money laundering as a rare example of an international crime.

## The collective power of nation states

We need to recognise that the people of Moneyland live in real countries, where they can be arrested and prosecuted. Their assets are also in real countries. While some will be cash, the vast majority will be real estate that can be frozen and confiscated. It is only the financial *information* that is in Moneyland.

As well as good law, the organisational infrastructure to get financial intelligence in most countries is good (but could be better). Every country has an FIU which is normally well resourced. Their task is to collect financial intelligence and pass it to the 'competent authorities' for financial investigation and asset recovery. There is, unfortunately, a gross imbalance between intelligence investment in prevention compared to enforcement. The SAR regime is excellent; it should be after decades of development to create it. We recommend that there is some small investment needed to connect the system so that the end-user actually gets to see the information being generated. We also recommend that the lavish investment in high-tech resources that is currently developing better SARs is diverted to develop end-user intelligence, so that existing SARs that contain information about suspicious money can be connected with information about suspicious people.

Moneyland is an international place where information about the proceeds of crimes, like international tax evasion, can still be accessed. We recommend a real effort to create a genuine international enforcement infrastructure to do this work. This should match the prevention infrastructure already created by the FATF; so, it would make sense for the FATF to use their expertise to create this new infrastructure. This solution would involve prevention and enforcement having equality in the agendas of meetings of the FATF and FSRBs. The Egmont Group and its FIUs would need a matching enforcement network, probably styled on the European Union Asset Recovery Offices, but with more staff. Each national FIU should have a partner Asset Recovery Office *comprised of at least the same number of staff* – in each country. This would require investment, but this is to do justice to the existing investment in FIUs. We think that the FIUs are generally 'operationally independent' (which is a good thing), but that they have been 'operationally abandoned' by their national governments (which is a bad thing). We think no one has the courage to say what we see as the truth.

The EU has a lot to offer in terms of international good practice. A significant problem is the sloth of international mutual legal assistance (MLA). MLA is often too slow, complicated and inflexible to cope with international illicit financial flows. We think that the EU Joint Investigation Team (JIT) model has the potential to be more effective in international financial investigation. The legal umbrella of a JIT, within which evidence and intelligence can be swiftly exchanged between countries, is well suited to the fast-moving, covert world of international financial investigation.

The FATF's MER system needs to develop beyond a regime fixed on evaluating individual countries to one that evaluates international illicit flows between countries. This should not be too hard; the MER system is highly developed and already has international assessment embedded in its 'operational effectiveness' approach. One way to think of Moneyland is to recognise that

Moneyland is where illicit financial flows happen, so our global evaluation process should focus on it.

We see the global financial sector as a generator of powerful information for a criminal justice engine that needs to be fully switched on. To make this happen we need to provide the global financial sector with the conceptual support, hard information and practical guidance so it understands why it should divert a modest 10% towards connecting this power up to the criminal justice system. To put this in money terms, we suggest that instead of spending US$210 billion a year on prevention (whose level of efficacy is hard to even guess), we reduce this by 10% to US$189 billion. We should divert US$0.5 billion to connect SARs to police and prosecutors and another US$20 billion on extra financial investigators and prosecutors to develop them into prosecution casework. A remaining US$0.5 billion is for research to see whether this modest adjustment actually works. To put this modest transfer of just 10% of the current cost of prevention into context, it is useful to know that the *entire budget* of the UK's National Economic Crime Centre (part of the National Crime Agency) in 2020/21 was just under US$0.05 billion.[3]

We anticipate that a few years after this initial investment, the value of assets recovered would substantially reduce the need for this seed funding.

## More research

In this book we have set out, in chapter after chapter, a world where hundreds of thousands of people are devoting some or all of their effort into systems which do not connect with the problem that they are trying to solve. There is far too little review of the logic of what all these people are doing. There are knowledge gaps everywhere and hardly anyone is engaged in researching practical solutions to everyday issues.

We see a need for much better knowledge of what works. There is a desperate need for research at every stage of the process and a mechanism to share good practice around the world. Assumptions include that asset recovery changes criminal behaviour, but we have not engaged researchers to ask criminals if it does. We seem to have assumed that asset recovery is a single thing whereas, in fact, there are levels of asset recovery. Perhaps some forms of asset recovery are more effective than others. We just do not know, and we have scarcely begun to research the effect of what we are doing in over 200 different countries.

We have, however, started to realise that there are 'illicit financial flows' between countries. But we understand little about how these flows actually work. We recognise that cash seems to end up in vast quantities in particular countries without examining how or why it got there.

We work hard to produce millions of SARs for the end-users but have failed to realise that hardly any of them get to the front line because there is a break in the line of communication between the FIU and the end-user. When the SAR intelligence does get through, there is no one there to use it. When we do achieve asset recovery, we choose not to research how success was achieved and how we could be even better at what we did. We have not even worked out how to consistently count what we have done. We should research what we are doing and agree how to account for it.

## Creating a virtuous circle from a vicious one

Crime and corruption drain resources away from poor people and leave them poorer, but it does not have to be this way. Asset recovery is treated as a by-product of expensive criminal justice; it is not viewed as a success in its own right that should be reinvested in better, more effective justice. The harm done to specific communities by crime could be repaired by recycling recovered assets or money, but again, we fail to do this. Instead, the money goes back to the general public purse, as if there was nothing special about it. We think it is special; it represents the misery and harm caused by crime and should be used to compensate specific victims, if they can be identified, or communities if they cannot. Alerting communities that they can fight back against crime and be compensated for doing so seems an important way to improve the world.

# Conclusion: A call to arms

Dirty money is a stain on society. It is literally destroying the planet and strangling efforts by good people to do good things. Its malign influence taints everything. Illicit financial flows of dirty money undermine honesty, integrity and good business practices. Yet, the parasitic people creating and moving dirty money *can be identified and stopped.*

The AML regime created over three decades by the FATF and other national and international bodies has developed the technical tools and the legal framework to tackle money laundering effectively, but the regime as a whole does not work. We think it lacks a moral and geographical compass. A moral compass would point to the global evils of corruption, environmental crime, tax inequality, organised crime and all other crimes that *could all be exposed, tackled, and reduced* by focusing on the dirty money that is both the root cause and the product of these evils. A geographical compass would point, not towards individual countries, but towards the illicit financial flows between them. Better still, the regime's compass could identify 'Moneyland', that artificial legal construct where bad people hide their bad money.

Yet, at the end of 30 years, the AML regime has ended up in a box, separated from crime altogether, filled with compliance specialists who are correctly regarded as an expensive 'cost of doing business'. Their product is not valued or understood outside their own profession and is rarely even seen by the front line against crime. Ironically and unfairly, they are frequently judged not by their prevention efforts but by those on the enforcement side of the regime, who recover pitifully small amounts of money from criminals compared to the huge illicit financial flows estimated to exist. We should return to the fundamental principles that were present when the FATF was created, the twin ideas that crime must not pay and that money laundering is integral to crime.

The AML regime is now fully in place across the world, its institutions have been created and matured, its people recruited and trained, its legal framework tried and tested. This is no mean feat, so congratulations go to the FATF. The AML regime is like a giant global machine, ready and able to tackle the evil of dirty money, if only we could find the switch to turn it on. Making crime not pay can be done. To this end we need to exploit our new ability to confiscate personal assets from criminals and return them to crime victims and wider society in a 'virtuous circle' that is fundamentally fair and positive. Most of all we need to change what we are doing, because it is unfocused, repetitive and, above all, it simply does not work. In this book we have set out a way to do this.

Each chapter had a 'Solutions toolbox', totalling over a hundred potential solutions set out in different contexts. Here these solutions are brought together as a cohesive package. Overall, we have shown that money laundering has been poorly defined from its inception and fundamental issues have been left unaddressed. We do not blame anyone for this, we understand it can appear confusing and complex and it is very difficult to always see the whole picture. We fully accept that there are gaps in global knowledge and that far more research is needed into, for example, the impact of confiscation on criminals, why cash seizure remains so important and how grand and petty corruption fit together. The lack of research into money as a cause of crime is astonishing and shameful. So too is the lack of research into money laundering as a series of transfers and purchases.

Our conclusions have been reached after years of specialist analysis, practical casework and problem-solving with experts across multiple professions around the world. We have focused on the practice of tackling dirty money to reach this modest and probably flawed proposal, but it is, in our view, a calculated and realistic way forward.

## What should we do then?

The idea that money laundering is complicated, undertaken through sophisticated activities aligned to typologies, needs to be reassessed. The global push to understand money laundering has focused the ideas and beliefs into tightly knit groupings. Money laundering is no longer a three-stage process, so research is urgently needed to understand the *who*, *how* and *why* behind today's money laundering practices. No easy task, but it is this *reset in thinking* that will set the foundation for everything that then follows.

The global AML regime costs billions and engages hundreds of thousands of people in many full-time professional roles aimed at preventing money laundering and enforcing the law when prevention has failed. We salute everyone who is engaged in this effort, and we think that they deserve better. Yet the benefits from their work are hard to identify. Everyone in charge has a duty to fix this cost/benefit failure. We think that there is a massive imbalance between the huge resources applied to prevention and the scraps given to enforcement. This imbalance should be addressed by some of the resources being moved from prevention to enforcement. Enforcement should be against money laundering and money launderers rather than, for example, the owners of banks. The key method of enforcement should not be a monetary fine against any institution but the confiscation of personal assets from perpetrators. We have set out the levels of confiscation ability that countries possess. Every country should aspire to the highest level of competence, but especially the 80% of countries that do no confiscation at all and choose instead to let crime pay. To raise public confidence, the FATF should mandate the collation and publication of confiscation statistics. This is the bedrock of evidence-based decision making.

The financial sector's compliance regime is by far the biggest user of resources. We challenge this division of resources. The RBA needs to focus on the actual risk, not the box marked 'risk'. Regulators in particular should reward proper RBA and penalise box-ticking. We should identify true risks: the availability of large denomination notes; large cash transfers and purchases; the irresponsible registration of anonymous companies; tax-dodging accountancy 'standards', the 'double indemnity' from prosecution enjoyed by companies, and so on, and so on.

Currently the benefits of money laundering prevention are illusory. We advocate that the resources should be moved to enforcement against money launderers. In particular, the 'RegTech' solutions and the heavily computerised financial sector could be usefully diverted towards developing the largely computer-free world of policing and prosecution. The analytical power and skill of FIUs and the financial sector could be diverted to the crime front line. The front line itself could be strengthened by using financial investigation against all crimes, on the reasonable grounds that it is quicker, cheaper and more effective than traditional methods. The other 99% of detectives and their leaders who already investigate predicate crimes should be deployed against the money from those crimes (something called parallel investigation).

The effectiveness of financial intelligence and financial evidence is poorly understood by prosecutors, police managers and judges. So international guidance and support is needed to develop national leadership strategies and skills. The AML regime has enormous resources, but they are pointing in the wrong direction; we need to move from 'prevention' to 'enforcement'.

## So how should we do it?

The definition of money laundering as 'placement, layering and integration' is misleading and obstructive. It should be scrapped and replaced by the United Nations' Conventions wording: 'The acquisition, possession or use of any property derived from or obtained, directly or indirectly, through the commission of an offence.'[1]

In this way the AML regime of each country, currently split between prevention and enforcement, can be united under one set of words that should be written into every country's criminal code. The compliance sector can then focus on suspicious transfers and purchases in cooperation with the enforcers. The universal terminology will facilitate international cooperation so that countries can support one another. Having started so well with finding agreement for the conventions against narcotics, transnational organised crime and corruption, it is the United Nations which has a specific role to play to make the words of those conventions work. Its agencies could be tasked with ensuring that key definitions – like money laundering – are incorporated into criminal codes, word for word, and that they are enforced. It is simply not enough for legal definitions to be 'similar'; to work across national frontiers they must be the same. It is not good enough for UN members to sign a UN Convention into law and then ignore it.

Remember that money laundering is integral to every crime motivated by money and that we now have the computer power and a legal framework to actually tackle it for the first time in history. For too long, countries have claimed success in fighting money laundering on the basis of isolated, individual cases, reported out of context without any regard, rather than what, if anything, they achieve.

## And when and where should we do it?

Incrementally, everywhere. The war on dirty money is being fought country by country and against the illicit financial flows running between some countries. This provides over 200 places where different AML techniques can be tried. We have an established mutual evaluation system which could be tweaked to detect international illicit financial flows and how they are being tackled, to identify and promote good practice and to detect weak spots that could be supported by international donors and organisations.

The 'country watchlist' approach by the FATF and other regional and international bodies feels biased, politicised and counterproductive. Perhaps listing the countries at both ends of an illicit financial flow might identify genuine risk and inspire cooperative action. The FATF greylist and blacklist 'one-size-fits-all' approach needs to be scrapped in order to reflect a collective responsibility for illicit flows between countries, and the unique local circumstance of local countries.

Between the two halves of the AML regime – prevention and enforcement – is a gap which money launderers exploit, because their task is to separate the information about the money from the information about the crime. For this reason, the FATF should recommend the combining of SAR data with police intelligence data (with appropriate safeguards) as a key way to evaluate a country's effectiveness.

Information sharing is notoriously difficult, so successful instances should be documented and promulgated through the MER system.

## Who should do it?

The FATF has a global network, but its members include other global, regional and international organisations. These could work easily together to provide expertise for countries which lack their own resources. What is lacking is a global strategy that identifies specific roles for specific bodies. The FATF should be tasked by its international members to create that strategy for the general 'good of all'.

Cohesion and a collectiveness among academic and 'ground level' professionals could be the key to identifying why some cases and national approaches succeed. This should be undertaken both in real time and through cold case reviews. Currently, successful cases are simply filed and ignored, yet they hold immense value. Successful countries are not recognised – even by themselves – because there is still no forum, no mechanism to learn and develop. Learnings from this process would inspire a new approach to preventing and investigating, as well as creating NRAs that detail *how* money laundering manages to remain so successful within national contexts. The FATF needs a well-resourced academic research arm to identify what works and promulgate good practice.

Regulators discover failures to comply with a 'risk-based approach' and impose fines, but their budgets depend on these fines. This has created a risk of its own. The reputation of the global AML regime has been damaged by weak enforcement, deferred prosecution agreements and expensive, ineffectual prevention. The huge fines imposed in recent years have made no apparent difference to criminal behaviour; no one is even claiming they have. They serve, instead, to indicate the monetary value of the corruption, environmental crime and organised tax evasion that is being permitted, even perpetuated, by an ineffective AML regime. This needs to be stopped and a shift in focus quickly applied.

The crime of tax evasion failed to make the list of predicate crimes for dirty money purposes for two decades, before finally being included in 2012. It is still viewed generously by government tax authorities who favour encouragement to pay over enforcement. We think corporate tax evasion has now become such a serious crime that it deserves special and serious treatment not by tax collectors but by organised crime investigators and prosecutors.

## The need for a level playing field

The prevention side of AML is lavishly equipped with an entire compliance industry supported by national FIUs coordinated by the Egmont Group Secretariat, the Association of Anti-Money Laundering Specialists (85,000 members), the FATF itself and its FSRBs, all coordinated by a permanent Secretariat. Its annual budget is well over US$210 billion.

The enforcement side of AML has some regional informal networks called Asset Recovery Interagency Networks, composed of a volunteer prosecutor and a law enforcement official per country, and no formal global structures or professional groups at all. The front line, where the actual war on dirty money takes place, hardly exists. Its annual budget is not even known.

So, here lies the key problem. The FATF has built a global infrastructure in two distinct halves, 'prevention' and 'enforcement'. It is not clear if prevention works or not, but it has become clear that the enforcement half does not work. Nor can it, with so little support. Enforcement needs the same international infrastructure as the prevention side. It needs resources, coordination and cooperation. The 'good guys' are not out-resourced – instead, resources are ill-aligned. The laws, the reporting systems, excellent skills and good people are all in place, they are just too few. It is a global mechanical giant that is half asleep. It is time to turn it on and finally begin the 'war on dirty money'.

# Notes

## Foreword

1. Global gross domestic product in 2020 is estimated to be some US$85 trillion. See: https://www.statista.com/statistics/268750/global-gross-domestic-product-gdp/
2. OECD data 2019–2020 average. See: https://public.tableau.com/views/AidAtAGlance/DACmembers?:embed=y&:display_count=no?&:showVizHome=no#1
3. See: https://www.unodc.org/documents/data-and-analysis/Studies/Illicit_financial_flows_2011_web.pdf
4. Memorandum by the National Criminal Intelligence Service to the House of Commons International Development Committee inquiry on corruption, 2000–01, HC 39-II, March 2001.
5. See: https://www.nationalcrimeagency.gov.uk/who-we-are/publications/546-national-crime-agency-annual-report-and-accounts-2020-21/file
6. See: https://www.fatf-gafi.org/media/fatf/documents/reports/mer4/MER-United-Kingdom-2018.pdf
7. See: https://www.gov.uk/government/news/uk-takes-top-spot-in-fight-against-dirty-money

## Chapter 1

1. 1930, March 16, Los Angeles Times, Twain Letter Unearthed by Neeta Marquis, Section 3, Quote Page 22, Column 1 and 2, Los Angeles, California. See: https://www.newspapers.com/clip/55822232/the-los-angeles-times/
2. Bible, 1 Timothy 6:10.
3. LexisNexis Risk Solutions (2021) *True Cost of Financial Crime Compliance Global Report*. This report by a respected industry specialist estimated that the global cost rose from US$180.9 billion in 2020 to US$213.9 billion in 2021.
4. Quote from David Lewis at the Royal United Services Institute, London, 18 November 2019. See: https://www.fatf-gafi.org/publications/fatfgeneral/documents/rusi-fatf-strategic-review.html. Accessed 3 October 2021.
5. See: https://www.fatf-gafi.org/glossary/d-i/. Accessed 6 July 2021.
6. Health & Safety Matters (2021) 'Waste boss ordered to repay £800k'. See: https://www.hsmsearch.com/Waste-boss-ordered-repay-800k

[7] Young, M.A. and Woodiwiss, M.J. (2020) 'A world fit for money laundering: the Atlantic alliance's undermining of organized crime control'. *Trends in Organized Crime*, doi:1.1007/s12117-020-09386-8

[8] 'Staff Study of the Crime and Secrecy: The use of offshore banks and companies. Made by the Permanent Sub-Committee on Investigations of the Committee on Government Affairs, United States Senate', 1983. See: https://babel.hathitrust.org/cgi/pt?id=pst.000017389921&view=1up&seq=1

[9] See: https://tristramhicks.com/2020/05/01/as-covid-19-resets-our-world-its-time-to-reset-our-aml-toolbox/

[10] Pol, R.F. (2018) 'Uncomfortable truths? ML = BS and AML=BS²', *Journal of Financial Crime* 25(2): 294–308.

[11] The Council of the EU (2012) 'Final report on the fifth round of mutual evaluations – Financial crime and financial investigations'. See: https://data.consilium.europa.eu/doc/document/ST-12657-2012-REV-2/en/pdf

[12] Ramay, S.A. (2021) 'Op-Ed the FATF choosing to be unfair', *Daily Times* (of Pakistan), 3 July.

[13] 'De-risking' is a compliance technical term whereby a bank ends a customer relationship because the perceived risk of continuing it might put the bank in technical breach of regulations. There is criticism that de-risking is done based on perceived rather than actual problems.

[14] Quotation from The Royal United Services Institute webinar 'The FATF Standards and unintended consequences', Part 1. 8 July 2021.

[15] FATF (2021) *High-Level Synopsis of the Stocktake of the Unintended Consequences of the FATF Standards.*

[16] See: https://www.fatf-gafi.org/media/fatf/documents/Unintended-Consequences.pdf

[17] The technical term 'competent authorities' is used by the FATF to describe all government bodies which do, or could, intervene against money laundering. We cover misleading jargon in Chapter 2.

[18] *Rapport de stratégie, Stratégie anticorruption de la France dans son action de coopération 2021–2030*, 2 June 2021. See: https://www.diplomatie.gouv.fr/IMG/pdf

## Chapter 2

[1] The author's first-hand knowledge of resolving this case.

[2] More jargon: a *predicate* crime is one that generates money that can be laundered.

[3] International Letter of Requests

[4] Robinson, J. (2020) 'No! Enough, basta'. LinkedIn. See: https://www.linkedin.com/pulse/enough-basta-one-more-time-al-capone-money-launderer-anyone-robinson-1f/?trackingId=%2BqaEBMwr2V9E4JvAzkm%2F7g%3D%3D

[5] United Nations (1988) (Vienna) Convention against illicit traffic in narcotic drugs & psychotropic substances, Article 1(p).

[6] Hicks, T. (2015) 'It's all about Eve, the first money launderer', *Money Laundering Bulletin*, May.

7   Royal United Services Institute (2022) 'The future of economic crime policing' (webinar, 28 April 2022).

8   Unless you are dealing with the World Bank who, uniquely, have decided to use the term to describe only the recovery of the proceeds of corruption. Insert the emoji of your choice here.

9   The UN Conventions say that property means assets of every kind, whether corporeal or incorporeal, movable or immovable, tangible or intangible, and legal documents or instruments evidencing title to, or interest in, such assets.

10  See: https://fsi.taxjustice.net/en/

11  Bullough, O. (2019) *Moneyland: Why thieves and crooks now rule the world and how to take it back*. Profile Books.

12  See: https://www.statista.com/statistics/264806/worldwide-production-quantity-of-cocaine-since-1994/

13  Home Office (2017) *Asset Recovery Statistical Bulletin, 2011/12–2016/17*, HO Statistical Bulletin 15/17.

## Chapter 3

1   See: https://www.europol.europa.eu/activities-services/main-reports/europ ean-union-serious-and-organised-crime-threat-assessment

2   See: https://www.fincrimeworldforum.com/

3   See: https://www.interpol.int/en/News-and-Events/News/2022/INTER POL-launches-centre-against-financial-crime-and-corruption

4   The theory behind 'opportunity makes a criminal theory' was developed by the UK Home Office in the 1970s in which it was said that if an opportunity was available, then even those who had not decided to act unlawfully may nevertheless be inclined to if the circumstances were seen as favourable.

5   See: https://www.austrac.gov.au/new-financial-crime-guide-explains-cuc koo-smurfing

6   See: https://www.austrac.gov.au/business/how-comply-guidance-and-resour ces/guidance-resources/typologies-and-case-studies-report-2012

7   'Defence' – the suggestion that it is the libel laws of the UK which help you cover up any suggestion that there is anything untoward going on. The problem is this 'defence' addition muddies the already muddy waters of understanding.

8   See the video, 'How London became the dirty money capital of the world', *Financial Times*, 22 April 2022. See: https://www.ft.com/video/d3bafb94-9dbd-4c1e-8016-8cd8331960f1

9   Levi, M. and Reuter, P. (2006) 'Money laundering', *Crime and Justice* 34(1): 289–375.

10  Levi and Reuter 'Money laundering'.

11  See: https://www.ft.com/content/addd777e-de43-11e7-a8a4-0a1e63a52f9c

12  Leaving aside the issue of the integrity of this estimate, see RegTech Consulting LLC (2020) 'Measuring illicit financial flows – getting closer to a true estimate of global money laundering'. See: https://lnkd.in/gXqvzcB

[13] McGuire, M. (2018) *Into the Web of Profit*. An in-depth study of cybercrime, criminals and money. See: https://threatresearch.ext.hp.com/wp-content/uploads/2018/05/Into-the-Web-of-Profit_Bromium.pdf

[14] Self-laundering is considered the process of spending money on everyday smaller more discreet purchases such as fuel, food and cash payable services as opposed to laundering through the three-stage process of placement, layering and integration more commonly associated with higher amounts.

[15] Wathne, C. and Stephenson, M. (2021) 'Credibility of corruption statistics: a critical review of ten global estimates', U4 Anti-corruption Resource Center, U4 Issue 2021: 4.

[16] This assessment is based on the premise that illicit funds are almost always worthless until they have been successfully entirely laundered. It is true, there are options to 'self-launder' but if the holder wishes to purchase items and services, the illicit funds need to be cleaned – thus finally providing a reward from the predicate offence.

[17] See: https://www.reuters.com/article/us-danske-bk-moneylaundering-idUSKCN26F2SJ

[18] Jones, R. (2021) 'Cashless society draws closer with only one in six payments now in cash', *The Guardian*, 16 June. See: https://www.theguardian.com/business/2021/jun/16/cashless-society-draws-closer-with-only-one-in-six-payments-now-in-cash

[19] See report by Europol: https://www.europol.europa.eu/publications-events/publications/why-cash-still-king-strategic-report-use-of-cash-criminal-groups-facilitator-for-money-laundering

[20] See new story: https://amp.abc.net.au/article/101073180

[21] Gawande, A. (2011). *The checklist manifesto*. Profile Books.

[22] Initial FATF guidance released in 2006 only updated in 2020 with limited details on 'Trends and Developments', despite the fact that the FATF considers that it 'remains a profound and significant risk'. See: https://www.fatf-gafi.org/media/fatf/content/Trade-Based-Money-Laundering-Trends-and-Developments.pdf

[23] Money laundering is often described in two ways: scale, and value. Although interchangeable, scale is associated with the spread and frequency of money laundering, while value is the monetary amount laundered.

[24] See: https://www.fatf-gafi.org/publications/?hf=10&b=0&s=desc(fatf_releasedate)

[25] See: http://www.fatf-gafi.org/publications/fatfgeneral/documents/effectiveness-compliance-standards.html

[26] 2015 TedTalk. See: https://www.youtube.com/watch?v=udiTaS2wTAM

# Chapter 4

[1] See: https://www.imf.org/external/np/leg/amlcft/eng/aml1.htm/index.htm

[2] Although if you want to prevent and detect money laundering (and terrorism financing) you try to think like they do every single minute of your working day.

3   Snakes and ladders is a minimum two-player game in which each player takes turns to throw a dice. The number on the dice allows the player to move up the numbered board. Landing at the foot of a ladder allows them to climb higher while landing on a snake's head requires them to drop down the board. The winner is the first to number square 100.

4   The Fintel Alliance is a PPP led by AUSTRAC. Partners include businesses from the financial services, remittance and gaming industries as well as law enforcement and security agencies in Australia and overseas.

5   See: https://www.austrac.gov.au/sites/default/files/2022-04/AUSTRAC_FCG_PreventingCriminalAbuseOfDigitalCurrencies_FINAL.pdf

6   In the introduction to the report, we are informed, 'the pseudo-anonymous and borderless nature of digital currencies presents a risk for the facilitation of serious crimes, including: money laundering, the purchase and sale of illicit products, via darknet market places, terrorism financing, scams, tax evasion and ransomware'. Could this then suggest all other crime types are of a non-serious nature?

7   See: https://www.imf.org/external/np/leg/amlcft/eng/aml1.htm

8   See footnote 3 in the report titled: 'FinCEN advises increased vigilance for potential Russian sanctions evasion attempts'. See: https://www.fincen.gov/sites/default/files/2022-03/FinCEN%20Alert%20Russian%20Sanctions%20Evasion%20FINAL%20508.pdf

9   See: https://www.fatf-gafi.org/media/fatf/content/Trade-Based-Money-Laundering-Trends-and-Developments.pdf

10  Detect and Report Cuckoo Smurfing Financial Crime Guide (June 2021). See: https://www.austrac.gov.au/business/how-comply-guidance-and-resources/guidance-resources/cuckoo-smurfing

11  See: https://rusi.org/commentary/free-trade-zones-and-financial-crime-faustian-bargain

12  For the risk-based approach to be workable, there is a continuous need for the perception of risk by a reporting entity to align with regulatory expectations and pre-defined circumstances.

13  See: https://www.austrac.gov.au/news-and-media/media-release/austrac-releases-four-new-australian-banking-sector-risk-assessments

14  Anti-corruption judge-turned-MEP Eva Joly. See: https://www.youtube.com/watch?v=uSP_s6xXjIU

15  See: https://www.sra.org.uk/solicitors/guidance/money-laundering-terrorist-financing/

16  See: https://www.aml-analytics.com/solutions/financial-institution/red-flag-testing/

17  See: https://baselgovernance.org/news/new-four-part-series-spotlights-green-corruption-risks-and-what-do-about-them

18  Reid, A. and Williams, M. (2021) *Illegal Wildlife Trade and Financial Investigations in West Africa*, Royal United Services Institute, 29 April.

## Chapter 5

1   Marvin Comic strip by Tom Armstrong. See: https://www.washingtonpost.com/entertainment/comics/strips/?name=Marvin

2   The gender, occupation, age and ethnicity of recipients of confiscation orders are discussed in Chapter 14.

3   Europol Organised Crime Threat Assessment (2006).

4   BBC News (2022) 'Crypto money laundering rises 30%, report finds', 26 January. See: https://www.bbc.com/news/technology-60072195

5   Ridley, N. and Gilmour, N. (2015) 'Every day vulnerabilities, money laundering through cash intensive businesses', *Journal of Money Laundering Control* 18(3): 202–93.

6   Casciani, D. (2010) 'Organised crime fears ban €500 note sales'. BBC News. See: http://news.bbc.co.uk/1/hi/uk/8678886.stm. Accessed 19 December 2021.

7   This case has become the first conviction in the UK by the Financial Conduct Authority for a breach of money laundering regulations. NatWest Bank was convicted and fined £265 million. No individual person was prosecuted. The case is discussed in depth in 'The Dark Money Files' podcast: 'NatWest Bank and the Bradford laundromat'. Ray Blake and Graham Barrow https://podcasts.apple.com/gy/podcast/natwest-bank-and-the-bradford-laundromat-part-1/id1448635132?i=1000546793669

8   A cash courier hid £1.9 million in vacuum packs hidden in coffee en route between UK and Dubai. She admitted to smuggling another £3 million and was jailed in 2021. See: https://www.bbc.com/news/uk-england-leeds-57350863. Accessed 28 July 2021.

9   Home Office (2020) *Asset Recovery Statistical Bulletin 2014/15–2019/20*, Home Office 23/20.

10  Edmond Locard's criminological principle that 'every contact leaves a trace', first established in 1920.

11  Ashby, M. (2016) *Using crime science for understanding and preventing theft of metal from the British railway network*. Doctoral thesis. See: thesis_final_screen.pdf (ucl.ac.uk). This work is licensed under the Creative Commons Attribution 4.0 International Licence. To view a copy of this licence, visit http://creativecommons.org/licenses/by/4.0/

12  See: https://www.newsweek.com/2014/09/26/why-europes-super-rich-are-resorting-smuggling-cash-271540.html

13  UK Treasury, UK Home Office (2015) *UK national risk assessment of money laundering and terrorist financing*, Open Government Licence.

14  See: https://www.gov.uk/government/news/uks-first-ever-successful-prosecution-for-false-company-information. Accessed 1 August 2021.

15  NRA above.

16  Egmont Group Annual Report 2018/19.

17  Robert Magnus Martinson's 1974 study 'What Works?' was so influential, that it became known as the nothing works doctrine. He was studying

rehabilitation, but some people in law enforcement merely interpret his work to justify incarceration as the only possible response to crime.

18 Brown, R. and others (2012) *The contribution of financial investigation to tackling organised crime: a qualitative study*, HO Research Report 65.

19 European Commission (2011, 2013) *Eurostat Statistical Working Papers.*

20 Martin Woods, an AML compliance specialist.

21 Europol (2008) *European Union Organised Crime Threat Assessment.* The difficulty of cross-border cooperation has been a consistent theme since OCTAs were first published.

## Chapter 6

1 The European Economic Area includes members of the European Union and the European Free Trade Association.

2 FCA, 2020. See report: https://www.fca.org.uk/publication/final-notices/commerzbank-ag-2020.pdf

3 The 2016 Mossack Fonseca Panama Papers exposé relates to the leaking of 11.5 million financial and attorney-client records of over 214,488 offshore entities which were created by Panamanian law firm Mossack Fonseca in order to evade taxes and other money fraud. See: https://www.icij.org/investigations/panama-papers/

4 The results of which were nevertheless not fully recognised in their 2015 assessment. Followed by greylisting in 2016. Australian and US banks responded by closing their correspondent accounts in Vanuatu.

5 At the time – November 2021 – there were 23 countries on the greylist.

6 See: https://www.theguardian.com/world/2021/apr/23/malta-still-selling-golden-passports-to-rich-stay-away-residents

7 See: https://timesofmalta.com/articles/view/24-companies-renounced-malta-license-after-greylisting-pn.898591

8 See: https://www.linkedin.com/feed/update/urn:li:ugcPost:6853330461016518658?commentUrn=urn%3Ali%3Acomment%3A%28ugcPost%3A6853330461016518658%2C6855523072288542720%29. Accessed 12 May 2022.

9 See: https://www.moroccoworldnews.com/2021/02/336179/morocco-accused-of-pervasive-money-laundering-placed-on-greylist

10 Designated non-financial businesses and professions (DNFBP) is an FATF acronym applied to accountants, lawyers, real estate agents and similar, which in some countries are legally required to report the suspicious behaviour of their clients.

11 For Switzerland, see the 2016 FATF MER at: https://www.fatf-gafi.org/media/fatf/content/images/mer-switzerland-2016.pdf. For Luxembourg, see the 2014 FATF MER at: https://www.fatf-gafi.org/media/fatf/documents/reports/mer/FUR-Luxembourg-2014.pdf

12 'The impact of international anti-money laundering greylists on cross border payments: evidence from SWIFT data'. Presentation given at the 2021 Empirical Research Conference on Approaches to AML and Financial Crime in the Bahamas, 29 January 2021.

13   WIC News Reporter (2021) 'PM Harris outlines CARICOM meet as joint commitment to existential threat'. WIC News, 19 December.

14   UN (2019) Territorial Disputes, Weaponizing of Trade, Banking System Dominate Discussion by World Leaders, as General Assembly Continues Debate. Seventy-fourth Session GA/12196 (27 September 2019).

15   See: http://www.fatf-gafi.org/publications/mutualevaluations/documents/more-about-mutual-evaluations.html

16   See: https://www-bnnbloomberg-ca.cdn.ampproject.org/c/s/www.bnnbloomberg.ca/swiss-efforts-to-fight-money-laundering-are-a-failure-tdg-1.1496895.amp.html

17   This acronym includes a wide range of businesses and professions, but the significant ones in our view are lawyers, accountants and estate agents. These professions facilitate large transfers or purchases and are therefore important to this book.

18   See: Anti-money laundering and counter-terrorist financing measures – Australia. Mutual Evaluation Report April 2015. Australia has chosen, despite political pressure and its obligations as a signature member of the FATF not to implement legislation that incorporates DNFBPs into AML/CFT legislation. This means there are critical avenues for money laundering and terrorism financing that still exist in Australia because AML/CFT obligations are not applied to DNFBP's

19   Senate, Legal & Constitutional Affairs References Committee (The adequacy and efficacy of Australia's anti-money laundering and counter-terrorism financing (AML/CTF) regime) Live. The FATF has chosen not to add Australia to the FATF Grey List despite this obvious failing. This means Australia has dodge the international pressure of capturing DNFBP's in its national AML/CFT legislation.

20   Beneficial owner refers to the natural person(s) who ultimately owns or controls a customer and/or the natural person on whose behalf a transaction is being conducted. It also includes those persons who exercise ultimate effective control over a legal person or arrangement

21   For example, in July 2021, Luxembourg's Commission de Surveillance du Secteur Financier (CSSF) and Monaco's Service d'Information et de Contrôle sur les Circuits Financiers (SICCFIN) signed a Memorandum of Understanding (MoU) regarding the fight against money laundering and the financing of terrorism (AML/CTF).

22   Despite been neighbouring emirates, two of the seven which make up the United Arab Emirates, it was only in November 2021 that Dubai Police and the UAE FIU signed an MoU with the aim of cooperating in the field of money laundering crimes.

## Chapter 7

1   *CoE Parliamentary Assembly adopts Resolution on Financial Intelligence Units.* Strasbourg 13 April 2021. See: https://www.coe.int/en/web/moneyval/home/newsroom/-/asset_publisher/zTE3FjHi4YJ7/content/coe-parliamentary-assembly-adopts-resolution-on-financial-intelligence-units

2  We refer to SARs throughout the book, but acknowledge there are variations, such as suspicious transaction reports or STRs (United States) and suspicious matter reports or SMRs (Australia).

3  Egmont Group: FIU tools and practices for investigating laundering of the proceeds of corruption. According to the Egmont Group, the consequences of an FIU having their operational independence and autonomy compromised can impact on the credibility of an FIU with members of the private sector and domestic law enforcement. This can in turn influenced an FIUs ability to gather information it needs domestically to exchange information with international partners. Equally, it can have a negative effect on the quality and scope of investigations related to ML, TF, and predicate offences such as corruption and organized crime.

4  See: https://egmontgroup.org/about/financial-intelligence-units/

5  See: https://www.fincen.gov/reports/sar-stats

6  See: http://www.eu2015lu.eu/en/actualites/articles-actualite/2015/11/20-conseil-jai/index.html

7  goAML is UNODC's unique fully integrated software designed specifically for FIUs. The goAML solution is executed in three steps: data collection, analysis (rule-based analysis, risk-score and profiling) and dissemination (escalate to law enforcement and See: k feedback). See: https://unite.un.org/goAML/content/approach-and-benefits

8  At the time of writing, 56 of the 111 FIUs engaged with the OECD had deployed goAML.

9  See: https://www.unodc.org/unodc/en/global-it-products/goAML.html

10  Most AML SARs have to do with anomalous cash-use, deposits and withdrawals: for example, in Europe they account for 40% of all those issued annually, according to Europol (2017). In countries with higher levels of cash-intensity (that is, with a higher use of cash for payments), it is easier to integrate illicit proceeds into the legitimate economy, and the risk of money laundering is also higher.

11  AUSTRAC (2021) Public consultation: System Transformation Program – Your feedback will help to shape how you report to AUSTRAC. See https://www.austrac.gov.au/system-transformation-program-your-feedback-will-help-shape-how-you-report-austrac

12  See: https://www.politico.eu/article/europe-money-laundering-is-losing-the-fight-against-dirty-money-europol-crime-rob-wainwright/

13  See publication by the Egmont Group: 'Understanding FIU operational independence and autonomy'.

14  See: https://amlintelligence.com/2021/04/council-of-europe-calls-for-stronger-financial-intelligence-units-says-recent-scandals-like-fincen-have-exposed-an-aml-system-that-has-fallen-far-short-of-declared-objectives/

## Chapter 8

1  Speech by David Lewis FATF Executive Secretary AI & Blockchain Summit Smart City Expo World Congress Barcelona, 21 November 2019. See:

https://www.fatf-gafi.org/publications/fatfgeneral/documents/speech-digital-id-nov-2019.html

2   See: https://www.fatf-gafi.org/publications/fatfgeneral/documents/speech-digital-id-nov-2019.html

3   See: https://baselgovernance.org/news/basel-aml-index-2021-4-things-holding-back-global-fight-against-money-laundering

4   Unger et al. (2014) analyse the effectiveness of AML policies in EU member countries, but they are not able to conclude whether money laundering has been reduced. Levi et al. (2018) argue that the current AML framework cannot be evaluated without improved data. Unger, B., Ferwerda, J., van den Broek, M., and Deleanu, I. (2014) *The Economic and Legal Effectiveness of the European Union's Anti-Money Laundering Policy*, Edward Elgar Publishing. Levi, M., Reuter, P., and Halliday, T. (2018) 'Can the AML system be evaluated without better data?' *Crime, Law, and Social Change* 69(2): 307–28.

5   See: The Wolfsberg Group – Demonstrating Effectiveness. Yet it is the very same 'outcomes', that when correctly aligned, influence how money laundering and terrorism financing activities are prevented and detected.

6   The term enabler has become synonymous with the practices of lawyers, accountants and real estate agents aligned to anti money laundering practices and international preventative efforts. Unfortunately, the term distracts from the fact some in these professions are actually money launderers. If they enable money laundering are they not then a money launderer? We see the distinction between and enabler and a money launderer is not as we are made to believe and the reason for this is perhaps because we still see money laundering as a three stage process.

7   An internal investigation found several historical deficiencies in Swedbank's AML compliance systems and controls. A report by Clifford Chance, one of the world's pre-eminent law firms, according to their website, found further failings during their investigation.

8   See: https://www.theguardian.com/australia-news/2019/oct/15/calls-for-crown-casino-inquiry-after-leaked-video-of-bricks-of-cash-in-junket-room

9   See: https://www.fatf-gafi.org/publications/fatfgeneral/documents/speech-digital-id-nov-2019.html

## Chapter 9

1   FATF report July 2021, 'Opportunities and challenges of new technologies for AML/CFT'. FATF (2022) *Opportunities and Challenges of New Technologies for Aml/Cft*. See: https://www.fatf-gafi.org/publications/fatfrecommendations/documents/opportunities-challenges-new-technologies-for-aml-cft.html

2   See: https://globalanticorruptionblog.com/2021/05/31/ml-for-aml-is-artificial-intelligence-up-to-the-task-of-anti-money-laundering-compliance/

3   'RegTech Adoption Practice Guide Issue #2: Anti-Money Laundering/Counter-Financing of Terrorism', July 2021. Hong Kong Monetary Authority (2021) *Regtech Adoption Practice Guide. Issue #2: Anti-Money*

*Laundering/Counter-Financing of Terrorism* (July 2021) See: https://www.hkma. gov.hk/media/eng/doc/key-information/guidelines-and-circular/2021/202 10726e1.pdf

4 See: https://www.dfsa.dk/-/media/Nyhedscenter/2021/Consultation_ Project_AML_TEK.pdf

5 For more details, see Morris-Cotterill, N. (2014) *Understanding Suspicion in Financial Crime*, Createspace Independent Publishing Platform.

6 What advocates for technology will now say is that no, the customer's 'unusual transaction' will be mitigated by an inspection of their transaction history. But what if that history is not sufficient, purposefully made complicated and a result of changes within society?

7 FATF technology report. See: https://www.fatf-gafi.org/media/fatf/docume nts/reports/Opportunities-Challenges-of-New-Technologies-for-AML-CFT.pdf

8 Ibid.

9 The TMNL is a joint intelligence-sharing initiative of five major Netherlands-based banks: ABN AMRO, ING, Rabobank, Triodos Bank, and de Volksbank. These banks have agreed to collectively monitor activity across their institutions.

10 See: https://www.rtassociates.co/2021/05/whats-new-in-financial-crime-regtech/

11 The term 'PrevTechAML' or preventative technology is attributed to the analysis of the authors' previous research findings and professional experience.

## Chapter 10

1 30.6 million SARs in 2018/2019 according to the Egmont Group, the global network of FIUs.

2 See: https://insight.thomsonreuters.com.au/business/posts/fincen-leaks-expose-personal-risk-of-aml-ctf-compliance-enforcement

3 See: https://www.linklaters.com/en/insights/blogs/businesscrimelinks/ 2019/august/suspicious-activity-overhaul-of-the-sar-process

4 These are sometimes called 'Suspicious Transaction Reports' or 'Suspicious Activity Reports' (to avoid the need for multiple reports of single transactions). The Dutch call them Unusual Transaction Reports and the Australians Suspicious Matter Reports. These all require a degree of subjective opinion and should not be confused with Currency Threshold Reports which require reporting all transactions over a monetary threshold.

5 For the most relevant judgment on the meaning of suspicion, see: *R v. Da Silva* [2006] EWCA Crim 1654.

6 Mason, P. (2020) 'Twenty years with anticorruption. Part 9: The UK's changing anti-corruption landscape – new energy, new horizons', U4 Practitioner Experience Note 2020: 9. U4 Anti-Corruption Resource Centre, Chr. Michelsen Institute.

7 The system was developed for FIUs by the United Nations Office on Drugs and Crime: Global Programme Against Money Laundering, Proceeds of Crime, and the Financing of Terrorism (GPML).

[8] The leak of files from the USA's FIU to BuzzFeed investigative reporters was so large that it could only be handled by an International Consortium of Journalists. See: https://www.icij.org/investigations/fincen-files/as-reforms-sparked-by-fincen-files-roll-out-a-year-on-key-source-is-behind-bars/. Accessed 21 May 2022.

[9] Oliver Bullough in *Prospect Magazine*, May 2019.

[10] Around 3,000 foreign individuals were given UK residency in return for a promise to invest millions in the country. The absence of due diligence around the scheme was exposed in Bridgewater, K. and Maxwell, N. (2015) *Goldrush: Investment visas and corrupt capital flows into the UK*, Transparency International UK.

[11] Egmont Group (2019) *Egmont Group of Financial Intelligence Units, Annual Report 2018/19*.

## Chapter 11

[1] The authors are not suggesting that the current situation is a deliberately contrived one. But if you do not highlight something as a problem, then the problem is not a problem. Well not for those on the outside looking in.

[2] See: www.fatf-gafi.org/publications/fatfgeneral/documents/chatham-house-march-2021.html

[3] A project driven by the Netherlands' data protection authority to allow more than 160 financial institutions to share information about fraudsters to help fight financial crime.

[4] FATF's immediate outcomes are explained in more details here: https://www.fatf-gafi.org/publications/mutualevaluations/documents/effectiveness.html

[5] See: https://www.reuters.com/business/finance/how-little-known-g7-task-force-unwittingly-helps-governments-target-critics-2021-08-05/

[6] Wikipedia provides various generic explanations that are not always written by those with expert knowledge or are independently verified.

[7] See: https://www.theguardian.com/politics/2008/jun/12/defence.terrorism

[8] Examples are everywhere: drug and people trafficking; organised crime working with money laundering syndicates; drug importation, distribution and sales.

[9] See: https://lnkd.in/e4bXsHR

[10] See: https://www.europol.europa.eu/publications-events/publications/shadow-money-international-networks-of-illicit-finance

## Chapter 12

[1] Keppel, R.D. (1996) *The Riverman: Ted Bundy and I Hunt for the Green River Killer*, Arrow Books.

[2] The United Nations defines money laundering using identical wording across its conventions. For example: United Nations Convention Against Corruption, Article 23(1)(b)(1): The acquisition, possession, or use of

property, knowing, at the time of receipt, that such property is the proceeds of crime.

3    Brown, R. and others (2012) *The contribution of financial investigation to tackling organised crime: a qualitative study*, HO Research Report 65.

4    UN Convention Against Corruption, Article 28; UN Convention Against Transnational Crime, Article 3(3); UN Convention Against Narcotics, Article 5.2.

5    See: https://www.planetclaire.tv/quotes/sherlock/series-two/the-hounds-of-baskerville/

6    O'Connor, D. (2005) *Closing the gap: a review of the fitness for purpose of the current structure of policing in England & Wales*, HM Inspectorate of Constabulary.

7    The Camden Asset Recovery Inter-Agency Network (CARIN) now has regional equivalents across the globe and is the first port of call for all international requests to freeze and seize criminal assets.

8    'Collar' is a local term for an arrest, derived from restraining a person by their collar. Please forgive the gender-biased language, it is intended to illustrate the unenlightened thinking of the times.

9    The UK's ministry of the interior.

10   *Home Office Working Group on Confiscation Third Report: Criminal Assets*, November 1998.

11   Home Office statistics retrieved via a Freedom of Information Act request.

## Chapter 13

1    Mehmet ildan (2021) *Aforizmalar (Aphorisms)*. Publication by Siyah Beyaz Publishing House.

2    Immediate Outcome 7, in the Methodology for assessing technical compliance with the FATF recommendations and the effectiveness of AML/CFT systems, 2012.

3    Brown, R. and others (2012) *The contribution of financial investigation to tackling organised crime: a qualitative study*, HO Research Report 65.

4    Hawley, S. and Hames, D. (2020) *Strengthening the UK Deferred Prosecution Regime*. See: https://www.transparency.org.uk/publications/airbus-uk-deferred-prosecution-agreement-dpa-bribery-sfo-lisa-osofsky/. Accessed 13 May 2022.

5    Immediate Outcome 7, in the Methodology for assessing technical compliance with the FATF.

6    Sir Robert Peel founded London's police in 1829. His 'Instruction Book', issued to every constable begins:

> It should be understood, at the outset, that the principal object to be attained is the 'prevention of crime'. The security of person and property, the preservation of public tranquillity, and all the other objects of a Police Establishment, will thus be better effected, than by the detection and punishment of the offender, after he has succeeded in committing the crime.

[7] Justia website. See: https://www.justia.com/criminal/docs/rico/. Accessed 13 September 2021.

[8] The Communist Party was and remains a mainstream political party in Italy.

## Chapter 14

[1] Wilson, M. (2006) 'Public attitudes towards crime and recovery of assets by the Assets Recovery Agency in Northern Ireland: findings from the July 2005 Northern Ireland Omnibus Survey', *Research and Statistical Bulletin* 1/2006, Northern Ireland Office.

[2] Gottschalk, E. (2009) *Public attitudes to asset recovery – results from an opinion poll*, UK Home Office.

[3] Council of Europe (2011) *Technical Paper: Public opinion survey about the implementation of the law on seizure and the confiscation of the proceeds of crime.* Project on Criminal Asset Recovery in Serbia (CAR Serbia).

[4] Dordević, S. (2022) 'Resilient Balkans: Social Reuse of confiscated assets'. Global Initiative against Transnational Organized Crime.

[5] The authors have maintained a Google alert for the word 'confiscation' for the last three years, so this is a summary of what is reported worldwide in the English-speaking press.

[6] Levi, M. and Osofsky, L. (1995) *Investigating, seizing, and confiscating the proceeds of crime.* Crime Detection and Prevention Series paper 61, Home Office.

[7] Reminder: asset recovery is the umbrella term for different ways to recover assets, of which confiscation following a criminal conviction is one.

[8] Stessens, G. (2000) *Money Laundering: A new international law enforcement model*, Cambridge University Press.

[9] The Proceeds of Crime Act, 2002, text is available here: https://www.legislation.gov.uk/ukpga/2002/29/contents

[10] Unger, B. (ed.) (2013) *Research Handbook on Money Laundering*, Edward Elgar Publishing Co. Mühl, B. (2013) *Access by Law Enforcement Agencies to Financial Data*, Edward Elgar Publishing Co.

[11] An undercover police action called 'Operation Julie' led to the case of *R v. Cuthbertson*, in which the defendants, although imprisoned, kept nearly £1 million in drugs proceeds. The Hodgson Report recommended legal reform – the Drug Trafficking Offenders Act 1986.

[12] National Audit Office (2013) *Confiscation Orders*, House of Commons 738.

[13] UK Prime Ministers Performance and Innovation Unit (2000) *Recovering the proceeds of crime* (Cabinet Office)

[14] Pol, R.F. (2018) 'Uncomfortable truths? ML = BS and AML=BS$^2$', *Journal of Financial Crime* 25(2): 294–308.

[15] Fitzpatrick, D. (2017) 'A "think piece" on intelligence, investigation and prosecution', *Journal of Financial Crime*, 24(3): 449–60.

[16] About US$75 million.

[17] Home Office (2021) *Asset Recovery Statistical Bulletin: Financial Years Ending 2016 to 2021.*

## Chapter 15

[1] For the full text of President Bush's speech, see: https://www.theguardian.com/world/2001/sep/21/september11.usa13. Accessed 24 October 2021.

[2] The Camden Asset Recovery Inter-Agency Network was named after the Camden Court Hotel, where the delegates were staying.

[3] The National Terrorist Financial Intelligence Unit was created in 2001.

[4] The 9/11 Commission Report (2003), National Commission on Terrorist Attacks Upon the United States (Established by Public Law 107-306, November 27, 2002).

[5] Peters, G. (2012) *Haqqani Network Financing: The Evolution of an Industry*, US Military Academy.

[6] FATF (2015) *Financing of the Terrorist Organisation Islamic State in Iraq and the Levant (ISIL)*, FATF.

[7] Oftedal, E. (2014) *The Financing of Jihadi Terrorist Cells in Europe*, Forsvarets forskningsinstitutt.

[8] Oftedal, *The Financing*.

[9] Oftedal, *The Financing*.

[10] Othman, R. and Ameer, R. (2014) 'Institutionalization of risk management framework in Islamic NGOs for suppressing terrorism financing', *Journal of Money Laundering Control* 17(1): 96–109.

[11] Othman and Ameer, 'Institutionalization of risk management'.

[12] Stewart Bell, Global News. See: https://globalnews.ca/news/5893768/irans-properties-in-canada-sold/. Accessed 26 October 2021.

[13] Carnegie Endowment for International Peace accessed 26 October 2021. See: https://carnegieendowment.org/sada/77427

[14] Blum et al. (2011) *OSINT Report* 2/2011, International Relations and Security Network.

[15] UN (2008) *Survey of the implementation of Security Council resolution 1373* (2001), United Nations Security Council S2008/379.

[16] FATF (2021) *Fourth Round Ratings*, FATF.

[17] Anderson, D. (2015) *Fourth Report on the operation of the terrorist Asset Freezing, etc. Act 2010*, UK Treasury.

## Chapter 16

[1] Sinclair, U. (1934) 'I, candidate for governor and how I got licked', *Oakland Tribune*, 11 December, page 19, column 3 (Newspapers.com).

[2] RUSI Get Serious: Illicit Finance is a UK national security threat. See: https://rusi.org/explore-our-research/publications/commentary/get-serious-illicit-finance-uk-national-security-threat

[3] See: https://www.fatf-gafi.org/publications/fatfgeneral/documents/chatham-house-march-2021.html

[4] Joshua Kirschenbaum, Senior Fellow at the German Marshall Fund, and a former US Treasury official at the Financial Crimes Enforcement Network (FinCEN) https://www.youtube.com/watch?v=1QvXtLvTFyo

## Chapter 17

1. Tax Justice Network (2021) *The State of Tax Justice 2021*. See: https://tax justice.net
2. Source Europol. See: https://www.europol.europa.eu/crime-areas-and-trends/crime-areas/economic-crime/mtic-missing-trader-intra-community-fraud. Accessed 24 November 2021.
3. Stern, D. (2019) 'The CumEx trading scandal', 5 St Andrews Hill. See: www.5sah.co.uk.
4. Swanberg, W. (1967) "Pulitzer", pp 402–3, published by Simon Schuster Trade (January 1, 1967).
5. Bullough, O. (2018) *Moneyland: Why thieves & crooks now rule the world and how to take it back*, Profile Books.
6. Vogl, F. (2021) *The Enablers: How the west supports kleptocrats and corruption – endangering our democracy*, Roman & Littlefield (as narrated by Alex Andreou, *The Bunker* Podcast, Episode 465).

## Chapter 18

1. See: https://www.transparency.org/
2. Withne, C. and Stephenson, M.C. (2021) 'The credibility of global corruption statistics', Chr Michelsen Institute, U4 Issue 2021/4.
3. World Bank (2012) 'Fighting corruption in public services: chronicling Georgia's reforms', Directions in Development Public Sector Governance 66449.
4. Nemtsova, A. (2021) 'Busted cop exposed, etc.', MSN News. See: https://www.msn.com/en-us/news/world/busted-cop-exposed-as-member-of-russian-elites-golden-toilet-fetish-club/ar-AAMpmZ7. Accessed 2 November 2021.
5. De Sousa, L. (2021) 'Reflections on the value, functions, and conditions for success of anti-corruption agencies (ACAs)', Centre for the Study of Corruption, University of Sussex.
6. National Crime Agency (2022) *Convicted money launderer who smuggled millions out of UK wanted by NCA*, website. See: https://jnews.uk/convicted-money-launderer-who-smuggled-millions-out-of-britain-wanted-by-nca/
7. Tankebe, Justice (2010) 'Public confidence in the police', *British Journal of Criminology* 50(2): 296–319.

## Chapter 19

1. The FATF Recommendations: International Standards on Combating Money Laundering and the Financing of Terrorism & Proliferation (2012, p 9).
2. See: https://www.ft.com/content/7ece4a22-29b7-4539-bf79-2cb3b6cc4add
3. Barrington, R. (2018) 'London, the money laundering capital', Chatham House. See: https://www.chathamhouse.org/publications/the-world-today/2018-04/london-money-laundering-capital
4. See: https://www.occrp.org/en/daily/9191-estonia-vs-denmark-the-battle-for-danske-blame-begins

5  See: https://www.handelsblatt.com/politik/international/illegale-geldtransfers-geldwaesche-republik-deutschland-wie-die-eu-durchgreifen-will/27432240.html?ticket=ST-11028076-nizXSSvWWlG5jMU5Bdwt-ap1

6  See: https://www.linkedin.com/posts/authorjeffreyrobinson_fca-fsa-money-laundering-activity-6852377557455654913-ulpd

7  The EBA has been heavily criticised for failing to act against Danske Bank over its €200 billion money laundering scandal and address money laundering scandals at Swedbank, Nordea Bank, ING and Deutsche Bank.

## Chapter 20

1  See the *Financial Times* article titled 'ABN Amro reaches €480m anti-money laundering settlement'. Nicholas Megaw and Oliver Ralph in London and Richard Milne in Oslo (April 19 2021). See: https://www.ft.com/content/fd891e4d-8438-4887-82cd-096b3f248592

2  See: https://www.news.com.au/finance/business/banking/westpac-pays-up-for-austral-scandal/news-story/4161d88925180d6dd70a124b8fafdb8e

3  2010, The Ultimate Quotable Einstein, edited by Alice Calaprice, *Section: Misattributed to Einstein*, Quote Page 474. Princeton University Press, Princeton, New Jersey.

4  Protess, B. and Silver-Greenberg, J. (2012) 'HSBC to pay US$1.92 billion to settle charges of money laundering', *New York Times*, 10 December. See: https://dealbook.nytimes.com/2012/12/10/hsbc-said-to-near-1-9-billion-settlement-over-money-laundering/

5  See: https://www.theguardian.com/commentisfree/2021/oct/06/crackdowns-finance-government-laws-regulation-pandora-papers

6  Failures at RaboBank in 2018, US Bancorp in 2017, HSBC in 2012 and similar did not lead to a single bank employee receiving a conviction for money laundering.

## Chapter 21

1  See: https://blog.nationalarchives.gov.uk/beveridge-report-foundations-welfare-state/

2  LexisNexis Risk Solutions (2021) *True Cost of Financial Crime Compliance Global Report*. This report by a respected industry specialist estimated that the global cost rose from US$180.9 billion in 2020 to US$213.9 billion in 2021.

3  Parliamentary Question by Mr Hollinrake MP, UIN 35778, tabled on 19 July 2021.

## Conclusion

1  This definition contains the main points to prove an offence contained in the UN Conventions: Against Corruption (Article 32.1 (b)(i) and Article 2 (e)); Illicit Traffic in Narcotics and Psychotropic Substances (Article 3 (b), (c) and Article 1(p)); Transnational Organised Crime (Article 6.1 (b)(i) and Article 2 (e)). These three conventions are, very helpfully, drafted using almost identical text.

# Index

References to figures appear in *italic* type;
those in **bold** type refer to tables.

As 'money laundering' and 'AML/CFT' are the main topics of the book,
entries under these headings have been kept to a minimum. Readers are
advised to search under more specific terms.